THE MUSEUM OF
OTHER PEOPLE

THE
MUSEUM
OF OTHER
PEOPLE

FROM COLONIAL ACQUISITIONS
TO COSMOPOLITAN EXHIBITIONS

ADAM KUPER

PANTHEON BOOKS
New York

Library of Congress Cataloging-in-Publication Data
Name: Kuper, Adam, author.
Title: The museum of other people : from colonial acquisitions to
cosmopolitan exhibitions / Adam Kuper.
Description: First American edition. New York : Pantheon Books, 2024.
Identifiers: LCCN 2023039861 (print). LCCN 2023039862 (ebook).
ISBN 9780593700679 (hardcover). ISBN 9780593700686 (ebook)
Subjects: LCSH: Ethnological museums and collections—History. |
Ethnological museums and collections—Moral and ethical aspects. | Museums—
Acquisitions—Moral and ethical aspects. | Cultural property—Government policy. |
Cultural property—Moral and ethical aspects. | Cultural property—Protection. |
Cultural property—Conservation and restoration.
Classification: LCC GN35 .K87 2024 (print) | LCC GN35 (ebook) |
DDC 305.80075—dc23/eng/20231019
LC record available at https://lccn.loc.gov/2023039861
LC ebook record available at https://lccn.loc.gov/2023039862

www.pantheonbooks.com

Jacket photograph: *Noire et Blanche*, 1926, by Man Ray. © Man Ray 2015
Trust/Artists Rights Society (ARS), NY/ADAGP, Paris, 2023. Digital image
© The Museum of Modern Art/Licensed by SCALA/Art Resource, N.Y.

Jacket design by Jenny Carrow

Printed in the United States of America

First American Edition
2 4 6 8 9 7 5 3 1

"There is no document of civilisation that is not at the same time a document of barbarism."

—Walter Benjamin

Contents

Acknowledgements   ix

1. The Museum of Other People   1

Part 1: Faraway People

2. Inventing the Museum of Other People   31
    Jomard in Paris—Siebold in Leiden—Thomsen in Copenhagen

3. Civilised and Uncivilised: The British Museum and
    the Pitt Rivers Museum   53
    *Prehistory, evolution and ethnography—the challenge of Pitt
    Rivers*

4. German Museums and the Cultural History
    of Humanity   73
    Humboldt's Legacy—Klemm in Leipzig—Bastian in Berlin

5. The Rise and Fall of the Musée de l'Homme   84
    *World's Fairs—the Trocadéro Museum of Ethnography—the
    Musée de l'Homme—Surrealism—Second World War*

Interlude: An American in Paris   103

**Part 2: Native Americans, Manifest Destiny and American
Exceptionalism**

6. The Smithsonian Institution Goes West: Or, How the
    West Was Spun   109
    *Origins—the Western Frontier—the Bureau of American
    Ethnology—the U.S. National Museum*

7. Franz Boas Challenges the Smithsonian   143
    The Boas myth in American anthropology—the great debate—
    evolutionary and regional models—Boas as collector
8. Harvard's Peabody Museum of American Archaeology
    and Ethnology   158
    Origins—Darwin and Harvard's scientists—Putnam and
    prehistory
9. The World's Columbian Exposition, 1893   173
    The Chicago Fair—the Smithsonian vs. Putnam and Boas—the
    American Museum of Natural History—the end of the Museum
    Age in Anthropology

Part 3: Divesting and Reinventing the Museum
10. Bones of Contention   193
    Collections of body parts—race studies—repatriation
    and burial
11. Trophies of Empire, African Court Art, and the
    Slave Trade   223
    Wars and looting—the history of restitution—the
    Benin Bronzes—the politics of restitution
12. But Is It Art?   251
    The invention of primitive art—from Paris to New York—
    museums of primitive or tribal art in the twenty-first century
13. National Museums and Identity Museums   290
    Culture and civilisation—European folk museums—identity
    politics in the late twentieth century—tribal museums and
    the National Museum of the American Indian—the dialogical
    museum
14. Show and Tell   316
    Exhibits, permanent and temporary
15. The Cosmopolitan Museum   342

Notes   357
Index   405

ACKNOWLEDGEMENTS

Two old friends of mine made their careers in the Museum of Other People: Igor Krupnik, chair of anthropology and curator of circumpolar ethnology at the National Museum of Natural History, Smithsonian Institution; and Enid Schildkraut, curator in the division of anthropology at the American Museum of Natural History from 1973 to 2005, and then director of exhibitions at the Museum for African Art in New York City until 2011. They were always ready to talk about museums, to discuss my findings, to challenge my judgements; and they read (and sometimes reread) all the chapters in the book. I also had a home team of experienced and equally uncomplaining and indefatigable readers: my older son, Simon Kuper, who is a wonderful writer; my cousin, Richard Kuper, who was head of a publishing house; and my partner, Jytte Klausen, who did her best to ensure that I didn't disappear down some rabbit hole.

Other colleagues came to my aid when asked, with information, criticism and, really quite often, encouragement. I am grateful to them all: Mary Jo Arnoldi, curator for African arts and ethnology at the National Museum of Natural History at the Smithsonian Institution in Washington, DC; Nigel Barley, assistant keeper of ethnography, British Museum; Margit Berner, curator, Museum of Natural History, Vienna; Lissant Bolton, keeper of the department of Africa, Oceania and the Americas at the British Museum; Laura van Broekhoven, director of the Pitt Rivers Museum, University of Oxford; Patricia Capone, curator, Peabody Museum of Archaeology and Ethnology, Harvard University; Nélia Dias, professor at the Centre for Research in Anthropology, Lisbon, Portugal; Rudolf Effert, Institute of Area Studies, Leiden University; Benoît de L'Estoile, CNRS, Paris; Carlos Fausto, professor of anthropology, National Museum, Federal University Rio de Janeiro; Thomas Fillitz, professor of anthropology, University of Vienna; Michael Fisher, former editor for science and medicine, Harvard University Press; Jonathan David MacLachlan Fine, head of the Ethnological Museum, Berlin State Museums; David Gellner, professor of social anthropology, University of Oxford; Clare Harris, curator for Asia at the Pitt Rivers Museum and professor of visual anthropology, University of Oxford; Kirsten Hastrup, professor of anthropology, University of Copenhagen and president of the Danish Royal Academy of Sciences and Letters, 2008–16; Karl-Heinz Kohl, professor emeritus of ethnology at Frankfurt Goethe University and former director of the Frobenius Institute for Research in Cultural Anthropology; Christine Laurière, CNRS, Paris; John Mack, keeper of ethnography at the British Museum, 1990–2004 and, since 2004, professor of world art at the University of East Anglia; Jonathan Marks, professor of anthropology, University of North Carolina; Pierre de Maret, emeritus professor of archaeology, Université libre de Bruxelles, former rector of the university, and president of the scientific commission of the Royal Museum of Central Africa in Tervuren; Malcolm McLeod, keeper of ethnography at the British Museum, 1974–90, director of the Hunterian Museum and Art Gallery, 1990–99; John Picton, emeritus professor of African art, University of London; Barbara Plankensteiner, director of the Museum am Rothenbaum World Cultures and Arts (MARKK) in Hamburg; Alexis von Poser, deputy director of the Ethnological Museum and the Museum of Asian Art at the Berlin State Museums; Gina Rappaport, head archivist, national anthropological archives, Smithsonian Institution; Antonio Saborit, director, National Museum of Anthropology, Mexico City; Anna Schmid, director of the Museum of Cultures in Basel; Robert Storrie, keeper of ethnology, Horniman Museum, London; Anne-Christine Taylor, director of research and education, Musée du quai Branly, 2005–13; Han Vermeulen, research fellow, Max Planck Institute for Social Anthropology in Halle, Germany; and Sarah Walpole, archives officer, Royal Anthropological Institute.

THE MUSEUM OF
OTHER PEOPLE

THE MUSEUM OF OTHER PEOPLE

Since at least the fifteenth century, Europe's 1 per cent collected Greek and Roman antiquities, Renaissance art and Chinese ceramics. Their gardens flaunted exotic trees. For entertainment, perhaps instruction, they had cabinets of "natural curiosities" and "artificial curiosities" with freaks of nature, bizarre devices, instruments of torture, titillating images.

In the last decades of the eighteenth century a few grand collections were put on public show. The venues came to be known as museums: shrines of the muses. At first only select visitors were admitted. The Hermitage insisted on court dress. The Louvre gave privileged access to artists. As late as 1808 anyone who wished to enter the British Museum had to submit a written application. Gradually more and more museums opened to the public, though children were not welcome.

In 1848 two Chinese scholars were dispatched to examine these new institutions. They reported that there were *jigulou*, "buildings for collections of bones," *wanzhongyuan*, "gardens of everything," *huage*, "pavilions of paintings," *jibaoyuan*, "courtyards of treasures," and *junqilou* "houses of military equipment." After visiting the British Museum, a Japanese delegation coined a new term, *hakubutsukan*, "mansion of boundless things."[1]

This book tells the story of yet another kind of museum. Benoît de L'Estoile identified it as le musée des autres. I call it the Museum of Other People.[2]

Conceived in the 1830s and 1840s, the Museum of Other People put on display an exotic world of "primitive" or "tribal" peoples who lived far away or long ago. Its golden age began with the wave of European colonialism in Africa and Oceania in the 1880s. It then went into decline in the era of decolonisation in the 1960s. Museums of ethnology and anthropology in the U.S.A. followed a similar trajectory, emerging at the height of colonisation of the territories west of the Mississippi ("Indian country"), and giving way to identity museums in the 1980s. By the twenty-first century the Museum of Other People confronted a full-blown crisis. This may be terminal.

The first plans for the Museum of Other People were drawn up in Paris, Leiden, Copenhagen and Dresden. In 1845 the British Museum installed an ethnographic gallery. In 1846 the Smithsonian Institution in Washington, DC, established a department of ethnology. At the same time, societies of anthropologists and ethnologists were founded, part of a new wave of learned societies that were coming to terms with an industrialising, urbanising, imperialist Europe.

Governments assumed responsibility for education, poor relief, public health and policing (functions once left largely to parish authorities). For reasons of state and commerce, European powers began a new round of land grabs in faraway lands. Modernising bureaucracies found themselves in urgent need of facts and ideas. In 1836, Lord John Russell, who served twice as prime minister of Britain, declared: "We are busy introducing system, method, science, economy, regularity [and] discipline."[3] A new breed of statisticians delivered the data. Positivists in France and Utilitarians in England proposed methods and theories—and a cluster of new sciences emerged. Michel Foucault called them human sciences, while admitting that he used the term "sciences" loosely: "the body of knowledge (though even that word is perhaps a little too strong: let us say, to be more neutral still . . . the body of discourse) that takes as its object man as an empirical entity."[4]

As the philosopher and historian of science Ian Hacking remarked, the new human sciences were *making up kinds of people*.[5] Ethnologists and anthropologists began to investigate the character, habits and customs of a very particular kind of people. Once known as savages, they were now, in a scientific era, identified as "primitive": stuck in an early stage of human development. These primitive people were distinguished by their "race," "culture," or degree of "civilisation," terms coined in the last decades of the eighteenth century.

Anthropologists distinguished populations by race. Ethnologists concerned themselves with culture or civilisation. However, disciplinary labels were expansive, overlapping and often a matter of contention. William Edwards, son of a Jamaican planter, who founded the Société ethnologique de Paris in 1839, claimed that the term ethnology had the double advantage that it lent itself to generalisation and "designated indifferently the study of races or of peoples."[6] In 1843, James Cowles Prichard, author of the first English textbook in the field, defined ethnology as the study of the history of peoples, and laid down that it "must be mainly founded on the relations of their languages."[7] In 1859, Paul Broca, a professor of anatomy at the Sorbonne, set up the Société d'anthropologie de Paris, the first learned society to adopt the title "anthropology," an old term for the philosophical contemplation of the human condition. He dismissed the ethnologists as do-gooders, obsessed with slavery, their motivation not truly scientific. They were, he complained, deplorably reluctant to acknowledge the radical importance of biological differences.

Armed with eighteen signatures of potential members, Broca approached the Ministry of Public Education for permission to form his society. The minister hesitated. As a historian, Francis Schiller summed up official concerns: "Worse than ethnology, which smacked only of anti-slavery, anthropology suggested subversion and the spirit of 1848; something vaguely degrading to man's immortal soul, possibly in conflict with the teachings of the Church and the interests of the Empire." Permission was granted, but on two conditions: First, "they must never talk politics or religion." Second, "a plainclothes officer of the Imperial Police must be present at each session and report to headquarters."[8] (Broca enjoyed reminiscing about the time the attendant policeman asked whether he might be excused. "There will be nothing interesting to-day, I suppose? May I go?" "No, no, my friend," Broca replied, "you must not go for a walk; sit down and earn your pay.")[9]

In London too, ethnologists and anthropologists were at daggers drawn. In 1842 the Aborigines' Protection Society resolved that the best way to help native peoples was to study them.[10] This was contentious. The missionary element in the society resisted. A year later the secretary of the APS, Richard King, and two Quaker physicians, Thomas Buxton and Thomas Hodgkin, formed the London Ethnological Society. The members were anti-slavery and committed to the doctrine that all human races had a common origin.

In 1863, in the heat of the American Civil War, a frankly racist faction broke away and set up the Anthropological Society of London. A year later its leader, James Hunt, published *On The Negro's Place in Nature*, in which he asserted the separate origin of the various human races and defended slavery. The inner circle of the Anthropological Society formed "The Cannibal Club," which was called to order with a gavel carved in the shape of an African head.[11] Hunt was even more dismissive of the ethnologists than Broca had been. These "opponents of comparative anthropology" suffered "arrested brain growth" and "from what I will call respectively the religious mania, and the rights-of-man mania."[12]

Hunt died in 1869. In 1871, the year in which Darwin's *The Descent of Man* was published, the feuding London societies merged under the leadership of Thomas Henry Huxley, John Lubbock and General Augustus Lane-Fox (later Pitt Rivers). They were all Darwinians. Indeed, one commentator complained that the new society promised to be "little more than a sort of Darwinian club."[13] The choice of a name for the society was a final bone of contention. Lubbock, intervening in a heated debate at the British Association for the Advancement of Science, said that he "looked upon anthropology as an ugly name for ethnology . . .

[Ethnology] was an older word and a prettier word than anthropology."[14] But after much heart-searching, and despite a rearguard action by the fervently anti-racist Lady Lubbock, the new association was named "Anthropological."[15]

Museums of Civilisation (the Louvre, the British Museum, New York's Metropolitan Museum) embodied the Enlightenment theory of history. All human societies progress from a lower to a higher condition, some more quickly than others. Progress can be measured by the advance of reason in its cosmic battle against raw nature, instinct, superstition and traditional authority. The goal towards which all must travel is what French philosophers in the late eighteenth century began to call *Civilisation*. Civilisation had three peaks: ancient Greece and Rome, the European Renaissance, and, well, obviously, the great city in which is found the premier Museum of Civilisation—Paris, or London, or New York. The antithesis of civilisation, its foil, was represented by "Stone Age" or "primitive" societies. Their crude arts and artefacts belonged in a Museum of Other People, if not in a Museum of Natural History.

In the middle of the nineteenth century, the English philosopher Herbert Spencer proposed that societies were like living organisms. As they "evolve" they become more complex and efficient. The term "evolution" duly entered the vocabulary of speculative historians, alongside "progress" and "civilisation." Spencer's "evolution" was, however, radically different from Darwin's theory of natural selection. Darwin repudiated the idea that the development of natural organisms, let alone societies, follow the same path everywhere. Challenges are local and changeable. Particular adaptations cannot be foreseen. Outcomes are unpredictable. "What a chance it has been . . . that has made a man," Darwin mused. "Any monkey probably might, with such chances be made intellectual, but almost certainly not made into man."[16]

Yet Darwin pointed out that as human beings became toolmakers they were less exposed to a changing environment. Gradually they developed the means to engineer their own progress.

At that point, Darwin did buy into the civilisation narrative. He wrote, in *The Descent of Man*, that "man has risen, though by slow and interrupted steps, from a lowly condition to the highest standard as yet attained by him in knowledge, morals and religion."[17] And while he hated slavery, Darwin believed that there was a hierarchy of races. "It is very true what you say about the higher races of men, when high enough, replacing & clearing off the lower races," he wrote to the Christian Socialist, Charles Kingsley, in 1862. "In 500 years how the Anglo-saxon race will have spread & exterminated whole nations; & in consequence how much the Human race, viewed as a unit, will have risen in rank."[18]

In 1871 the father figure of English anthropology, E. B. Tylor, wrote in his *Primitive Culture*: "The educated world of Europe and America practically settles a standard by simply placing its own nations at one end of the social series and savage tribes at the other, arranging the rest of mankind between these limits according as they correspond more closely to savage or to cultured life."[19] Perhaps Tylor was being ironic, but this way of thinking had an obvious appeal to imperialists, though not necessarily to the foreigners over whom they ruled.

In the second half of the nineteenth century, as European powers were busily assembling tropical empires in Africa and Oceania, most Europeans were themselves living under imperial rule, subjects of the Austro-Hungarian, the Ottoman or the Russian empires. Central European intellectuals invoked the notion of *Kultur* to challenge the imperialist cult of *Civilisation*.[20] The identity of a *Volk* derived from its particular culture. This was rooted in blood and soil, fitted to a local environment. The *Volksgeist*, the national spirit, found expression in rituals, folk tales, music and crafts. Appeals to a universal civilisation were imperialist propaganda. There was no hierarchy of cultures, no universal historical dialectic leading peoples everywhere onwards and upwards to a civilised condition. "What does 'progress of the human race' mean?," demanded Johann Gottfried von Herder. "How are we to measure so many different periods and peoples, even with the best of outside information?"[21]

Proponents of local culture feared that their very identity was threatened by foreign powers and the insidious appeal of modernity. Suspicious of science, industry and commerce, they looked to the past for reassurance and inspiration. Champions of civilisation were full of optimism, confident of moving forward, making progress, certain that they were on the side of history. Civilisation trumped barbarism. Progress had its costs, no doubt, but resistance was futile.

And yet the opposed poles of Tylor's series—"savage or cultured life"—do not correspond to objective, readily specified historical conditions. Remarkably little is known about the way of life and beliefs of hunter-gatherers in Upper Palaeolithic times. We cannot say with any confidence what these societies had in common, apart from a dependence on hunting and gathering. (Who knows whether they had families, leaders, shamans, music?) Since they were first documented, pastoral nomads and many foraging peoples associated with farmers and even with city folk, and had done so for many generations, in some cases for millennia. Far from being very like the ancient Stone Age peoples who lived in a world of hunters and gatherers, they have more in common with their farming neighbours than with foragers and herders in other parts of the world.

"Civilisation," the Enlightenment antithesis to savagery or barbarism, is almost as hard to pin down. The term was applied at first to ancient Greece and Rome. In the nineteenth century, European scholars extended its range to include ancient Egypt and Israel, Babylon, Persia, China, Japan and Moghul India. Yet while all civilised peoples, ancient and modern, are assumed to share common features, there is little agreement about which features are decisive. "No civilised society would—" Fill in the blank according to taste.

In 1883, the English historian J. R. Seeley remarked that civilisation was associated with all sorts of conditions—"sometimes the softening of manners, sometimes mechanical inventions, sometimes religious toleration, sometimes the appearance of great poets and artists, sometimes scientific discoveries, sometimes constitutional liberty." However, these qualities did not necessarily occur together. Nor were they produced by a single cause. And "civilisation" certainly did not explain, let alone excuse, the remarkable expansion of the British Empire. ("We seem, as it were, to have conquered and peopled half the world in a fit of absence of mind," Seeley famously remarked.)[22]

Britain's medals to honour veterans of the First World War were inscribed "The Great War for Civilisation 1914–1919": but after the horrors of that war, the differences between civilisation and barbarism seemed less apparent. The father figure of American anthropology, Franz Boas, wrote in 1928:

> Anyone who has lived with primitive tribes, who has shared their joys and sorrows, their privations and their luxuries . . . will agree that there is no such thing as a "primitive mind," a "magical" or "prelogical" way of thinking, but that each individual in "primitive" societies is a man, a woman, a child of the same way of thinking, feeling and acting as a man, woman or child in our own society.[23]

Yet even in this passage Boas wrote unselfconsciously about "primitive tribes." The idea of a primitive kind of people still cast a long shadow when I was a graduate student of social anthropology at Cambridge University in the 1960s. British, French and Belgian colonies in Africa, the Caribbean and the Pacific were in the process of becoming independent states. And yet we were given to understand that out there, in the tropics and the antipodes, in countries that had until very recently been European colonies, functioning tribes could still be studied. To be sure, those people were now mostly Christians or Muslims. Their children went to school. But perhaps a residue of the old system could be discerned. Despite missionary disapproval, people sacrificed to their ancestors and tabooed animal totems. Tribal chiefs insisted on traditional prerogatives, even if they had to be propped up in office by colonial commissioners. Everyone had access to money and markets, and yet they practised barter and gift exchange.

Anthropologists did adapt to the post-colonial world. They dropped the fantasy of bounded tribes, each with its pristine culture, and began to study globalisation, hybrid religions, ethnic relations, urban life, the legacy of colonial structures. Some were drawn into projects of "modernisation" or "development" in the newly independent states. The description "primitive" was avoided. "Indigenous" might be preferred, though that term was applied to the same roll call of hunters and pastoral nomads whom the Victorians regarded as prototypical primitives.

Meanwhile, the Museum of Other People remained stuck in its ways. In 1969, William C. Sturtevant, long-serving curator of North American ethnology in the Smithsonian Institution in Washington, DC, asked his colleagues "to admit the minuscule role and the low prestige of museum work in present-day ethnology."[24] This was fair enough. Many museums continued to purvey timeless images of exotic ways of life (dioramas of waxwork figures hunting, praying, carving, weaving, cooking and sitting around camp fires). The mood music was no longer imperialist, however. Exhibitions communicated a benevolent universalism. Look at funeral practices around the world, beliefs in spiritual beings, music, dance, initiation rituals. See what we all have in common!

The prototype was the blockbuster "Family of Man" photographic show that travelled the world in the 1950s. Even at the time it was derided as a happy-clappy, all-in-it-together, Kumbaya *family* show. The critic Roland Barthes pointed out the ambiguity of its message:

the difference between human morphologies is asserted, exoticism is insistently stressed, the infinite variations of the species, the diversity in skins, skulls and customs are made manifest, the image of Babel is complacently projected over that of the world. Then, from this pluralism, a type of unity is magically produced: man is born, works, laughs and dies everywhere in the same way . . . Of course this means postulating a human essence, and here God is re-introduced into our Exhibition.[25]

"The Family of Man" was a huge success. It helped that the United States Information Agency funded a tour through thirty-seven countries that attracted over 7.5 million visitors.

The Museum of Other People gradually lost its moorings, drifting away from the new centres of research in anatomy, anthropology, archaeology, linguistics and history of art. In the 1920s and 1930s, ethnographers began to do long-term field-work. Studying social and cultural processes, drawing on a range of social science theories, they lost interest in what came to be called "material culture"—the sort of things to be found in the museums. In the second half of the twentieth century, racist, typological thinking was replaced by a statistically based population genetics. There was no longer a good reason to display skulls and skeletons. Yet while the old paradigms were abandoned in the universities, they had a half-life still in the museums, where dusty showcases and dioramas continued to purvey timeless images of exotic ways of life.

In the 1960s the Museum of Other People sailed into troubled waters. European colonies in Africa and Oceania became independent states. Indigenous peoples' movements emerged in the Americas and in Australia and New Zealand. In the late twentieth century, identity museums along the Mall in Washington, DC, called into question the very idea of a Museum of Other People. Curators of ethnographic and prehistoric artefacts were thrown, unprepared, into a cauldron of controversy about race, colonialism, cultural appropriation and the very nature of scientific authority. And to cap it all, by the twenty-first century they were themselves in the dock, charged with sequestering other peoples' heirlooms.

"The trustees of the British Museum have become the world's largest receivers of stolen property, and the great majority of their loot is not even on public display," claims Geoffrey

Robertson QC, a human rights lawyer.[26] Dan Hicks, a senior curator at Oxford's Pitt Rivers Museum, insists that European museums must atone for their colonial past, transform themselves into "sites of conscience" and "take action to make the 2020s a decade of restitution."[27]

An activist theatre group "BP or not BP" (a reference not only to Hamlet but to British Petroleum, a controversial donor) runs "stolen goods tours" of the British Museum. An Australian Aborigine man, resident in London, demands the return of a shield that was taken by Captain Cook in 1770. He claims that 250 years ago it belonged to his own ancestor, a warrior identified by Cook as Cooman. Next up, a woman introduced as a Maori calls on the museum to return 2,300 Maori artefacts. Then a British man with Greek Cypriot parents testifies that the Elgin Marbles belong back in Athens.

In a superhero film released in 2018, *Black Panther*, a visitor from a fictional African country, Erik "Killmonger" Stevens (played by Michael B. Jordan), confronts a curator in the "Museum of Great Britain." He tells her that a seventh-century war hammer on display with other African artefacts is wrongly labelled. It wasn't made in Benin. The British took it from his own people, the Wakanda. Now he is going to take it back. She protests that it isn't for sale. "How do you think your ancestors got these?," he replies. "Do you think they paid a fair price? Or did they take it . . . like they took everything else?" Killmonger poisons the curator's coffee, kills the guards, and makes off with the hammer.

Iconic museum pieces were acquired by force or shady dealing in the heyday of European imperialism, usually from rival empires. Famous examples are the Elgin Marbles, the Rosetta Stone and Qing dynasty treasures looted from the Chinese emperor's summer palace, which together are the pride of the British Museum.[28] (Even the word loot was appropriated. It comes from *lut*, the Hindi word for plunder.)

A corps of scientists accompanied Napoleon's military expedition to Egypt in 1798. They carried off antiquities, a number of which—including the Rosetta Stone—were seized by a British expeditionary force, shipped to London in a captured French frigate, *L'Égyptienne*, and ended up in the British Museum. In 1812, Lord Elgin, British ambassador to the Ottoman Empire, arranged for half the surviving sculptures of the Parthenon to be removed and sent to his private home in England. "Bonaparte has not got such a thing from all his thefts in Italy," he boasted.[29] In 1816 he sold his trophies to the British Museum. The imperial summer palace in the north of Beijing was plundered and then razed to the ground by British and French troops in October 1860 in revenge for the capture and torture of thirty-nine Europeans during the Second Opium War, only eighteen of whom survived. When the looting began, the soldiers were given a free hand. About one and a half million precious objects were taken from the palace complex. A great many found their way into European and North American museums.[30] The whole forty-acre imperial estate was then torched on the orders of the British high commissioner to China, Lord Elgin (son of the Lord Elgin of the Elgin Marbles). "We, Europeans, we are the civilised, and for us, the Chinese are the barbarians," Victor Hugo wrote to a correspondent. "Now see what civilisation has done to barbarism . . . One day I hope that France will return these spoils of war to China, cleansed and polished."[31]

"Throughout history, soldiers have claimed the spoils of war, and the plunder and sacking of cities has been as common as the practice of forcibly requisitioning food from the countryside," according to Sir Richard Evans, regius professor of modern history at Cambridge University.[32] Not only was looting a common accessory to warfare: it was regarded as right and natural. In his classic account of the laws of war and peace, published in 1625, the Dutch jurist Hugo Grotius recognised "the right to appropriate for oneself what one has taken from the enemy."[33]

Napoleon Bonaparte elevated looting to a patriotic duty. Following the example of the Roman Triumphs, he ritualised his appropriations. In 1798, on the anniversary of the fall of Robespierre and the end of the Terror, Paris celebrated a two-day "Festival of Liberty and Triumphal Entry of Objects of the Sciences and the Arts Collected in Italy." Among the prizes on show were four gilded Corinthian horses that a Crusader force seized from the Hippodrome in Constantinople in 1204 and carried off to Venice. French soldiers removed the horses from the porch of the cathedral of St. Mark and they were paraded through Paris beneath a banner that read: "Horses transported from Corinth to Rome, and from Rome to Constantinople to Venice, and from Venice to France. They are finally on free soil." A song written for the occasion had a refrain: "Rome is no more in Rome / It is all in Paris."[34]

Much of the plunder of Napoleon's campaigns ended up in the Louvre, renamed the Musée Napoléon in 1803. After the Battle of Waterloo, the Duke of Wellington insisted that the victorious allies "could not do otherwise than restore [works of art] to the countries from which, contrary to the practice of civilised warfare, they had been torn during the disastrous period of the French Revolution and the tyranny of Buonaparte."[35] Richard Evans notes, however, that "only about 55 per cent of the looted objects were returned; the rest had been sent out to provincial museums, beyond the ken of the occupying Allied armies."[36]

The Hague Conventions of 1899 and 1907 were the first international instruments to ban pillage. This in no way inhibited the Nazis from plundering masterpieces from museums and from Jewish families. As a young man Hitler dreamt of being an artist. In his last years, in the midst of a world war, he was planning a Führermuseum, to be built in Linz, near his birthplace in Austria. It would be a museum of looted art.

Following the defeat of Nazi Germany, the U.S. imposed a temporary embargo on trade in works of art and set up a mechanism for the collection and return of stolen goods (but that did not prevent Soviet troops from carting away truckloads of antiquities and works of art). Discussions in the United Nations and UNESCO led to the promulgation of the 1954 Hague

Convention for the Protection of Cultural Property in the Event of Armed Conflict. At the time of writing, 133 states are party to the convention. (The United States signed up only in 2009, and insisted on a waiver where nuclear weapons are deployed.)

This convention affirms that institutional and individual owners of stolen works of art (and their descendants) have the right to reclaim them, but it can be very difficult to recover treasures looted by the Nazis. "In many cases, the original owners were dead, and sometimes their heirs had been killed by the Nazis as well," writes Evans, an authority on the Third Reich.

> Entire families perished in very large numbers at Auschwitz, and while institutions, museums and galleries possessed the knowledge, the resources and the evidence to mount actions to try and regain what they had lost, the same was seldom true of individuals. As a result the number of restitution actions and claims fell sharply during the 1950s, at the same time as new international agreements protecting cultural property came into force.[37]

UNESCO's 1970 Convention on the Means of Prohibiting and Preventing the Illicit Import, Export and Transfer of Ownership of Cultural Property urged buyers to require proof that antiquities were acquired legally. The United States ratified the treaty in 1983, but it took Britain until 2002 and Germany until 2007 to sign it. In the meantime, countries rich in antiquities—Afghanistan, Iraq, Libya, Syria—were ravaged by invasions and civil wars. Rare and wonderful pieces soon appeared on the world market.[38]

Reviewing international conventions governing the ownership of "cultural property" (which he defined as "objects of artistic, archaeological, ethnological or historical interest"), the jurist John Henry Merryman distinguished two opposing points of view.[39] One school of thought treats cultural property as a shared endowment of humanity. Merryman dubbed this the cosmopolitan principle. An example is the preamble to the Hague

Convention of 1954, which states that "damage to cultural property belonging to any people whatsoever means damage to the cultural heritage of all mankind, since each people makes its contribution to the culture of the world." The other approach is nationalist. This underpins the UNESCO Convention on Cultural Property. The thrust here is on the retention of cultural property within national boundaries.

Whether nationalist or cosmopolitan, the status of these international conventions is uncertain. The International Court of Justice has not tested whether there is a duty under international law to return "cultural property" even if it was illegally acquired. James Cuno, president and CEO of the J. Paul Getty Trust and former director of the Harvard Art Museums, the Courtauld Institute and the Art Institute of Chicago, is disparaging. "It wouldn't be an exaggeration to see these many conventions as a bouillabaisse of good intentions and bureaucratic ambitions," he writes, "all of which are, in the end, unenforceable, except insofar as the States Parties themselves have imposed internal laws and sanctions governing the activities addressed by the Conventions."[40]

Some national legislatures did institute procedures for restitution. In New Zealand, Australia and Canada laws were introduced to protect the heritage of Indigenous peoples. In 1990 the U.S. Congress passed the Native American Graves Protection and Repatriation Act (NAGPRA). This provided a legal framework for the repatriation of Native American human remains and ceremonial objects held by museums. And social movements around the world demanded redress for the injuries of slavery and colonialism.

In July 2013, the hashtag #BlackLivesMatter kick-started perhaps the largest protest movement in the history of the U.S.A.[41] The killing of George Floyd by a police officer in Minneapolis on 25 May 2020 sparked massive demonstrations in nearly 550 locations across the United States. Halls of residence, lecture theatres and libraries donated to universities by slave owners were renamed. In June 2020, the statue of Edward Colson, a philanthropist who profited from the Atlantic slave trade, was toppled and thrown into Bristol harbour.

A spotlight then turned on museum collections, and in particular on West African court art that had been looted by British and French armies in the 1890s. In August 2016, the newly elected president of the Republic of Bénin, Patrice Talon, demanded that France restore trophies looted by a French expeditionary force in 1894 from the ancient kingdom of Dahomey. France's Foreign Ministry made the customary response: objects deposited in French museums are inalienable national possessions. However, on 28 November 2017, during a visit to Burkina Faso, the newly elected president of France, Emmanuel Macron tweeted: "African heritage cannot be held prisoner by European museums."

Macron's intervention resonated with a general shift in public attitudes to race and imperialism. Veteran staff at the British Museum recalled with horror the campaign for the return of the Elgin Marbles to Athens launched in 1982 by the Greek film actress Melina Mercouri, her country's minister of culture. But Macron's démarche was more troubling, its potential constituency larger and more radical. The cultural establishment was thrown off balance. Some museum directors were dismissive. Others issued pious mission statements. A few proclaimed their solidarity, but did not undertake to surrender prized collections.

Parodying Macron's tweet, the former head of the Musée du quai Branly in Paris, Stéphane Martin, declared that "museums should not be held hostage to the painful history of colonialism."[42] He pointed out that one of the items demanded by the Republic of Bénin, a statue of the Dahomey god Gou that is in the Louvre, was sculpted by a man from a neighbouring country while he was a prisoner of the Dahomey king. The statue was found on a beach by a French sailor. Exhibited in the Louvre for 150 years it became an icon of modernism, revered by Picasso and Apollinaire.[43] Nevertheless, Martin came out in favour of the "circulation" of artefacts between museums. He added that African governments should be urged to treat curators with respect and pay them decent salaries.

Directors of other European museums were more diplomatic. Harmut Dorgerloh, the director-general of the Humboldt Forum in Berlin, promised that in future, labels would contextualise colonial artefacts and reveal their sometimes troubling provenance. "This will be done in a manner that displays the power relations between the colonists who brought the objects to Germany and the colonised," he declared.[44] The British Museum moved the bust of its founder, Sir Hans Sloane, from a pedestal near the entrance to a cabinet in the newly unveiled Enlightenment Hall. A text identifies him as a "slave owner" whose work was "enabled by the wealth and networks that grew out of European imperialism." "The British Museum has done a lot of work—accelerated and enlarged its work on its own history, the history of empire, the history of colonialism, and also of slavery," the museum's director, Hartwig Fischer, assured the *Daily Telegraph*. "We must not hide anything. Healing is knowledge."[45] In June 2020 he posted a pledge on the museum's website: "The British Museum stands in solidarity with the British Black community, with the African American community, with the Black community throughout the world. We are aligned with the spirit and soul of Black Lives Matter everywhere." And yet President Macron's initiative "does not change the policy of the British Museum, nor legislation in Great Britain," Fischer told *The New York Times*. The British Museum's trustees were of course open to all forms of cooperation. Nevertheless, "the collections have to be preserved as a whole."[46]

Imperial wars cast a long shadow over collecting activities in the colonial era. The argument is sometimes made that because there was a great disparity of resources between local people and foreign collectors, all acquisitions made by Europeans during the colonial period should be considered illegitimate. Ample evidence might be adduced in support of this syllogism. The ethnographer and surrealist poet, Michel Leiris, while serving as secretary to a collecting expedition under the auspices of the National Ethnographic Museum in Paris, wrote, in a letter to his wife in September 1931: "We pilfer from the Africans under the pretext of teaching others how to love them and get to know their culture, that is, when all is said and done, to train even more ethnographers, so they can head off to encounter them and 'love and pilfer' from them as well." And yet, Leiris noted in his diary, "even if we force them a little to turn over their objects (threatening them, for example, with the authority of the colonial administration), in the end it will not be to their disadvantage." And after all, "we paid for almost everything."[47]

But blanket condemnation of all transactions in the age of empire downplays local agency. Collectors were typically drawn into established systems of exchange. Leiris parodied this, imagining a scenario in which Europeans trade carnival masks in order to acquire masks of deities for museums back home, only to find that local entrepreneurs begin to trade in European masks and open their own museum of exotic crafts.[48]

Jenny Newell, co-manager of the Pacific collection at the Australian Museum in Sydney, cites an eighteenth-century account by the surgeon of a convict transport of what happened when his ship docked in a Polynesian port:

> Once the ship had come properly to anchor, the chiefly family of the region would go aboard, or arrange to meet the captain and officers on shore. Chiefs and their families would bring high-value gifts: items of regalia, large rolls of decorated tapa, ornaments, pigs and fruit that were specifically intended for establishing connections rather than the more common practice of barter. These people of rank would, after assessing the status and wealth of the crew members, select an appropriate taio [friend] each. They would wrap him in cloth, sometimes place a taumi (warrior's gorget of feathers and shark's teeth) around his neck and hand him other significant objects until, as one officer reported, he could be close to fainting from the heat and weight of them.

"With taio bonds established at all levels of the ship and the community on shore, the commodity and gift-exchanges would continue throughout the ship's stay," Newell adds. "Tahitians would at times ask the ships' carpenters to make up wooden chests in which to store the important goods they had collected." She cites George Tobin, a young lieutenant on Captain Bligh's *Providence* voyage, who remarked, after visiting Tahiti in 1792: "they have at O'tahytey their Collectors, and their cabinets of European curiosities."[49]

A handsome young aristocrat from an island near Tahiti, Omai, accompanied Captain Cook and Joseph Banks back to England in 1774, at the end of Cook's second Pacific voyage. Omai was presented to King George III, who made him an allowance and set him up in lodgings. His portrait was painted by Joshua Reynolds. A play about his life was performed at the Theatre Royal in Covent Garden. He was fêted in polite society, his courtesy and elegance widely admired. The very short-sighted Dr. Johnson told Boswell that when he dined with Omai and a British politician, Lord Mulgrave, one evening, "they sat with their backs to the light fronting me, so that I could not see distinctly; and there was so little of the savage in Omai, that I was afraid to speak to either, lest I should mistake one for the other."[50]

Omai returned to his home island of Raiatea in 1777 with a horse, armour and some curiosities. He set up a museum. "The helmet, and some other parts of armour, with several cutlasses, are still preserved, and displayed on the sides of the house now standing on the spot where Mai's dwelling was erected by Captain Cook," a missionary reported forty years after Omai's death. "A few of the trinkets, such as a jack-in-a-box, a kind of serpent that darts out of a cylindrical case when the lid is removed, are preserved with care by one of the principal chiefs, who at the time of our arrival considered them great curiosities, and exhibited them, as a mark of his condescension, to particular favourites."[51] Meanwhile, back in London, Joseph Banks donated to the British Museum a "very large Collection of Artificial Curiosities Utencils, dresses &c. from the South-Sea Islands."[52]

Dr. Newell also tells the story of Hitihiti, a young Society Islander, who accompanied Captain Cook on his second voyage as a translator and guide. When the ship visited Easter Island, Hitihiti exchanged Tahitian tapa cloths for carvings of human figures, "assuring us they would be greatly valued at Taheitee." He gave a life-size carved hand with long fingernails to the expedition's senior naturalist, Johann Reinhold Forster, who passed it on to the British Museum. It is now on display in the Enlightenment Gallery.[53]

A number of familiar anecdotes are cited to illustrate the bad faith of collectors in European colonies. Typical is the story of how colonial authorities in Nigeria apprehended Leo Frobenius, a prolific collector for German museums, when he was caught substituting a copy for an original Ife head.[54] Yet how representative are such examples? "Some objects were undoubtedly stolen and taken by force," writes Enid Schildkraut, who has studied collections made in the early twentieth century by Leo Frobenius, Emil Torday, a Hungarian ethnographer, and an American anthropologist, Frederick Starr. She points out, however, that

> often the most active collectors hung around, sometimes (as in the case of Torday) learning African languages, drinking, smoking, and dancing with Africans to convince them to exchange their objects for imported goods. Even when these collectors moved rapidly from village to village . . . or worked through local middlemen, as most did, they had to establish some rapport to extract the objects they were looking for.[55]

In the colonial period, collectors engaged with local people who were soon all too familiar with European interests. Some were shrewd traders. In November 1905, Frederick Starr recorded in his diary an attempt to buy esoteric items from an old man in a Congolese village:

> Afterward he showed the other bundle which contained a purplish mass. This had lost its efficacy so we proposed its purchase, a proposition that was promptly blocked by one of those present. After some little argument a small fetish figure was brought out and to show us how it was used the palm-oil bottle and cam-wood were produced: they were mixed in the palm and then carefully rubbed over the whole figure, suitable observations being addressed to it all the time. When the act had been gone through with we talked price; I finally offered 1½ francs for it alone or 2 in case the old man stood greasing it while we photographed him; he took the latter. This fetish he told us was for success in hunting.[56]

In a book published in 1907 Frobenius described bargaining for curios in the Congo:

> Slowly the tall sons of the Kukengo State approached and offered their ethnological stuff [*ethnologischen Kram*] for sale. I had sent my people into the country to invite the Bakuba and they came. But when they sell, the Bakuba are truly the worst Greeks. They begin by asking prices that are unheard of and don't bargain much. Then someone brings the same object and haggles over it such that the Ethnologist needs all his patience and passion for valuable collections in order to endure this ordeal. But in order to be able to acquire more I first had to pay higher prices and initially had to let much blood.[57]

The reference to blood-letting may not have been meant literally, but Frobenius was prepared to use force, particularly when it came to recruiting bearers, and he travelled with an intimidating private escort of "police soldiers."[58]

By the 1920s, trained ethnographers were embedded in faraway villages for months and years at a time, doing their best to fit in. Gregory Bateson and his wife, Margaret Mead, did fieldwork in New Guinea in the 1920s and 1930s. Bateson recalled that:

> in one of the big villages of the Sepik River headhunters, I was negotiating to buy a specially fine pair of secret flutes—highly decorated bamboo tubes, about 6 feet long and giving deep organ notes. The members of the clan which owned the flutes had two objections to the sale: "If you take these flutes away to your country *women* may see them," and "The flutes will never make music again. Who will know how to play them?" On the subject of women, I assured them—"No New Guinea women shall see the flutes and any women in my country who may see them will not know what they are." To the other objection my only reply was to take some lessons in flute playing.[59]

Melville Herskovits, a pioneer of African American studies, did fieldwork in the late 1920s among the Saramaka Maroons in a Dutch colony in South America, now the Republic of Suriname. He recalled that just as he prepared to depart:

> I was getting into the dugout canoe that I was to take for a final run through the rapids that lay between the base camp and the railhead. My field kit, my notes, my collection of carvings and specimens were being stowed away. I was saying my goodbyes. At that moment, an old woman came up to me. In her hands she held a fine food-stirring paddle, which I had tried in vain to buy from her earlier. "White man," she said, "take this. Ayobo made it for me before I came to live with him in his village. Put it in the big house, in your white man's country, where you told me beautiful things are kept. And write on a piece of paper that Ayobo made it."[60]

A trader sets out craft items for sale in the town of Ibantshe, in what
is now the Kasaï Province of the Democratic Republic of the Congo.
Leo Frobenius, who took the photograph during his 1904–6 expedition
to the Congo Free State, complained that the prices charged by Kuba
traders were far higher than he had expected. (By permission of the
Frobenius Museum, University of Frankfurt. Image: FoA 01–2229.)

The focus on the colonial period is arguably misleading. According to Maureen Murphy, a historian of African art at the Sorbonne, "70 per cent of the works preserved outside the continent 'departed' after independence in the 1960s."[61] Corruption, civil unrest and local wars fuel smuggling. John Picton recalls how during the Biafran war in the late 1960s, federal Nigerian soldiers looted Igbo sculptures "which ended up as trophies fixed to the fronts of military vehicles, while much else found its way into the international market."[62]

Christian and Islamic evangelists in Africa have instituted periodic purges of Satanic images. Marxist regimes in some West African countries banned polytheistic cults. (For instance, *Voudou* was banned in the Republic of Bénin from 1970 to 1990.) Each time, a surge of exports of antiquities followed.[63]

Iconoclasm may bring about even more serious losses than smuggling. In February 2001 the Taliban leader Mullah Omar decreed the destruction of pre-Islamic monuments and figurative art works in Afghanistan. In March, two monumental statues of the Buddha carved into a cliffside in Bamiyan between AD 570 and 618 were blown up. A team of Taliban inspectors then visited the National Museum in Kabul and ordered the curators to open locked cabinets of antiquities. "Here were drawers of extraordinary Bactrian artifacts and Ghandara heads and figurines," writes Kwame Anthony Appiah. "My friends recall the dead look in a curator's eyes as he described how the Taliban inspectors responded to these extraordinary artifacts by taking out mallets and pulverizing them in front of him."[64]

Modern art is also anathema to some authoritarian and clerical regimes. In the 1970s, when the Shah of Iran was in his pomp, courtesy of a boom in oil prices, his wife, Farah Pahlavi, went on a museum-building spree. Her signature project was the Tehran Museum of Contemporary Art. A team of curators was despatched to New York and Paris to buy works by great modernists including Picasso, Van Gogh, Pollock, Warhol and de Kooning. Among the more controversial paintings were *Gabrielle With Open Blouse*, 1907, by Renoir, and Bacon's 1968 triptych, *Two Figures Lying on a Bed With Attendants*. (The naked figures, both male, are posed facing one another.) Orientalist images included such challenging examples as Derain's *L'Age d'or*, an exercise in primitivism that featured androgynous, semi-naked figures play-fighting with wild animals.

A former curator of the Tehran museum, Roxane Zand, comments that here was "a major institution actually reflecting a reverse process, a reverse colonialism or reappropriation."[65] Iran's sudden openness to international movements in the arts was certainly remarkable. But everything changed when a fundamentalist regime came to power in 1979. Artistic representations, critical literature, even ancient texts were condemned as sacrilegious. In 1989, Ayatollah Khomeini issued a fatwa ordering Muslims to kill Salman Rushdie because his novel, *The Satanic Verses*, was blasphemous. Iranian politicians then joined a clamour over satirical cartoons featuring the prophet Muhammad that were published by the Danish newspaper *Jyllands-Posten* in 2005.[66] And the collection of the Contemporary Art Museum was shut away in a high-security vault. (It is now estimated to be worth £2.5 billion.)[67]

Shortly before the Islamic Revolution, the Shah had been negotiating with the British Museum for the loan of the Cyrus Cylinder, a clay cylinder inscribed with an account of the conquest of Babylon by Cyrus in 539 BCE. The new regime carried on with the negotiations. Some Iranian politicians even claimed that the Cylinder, excavated in Babylon in 1879, rightfully belonged to Iran, and demanded its permanent return. In 2010, following lengthy negotiations, a loan was agreed. The director of the British Museum, Neil MacGregor, claimed this as a diplomatic triumph. But there was an outcry in Iran because the ancient artefact shed a glorious light on a pre-Islamic dynasty. The director of the national museum was imprisoned.

Despite cautionary tales about smuggling, theft, iconoclasm, censorship and neglect, the force is with those who demand the restitution of colonial collections. The director of a major

European museum told me that her younger curators are convinced that every questionable piece in the collections should be
"returned." Yet it may not be a simple matter to restore antique
works of art, or even to identify who might be their rightful
owners, or reliable custodians. Do people who share a "culture"
(whatever that might mean), have collective rights in historical
artefacts that date back centuries? Do museums that preserved
and displayed foreign artefacts for a century or more retain no
legitimate claim to them?

"There have been bad arguments on both sides" when it
comes to Lord Elgin's Athenian booty, in the judgement of
Mary Beard. "Politicians have leapt on and off the bandwagon.
Successive Greek governments have found the loss of the Parthenon sculptures a convenient symbol of national unity, and
demands for their restitution a low-cost and relatively risk-free
campaign." Difficult questions of principle are at stake: "to
whom does the Parthenon, and other such world-class monuments, belong? Should cultural treasures be repatriated, or
should museums be proud of their international holdings? Is
the Parthenon a special case—and why?"[68]

By the 2020s pressure was building. The Smithsonian Institution in Washington, DC, and the Horniman Museum in
London announced that they would return Benin Bronzes to
Nigeria. There may even be a deal in the making to settle Athens's claim on the Parthenon Marbles in the British Museum.
At a meeting of UNESCO in May 2021, "every country there
ganged up against the UK," *The Times* reported. A poll published
by YouGov in November 2021 revealed that 59 per cent of British
respondents believed that the Parthenon statues should be
returned to Greece (18 per cent wanted them to stay in Britain;
22 per cent were don't knows). However, while Greece wanted
acknowledgement of its "ownership" of the marbles, Jonathan
Williams, deputy director of the British Museum, preferred talk
of loans. "There are many wonderful things we'd be delighted
to borrow and lend," he said. "It is what we do."[69]

While demands for restitution command the headlines, the crisis of the Museum of Other People is also, perhaps yet more fundamentally, an intellectual crisis. The museum is charged with disseminating racist and imperialist propaganda. Even if that broad-brush indictment may be countered, relativised or put into historical context, more insidious questions must still be addressed. Can we (Europeans, let us say) grasp the world view, the rituals, the customs, the arts of people with whom, it may seem, we have little in common, and who have reason to suspect us of racism, or at least condescension? Can we, should we, translate their ideas into our own terms? Some argue that the very act of observing and classifying others is a power play. If that is so, it may be impossible, in good faith, to undertake ethnographic research. But would you accept a stranger's self-representation on trust? After all, how many English people are able to provide reliable information on their country's history, literature, arts or religions?

Then there is the most challenging question of all. What is the Museum of Other People about? *What is it a museum of?* In 1988, the Victoria and Albert Museum in London commissioned six posters that advertised the V&A as: "An ace caff, with quite a nice museum attached." One poster asked: "Where else do they give you £100,000,000 worth of *objets d'art* free with every egg salad?" What slogan might be blazoned on a poster to advertise the Museum of Other People in the twenty-first century? (Under a different name, it goes without saying.)

PART 1

FARAWAY PEOPLE

INVENTING THE MUSEUM
OF OTHER PEOPLE

On 10 October 1789, the revolutionary French government seized the properties of the Church. In March 1792 the estates and goods of noble émigrés were confiscated. In October 1793 the republic claimed the belongings of people who had been guillotined, among them King Louis XVI and his queen, Marie Antoinette.

Church buildings, grand houses, parks, farmlands and forests were now at the disposal of the state. The authorities also found themselves in possession of sprawling assemblages of manuscripts, holy relics, jewellery, works of art, weapons, and zoological and botanical specimens. Some precious objects were sold off, but there was a high-minded view that the great collections should be accessible to everyone. The royal gardens were opened to the public together with the collection of natural curiosities, which became the National Museum of Natural History. The royal library became the National Library. In 1793, the Palace of the Louvre became a public museum of art and classical antiquities. ("The museum is not supposed to be a vain assemblage of frivolous luxury objects," Jacques-Louis David, the leading French painter of his generation, and a close ally of Robespierre, advised the National Assembly. "What it must be is an imposing school.")[1]

Putting things right was not always so straightforward, to be fixed by a change of name. A particularly intractable problem was posed by the French king's *Cabinet des médailles*, which was deposited in the royal library. A relic of the medieval treasury, it was originally a repository of antique and foreign coins, precious stones, and assorted seals and engravings.[2] By the time the royal library was transferred from Versailles to Paris in 1724, the *cabinet* functioned as a sort of royal attic, crammed to overflowing with a jumble of ancient and exotic artefacts.

In 1795, the committee of public instruction of the revolutionary National Assembly dispatched one of its members, a radical bishop, Villar de la Mayenne, to advise on the reorganisation of the royal library. He reported that the attic of the library was stuffed with idols, vases, busts and ancient lamps. Other antiquities and exotic objects were packed into an obscure and humid room on the ground floor.

In 1800, an audit was ordered. This recorded that the *cabinet* held over 6,000 Egyptian, Etruscan, Greek, Roman, Gallic, Indian, Chinese and Peruvian items, including sculptures, vases, hieroglyphic inscriptions, furniture, surgical instruments and weapons. The audit classified items according to the materials used in their manufacture (marble, silver, bronze, stone, etc.), and then by region of origin; but the principles guiding the classification were not made explicit.[3] Nor is it easy to reconstruct the logic behind the acquisitions. For example, in 1776, the royal library procured from Russia two calendars inscribed on wooden boards; an iron harness from Siberia; representations of deities from Siberia and Mongolia; and a Chinese balance. There were also unsolicited, sometimes idiosyncratic gifts from naval officers and travelling scientists. So in 1779, Joseph Dombey, an adventurous French botanist, donated a striking if miscellaneous assemblage of objects from Peru, including gold and silver ornaments and statuettes; vases made in "unusual, even bizarre" shapes; an ornamental wooden staff; and a superb embroidered poncho.[4] (The following year, Dombey dispatched botanical specimens from Peru to France. The ship on which they were transported was intercepted by a British vessel and the collection transferred to the British Museum.)

Villar de la Mayenne reported that the *Cabinet des médailles* was swamped, and yet more and more treasures were being brought in. Holy relics, sculptures and paintings were removed from churches. The cabinets of curiosities of nobles who fled the country or perished on the scaffold were confiscated. Revolutionary armies brought back spoils from sorties abroad, notably masterpieces of art from Belgium and Italy but also such specialist collections as the papal archive and the trove of orientalist manuscripts and maps assembled by the Stadtholder of the Netherlands. What was to be done with all these treasures?

In 1803, the secretary of the short-lived Société des Observateurs de l'Homme, Louis-François Jauffret, published a brief plan for an "anthropological museum." It would collect skulls and skeletons to allow the "naturalistic" study of humanity, and display "products made by savages" in order to promote an understanding "of the customs and usages of ancient and modern peoples."[5] Nobody took him up on it.

Choice carvings and sculptures might be acceptable to the Louvre. Anatomical, geological, zoological and botanical specimens could be passed on to the new National Museum of Natural History. But what was to be done with all those antiques and curios crammed into the attic of the National Library? Villar de la Mayenne proposed that a museum of antiquities be set up in one of the mansions recently confiscated from fleeing aristocrats.

The head of the library and curator of the *Cabinet des médailles*, André Barthélemy de Courcay, began to make arrangements for this museum of antiquities, which, he announced, would document "the customs and practices of peoples distanced by time and space" (*"les moeurs et des usages des peuples éloignés par les temps et par les lieux"*).[6] Pressed for space, the Museum of Natural History promptly offered unwanted "artificial curiosities" to Barthélemy. An employee of the *Cabinet des médailles* went through boxes of odds and ends in the museum and recovered "idols worshipped by savages, and weapons and furniture used by them . . . I also brought away a mummy, some Egyptian antiquities, and a mummified head . . . ."[7]

In October 1799, Barthélemy died suddenly of a stroke, surrounded by unopened boxes of curiosities. Without his commitment, the prospect of a museum of antiquities faded from view. And yet still more stuff was coming in. Napoleon's expeditionary force in Egypt sent boatloads of antiquities to France. Scientific and naval expeditions in Oceania, South America and the Far East brought home not just maps and ocean charts, and plants and seeds, but also antiquities, jewellery, weapons and miscellaneous arts and crafts. If these were not accepted by the Louvre, or offloaded on the *Cabinet des médailles*, they might be sold at auction. Napoleon's wife, the Empress Josephine, commandeered some particularly desirable pieces for her swanky new home, the Malmaison.

Every now and then a particularly significant cargo arrived, and concentrated minds. Typically, the Ministry of Public Instruction would appoint a commission to work out what should be done with it. In 1818, the French consul in Cairo offered a substantial but rather random collection of Egyptian objects. The ministry duly set up a commission. It advised that antiquities should be acquired for the Louvre. Plants, animals, and human skeletons and skulls should go to the Museum of Natural History. "As for the diverse objects, brought from Egypt, Nubia and Abyssinia, to wit: musical instruments, tools, arms and armour, clothes, cooking implements, vases and domestic objects, there is no establishment designed for their reception." The commission recommended that the authorities fund "a *special collection*, devoted to this third type of object."[8] In the event, the consul's collection was auctioned off. However, the secretary of the commission, Edme-François Jomard, would devote the rest of his life to the establishment of this *special collection*.

An engineer and cartographer, Jomard was one of the savants who travelled to Egypt with Napoleon's army. Later he coordinated the encyclopaedic official report on the country. In 1828, he was appointed curator of the *Cabinet des médailles* and charged with the organisation of a *dépôt de géographie* which would assemble "various objects and instruments yielded by scientific voyages."[9] From now on he was a man on a mission. He would create a museum dedicated to "this third type of object." And the timing was auspicious, Jomard noted. France was undertaking military operations in Algeria. "Science as well as commerce should profit . . . No doubt, objects would be collected from tribes in the interior . . . including much of interest in relation to the customs and traditions of the Berbers and other peoples of the Atlas, such as arms, vases, and instruments of various kinds."[10]

Like Barthélemy before him, Jomard planned to exhibit ethnographic and ancient artefacts side by side. The royal library possessed a Nubian lyre with five strings and a sound board made from a turtle shell. Studying it, Jomard had an epiphany. "*Voilà*, I said to myself, the lyre of Mercury, found far from the lands of Greek mythology. And so I began a collection, whose utility for the study of man and his diverse races I sensed at once."[11] This collection of ancient and exotic "instruments, weapons and costumes . . . would give an idea of the customs and usages or the degree of civilisation of peoples."[12]

But almost immediately Jomard had competition. The Bourbons were back on the French throne. In 1827, King Charles X ordered the establishment of a naval museum (Musée de la Marine) within the Louvre. The museum would be mostly about ships, sea battles, ocean charts and so on, but it also took in naval exploration, and so it would exhibit "ethnographic" materials collected by the French navy in faraway ports. Admiral Dumont d'Urville presented more than a hundred objects from Oceania.[13] Royal collections and other national depositaries handed over specimens that seemed suitable, including vases from Chile, snowshoes from Canada, a Hawaiian helmet and a magnificent Sioux costume. The king had high hopes for the new museum. He named it for his son, the dauphin. There seemed little chance that Jomard would get his hands on its ethnographic specimens.

In 1828, a remarkable collection of religious materials from India was offered to the French state. Several museums put in bids. The ministry duly set up a blue-ribbon commission, including both the great naturalist Georges Cuvier and Jomard. It recommended that:

1. An ethnographic collection should be established in Paris to illustrate the history of *"l'homme physique et l'homme moral,"* the physical man and the moral man.
2. This depositary should be placed within the Royal Library.
3. "Objects of a kind appropriate to this collection that are presently dispersed in various public establishments in Paris . . . should be brought to the Royal Library."[14]

Jomard must have been encouraged, but the Louvre was unimpressed. Ministerial budgets were tight. And then, in 1830, there was a political crisis. The Bourbons were driven out. The new citizen king, Louis Philippe, had other things on his mind. Nobody had time to spare for Jomard's project.

Before there were ethnographic museums, they could be imagined. In 1831 Jomard published one of the first—perhaps the very first—coherent plan for the identification, classification and arrangement of "ethnographic" objects.[15] The Baron de Férussac, a veteran of Napoleon's campaigns, and the director of the naval museum in the Louvre, reprimanded Jomard for wanting to poach its ethnographic collection.[16] A distinguished naturalist accused him of trying to expand and glorify his niche in the *Cabinet des médailles*.[17] But rising above these local jealousies, Jomard made a coherent, considered argument. His essay initiated a debate that would resonate throughout the nineteenth century.

Even the most isolated societies were adopting European languages, customs and techniques, Jomard began. It was therefore urgently necessary to collect artefacts that bore witness to their unspoilt aboriginal condition. Such a collection would serve both philosophical and practical purposes. France was expanding its trade with faraway countries and acquiring tropical colonies: French traders and officials should learn more about those remote lands. Finally, the clincher. There were substantial ethnographic collections in St. Petersburg, Berlin, London and even in the capital cities of small Scandinavian countries. Surely Paris, which Jomard called "the capital of civilisation," should have its very own museum of ethnography?[18]

Jomard's central claim was that this "third type of object," these "ethnographic" artefacts, were indeed distinctive. Although often fashioned from natural materials, they were not "natural," and so they did not belong in a museum of natural history. Nor were they antiquities. After all, they were still being made. No more were they works of art. Any aesthetic qualities were incidental. Ethnographic objects were rather to be regarded as tools or instruments (although Jomard did note that even useless fripperies might help philosophers to understand the "moral man"). The conclusion was evident. Ethnographic objects belonged in a museum of ethnography.

As to what objects should be selected, that "depends on the specification of the goal," Jomard wrote. "This goal is essentially *scientific:* it concerns, principally, coming to know, in a precise and positive manner, the degree of civilisation of peoples who have made little progress at the social level."[19] A "philosophical observer" who made a study of the artefacts of such peoples could not fail to be impressed by the progress of humanity.[20]

And how were these ethnographic objects to be ordered and displayed? It was here that Jomard made his most influential contribution. In the early nineteenth century, the orthodox taxonomic system in the natural sciences was still that of Carl Linnaeus, but Georges Cuvier, the most celebrated natural scientist in France, argued that what mattered most was not form, or presumed family relationships (genus, species, variety), as in the system of Linnaeus, but rather function. Indeed, Cuvier argued that function determined form.[21] A professor in the Museum of Natural History, he had reordered the museum's collections of animal skeletons, paying particular attention to the function of organs, and to what he termed the correlation of parts.[22]

Cuvier, a weighty figure in scientific circles, was a supporter of anthropology and ethnology. Jomard served alongside him on official committees, including the commission in 1828 that recommended the establishment of a museum of ethnography. In 1830, Cuvier took on a more orthodox naturalist, Geoffroy St. Hilaire, in a historic debate about scientific taxonomies.[23] Jomard's brochure appeared a few months later. It applied Cuvier's method to the classification and comparison of ethnographic materials. Function was the key.

All human beings share certain common needs, Jomard began. Even "savages" make tools that help them to satisfy these needs (for food, shelter, defence and so on). At a more advanced stage, the arts, sciences and religion develop. Objects of the same "genre," which perform similar functions, should be placed together. So, for instance, Jomard proposed to exhibit weapons from around the world—antique or ethnographic—in a single display, arranged in a series from "primitive" to "civilised." And there would be virtually no limit to the geographical range of the collection. "With the exception of civilised Europe, practically the whole of the inhabited globe furnished suitable materials."[24] So there, in plain sight, was the Other: the whole world beyond "civilised Europe."

Jomard's brochure caught the attention of Philipp Franz Balthasar von Siebold, a medical doctor, cosmopolitan adventurer, and dealer in oriental antiquities who had plans for an ethnographic museum in the university city of Leiden in the Netherlands. Born in the bishopric of Würzburg in 1796, Siebold was twenty years younger than Jomard.[25] He came from a family of doctors and duly qualified in medicine, but his ambition was to become a traveller and scientist like his hero, Alexander von Humboldt. He made a promising start. Recruited to serve as a doctor with the Dutch military in the East Indies, he was immediately promoted by an officer who had been treated for a gunshot wound by Siebold's grandfather. Soon the young Siebold was a colonel.[26]

After the fall of Napoleon, the Dutch East India Company retained a precarious foothold in Batavia, its headquarters in the Far East, and managed to hang on to a potentially valuable base in Dejima, an artificial island at Nagasaki that was the only site of direct trade between Japan and the outside world during the Edo period. In 1822, Siebold was sent out to Indonesia as a military surgeon. He made a good impression on the Dutch governor-general and was dispatched to Dejima with the expectation that he would practise medicine while dabbling on the side as a commercial agent and collector. Conveniently, he was permitted to give instruction in medicine in Nagasaki, so he was able to develop a wide acquaintance with local scientists, and he set up house with a Japanese woman. (Their daughter, Kusumoto Ine, became the first female doctor in Japan qualified in Western medicine, and she was appointed a physician to the Japanese court. Her story has inspired plays, musicals, TV dramas and a novel by a famous Japanese author, Akira Yoshimura.)[27]

Siebold did not master the Japanese language: he explained that the "perverted pronunciation is impossible for a European in so short a time."[28] However, he collected flora, fauna, scientific instruments and arts and crafts, apparently all part of his intelligence gathering on behalf of the Dutch East India government.[29] Then he went too far. Permitted to visit Edo (the modern Tokyo), he acquired maps of Japan. This led to his detention on a charge of espionage, house arrest and expulsion from the country. In retribution, Dutch trade with Japan was halved for a time, but Siebold was treated leniently by the Dutch authorities. In 1830, he returned to Europe with a remarkable haul of paintings, books, and botanical and ethnographic specimens. He began at once to compile and publish extensive though prolix and poorly organised reports on Japan.[30] (His model was Humboldt's volumes on Mexico and Cuba.)[31] And he now began a sustained push to market his materials.

When Napoleon occupied the Netherlands, the Dutch Stadtholder, William V, fled to England. His natural history cabinet was seized, packed into 150 chests, and taken to France, together with a large portion of his magnificent hoard of oriental manuscripts and treasures.[32] Following Bonaparte's defeat in 1813, the Stadtholder's son, William, Prince of Orange, returned as the first king of the United Netherlands, bringing with him collections that his father had managed to take with him into his exile. Under pressure from the Duke of Wellington, who was instrumental in the defeat of Napoleon, the Louvre returned choice items that had been seized by Napoleon's agents. In 1816, King William established the Royal Cabinet of Rarities (*Het Koninklijk Kabinet van Zeldzaamheden*). In 1821 it was moved to the restored Mauritshuis in the Hague, alongside the royal art collection. A year later it opened for public viewing.

Reinier Pieter van de Kasteele, a minister of the Dutch Reformed church, was put in charge of the cabinet of rarities. Confronted with the task of putting this very mixed bag in order, he wrote, rather desperately, to a colleague, that: "now, like when one moves house, things are pulled out of the sacks and not yet placed in order in the new house."[33] Yet the king was soon busily making further acquisitions: "rarities, antiquities, products of nature, art and taste," according to Kasteele.

Kasteele had studied geography and ethnography in Halle, in Germany, and he noted that the collection represented "the morals, habits and religions of all extant peoples since the Middle Ages and those of the Fatherland."[34] Given Holland's historical investment in the Far East, the Orientalist selection was particularly rich. The king now commissioned further purchases of Chinese and Japanese materials by agents of the Dutch East India Company operating out of Dejima.

In 1831, the king bought a large selection of books and artefacts from Siebold. While the king would remain his most important client, Siebold sold choice items from time to time to collectors in Russia and Germany, much to the irritation of the Dutch authorities. Nevertheless, he was not content simply to be a dealer. He had scientific pretensions. And he hoped to direct a new museum in Leiden that would bring together the king's Japanese collections and his own. Meanwhile, he opened his personal stock of East Asian materials to visitors to his home.

In 1834, Siebold circulated a prospectus for an ethnographic museum that would display objects from certain countries beyond Europe, in particular from Dutch colonies and trading partners in the East.[35] Setting out his stall, he proclaimed that "Humanity in its many-sided development in foreign climes is therefore *the main subject matter* of an ethnographic museum." Drawing on contemporary German geographical discourse, he distinguished the study of "lands and peoples" from environmental studies, which were a topic for natural history.

But Siebold was not concerned solely with science. "The purpose of an ethnographic museum is the expansion of knowledge of lands and people in general . . . such a development of geographical knowledge would be without question of the greatest utility for a country that depends on trade and seafaring."[36] His museum would showcase "commercial trade products" of little-known faraway countries, selecting those that would be "beneficial to the economist, the artist, the manufacturer and the master builder alike." Prehistoric artefacts were excluded. Siebold declared that they belonged in a different kind of museum: a museum of antiquities, or a natural history museum.[37]

In 1838, Siebold finalised a large sale of his Japanese materials to the Dutch king. He continued to lobby for a publicly funded museum under his leadership, but vacillated between the project for a museum of Japan and vaguer plans for a more broadly conceived ethnographic museum.

In 1843, Siebold visited Jomard in Paris. He then published a pamphlet on the subject of museums of ethnography. Formally addressed to Jomard, it should be read in the context of his long-running campaign for a museum in Leiden. Siebold took up Jomard's suggestions critically, but courteously, and at some length.[38] On what was perhaps the crucial issue, he agreed that there was a pressing need for ethnographic museums, in order to inform colonial officers, missionaries and traders about the character of a particular population with which they had dealings. Indeed, Siebold's pamphlet was entitled: "on the utility of ethnographic museums and the importance of their creation in European states that possess colonies or which maintain commercial relations with other parts of the world."

Ethnographic museums would also serve a more philosophical purpose. Scholars generally neglected the civilisations of East Asia and the Americas, wrote Siebold. However, he had himself lived for many years in Japan, which, he judged, represented "the summit of Far Eastern civilisations." He noted that Jomard was well acquainted with Egypt, a country once highly civilised, though now occupied by "barbarous tribes." Both he and Jomard had accordingly developed a sympathetic appreciation of very different civilisations.[39] But Europeans were apt to neglect less spectacularly endowed societies. "Other non-European peoples were almost forgotten," Siebold noted, "and the epithet 'savages,' vulgarly applied to them, was sufficient in itself to put off the learned world." Cabinets of "curiosities" or "rarities" included weapons, costumes, sacred objects and utensils of "savage peoples," but the "most hideous examples were specially chosen, in order to certify the bizarre character and the inhumanity of their customs, and when it came to their religious and moral institutions, or their principles of government and administration, interest was shown only in pagan edifices and despotic maxims."[40]

Yet while Siebold agreed with Jomard that the time had come for dedicated museums of ethnography, the two men had very different ideas about how ethnographic collections should be classified and displayed.[41] Jomard advocated a "functional" classification, on the model of Cuvier. Siebold took the view that a museum of ethnography should focus on objects made within particular geographical regions. He recognised that similar artefacts might well turn up in very different locations, but he assumed that this was because they had been borrowed. For example, the zodiac of the Chinese, or so it seemed, had been found among the Aztecs. (When Siebold showed Japanese colleagues Humboldt's illustrations of Aztec "zodiacs" they immediately recognised the similarities.)[42]

Summing up, Siebold wrote to Jomard:

> You and I elect different systems for the classification of eth-nographic objects. Yours facilitates comparison by bringing together objects of the same nature, that serve the same purpose, as they exist among different peoples; mine, on the contrary, is ordered geographically, and brings together the productions of one and the same nation . . . One room in my collection shows the richness and high perfection of Japanese technology; another room, dedicated to the peoples of New Guinea, reveals the poverty and imper-fection of the utensils, clothes and other objects that are indispensable even among the most savage of men.[43]

Siebold remarked that when he visited Jomard's collection he saw some Japanese bronze mirrors. Jomard put them together with ancient Roman mirrors. In his own museum, Siebold set Japanese mirrors within a broader display of Japanese luxuries. Perhaps, Siebold suggested, he and Jomard were practising dif-ferent sciences. "One might call the juxtaposition of objects of the same nature among different peoples the ethnological method," Siebold wrote, "while the practical study of peoples taken separately is the ethnographic method, and I think it should be preferred."[44]

In February 1848, Siebold was at last informed by the minister of the interior that the Dutch king planned to unite the royal collections of Japanese and ethnographic artefacts with Sie-bold's collections in Leiden. Siebold was to be the director of the new museum. As part of the deal, Siebold agreed to sell all his materials to the state, although he continued to deal in

Japanese artefacts, despite the objections of the responsible Dutch bureaucrats.[45]

In the 1850s, responding to American and British pressure, Japan relaxed its restrictions on foreigners. Siebold was permitted to return to the country in 1859. He remained for three years and accumulated another large collection. In the meantime, back in Holland, Conradus Leemans, director of the Museum of Antiquities in Leiden, took custody of Siebold's Japan museum. In 1864 it became the basis for a national museum of ethnography under Leemans's leadership.

Thwarted in his ambition to establish a public museum under his own direction, Siebold offered his new collection to the Dutch authorities. They baulked at the asking price. He then sent catalogues to leading European museums and bustled about trying to promote commercial exchanges with Japan, which was now at last opening up to foreign trade.

The French novelist Alphonse Daudet, who had a position in the court of Napoleon III, and who Siebold briefly employed as a secretary, published an ironic account of a visit to Paris in 1866 by "M. Le Colonel de Sieboldt," a grand old man with a long white beard, "firm and upright despite his seventy-two years," who was accompanied "by a young demoiselle from Munich whom he presented as his niece." (According to Rudolf Effert, Siebold was accompanied only by his youngest son, who had long blonde hair. It seems that Daudet was playing games with the reader.) Siebold's purpose was to interest the emperor in an international business consortium that would invest in Japan. Daudet had some fun with that:

> Poor old Sieboldt! I still see him on his way to the Tuileries, his medals pinned to his chest, in his fine colonel's dress uniform. He returned in triumph that evening: Napoléon III had received him, heard him out for five minutes, and sent him on his way with his favourite phrase: "I will see . . . I will reflect" . . . I had the greatest difficulty to make him understand that His Majesty might take quite a while for

reflection, and that he would be well advised to return to Munich, where the legislature was at that very moment voting funds to buy his vast collection.[46]

A few months later Siebold, caught up in the Prussian invasion of Bavaria, died suddenly of a stroke. The Bavarian authorities did buy a large haul of Japanese materials from Siebold's estate, but Maximilian Buchner, who became director of the Munich Ethnographic Museum in 1887, described it as "the collection of a natural-history researcher, who was far from artistically inclined, and who tried to substitute in quantity what it lacked in value and quality."[47]

Christian Jürgensen Thomsen, the director of the newly established Royal Museum of Nordic Antiquities in Copenhagen, was in correspondence with Jomard and Siebold, and he visited them both in 1841 and 1842. The three men were fellow pioneers in the still novel field of ethnographic and archaeological museums, but they had very different ideas about what these museums should collect and how collections should be arranged. Like Siebold, Thomsen preferred to show ordinary and common objects, "used by the entire people." He hid away his museum's holdings of "unusual and rare" curiosities.[48] On the other hand, he agreed with Jomard that the ideal museum of antiquities should illustrate "the gradual development of humanity."[49] Accordingly, he did his best to order archaeological and ethnographic specimens in a chronological series.

Thomsen was the eldest of six sons of Christian Thomsen, merchant, shipowner and one of the first five directors of the National Bank of Denmark, which was founded in 1818. After his father's death, he ran the family firm for a decade before selling it in order to devote himself to the development of a national collection of ancient Nordic artefacts.[50] This was a patriotic cause. Although Denmark had done its best to stay on the sidelines during the Napoleonic wars, the British authorities suspected that the country was being drawn into an alliance with France and Russia against Britain. In 1801, Royal Navy ships entered the Sound and destroyed the Danish fleet in Copenhagen harbour. In 1807, British forces occupied Zealand, imposed a naval blockade and bombarded Copenhagen, laying waste to large parts of the city.

In reaction, there was a surge of patriotic interest in the ancient world of the sagas. Adam Gottlob Oehlenschläger's epic poem, published in 1802, "The Golden Horns," became a popular sensation. Its occasion was the theft from the royal *Kunstkammer* of two golden prehistoric drinking horns which had been discovered in Jutland in the seventeenth century. (Thomsen attempted to discover the thieves. The horns themselves were soon found, but they had been melted down.)[51] Oehlenschläger represented the horns as gifts from the Nordic gods, and lamented that modern Danes had shown that they were too materialistic to appreciate their true value.

But romantic antiquarians were confronted by sceptical historians. There was a culture war in progress, a struggle for the past. The new German critical historical scholarship was devoted to documentary research. It was conceded that there was an age before writing, but this had no place in history, certainly not in historical scholarship. A critical historian, August Ludwig Schlözer, wrote in 1772: "I am allowed to separate all history from the beginning of the world to the beginning of Rome—or rather the poor leftovers of it—from the rest of world history, and to call it prehistory (*Vorgeschichte*)."

Schlözer, who spent many years in Sweden, judged that there could be no northern history before the ninth century, when Scandinavia became Christian. There could be no "internal history" because there was no writing. And there could be no "external history" because there were no contacts with the civilised, literate, Christian south of Europe.[52] A professor at the University of Copenhagen, Christian Molbech, who founded the Danish Historical Association in 1839, insisted on the need to "separate the absolute historical night" of prehistoric times from real history. Prehistory "can be the object of mythical poetry

or of speculation in natural philosophy, but never of historical knowledge."[53] Odin, the wise, one-eyed Norse god, was a
legend, not a real person.

The sagas mixed myths and legends together with what
were perhaps historical episodes, but the austere new doctrine
seemed to leave no place for scholarly research on ancient
Nordic times. However, a few enthusiasts began to collect relics
of those ancient days, not just runic inscriptions but also stone
implements. These were not "thunderstones" that dropped
from the sky, as folklore had it: they were the work of Nordic
craftsmen.[54] What insights might these artefacts give into pagan
Scandinavia?

In 1806, Rasmus Nyerup, the librarian at the University
of Copenhagen, published a book urging the protection of
monuments and the establishment of a national collection of
antiquities. A Royal Commission for the Preservation and Collection of Antiquities was established in 1807, with Nyerup as
secretary. It soon put together a substantial collection.

Thomsen was brought in as Nyerup's deputy. In 1816 he was
invited to help catalogue the commission's collection of antiquities and to arrange for its exhibition. He was just twenty-seven
years old, and with a commercial rather than an academic education. A sniffy Copenhagen professor remarked that he was
"only a dilettante" but, he conceded, "a dilettante with many
qualifications." His business training was certainly an asset. He
introduced budgetary controls, created a register of acquisitions, and instituted an energetic programme of acquisition.[55]

In 1819, Thomsen supervised the opening of the grandly
named Royal Museum of Nordic Antiquities. Popular with visitors, the museum attracted donations. Within a few years its
display cabinets were overflowing. Thomsen began at once to
develop a system of classification. This was based, first, on the
materials used to make artefacts, and then by function. In 1820, an
English visitor to the museum noted: "the collection of heathen
antiquities is the most complete: in one cabinet are only things
of stone, in relation to religious matters . . . In another cabinet

are only stone weapons. . . . After this follows in a third cabinet antiquities of metal, in relation to religious worship (idols, sacrificial vessels, etc.) and in a fourth cabinet are weapons and tools of metal."[56] When the collection was moved to Christiansborg Castle in 1832, Thomsen arranged it into Stone Age, Bronze Age and Iron Age sections. This came to be known as the "Three Age System."[57] In 1837, the Royal Society for Ancient Nordic Texts put together a collective volume, *Guideline to Knowledge of Nordic Antiquity*. Thomsen contributed an essay setting out the Three Age System. This was immediately translated into German. An English translation followed in 1848.[58]

Thomsen's model was not entirely original. It might even be traced back to the long poem, *De Rerum Natura*, written in the first century BCE by Lucretius, which contrasted stone, bronze and iron decorations and weapons. This text was familiar to classically educated people. In 1813, a colleague of Thomsen on the Royal Commission for the Preservation of Antiquities, Vedel Simonsen, suggested that it might be applicable to the commission's collection.[59] But it was Thomsen who demonstrated that the model worked. It imposed a coherent chronological narrative on his museum's large and variegated holdings.

Thomsen nevertheless recognised that the boundaries between the three stages were far from watertight. "Bronze and stone artefacts had continued to be made in the Iron Age, just as stone tools had been used in the Bronze Age," writes Bo Gräslund, a Swedish archaeologist. "The challenge was therefore to distinguish bronze tools made during the Iron Age from those made during the Bronze Age and to differentiate which stone tools had been made in each period. There was also the problem of assigning objects made of gold, silver, glass and other substances to each period."[60] Within these three periods, Thomsen arranged artefacts into functional categories (tools, weapons, cooking implements, jewellery, cult objects, and so on), and then by shape and decoration, which were also a guide to periods, giving clues, for example, as to which objects made of stone were actually associated with Bronze Age objects.

In 1825, Thomsen wrote to a German colleague: "It appears clear to us, that in an early period the whole of the northern part of Europe: Scandinavia, most of Germany, France and England, was occupied by very primitive peoples, who all resembled one another a great deal." And, he added, "It is certain that they resembled the savages of North America in many respects."[61] Perhaps, then, exotic "ethnographic objects" should be exhibited alongside Nordic relics of the Stone Age.

Crammed initially into an attic in the university library, the Royal Museum of Nordic Antiquities was moved to the more glamorous royal castle Christiansborg in 1832. In 1839, Thomsen was given control of the ethnographic collections in the Danish royal *Kuntskammer*. Between 1845 and 1847 a corvette, the *Galathea*, sponsored by King Christian VIII, travelled to India, China, Tahiti and South America with five researchers on board. It returned with a large haul of zoological, botanical and also ethnographic materials to add to Thomsen's collection. When, in 1849, the museum reopened as the "Royal Ethnographic Museum" in forty-four rooms in the Prinsens Palace, neighbouring Christiansborg, exotic ethnographic items were exhibited together with archaeological finds from Europe.

Thomsen's one-time assistant, Jens Worsaae, was appointed to the first chair in archaeology at the University of Copenhagen in 1855. He conducted excavations in Scandinavia and in Viking settlements in England and Scotland and confirmed that the Three Age System could be applied to archaeological sites throughout northern Europe. He also launched a devastating critique of antiquarians who treated the Nordic sagas as historical sources.[62]

The Danish king was delighted when Worsaae showed him that some allegedly runic inscriptions were in fact natural faultlines in the stones. Worsaae recalled:

After a while the King said "I both thank and congratulate you. From now on, nobody will be able to make me believe that there is even a single runic letter at Runamo. I would

C. J. Thomsen i Oldnord. Museum
paa Christiansborg.

Christian Jürgensen Thomsen welcoming visitors to the
Royal Museum of Nordic Antiquities in Christiansborg
Palace, Copenhagen. Drawing by P. Marquardt, 1846.

never previously have thought it credible that it was so clear a product of nature." At this he began to laugh so strongly that in the end he clutched his stomach, repeating *"oh these academics"* and . . . *"This is definitely an unmatchable story."*[63]

The Three Age System was quickly adopted by Scandinavian scholars. Worsaae was by now a firm favourite of the Danish king, who sponsored his visit to the British Isles in 1846–7. In London he met prominent British antiquarians, and was not impressed. "The British Museum is an utter shambles!" There was not even a room dedicated to British antiquities. Worse still, "there was absolutely nothing in the way of a generally accepted archaeological system. [The curators were] utter dilettantes, who had no concept of the chronological sequence of the monuments and antiquities . . . I think I can state without being immodest my trip was a sort of archaeological Viking raid, which served . . . to establish the foundations of the Danish system's influence on the British Isles."[64]

In fact, as Peter Rowley-Conwy has shown, British antiquarians were by no means persuaded that the Three Age System was an improvement on their established, if imprecise, notions of a "Celtic" past. They took the Danish model more seriously after the shock discovery of Stone Age implements and human remains in Brixham cave in Devon in 1858, and the publication in 1865 of John Lubbock's *Pre-Historic Times*. But while Lubbock endorsed the Three Age System, he set it within a broader framework, a more ambitious, "evolutionist" way of thinking that made the Copenhagen approach seem rather limited and old-fashioned.

Neither Thomsen nor Worsaae took on board the vast time-scale of life on earth that was being revealed by geology. Nor did they challenge the orthodox theological view that the world had been created very quickly, complete with human beings, no more than about 6,000 years ago. Thomsen was also uncertain about how to date the end of the Stone Age. In common with other scholars at the time, he fell back on "legends about Odin as the 'creator' of the Nordic metal technology in the last century before the birth of Christ."[65]

Yet the Nordic antiquarians were on to something. "By ironic coincidence," explains a distinguished archaeologist, Bruce Trigger, "Scandinavia, Scotland, and Switzerland had all been covered by glaciers during the Würm glaciation and to this day have produced little evidence of human habitation prior to the Holocene epoch. [The Holocene is the current geological epoch. It began about 11,600 years ago, at the end of the last Ice Age.] Hence the absolute chronology imagined by the Scandinavians, Scots, and Swiss for their finds was not significantly out of line with reality as we currently understand it."[66]

Jomard proposed a museum that would illustrate the progress of civilisation from its distant savage origins. (Thomsen's three-stage model was one version of this paradigm.) Following Humboldt, Sieboldt advocated a geographical arrangement of cultural traditions. Until the second half of the twentieth century, any Museum of Other People would adopt one of these two models: "evolutionist," or alternatively "cultural" or geographical. From time to time, there would be flip-flops from one model to the other. After Thomsen's death in 1865, Worsaae became director of the Copenhagen museum. He abandoned Thomsen's system and rearranged the exhibits on a geographical plan.

CIVILISED AND UNCIVILISED: THE BRITISH MUSEUM AND THE PITT RIVERS MUSEUM

Almost as if designed to illustrate some stereotype of contrasting national cultures, the post-revolutionary museums in Paris were rationalist and modernist, but susceptible to shifts in ideological fashion. The British Museum was economical, classicist, stuck in its ways. The French naturalist Georges Cuvier visited in 1818 and remarked: "we saw very nice things in Natural History, especially amongst the fossils. Their collections, however, are not to be compared with ours . . . they don't even know the value of their treasures. In general, the scientific institutions are nearly zero in Great Britain; the government is just interested in the art of earning money . . . All is a question of money."[1]

Unlike other great European museums, the British Museum did not grow out of a royal collection. It was created by parliament to house the vast but idiosyncratic collection of a self-made man, Sir Hans Sloane. An Irish apothecary, Sloane became a London society doctor, served as president of the Royal College of Physicians and succeeded Isaac Newton as president of the Royal Society. In 1712 he bought Chelsea Manor, a grand house in London. (Once a residence of Henry VIII, it occupied what is now Cheyne Walk.) In 1716, he was made a baronet. In the 1720s, "his private fortune grew and he became a gentleman of singular public standing," writes his biographer, James Delbourgo.[2] He died in 1753, at the age of ninety-three. In his will he arranged for his collections to be sold to the nation (he claimed that he only demanded a quarter of their real value), but stipulated that they should be open to the public. Parliament lent its support, and in 1753

George II gave royal assent to the British Museum Act. The purchase was financed by a public lottery. ("Even by the gamble-happy standards of the eighteenth century," Delbourgo remarks, "the British Museum lottery was widely seen as scandalous.")[3]

Sloane published little, and what he wrote did not impress the experts. "No article Sloane published better exemplified his enthusiastic curiosity-mongering—and its sometimes rocky reception—than the four-part illustrated essay that described what he called a 'China Cabinet,'" Delbourgo writes. Presented to the Royal Society by a surgeon with the East India Company, this China cabinet included rustproof razors, brass and steel knives, bezoar stones, tweezers, combs, ink and paper and assorted anatomical specimens. In Sloane's view, "the most unusual instruments that came over in this cabinet were those contrived for the taking any substance out of the ears, or for scratching or tickling them, which the Chinese do account one of the greatest pleasures." A Chinese figurine was included, "using one of these instruments, and expressing great satisfaction therein"; but, as a good doctor, Sloane warned about the "misfortunes" that follow from people "picking their ears too much."[4]

Almost as a parody of Sloane's collection of curiosities, one of his former servants, James Salter, set up "Don Saltero's Coffee House," where he exhibited, according to one visitor, "all manner of exotic beasts, such as crocodiles and turtles, as well as Indian and other strange costumes and weapons."[5] But distinguished guests up to and including the Prince of Wales accepted invitations to Chelsea Manor to view Sloane's cabinets. "These remarkable collections, perhaps the largest assembled by a single individual in the eighteenth century, Sloane assembled using the substantial sums he earned as a society physician, income from Jamaican slave plantations, rent collected on land in London and salaries from public offices," Delbourgo writes.[6] Sloane did very little first-hand collecting; Delbourgo describes him as "a collector of collectors."[7] He was ideally situated: his "prominence at the heart of London life placed him at the centre of Britain's empire. This was an empire of peoples and goods and . . . an empire of curiosities."[8]

Despite his exalted connections in the Royal Society, Sloane's collection was more like an old-fashioned cabinet of curiosities than a nineteenth-century museum. He hired learned assistants to see to the cataloguing, but there was no master plan, no scientific classification. There were odd juxtapositions. For instance, the collection of musical instruments included smoking pipes. As Delbourgo remarks, there was a "recurrent drift towards miscellaneousness."[9]

H. J. Braunholtz, appointed keeper of the British Museum's department of ethnography when it was created in 1946, noted that Sloane's exotica included "miscellaneous items such as shoes, tobacco pipes, bows and arrows, &c., from India, Persia, China, Japan Turkey, and Russia. It is not always clear whether the unlocalised objects described as 'Indian' are from India proper or America . . ." In fact, "a drum from Virginia which, though described by Sloane as 'Indian,' is characteristic of recent Ashanti work in the Gold Coast, and was almost certainly introduced or made by a slave from West Africa."[10]

Braunholtz lamented that the growth of the museum's ethnographic collection was "spasmodic and fortuitous, depending mainly on the chance 'curiosities' brought home by travellers and explorers."[11] Much of the early collecting was orchestrated by Sir Joseph Banks. President of the Royal Society, a trustee of the British Museum and informal director of Kew Gardens, Banks sailed on Captain Cook's famous first voyage (1768–71). He arranged for the transfer of the Royal Society's "artificial curiosities" to the British Museum, and in 1780 he led officers and men from Cook's last voyage in the donation of a "very large Collection of Artificial Curiosities Utencils, dresses &c. from the South-Sea Islands, the West Coast of North America and Kamschatka lately visited by His Majesty's Ships the Resolution & the Discovery."[12] Sea captains and explorers regularly asked his advice on the disposal of collections they brought back to England. "I look up to you as the common Centre of

we discoverers," he was told by James King, another veteran of
Cook's first voyage. Banks would advise them to direct artificial
curiosities to the British Museum.

George Dixon—yet another veteran of the Cook voyages—
brought back a typical mixed bag from the Northwest coast of
America. Banks passed the artificial curiosities on to the British
Museum. They are listed in the museum's minutes:

> Various Articles from the N:W: Coast of America brought
>   by Capt. Dixon, and presented by Sr. Joseph Banks, viz
> An Ornament worn by the women, on the under Lip.
> A large Ladle made of horn, probably of the American
>   Buffaloe.
> A Messing Bowl, or Porringer, in the form of an human
>   Figure.
> Stones impregnated with Pyrites and fires of Plants, used
>   as flint, steel and Tinder.
> A Stone of green Granite.
> A Paper of Tobacco, such as the natives Chew.
> A Piece of rock Crystal, and some Beads.
> Thirty four small Cylinders of Wood, variously marked,
>   used in playing at a game.[13]

The British Museum's holdings were initially divided between
three departments:

1. Manuscripts and coins. This included Sloane's books and
    manuscripts together with two other private collections.
    (The library of George III was added in 1823, doubling the
    size of the museum's library.)
2. "Artificial and natural productions." Drawn mostly from
    Sloane's collections, the "artificial productions" included
    artefacts from Mexico and Peru; a model of a Japanese
    temple; and a miscellany of baskets, pipes, hookahs, amulets
    and charms, instruments of punishment, classical sculptures,
    and "American idols."

3. "Modern curiosities." Here Sloane's tastes and prejudices were on full display. He scorned what he called sorcery and magic, and collected a variety of esoteric charms together with "articles in great esteem among many Roman Catholics, as relics."[14] There were also Native American feather headdresses, Wampum beads and scalps; European bronzes and ivories; Chinese deities; "a cyclops pig, having only one eye, and that in the middle of the forehead"; and the horn of a horned lady.[15]

In 1807, the collections were reorganised into three largely independent baronies: the library, natural history, and "antiquities." The department of antiquities bought the Parthenon sculptures from Lord Elgin in 1816 and acquired magnificent Assyrian reliefs and statues excavated by Austen Henry Layard in 1847, but it had very little to show from China or India.[16] (The East India Company set up an India museum in its premises in Leadenhall Street in 1801. Much of its substantial but poorly organised collection was transferred to the Victoria and Albert Museum in 1880.) And most scandalously, the British Museum, the premier national museum, had a meagre collection of prehistoric British items. When Christian Jörgensen Thomsen, director of the National Museum of Denmark, visited the British Museum in 1843 he found "the British antiquities everywhere covered in dust and not much esteemed," and the curators ill-informed.[17]

Sloane's ethnographic collection was consigned at first to the department of natural history. It was greatly enhanced by Polynesian items collected by Captain Cook and Joseph Banks, and in 1778 "The Otaheiti or South Sea Room" was opened. Immediately popular with visitors, this was, however, another mixed bag. "In the left corner is the mourning dress of an Otaheitean lady; opposite are rich cloaks and helmets of feathers from the Sandwich Islands," a guidebook reported. "Over the fire place are the Cava bowls and, above them, battoons [i.e., batons, and] various other implements of war. The idols of the various islands, present, in their hideous rudeness, a singular contrast with many of the works of art."[18] Further donations of sculptures, weapons, clothing and assorted curiosities from West Africa, the Arctic, Mexico and Australia were gradually introduced into the South Sea room.[19]

In 1836, this sprawling, poorly documented, incoherent assemblage was transferred—together with other "artificial productions"—from the department of natural history to the department of antiquities. They were not a good fit, however, for a department dominated by Mediterranean and Near Eastern sculptures and monuments. Ethnology was shunted into a sub-department along with British Roman and medieval materials, constituting one half of a very odd couple: "ethnography and medieval antiquities." The only thing that these two assemblages had in common was that they were both orphans in the storm. Scorned by the powerful librarian, Anthony Panizzi, the head of the museum, and looked down upon by the classicists, they were under constant threat of banishment.

In 1851, Augustus Wollaston Franks was appointed to take charge of this marginal section, with a particular brief to develop the museum's holdings of pre-Roman and Roman Britain. "The choice of a young mathematics graduate with an interest in monumental brasses for such an appointment might now seem odd," Jill Cook concedes, but she added that although Franks was not a classicist, he was a devoted collector of curiosities and "had shown a general interest in antiquities."[20]

As it turned out, what mattered rather more was that he had a large private income and moved easily in society. "At the time it was thought probable that I should succeed to a very considerable estate," Franks recalled, "and I very well remember the grave consultation as to whether it would not be infra dig for me to take a post in the Museum." Fortunately one of his father's trustees "discovered that a Suffolk man (Mr. Barnwell) had been employed at the Museum; so it was decided that I might accept the appointment."[21]

The young man turned out to have a talent for bureaucratic

infighting. This was vital as the various departments jostled in the more and more packed exhibition rooms of the museum, triggering a struggle for survival. The "ethnographical gallery," opened in 1845, was soon packed to capacity. When Franks joined the department of antiquities in 1851 the British Museum held some 3,700 "ethnological" or "ethnographical" artefacts. When he retired in 1896 there were more than 38,000. Franks personally donated some 9,000 of these.[22]

In the 1850s, the British Museum began a massive makeover. Its crowded old home was rebuilt and expanded. And it rebranded itself as a museum of civilisation (while embracing, or at least tolerating, its antithesis, the uncivilised). The museum's new mission, its vision of its future, was set in stone. Completed in 1852, the reconstructed museum building was fronted by Ionic columns copied from the temple of Athena Polias at Priene. These were topped by a triangular pediment with an allegorical sculpture by Sir Richard Westmacott entitled *The Progress of Civilisation*. Westmacott, who studied under Antonio Canova in Rome, was a committed classicist. He advised the British Museum on the acquisition of Greek and Roman sculptures, and designed a special room for the first display of the Elgin Marbles. His pediment incorporated four female figures copied from the Parthenon, though he replaced their diaphanous tunics with heavy drapery.[23] As he himself explained in a letter to Sir Henry Ellis, a classicist and principal librarian (in effect, director) of the British Museum, the sculptured pediment told a story with a moral:

> Commencing at the Eastern end, or angle of the Pediment, Man is represented emerging from a rude savage state through the influence of Religion. He is next personified as a Hunter, and a Tiller of the Earth, and labouring for his subsistence. Patriarchal simplicity then becomes invaded, and the worship of the true God defiled. Paganism prevails, and becomes diffused by means of the Arts.

The worship of the heavenly bodies & their supposed influence led the Egyptians, Chaldeans, Assyrians and other nations to study Astronomy, typified by the centre statues; the key stone to the composition.

Civilisation is now presumed to have made considerable progress. Descending towards the Western side angle of the Pediment, is Mathematics; in allusion to science being now pursued on known sound principles. The Drama, Poetry, and Music balance the group of the Fine arts, on the Eastern side, the whole composition terminating with Natural History of which such objects or specimens only are represented as could be made most effective in sculpture.[24]

Despite the expansion of the Bloomsbury site, it was generally agreed that the only solution to the space problem was to build a second museum, perhaps in South Kensington. But which collections might be sent away? Natural history was an obvious candidate, since it was large, growing fast, and did not interest the classically educated gentlemen who set the tone in the British Museum. However, ethnography was perhaps even more anomalous, and had fewer defenders. A parliamentary select committee on the British Museum met in 1860 and reported that it had "received evidence from every witness examined on this subject in favour of the removal of the ethnographical collections. Great additional space would be required, if it be intended that the British Museum should be the depository of a complete ethnographical collection, and it is probable that a more suitable receptacle might be found for it elsewhere."[25]

The *Handbook to the Ethnographical Collections* published by the British Museum in 1910 explained the rationale for keeping ethnography in Bloomsbury rather than sending it to South Kensington along with the natural history collections:

Want of space is a drawback for which there can be no compensation; yet there is some advantage in the exhibition of ethnographical specimens under one roof with those illustrating the art and industry of the great ancient civilisations. It is now realised that these civilisations, even that of Greece, arose gradually from primitive stages of culture; the instruments and utensils of savage or barbarous peoples are therefore not without their relation to the study of antiquities. With prehistoric remains the points of comparison are numerous and are especially instructive in the case of stone implements.[26]

Franks not only staved off the threat of expulsion. He kept his hodgepodge of collections together in the British Museum and greatly expanded their holdings. This was a tribute to his perseverance and diplomatic talents, but he also had two great pieces of luck. The first was that, after some vacillation, the formidable head of the natural history section, Professor Sir Richard Owen, decided to grasp the opportunity to transfer the collection to South Kensington, where he would be master of all he surveyed. This freed up a vast exhibition space in the British Museum's Bloomsbury headquarters. Franks's second piece of luck was the acquisition of the large, important, and generously funded Christy collection in 1865. This would eventually be moved into galleries vacated by the department of natural history.

Henry Christy, son of a Quaker manufacturer and banker, followed his father into the bank. In his forties, he began to collect folk art and fabrics from the Middle East, some of which were shown at London's Great Exhibition in 1851. Christy then broadened his range. In 1857 he met, by chance, on a bus in Havana, a young Englishman, Edward Burnett Tylor, who was travelling to get over a bout of illness. (Tylor heard one of the passengers talking English and using *thee* and *thou*, and realised that Christy was a fellow Quaker.) Together they visited archaeological sites in Mexico, and Christy smuggled some antiquities out of the country.[27]

Tylor, one of the first curators of the Pitt Rivers Museum

in Oxford, was to become the intellectual leader of the founding generation of British anthropologists. Christy promoted the new field of European prehistory. This was a heroic moment in European archaeology. Excavations in France uncovered human remains and artefacts in ancient geological formations. In 1863, Christy supported Édouard Lartet's pioneering excavations in the Dordogne, but then, two years later, visiting prehistoric cave sites in Belgium, he contracted pneumonia and died. He left his collection in the care of four trustees, including Franks, with instructions to offer it to the British Museum. A generous endowment allowed Franks to purchase some 20,000 additional artefacts.[28]

For two decades the collection was maintained in Christy's former home in Victoria Street, Westminster, where it was open to visitors one day a week. It was transferred to the premises of the British Museum only in 1883, when the natural history collections were at last moved to South Kensington. But Franks immediately gained credit for the Christy bonanza. In 1866, the year after Christy's death, he was promoted to the rank of keeper and put at the head of a new full section: "British and Medieval Antiquities and Ethnography."

Franks acknowledged that his new section was a muddle. He wrote to a correspondent that "it might with equal propriety be termed the Department of Miscellaneous Antiquities."[29]

> It consists of the following sections: 1. Prehistoric antiquities of all nations . . . In this of course are included prehistoric objects from Egypt and the East generally. 2. British Antiquities, vizt early British, Anglo Roman, and Anglo Saxon. 3. Medieval Antiquities, a small section here owing to the costly nature of the objects . . . 4. Glass and ceramic collection . . . includes objects in this material of all ages and countries . . . 5. Asiatic. This includes all the antiquities of India, illustrations of the Buddhist and Hindu religions, Chinese and Japanese works of art and pottery etc.

6. Ethnographical, including the productions of the uncivilized races of the whole world . . . 7. American antiquities.
This is a very large subject and one to which very little
attention has hitherto been paid in England . . . [30]

Franks's assistant (and in time his successor), Charles Hercules
Read, remarked that in the eyes of the public "the ethnographical
collections come next in interest to the Egyptian mummies."[31]
But visitors were not helped to make sense of what they were
seeing. The exhibits were loosely arranged by geographical area,
but disparate collections were bolted together, either because
of constraints of space or else to accommodate the demands
of family trusts. Writing to the keeper of antiquities in 1866,
Franks explained why the Indian and Chinese collections were
displayed in the "ethnographical room." "There was nowhere
else physically for them to go. If only on security grounds,
because the need to restrict access to locked cases meant that
two departments could not easily own objects in the same case."
Moreover, "separation of Indian antiquities and Ethnography
would involve the breaking up of the Raffles collection from
Java (contrary to its donor's wishes) and in any case, so far as
Arabic inscriptions were concerned, there was little before the
medieval period . . ."[32] In 1921, "British and Medieval Antiquities"
became a department in its own right. Ethnography remained
behind, obliged to cohabit with oriental ceramics.[33]

Meanwhile, ethnography and prehistory were being transformed by fresh discoveries and challenging new ideas. Charles
Lyell's *Principles of Geology*, published in three volumes between
1830 and 1833, laid down a new scientific paradigm. He established the great age of the earth. He also identified successive
geological strata, which allowed for the relative dating of fossils
and archaeological findings. Lyell's *Principles of Geology* accompanied the young Charles Darwin when he sailed on HMS *Beagle*.
Excavations in continental Europe turned up human remains
and artefacts in ancient geological formations and in association

with fossils of extinct animal species. It is "probable that man was old enough to have co-existed, at least, with the Siberian mammoth," Lyell told a major scientific gathering in 1859, after inspecting the excavations at Brixham cave.[34] Charles Darwin's *On the Origin of Species* was published at the end of the same year.

In 1863, Lyell's *Geological Evidences of the Antiquity of Man* endorsed the new ideas about ice ages, evolution and the long history of the human species, all matters on which he had previously been a prominent sceptic. In the same year, Thomas Huxley's *Man's Place in Nature* drew attention to anatomical similarities between humans and apes, clear indications of a common ancestry. In *The Descent of Man* (1871), Darwin argued that the earliest human beings must have lived rather like African apes.

A revolution followed in archaeology. Human history could not be confined to the brief chronology of the Old Testament. It was now possible to arrange archaeological sites in a time series with reference to geological sequences. Once this was done, it seemed incontrovertible that civilisation was a very recent development. For most of their long history, human beings had been hunters and gatherers, dependent on tools made from stone, wood, shells and bones.

The epoch before the rise of civilisation was given a new name: it was the age of "pre-history."[35] The term was first coined to refer to pre-Roman Europe. It gained currency with the publication in 1865 of John Lubbock's *Pre-Historic Times*, which adapted the Scandinavian tripartite model of Stone, Bronze and Iron Ages. (According to Bruce Trigger, this was "almost certainly the most influential work dealing with archaeology published during the nineteenth century.")[36]

Lubbock was Darwin's ally and his neighbour. He was also a member of parliament, where he promoted Darwin's projects. He bought the fields containing the Avebury ruins in order to protect them. In 1882 he masterminded the passage of the Ancient Monuments Protection Act (seven decades after

a similar act had been passed in Denmark). Lubbock's second—
and much younger—wife was the daughter of the great collector
General Pitt Rivers, and he saw to it that his father-in-law was
appointed the first inspector of ancient monuments.

One of the four trustees of the Christy collection, Lubbock
shared Christy's respect for Thomsen's three-stage theory of
history. In 1861 Christy invited Thomsen's assistant, Carl Ludvig
Steinhauer, to catalogue his collection, which he then arranged
into Stone Age, Bronze Age and Iron Age sections. Following
Lubbock's lead, Christy accepted that hunter-gatherer tools from
Australia and the Americas could shed light on the manufacture
and use of prehistoric European artefacts, and he expanded his
collection to include ethnographic specimens.

Yet visitors to the British Museum were not exposed to
new ideas about "pre-history." Franks kept a careful distance
from the epic debates around evolutionary theory that raged
in the 1860s and 1870s in the learned societies of which he was
a leading member. He was director of the Society of Antiquaries, a council member of the Ethnological Society, and later a
vice president of its successor organisation, the very Darwinian
Anthropological Institute.[37] In this milieu, there was no escap-
ing debates about evolution. Franks's problem was that the new
ideas were very controversial. Richard Owen, the influential
keeper of natural history in the British Museum, was a leader
of the scientific resistance to Darwinian theory. He stuck to the
earlier orthodoxy that species were immutable, and he was even
accused of hiding specimens that seemed to provide evidence of
transmutation.

Church leaders also found Darwinian theory unsettling,
even heretical. A vocal clerical opponent of Darwinism, Bishop
Wilberforce, was a trustee of the British Museum. The Arch-
bishop of Canterbury was a trustee *ex officio*. And they had
weighty political backing. Some of the most influential, educated and worldly men in England were quite sure that the
history of the world had been packed into a few thousand years,
as testified by the book of Genesis. William Gladstone, who

served four terms as prime minister of Britain between 1868 and 1894, described Genesis 10, an account of the world after the flood, as "the most valuable document of ancient ethnography known to man."[38]

So Franks had good reason to keep his head down. He could not, however, escape criticism from the evolutionist camp in the London Ethnological Society, spearheaded by Huxley, Lubbock and a formidable polemicist, General Pitt Rivers. A combative advocate of evolutionism, Pitt Rivers dismissed the British Museum as an "ethnological curiosity" in a "molluscus and invertebrate condition of development. For the education of the masses it is of no use whatsoever. It produces nothing but confusion in the minds of those who wander through its long galleries with but little knowledge of the periods to which the objects relate."[39]

Born in 1827, Pitt Rivers—or Augustus Lane-Fox as he was named until he was in his middle fifties—was a younger son in a hard-up family with aristocratic connections. He became a military officer and rose in the ranks, mainly by buying promotions, as was customary, ending up as a general. It was probably a visit to the Great Exhibition of the Works of Industry of All Nations, held in the purpose-built, ultra-modern, plate-glass and cast-iron Crystal Palace in London in 1851, that turned the general into a serious collector. The very first World's Fair, it attracted over 5 million visitors. (The Tory leader, Benjamin Disraeli, complained that it was "a godsend to the Government, diverting public attention from their blunders.")[40] Presided over by Queen Victoria's consort Prince Albert, this great show was designed "to present a true test and living picture of the point of development at which the whole of mankind has arrived . . . and a new starting-point, from which all nations will be able to direct their further exertions."[41] Over 13,000 exhibitors represented Britain, British colonies and forty-four foreign states.

Industrial machines and products were arranged according to a classification developed for the occasion by Lyon Playfair, president of the Chemical Society, fellow of the Royal Society, gentleman usher to Prince Albert, and a Liberal member of parliament. Playfair had once been the manager of a calico works in Lancashire, and he settled on the common-sense categories of the industrialist: raw materials, machinery, manufactures and fine arts, each in turn subdivided. Every category of exhibits was arranged to demonstrate the progress of a particular branch of technology. Cumulatively, the exhibition would celebrate the advances made by humanity—most particularly, in Victoria's England. (The historian Asa Briggs remarked, however, that "many of the machines displayed were more clever than useful" instancing "an alarm bedstead, causing a person to arise at any given hour," and a "cricket catapult, for propelling the ball in the absence of a first-rate bowler.")[42]

Also in 1851, the general served as a member of an army commission looking into rifle design. He now began to collect firearms, then all sorts of weapons, from boomerangs to spears, and, eventually, practically anything in the line of antiquities and ethnological artefacts. In time he became one of the great private collectors of antiquities and ethnography in England.

In 1879, completely unexpectedly, the general's fortunes were transformed: he inherited a large income and Cranborne Chase, a 32,000-acre estate in Wiltshire, from Lord Rivers, a cousin on his mother's side of the family. By the terms of the will he had to change his name, and he became Augustus Henry Lane-Fox Pitt Rivers. Now he went into collecting overdrive, sourcing more and more ethnological and antiquarian objects from a network of agents, and excavating Roman and Saxon sites on his estate.

"The General was a man of fierce temper, not untinged with violence," according to a biographer, "unsociable with his peers, a domestic tyrant."[43] Bertrand Russell, the nephew of the general's put-upon wife, Alice Pitt Rivers, recalled that he "spent every penny he could spare on excavating antiquities, much to the annoyance of his large family. My Aunt Alice—presumably as a result of his expenditure—practised petty economies to an almost incredible degree."[44] So the general was not a man to brook opposition to his designs, certainly not when it came to his great project, a museum of anthropology.

Pitt Rivers was determined to order his collection of ethnology and antiquities on a coherent plan, guided by a theory that, he imagined, was at once scientifically and ideologically correct. This was the conception of "evolution" or "progress" that he came across through Herbert Spencer, whom he knew personally, and then from the Darwinians, with whom he mingled in the Ethnological Society of London. He particularly liked the Darwinian insistence on slow, steady changes rather than sudden, revolutionary leaps. The general understood this doctrine to represent a scientific refutation of radical proposals for political reform. Revolution was contrary to the laws of nature. He designed public exhibitions of technological advances in order to demonstrate to the lower classes the inevitability of gradual progress and the folly of radical change.

Pitt Rivers was particularly fascinated, even obsessed, by weapons, but he divided all human productions—ancient and modern, native and exotic—into types, according to their uses or functions. Indeed, he claimed that he was the first person to use the term "typology" for a system of classification of human productions.[45] Objects within each type were to be ordered in a series from the simplest to the most complex, to illustrate the universal process of gradual improvement.

The guiding principles behind Pitt Rivers' typology were familiar enough, a mix of Linnaean taxonomy and Herbert Spencer's organic analogy. Ideas and techniques could be classified in the same way as natural species and they advanced exactly as natural species evolved. "Human ideas, as represented by the various products of human industry, are capable of classification into genera, species, and varieties in the same manner as products of the vegetable and animal kingdoms, and in their development from the homogeneous to the heterogeneous they obey the same laws," Pitt Rivers wrote.[46]

This may recall Jomard's "Plan d'une Classification Ethnographique." William Ryan Chapman has established that Jomard's plan was familiar to the small British community of ethnologists. Pitt Rivers himself had met and talked with Jomard on several occasions. However, Chapman is inclined to accept Pitt Rivers' own claim that Jomard's model merely confirmed an idea he had arrived at independently. "Given the popularity of biological schemes at that time, there is little reason to believe otherwise."[47]

Since the Jomard/Siebold dialogue in the 1840s, there were two competing models for a museum of ethnography. It could be arranged on evolutionist principles, or on a geographical plan. Franks defaulted to a geographical arrangement, though he was sometimes frustrated by stipulations that large donations should not be split up. Pitt Rivers tried to imagine how typological and geographical displays might be combined. At one time he envisaged what he called a rotunda arrangement. Items would be classified by function (weapons, musical instruments, etc.), then arranged longitudinally to demonstrate technical advances, and, finally, divided horizontally by region of origin.[48]

The general's collection soon took over his London house. In 1874, he loaned a large selection of artefacts to the Bethnal Green annexe of the South Kensington museum (now the Victoria and Albert Museum) on condition that they were arranged in accordance with his typology. As he compulsively delivered more and more specimens, the museum rebelled. Pitt Rivers then offered to donate his collection to the nation.

A government commission considered the matter. Franks was a member. He put it on record that he was "placed in a somewhat delicate position, for as Keeper of the National Collection of Ethnography I should naturally view with some dissatisfaction the ultimate creation of a second government collection, having much the same scope as our own, even though arranged on a system different from that adopted in the national collection, as such a result might lead to grave complications."[49] In other words, the collection would come encumbered with the general's evolutionist baggage. Lubbock and Huxley, also members of the commission, both close allies of Darwin, were inclined to accept Pitt Rivers' conditions, but the responsible parliamentary committee decided against them.

In 1884, Pitt Rivers persuaded Oxford University to take the bulk of his collection and to exhibit it in perpetuity, on the typological–ideological lines that he had developed, in an institution to be called the Pitt Rivers Museum.[50] He added a clause in his deed of gift that "a Lecturer shall be appointed . . . who shall yearly give Lectures at Oxford on Anthropology." Edward Burnett Tylor, Christy's old travelling companion, was appointed, and he held the post of "reader in anthropology" from 1884 to 1895. This was the first position in anthropology in a British university.

The Pitt Rivers Museum duly installed typological, evolutionary displays that covered almost every imaginable field of human activity—including a display case that became a favourite of visitors, "On the treatment of dead enemies," with items ranging from shrunken heads from Ecuador to skulls and scalps from Papua New Guinea, South Sudan, Nagaland, North America and Brazil.

The first curator of the museum, Henry Balfour, was not committed to the grand vision of Pitt Rivers. Indeed he was sceptical of all big ideas. "I don't want to theorize and shall stick to description as far as possible," he wrote in September 1898 to his friend Baldwin Spencer, a pioneering ethnographer of Australia. "The more I go on the more I see that it is still dangerous to form theories, and I prefer to collect and collate and leave the theories to fit themselves onto masses of facts."[51]

Pitt Rivers complained that Oxford had let him down.

I soon found out that it was quite impossible that a method communicated by one person should be worked out effectively by others . . . Oxford was not the place for it, and I should never have sent it there if I had not been ill at the time and anxious to find a resting-place for it of some kind in the future. I have always regretted it, and my new museum [on his estate] at Farnham, Dorset, represents my views on the subject much better.[52]

The museum at Farnham kept going until the 1960s, when the family sold the collection.

In 1963, Bernard Fagg, the director of the National Museum of Nigeria, was appointed curator of the Pitt Rivers Museum. Oxford University was considering moving the collection to a new site on the Banbury road. Fagg embraced the opportunity to reimagine the museum in a new custom-built home that would also accommodate the university's departments of social and biological anthropology.

Fagg was inspired by the general's plan for a rotunda. The celebrated engineer Pierre Luigi Nervi produced a mock-up of a modernist, concrete rotunda design.[53] It was topped by a dome under which tropical and subtropical plants were to be grown. Two floors would contain separate galleries for ethnology and prehistory. "A visitor taking a circular path around the planned ethnological floor would find the original display by type of object preserved, the largest (such as canoes) being on the outermost concentric circle, the smallest (jewellery) on the innermost," explains Michael O'Hanlon, director of the Pitt Rivers Museum from 1998 to 2015. Moving inwards to the centre of the rotunda, the visitor "would find collections arrayed by geographic region, each wedge-shaped segment of the rotunda displaying all the items from a particular cultural area." On the prehistory floor the wedges would also be geographical, but the visitor would move outwards and onward in time from the oldest items, which were at the apex of the wedge.[54]

The building was budgeted to cost £3 million. The university refused to underwrite it. In 1968, Fagg had a stroke. Deprived of his leadership, the project lost impetus. There was in any case resistance from various quarters against upsetting the long-established arrangement of specimens. The crammed old showcases were familiar, even hallowed. So the great change never happened.

It has sometimes been argued that the terms of the general's deed of gift prohibited Oxford University from making any changes to the arrangement of his collection. The relevant article in the original "Indenture" provided that:

> The general mode of arrangement at present adopted in the said Collection shall be maintained and no changes shall be made in details during the life time of the said August Henry Lane Fox Pitt Rivers without his consent and any changes in details which may be made after the death of the said August Henry Lane Fox Pitt Rivers shall be such only as shall be necessitated by the advance of knowledge and shall not affect the general principle originated by the said August Henry Lane Fox Pitt Rivers.

That may appear to offer an ample get-out. However, the deed has been invoked again and again to discourage any change. In consequence, the Pitt Rivers Museum is perhaps the most perfect example of a museum that belongs in a museum.

GERMAN MUSEUMS AND THE CULTURAL HISTORY OF HUMANITY

In the nineteenth century, the great cultural institutions of France were sited, as a matter of course, in Paris. The British Museum, the Museum of Natural History, the Victoria and Albert Museum and the National Gallery were in London. In contrast, the thirty-nine states that made up the loose German confederation funded their own universities, art galleries, museums, concert halls and opera houses. Even after the unification of Germany in 1871, cultural affairs were controlled by the regions.

The ducal city of Weimar hosted the greatest writers in Germany: Johann Wolfgang Goethe and Friedrich Schiller. The king of Prussia took great pride in his reluctant courtier, Alexander von Humboldt, who combined scientific expertise, humanist sensibility and the glamour of an explorer. Humboldt was a friend of Goethe. The young Charles Darwin was inspired by his travel writing. Thomas Jefferson said he was "the most scientific man of his age." Yet whenever Humboldt was back home from his travels, he was expected to be in attendance at the Berliner Schloss, dressed in court uniform, and prepared to read to the king after dinner.[1]

It was not only the courts that looked to the sciences and the arts to confer prestige. Good taste, intellectual sophistication and artistic connections were marks of caste for the rising educated bourgeoisie.[2] Societies sprang up to support causes ranging from Richard Wagner's music festivals in Bayreuth to art galleries, aquariums, zoological gardens—and rival ethnographic museums in Berlin, Dresden, Hamburg, Leipzig and Munich.

Gustav Klemm (1802–67), director of the royal library in Dresden and inspector of the royal porcelain collection, was the epitome of the court intellectual. Naturally, he collected antiquities and wrote history books.

Klemm's first monograph was a study of Attila the Hun. By his own account, this led him to "compare the ancient Germanic monuments with those of other peoples—and since I had been given the task of rearranging and exhibiting the royal porcelain collections, this became connected with renewed studies of China, and reflections on the technical production of porcelain."[3] He traced the development of pottery from prehistoric German clay vessels to Chinese porcelain, which, he explained, was perfected in Meissen in Saxony. Between 1843 and 1852 he published a *General Cultural History of Mankind (Allgemeine Kulturgeschichte der Menschheit)*, and followed up with a two-volume *General Science of Culture (Allgemeine Kulturwissenschaft*, 1854–5).

Klemm's theory of cultural history was conceived on a grand scale, but it was an amalgam of ideas that were current in educated, liberal circles at the time, notably Alexander von Humboldt's global environmentalism and Enlightenment accounts of the evolution of civilisation. To this he added Thomsen's Three Age System. The whole concoction was topped off with newly fashionable racial theories.

"We will set aside the usual geographical, ethnographical, and synchronic arrangements," Klemm wrote, "and divide the races of men into three fundamental classes—the savage, the barbarians, and the enlightened (represented in time, roughly, by the stone, the bronze, and the iron age)."[4] Races were further divided between the "passive" and the "active," which Klemm also characterised as feminine and masculine.

> . . . man is not only different from woman in his strengths, but also in his inclinations. He is disposed to lead enterprises and adventures of all kinds. He also does not shy away from using intoxicating and narcotic means to raise his spirits and enhance them to a wild exuberance . . .

Woman, whose gentler and milder nature announces itself through softer and more rounded forms, offers compassion and mercy: where man in blind passion often only becomes destructive, woman preserves with love, what man recklessly drives to ruin.[5]

In the Lamarckian tradition, Klemm assumed that physical and psychological features were shaped by the environment. Feminine, passive, dark-skinned races were forest-dwellers. Conservative, placid and timid, they made a living by hunting and fishing. More advanced passive folk lived in open prairies, domesticated animals and became nomads. At last the farmers appeared, the supreme representatives of the passive races.

Active, light-skinned, masculine races flourished in challenging environmental conditions. They tended to be violent, impulsive, destructive. But then came a world-historical dialectical advance: the active, masculine races conquered and subdued passive, feminine races. At first, a caste system developed. In yet more progressive societies there was a happy marriage of the best of the masculine and feminine qualities. This was Klemm's ideal: "I see in this mixture of the originally divided active and passive races the fulfilment of the purpose which nature pursues in all branches of its organic creation. Just as each male or female individual does not fulfil the purpose of nature if they remain alone, so too is a people, which is only made out of the active or only from the passive races, something unfulfilled, something halved." And where was this happy synthesis achieved, advancing humanity to its highest stage of development? Klemm had no doubt. "We therefore find in Germanic Europe, where the active and passive races are perhaps most equally mixed, true culture, true art, true science, and the most life, law and freedom."[6]

Klemm was no traveller. The only journey he made in his whole life outside Germany was a brief visit to Italy in 1838 in the entourage of the Saxon royals. But he had an interest in exotic lands—he claimed that this was triggered when as a boy he saw foreign troops in their colourful uniforms marching through his home town of Chemnitz during the Napoleonic wars.[7] He collected Germanic, Chinese, South Pacific, African and Arctic antiquities and crafts. He wrote a pioneering history of German cabinets of curiosities. And then he developed his neo-Hegelian theory of culture history. This trajectory was nicely character-ised by that great historian of classical European scholarship Arnoldo Momigliano: "As soon as the antiquarian leaves his shabby place which preserves something of the eighteenth century and enters modern life, he becomes the great collector, he is bound to specialize, and he may well end up as the founder of an institute of fine arts or of comparative anthropology."[8]

"Klemm's vision of human history," Peter N. Miller remarks, "was a collector's vision."[9] In 1843, Klemm published a "Fantasy Museum of Culture History" as an appendix to the first volume of his sprawling, ten-volume *Cultural History of Mankind*.[10] Each room in this fantasy museum was designed to illustrate a volume of the *Cultural History*.[11] Room 1: natural products. Room 2: "wilder" examples of the "passive race" (fishermen and hunters from America and the polar region, African and Asian nomads, South Sea islanders). Room 3: Mexico, Egypt and India. Room 4: China, highest level of the culture attainable by the "passive peoples." Room 5: Original state of the "active race" (Circassians and Tatars, followed by Arabs, Persians and Turks). Room 6: Cultures of classical antiquity, Greeks and Romans. Room 7: Original condition of Germanic and Scandinavian nations. Room 8: the Germanic and the Romanesque-Christian Middle Ages. Room 9: modern times.

This fantasy museum was a blown-up, idealised counter-part to Klemm's personal collection, and both were supposed to illustrate and support his theories. By his own account, he collected "industrial and artistic products from all times and all areas" in order to "establish a cultural science whose foundations shall be built by the ten volumes of my Cultur-Geschichte . . . With the help of God and numerous benevolent friends, we have managed, in the course of more than twenty-five years, to come as close to this goal as is possible."[12]

Klemm's collections soon overflowed the rooms of his apartment. In 1840, he bought a large house in the north of Dresden and dedicated five rooms to his personal museum. It was described in 1864 in a popular weekly journal of geography, *Das Ausland*. Bursting at the seams, "the collection is currently packed around five moderately sized rooms, but a complete arrangement would require a six-fold greater space." Yet even in these cramped conditions a philosophical design was apparent. The exhibits illustrated the progress of humanity from a state of nature to a cultured condition. The visitor proceeded past "rocks; skulls, busts and body parts; natural material used by humans; tools and weapons; examples of habitation, transport, clothing and jewellery; objects related to private, public and religious life; and finally a set of history 'relics,' including Napoleon's pen-stand and the Empress Marie Theresa's shoes."[13]

"By the time he died in 1867, the Museum Klemmium was one of the largest private collections in Europe, containing almost eight thousand classified objects and sixteen thousand other pieces," Chris Manias writes. Adolf Bastian described it as the first major museum of its kind in Europe. Visitors were permitted, though they were not always welcome. Klemm complained in a letter to a friend that a collector's "worst enemies are visitors who pick up everything with their hands, and doubt the accuracy of widely proven things, confusing bronze with stone or iron, or asking if Luanda is in America or Asia."[14]

A year after Klemm's death, his son sold his German antiquities to the British Museum. (Franks travelled to Dresden to make the selection himself.) The University of Leipzig refused to buy the rest of the collection, but public-spirited citizens set up a voluntary association and acquired it for what became the Museum für Völkerkunde zu Leipzig. Adolf Bastian advised the committee, and when the Leipzig museum was finally opened in 1895 it was arranged on geographical principles. Klemm's stages of culture history were abandoned. His fantasy museum died with him. In the twentieth century the Nazis would claim Klemm as a forerunner of their racial ideas.

The most important museum of ethnology in Germany—and, for a while, by far the largest in the world—was established in Berlin by Adolf Bastian. Bastian was born in 1826, a quarter of a century after Klemm, into a prosperous merchant family in the Hanseatic city of Bremen. Independently wealthy, he could study and travel as he wished all his life. In the German tradition of the wandering student he attended five universities and followed various courses before eventually graduating in medicine at the University of Würzburg under the guidance of Rudolf Virchow, a distinguished anatomist, anthropologist and liberal politician who became a lifelong friend and mentor.

Bastian described Alexander von Humboldt as the "hero of our age." He "provided the platform on which to erect the temple of the harmonious cosmos by inductive research."[15] On graduation, Bastian set off to become a world traveller in the mould of Humboldt, sailing around the world for eight years as a ship's doctor. On his return he published a ponderous, abstract three-volume treatise on humanity, which he dedicated to Humboldt. Then he travelled for five years in east Asia, where, among other adventures, he passed several months in the compound of the Mandalay palace as a reluctant guest of the king of Burma, obliged to spend several hours every day in the study of Buddhism. This Asian journey resulted in a six-volume compendium, *Die Völker des Östlichen Asien.*

Back in Germany, Bastian joined his old teacher, Rudolf Virchow, on the faculty of Berlin University. (The creation of Willem von Humboldt, Alexander's brother, Berlin University was the model for the research universities of the future.) Virchow and Bastian founded the Berlin Society for Anthropology, Ethnology and Prehistory, the first important German learned society in the field, and began to campaign for a dedicated museum of ethnology. In 1868, Bastian was made curator of ethnology at the Royal Berlin Museum where (E. B. Tylor records) "he found the Ethnological collections confined to two galleries and a very inadequate workroom."[16] In 1873 a specialist ethnographic museum, the Königlichen Museum für Völkerkunde, was founded in Berlin. Bastian became the first director. The museum's collections had to be built up almost from scratch, and it only opened to the public in 1886. Meanwhile, Bastian regularly took time out to write very long books and to continue his self-financed travels around the world, voyaging to West Africa, Polynesia, and South and Central America. He died in Trinidad in 1905, at the age of 78.

Bastian published thirty volumes on his travels, and capped these off with a Humboldtian five-volume account of global history. These books sold rather well, but were perhaps not widely read. A later generation found them impenetrable. "Who now reads Bastian?," asked Robert Lowie, a member of the inner circle that formed around Franz Boas, the leader of the most important early twentieth-century school of anthropology in America. "Two factors invested Bastian with a comic halo in the judgment of irreverent posterity—his determined opposition to Darwinism and his style." Lowie quoted Darwin's German disciple Ernst Haeckel, who described Bastian as *"Geheimer Oberkonfusionsrat"*—Secret Upper Confusion Counseller.

In fact opposition to Darwinism was common in scientific circles in France and Germany at the time. Bastian's mentor, Virchow, was a leading Darwin sceptic. Bastian's style was a more intractable problem. "At its worst it is surely inconceivably crabbed," Lowie wrote. "To confront Bastian in some of his lucubrations is a never-to-be-forgotten experience . . . there is no intelligible organization: ideas turn up on the principles of free association, with favorite propositions recurring at irregular intervals like the leitmotifs of a music drama."[17] Lowie conceded that the travel books were sometimes entertaining, but he complained that Bastian "became confused in proportion as he discussed theory."[18]

Bastian absorbed his mentor Virchow's liberal ideas on race.

All branches of the human species had a common origin. There are no pure races. Racial mixing is a source of strength and renewal. And there is no correlation between race, language and culture. Bastian also adopted the related doctrine of the "psychic unity of mankind," formulated by the pioneering German psychologists Theodor Waitz and Wilhelm Wundt.

Bastian's signature contribution was his notion of "elementary ideas" (*Elementargedanken*). The basic proposition here was that if indeed all human beings have a similar mind set (the "psychic unity of mankind"), then they must share some fundamental ideas. This was, after all, a fairly orthodox reading of Immanuel Kant's theory of knowledge. Kant argued that intuitions about space, time and causation were innate and universal. But Bastian's presentation of the *Elementargedanken*, which he called "a monotonous substratum of identical elementary ideas," was notably lacking in specificity. Klaus-Peter Koepping, who wrote the only monograph on Bastian's theories, asked: "did he ever delineate any particular elementary idea in living reality, or was it a term with only theoretical significance?"[19]

In any case, according to Bastian, there was no way in which these elementary ideas could be studied directly. They "never occurred as such but were always clothed in a unique fashion and expressed as folk ideas" (*Völkergedanken*).[20] So what were these folk ideas? "I say folk ideas where others use the term world view," Bastian wrote.[21] World views, shaped by the environment, were held in common among people who lived within the borders of what Bastian termed a "geographical province." Amounting to something very like environmental determinism, this proposition fitted in with the doctrines of the Humboldtian school of German geographers.

According to Bastian, people invent technological fixes when they face environmental challenges. New techniques might be adopted in simple societies through "transactions with neighbours," but he insisted that for most of human history people made do with their own inventions.[22] A rival school of geographers, led by Friedrich Ratzel, thought it unlikely that pre-modern populations were very inventive. New ways of doing things were borrowed or imposed. Great changes followed conquests and population movements. "The fundamental theory of world-history is the history of migration," Ratzel wrote.[23]

In 1886, under Bastian's direction, the monumental new home of Berlin's royal museum of *Völkerkunde* was formally opened at last. Glenn Penny vividly evokes the grand ceremony. The elite of Prussia was present, including the crown prince, in full military rig, and Otto von Bismarck, the architect of German unification. "After the audience was assembled—state officials seated to the left, members of the military and foreign office to the right, Bastian, the architect, and other scientists toward the front, and other guests, including many of the construction workers, toward the back—the royals took their place on the podium." They were addressed by the minister of culture, Gustav von Gossler. He heaped praise on Bastian who, he said, had transformed piles of "rarities" and "curiosities" into a scientific collection.[24]

This judgement was premature. Bastian's motto was "collect everything."[25] "The last moment has come, the twelfth hour is here!" he declared. "Documents of immeasurable, irreplaceable value for human history are being destroyed. Save them! Save them! before it is too late!"[26] He recruited hundreds of people—ship's captains, representatives of trading houses, travelling students—to collect for his museum. Wealthy Berliners were tapped for funds to buy whole collections and to bid at auctions in London and Paris. As Bismarck's overseas empire grew, colonial governments were directed to transfer ethnographic collections to the Berlin museum. By the time of his death Bastian had created what Lowie called "the largest emporium of ethnographica in the world."[27] A decade after the grand opening, a British Museum curator estimated that Berlin's ethnographic collection was ten times the size of London's.[28] But while acquisitions kept streaming in, there was not enough time or space to put them in order.

Bastian gave two reasons for this manic hunting and gathering of exotic artefacts. The first was that "Native tribes disappear like snow in the midday sun. The demise of primitive societies is foreshadowed by historical laws which can neither be halted nor diverted. The sole justification for our interference in them can be the goal of salvaging the lingering last survivals of those originals which are now swiftly disappearing, and putting them on paper or in museums." The second was that a museum collection had to be exhaustive if it was to serve science. The inductive method required that everything of any possible relevance must be subjected to detailed study. It was folly to decide in advance that something would turn out to be irrelevant. Since pristine, unadulterated ethnographic products were on the point of disappearing, *everything* should be collected. "In this way," Bastian concluded, "we can provide future generations with research materials which they will not be able to gather, but from which they—working inductively—will be able to write a history of mankind."[29]

Germany's ethnographic museums were launched with great expectations, but by the end of the nineteenth century they were in a state of near collapse. The failure of Bastian's museum was a parable of the dangers of unchecked empiricism. If everything was to be collected, in the absence of clear guiding principles, chaos would surely follow. And indeed it did. Again and again, updates of the official museum guide had to be postponed because it was impossible to keep up with the flood of new acquisitions. Bastian was committed in theory to arranging the collections geographically, but according to a guidebook, "cabinets containing collections from completely different areas of Africa are often standing next to each other."[30] Display cases were increasingly crammed. Ambitious plans for a display of skulls and skeletons had to be put on hold.

The entire ground floor was given over to the prehistory of Europe. (The highlight was a display of Schliemann's finds from the hypothetical site of ancient Troy.) Bastian hoped that visitors would draw comparisons between the relics of ancient Europe and often strikingly similar contemporary ethnographic artefacts from faraway places. But lacking a clear message, packed and disorganised, the Berlin museum confused and repelled visitors. Journalists began to carp. "Should these scientific collections from throughout the world be permitted to be mixed together like cabbages and turnips?"[31]

Meanwhile, the unchecked stream of uncatalogued specimens overwhelmed the curators. "Just a little over a decade after the grand opening, Bastian and his assistants declared conditions in the museum 'unbearable,'" Glenn Penny writes.[32] By 1905, when Bastian died, "Berlin's celebrated museum—the world's first self-standing ethnographic museum and by far the largest museum of its kind—had become a spectre in the world of ethnology."[33] The director of the royal museums, Wilhelm von Bode, an art historian, wanted the jumble to be cleared and replaced by a *Schausammlungen*, an artistic exhibition of aesthetically remarkable treasures. A century later, von Bode's vision was realised. The Humboldt Forum in Berlin, a vastly expensive showroom, is dedicated to artistic masterpieces from faraway places. Most of the ethnographic materials assembled under Bastian's direction remain in store in suburban Dahlem.

The other major German ethnographic museums were also in poor shape by the end of the nineteenth century. The Leipzig museum abandoned Klemm's developmental formula but did not attract public support. In Munich, the director observed that his curators were, to a man, classicists, and that the public was far more interested in art than in ethnography.[34]

THE RISE AND FALL OF THE
MUSÉE DE L'HOMME

In 1851, London's Great Exhibition of the Works of Industry of All Nations showcased wonders of modern technology, contemporary arts and exotic crafts. It attracted some 6 million visitors and triggered a world series of competitive, exorbitantly expensive festivals.

Napoleon III was determined to outclass London. In 1855, he presided over an Exposition Universelle des Produits de l'Agriculture, de l'Industrie et des Beaux-Arts in Paris. (One enduring innovation was a classification of fine wines from Bordeaux.) Just under 6 million visitors turned up. The emperor insisted on an even grander repeat performance in 1867. This attracted 11 million visitors. (Walter Benjamin remarked that World's Fairs became "places of pilgrimage to the commodity fetish.")[1] In addition to new technical marvels this exposition displayed recently discovered prehistoric finds curated by a leading French archaeologist, Boucher de Perthes. The Suez Canal Company contributed a display of ancient Egyptian monuments. Consular officials in Peru and Bolivia despatched sculptures, ceramics, fabrics, jewellery, skulls and mummies.[2] Colonial governments submitted arts and crafts. After the fair was over, choice archaeological and ethnographic items were divided between the Museum of Natural History, the Louvre and various provincial collections.

Among the prodigies of industrial ingenuity on display in Paris was a giant cannon, exhibited by the German arms merchant Krupp. Three years later, in 1870, the great gun played a

ghastly part when Prussia invaded France, laid siege to Paris,
humiliated the French army and imposed a crushing indemnity.
Napoleon III was captured in the Battle of Sedan. He went into
exile in England where he died two years later.

In 1873, following the defeat of France and the unification
of Germany, Berlin published a prospectus for an ambitious
Museum für Völkerkunde. Back in 1831, Edme-François Jomard
had launched his quixotic one-man campaign for a museum of
ethnography in Paris. He died in 1862, with a sad adieu to this
dream of a "museum of geography and travel, long hoped for,
awaited in vain."[3] But Paris could not now permit itself to fall
behind Berlin in the cultural stakes. In 1874, Ernest-Théodore
Hamy, a curator in Paris's Museum of Natural History, was sent
to inspect Scandinavian museums of archaeology and ethnology. He was particularly impressed by the "magnificent" Royal
Ethnographic Museum in Copenhagen. Could something
similar be done in Paris? Jomard had got nowhere, but Hamy put
the blame on Jomard himself. His plan had been "ill-conceived,
poorly presented, and unlikely to prove a success."[4] Moreover,
his "personality presented an insurmountable obstacle to an
agreement with the Naval Museum and the Louvre."[5]

Hamy found a patron. Oscar-Amédée de Watteville, director of science and letters in the Ministry of Public Instruction,
amateur archaeologist, author of a monograph on "war-cries
among different peoples," came out in favour of setting up a
museum of ethnography in Paris. And now, providentially, an
opportunity presented itself. Yet another Exposition Universelle
was held in Paris between May and November, 1878. (It attracted
16 million visitors.) This World's Fair bore witness to the recov-
ery of France, celebrated the return of democratic government
under the Third Republic, and advertised the rapidly growing
overseas empire. Colonial governments sent along works of art,
crafts, antiquities, and teams of musicians and dancers.

Hamy was tasked with setting up a provisional Musée ethnographique des missions scientifiques. The centrepiece of this
temporary museum was a display of American antiquities and

ethnographic artefacts, mostly from Peru and Mexico. Hamy also assembled small collections of European, Asian and West African arts and crafts.[6] Press coverage was favourable. After a few months the exhibition was transferred to the Champs de Mars for the Exposition Universelle, where again it proved to be very popular.

Watteville now proposed that some of the choicest exhibits should form the basis of a permanent ethnographic museum. He promised that there "would be not only a brilliant collection of objects of luxury and great value, but above all a scientific museum, which will not disdain the most insignificant object if it is possible to follow its evolution."[7] The Ministry of Public Instruction was persuaded. Hamy was appointed director. He would preside over the museum until a year before his death in 1908.[8]

The Trocadéro Palace, a sprawling mish-mash of Byzantine, Gothic and Moorish styles overlooking the Champ de Mars, had been built for the Exposition Universelle. The ministry agreed that the museum of ethnography could be accommodated in one wing. (The other wing was reserved for a collection of "monuments of France": plaster casts of sculptures and tombs taken from churches and palaces.)

An argument immediately started up about what sort of things properly belonged in an ethnographic collection. In particular, why should the American materials that Hamy had exhibited on the Champs-Élysées be handed over to the Trocadéro Museum? Were these in fact "ethnographic" objects? The matter was referred to France's highest court, the august Conseil d'État. "The American collection forms a whole, and apart from some pieces such as fabrics and various utensils, most of it is not in truth ethnographic," the court advised. "There is an American archaeology and mythology, an American art . . ."[9]

Perhaps the collection should be offered to the Louvre. It seemed the obvious place. But Jules Ferry (minister of public instruction, soon to be prime minister) demurred. The Louvre was dedicated to the history of art. Ferry believed that a new kind of museum was required to document "the history of the manners and customs of peoples of all historical periods."[10] This stand-off lasted for five years. Eventually the American collections were transferred to the new Museum of Ethnography, together with pre-Columbian items from the Louvre. The Trocadéro Museum now held around 10,000 American objects, mainly from Peru and Mexico.[11] Hamy claimed that it was one of the finest collections of Americana in the world.[12]

But the ethnographic coverage of the Trocadéro Museum was lopsided. Asia was largely excluded until the reorganisation of the museum in 1928. (The independent Guimet museum had a significant collection of Asian art.) At first there was little in the way of African exhibits. Colonial sources only gradually supplemented the collections with artefacts from French territories in West Africa, Oceania and Indochina.[13] A European hall, opened in 1884, showed traditional crafts and costumes from Greece, Italy, Spain, Portugal, Russia, and, later, Scandinavia. Another hall, dedicated to French folk arts and crafts, was dominated by materials from Brittany, which was regarded as a particularly backward and picturesque region of the country.

Displays were austere. Rather than highlighting individual masterpieces, showcases were packed with everyday utilitarian objects. Hamy followed Jomard's playbook, even echoing Jomard's language.[14] Ethnographic and archaeological artefacts were exhibited together. They were arranged to demonstrate that while basic human needs were essentially the same everywhere, now and in the past, they became more refined, and tools and arts became more sophisticated and efficient, as societies advanced along the long and winding upward path to a civilised condition.

The Trocadéro Museum began well. Hamy reported early on that there had been 4,000 visitors in a single day. One journalist who apparently caught the popular mood compared a visit to the museum with "a journey to the midst of Barbary."[15] But by the early twentieth century the museum was in a sad state.

The Trocadéro Palace proved an unsuitable venue. The vast halls, impossible to heat, dwarfed the crammed ethnographic showcases. The budget was barely sufficient to maintain the operation, let alone to fund new acquisitions. Hamy resigned in 1907 in protest against financial cuts. But money wasn't the only issue. Ethnology was undeveloped in France in comparison to Germany, Britain and the United States. The museum failed to define a distinctive mission.

Then came the horrors of the First World War, followed by a financial crisis. In the 1920s, the museum's income did not even cover its running costs; the staff was down to two curators and three guards; there was no catalogue and no library; the galleries were open to the public only two days a week. Arnold van Gennep, an authority on European folklore, said it was a "bad joke." A government minister called it a "national disgrace."[16] "It would be better to close the museum than to maintain it in its present state," judged Marcel Mauss, a leading social scientist. "It cannot be heated, it cannot be opened, it cannot be displayed to the public. It cannot be guarded. There have been serious thefts."[17]

The glory years came later, in the fraught decade that followed the stock market crash of 1929, France's *années folles*. Marcel Mauss presided over the professionalisation of French ethnography. In 1937, a modernised Musée de l'Homme replaced the old ethnographic museum. Young ethnographers mingled with progressive politicians, colonial reformers, and avant-garde artists and writers. It seemed the beginning of a golden age, but this brief, brilliant efflorescence came to an end with the German occupation in 1940.

French ethnology began as an austere science, a stepchild of the comparative, positivist sociology of Émile Durkheim. The *Année Sociologique*, the journal of Émile Durkheim's circle, devoted roughly a third of its pages to ethnology. Publication stalled after Durkheim's death in 1917. A new series began in 1925, edited by Durkheim's nephew and intellectual heir, Marcel

Mauss. The initial issue featured Mauss's masterpiece, the *Essay on the Gift*, which reworked ethnographic studies by Boas and Malinowski.

Mauss noted that although he himself had "a modest chair bizarrely labelled 'History of the religions of uncivilised peoples,'" there was not a single professorship dedicated to ethnography or sociology in all the institutions of higher education in France.[18] In 1925, at the same time as he relaunched the *Année sociologique*, Mauss set up the Institut d'ethnologie. Associated with the Sorbonne, funded by the Colonial Ministry, this was France's first teaching centre in the discipline.[19] Its president was Lucien Lévy-Bruhl, a professor of philosophy at the Sorbonne, author of influential studies of "primitive mentality" (1922) and the "soul of the primitive" (1927).[20] Mauss conceded formal leadership to Lévy-Bruhl, out of respect for his seniority, but he told an American colleague that he himself did "practically all the work . . . I'm the whole show."[21] The institute also had the very good luck to recruit a brilliant and efficient secretary, Paul Rivet. A medical doctor, Rivet had gone out to South America as a comparative anatomist in the tradition of Broca. After five years in Peru, he returned as an ethnologist.[22]

"Mauss savait tout," wrote Lévy-Bruhl, and he seemed to expect his students also to know everything.[23] According to a favourite student, Jacques Soustelle—a brilliant young philosophy graduate—Mauss told his class that there was no point in tackling ethnology without, at a minimum, a knowledge of Latin and ancient Greek plus Sanskrit, Hebrew and Chinese, not to mention German, English and Dutch. Another student reported that after his first course with Mauss, "I was groggy. What had he talked about? I had never come across such a flow of jokes and allusions in a lecture."[24] But Mauss gave detailed instructions about collecting and documenting ethnographic objects, and told his students to record everything: one can never be sure what might turn out to be important. "Pay attention to the latrines. That is where Griaule found some of his finest Dogon masks." He also warned them not to pursue the chimera of "the pure indigenous society . . . A state of transition is as interesting as a state of stability."[25]

In 1928, Rivet, the administrator of the Institut d'ethnologie, was appointed director of the National Museum of Ethnography, which now came under the control of the Natural History Museum. He changed the title of his chair from "anthropology" to the "ethnology of contemporary and fossil humans," set about remaking the Trocadéro as a museum of human evolution, and launched a massive effort to restock its collections.

Mauss's Institute of Ethnology and Rivet's Museum of Ethnography at Trocadéro—students called them the "*Insti*" and the "*Troca*"—now drove the professionalisation of French anthropology. The students at the Insti were fascinated by Mauss's flow of ideas. They valued his detailed instructions on scientific method (although Mauss never ventured into the field). They sympathised with his socialism. At the same time, they were enchanted by the subversion and creativity of the surrealists whose first manifesto was published in 1924, just a year before the Insti was founded.

There was a vogue for African art and African American music and dance.[26] The ballet *la Création du monde*, which had its première in Paris in 1923, was a treasury of what began to be known as *l'art nègre*. The score, by Darius Milhaud, incorporated jazz rhythms. The book, by Blaise Cendrars, recast Baoulé folk tales. The curtains, décor and costumes designed by Fernand Léger referenced African masks. In 1925, fashionable Parisians flocked to the *Revue nègre* at the Théâtre des Champs-Élysées to see the African American dancer Josephine Baker. "She appeared dressed just in ostrich feathers on her behind and some bananas suspended I don't know where," the young ethnologist André Schaeffner recalled. "She sang, or rather she gave out little cries; she danced . . . imitating a chicken . . . She did nothing else. She was irresistible."[27] Georges Henri Rivière, deputy director of the Museum of Ethnography, wrote songs for her to sing, including a popular, risqué number "Josephine, Josephine."

Mauss was less enchanted by the vogue for *l'art nègre*. He warned his students against dilettantism. ("On no account become *un amateur d'art*.")[28] But the young ethnologists liked to think of themselves as at once artists and scientists, with a mission to bring together a new science and a modern humanism.[29] Schaeffner, an associate of Darius Milhaud and Igor Stravinsky, wrote the first French study of jazz (published in 1926), and he became a pioneering ethnomusicologist. Leiris, a poet, was drawn to ethnology by his ties with the surrealist movement, "which represented for me the rebellion against the so-called rationalism of Western society and therefore an intellectual curiosity about peoples who represented more or less what Lévy-Bruhl called at the time the *mentalité primitive*. It's quite simple."[30]

The director of the Trocadéro Museum, Paul Rivet, was ambivalent about the aesthetic approach to ethnographic objects, but he recognised that the museum had to cater for fans of primitive art, among whom were rich and influential patrons and collectors.[31] To bridge the gap between the ethnologists, the aesthetes, and the beau monde, he recruited a flamboyant young dilettante, Georges Henri Rivière, to be his deputy director. Alice Conklin observes that "a thirty-year-old bourgeois aesthete and jazz enthusiast with no scientific training, settled profession, or political principles, was an unusual choice."[32] Rivière himself would claim that his appointment illustrated "the conjunction of science and culture in France at that time . . . A scholar of standing . . . was able to recruit a man of thirty, without any scientific qualifications, whose musical vocation had not been wholly concealed by his training at the École du Louvre."[33] But Rivet did not expect his deputy to become a scientist. "I will do science; you will do everything that has to do with the popular translation of that science," he told Rivière. "I am a man of the people. I want to found a great museum of popular culture." He added that Rivière should take responsibility for raising money to support this, "the poorest of museums."[34]

Rivière's connections to artists, collectors and donors were invaluable to the struggling museum. He had been secretary to

David David-Weil, chairman of the Lazard Frères bank, art collector and patron of museums, including the Trocadéro. And he was involved with a short-lived breakaway surrealist magazine, *Documents*, edited by Georges Bataille, "and myself to do the work." *Documents* had a remarkably eclectic remit. According to the journal's strapline, it covered "Doctrines, archaeology, fine arts, ethnography." "In its illustrations," Rivière recalled, "could be seen side by side a Zapotec urn and a scene from the Folies Bergères."[35]

Documents became almost a house organ of the Museum of Ethnography. The museum's director, Rivet, was on the editorial board. Two of his curatorial staff, Michel Leiris and André Schaeffner, were regular contributors. So was Marcel Griaule, one of the first professional ethnographers in France. Soon the surrealist Ciné-Club was having its regular film showings at the Trocadéro Museum.[36] (Bataille defined a museum as "a colossal mirror in which a person contemplates himself at last in all his facets, finds himself literarily admirable, and abandons himself to the ecstasy described in all the art magazines.")[37]

Rivière cultivated a spirit of camaraderie in the museum. In 1929, he set up a canteen with long communal tables. Financed by a grant from his carefully nurtured Society of Friends of the Museum, it provided free meals to a friendly crowd of curators, fieldworkers, avant-garde artists and writers and society ladies. The guards were treated as colleagues, and encouraged to help with the displays. Ping-pong tables were installed among the Mexican figures in the stores. Rivière arranged evening concerts, dances and film shows. "A strong endogamy reigned at the Trocadéro," writes Christine Laurière, "and not only among the young ethnologists. Couples formed and broke up."[38]

Rivet insisted that the Trocadéro was a scientific museum. And ethnography was not art history. Its subject matter was the stuff of everyday life. Yet Rivet felt obliged to accommodate the connoisseurs of primitive art. He directed Rivière to set up a "Hall of Treasures." Influenced by a path-breaking exhibition of primitive art in New York's Museum of Modern Art in 1932,[39] Rivière dedicated his "small kingdom," which enjoyed "extra-territorial rights," to objects that were "remarkable from an artistic point of view . . . gathered purely for the pleasure of the eye." It was set "free of all scientific and classificatory appara-tus." The sculptor Jacques Lipchitz designed the stage set.[40]

Among the objects on display, selected for their aesthetic appeal, mystical allure, rarity and value on the current art market, Alice Conklin notes particularly a Hawaiian feathered helmet, a Tiki god statue from the Marquesas Islands, a golden pendant from Colombia, a crystal skull from Mexico, an Aztec feathered serpent, two masks from pre-Columbian Mexico, a Mexican pyrite mirror, a great cloth from ancient Peru, and an obsidian block carved with a sign from the Aztec calendar. From Africa there was a sixteenth-century Benin bronze, an ivory carving from the Belgian Congo and a gold mask from the Ivory Coast.[41] There was also a display of fakes, designed to challenge superficial notions of authenticity.

But there was a reaction. "Rivière decided to get rid of the wooden cases and install metal ones, in order to make them look more sober and austere and severe," Leiris recalled. "And then there was the anti-aestheticism of Rivière and his peers at the time. They didn't want to hear any talk of 'art nègre'; it had become too fashionable. Besides, anthropology couldn't be reduced to what was called 'art nègre' or to the study of exotic arts. We were against both the explorers who wanted above all to romanticize and glorify relations with the people under study and the aesthetic view of these peoples' material products."[42]

In an article published in *Documents* in 1930, Marcel Griaule, a leading Africanist, wrote:

Ethnography—it is quite tiresome to have to keep repeat-ing this—is interested in the *beautiful* and the *ugly*, in the European sense of these absurd words. It has, however, a tendency to be suspicious of the beautiful, which is rather often a rare—that is monstrous—occurrence in a civilization. Ethnography is suspicious, too, of itself—for it is a white science, i.e., stained with prejudices—and it will not refuse aesthetic value to an object because it is up to date or mass produced.[43]

And he ridiculed connoisseurs who questioned "the authenticity of a Baoule drum because the figure carved on it is holding a rifle."[44]

Jacques Soustelle took over from Rivière as deputy director of the Trocadéro Museum in 1936. He was at the time close to the Communist Party, and he proclaimed that the museum "resolutely addresses the labouring and school-age masses."[45] He led evening tours of the exhibits for manual workers. And he shut down the Hall of Treasures.

In the 1930s the museum organised collecting expeditions. These saved a lot of money, because the fashion for "primitive art" led to price inflation. They also provided young graduates of Mauss's ethnology programme with the opportunity to do fieldwork, which might lead in turn to an appointment at the Trocadéro.

To raise money for the museum's first major collecting expedition, the Mission Dakar–Djibouti, Rivière arranged a boxing match at the Cirque d'Hiver that featured the world bantamweight boxing champion, an African American, "Panama Al Brown." (According to legend, Marcel Mauss got up on stage and shadow-boxed with him.) For the opening of a new Oceania Hall at the museum "there was a parade of mannequins from the great fashion houses dressed in alluring pareos [sarongs]," Rivière recalled. "A combination of productive modishness and scientific policies went hand in hand to promote ethnology and primitive art."[46]

The Paris Ethnographic Museum directed or sponsored around a hundred collecting expeditions between 1928 and 1937, most famously the Dakar–Djibouti expedition led by Marcel Griaule (1931–3) and Claude Lévi-Strauss's forays into the interior of Brazil in the late 1930s.[47] Promising students from the

Institut d'Ethnologie got their first breaks mounting collecting expeditions for the museum. Both Schaeffner and Leiris joined Griaule's African expedition and soon after were taken on as curators at the Museum of Ethnography, Schaeffner becoming the first curator of ethnomusicology.

Leiris remarked that some mundane artefacts were brought back by the Dakar–Djibouti expedition, but only in deference to Mauss, who insisted on documenting everyday objects.[48] Marcel Griaule later spent many months in Dogon country in southern Mali. He collected magnificent masks and carvings, but notwithstanding Mauss's directive, he did not bring a single hoe back home, although the Dogon were hoe-farmers.

The three Amazonian expeditions led by Lévi-Strauss spent most of their time in government designated "zones of contact" operated by missionaries or the telegraph company. Their main business was to collect objects for the Musée de l'Homme, which provided the funding. Forays into the interior were brief, though remarkably elaborate and expensive. A young Brazilian ethnographer, Castro Faria, who accompanied Lévi-Strauss's first expedition, remembered that it "was more like travelling than doing fieldwork: there were months of preparation for very brief periods with indigenous groups."[49] Lévi-Strauss did not collect any of the hybrid artefacts that the Indians were busily improvising, and turned his camera away from any evidence of what he took to be impurity and decline.[50] Remarkably, the expeditions of Lévi-Strauss and Leiris both yielded landmark works of literature: *L'Afrique fantôme* by Leiris (1934), and *Tristes tropiques* by Lévi-Strauss (1955).

The ethnographic museum sometimes presented exhibits in an evolutionary framework, sometimes arranged by culture area. These strategies corresponded to two very different, even contrary, colonial ideologies. The evolutionist model assumed that there was a single human civilisation. It was, however, unequally developed in different parts of the world. France should assist its colonial subjects to progress towards a higher stage. Some ethnologists took the contrary view that human cultures are radically different, and yet perhaps equally valuable. This fitted in with the policy of "Indirect Rule," introduced in British colonies in the 1920s, which influenced some French colonial governors in the 1930s.

Both the Institute of Ethnology and the Museum of Ethnography at Trocadéro—the "Insti" and the "Troca"—were dependent on funding from the Ministry for the Colonies. A third of the students at the institute came from the colonial service. Mauss and Rivet were critical of old-style colonial policies but hoped that the Popular Front, the left-wing coalition that came to power in 1936, would introduce a progressive colonial policy. Both men were close to the new political leadership.

Haunted by the recent horrors of the First World War, the young ethnologists were critical of France's "civilising mission." In northern Cameroon, Michel Leiris wrote in his diary: "Collecting taxes is the one great preoccupation. Pacification and medical aid have only one purpose: to soften up the people so that they offer no resistance and pay their taxes. Official tours, sometimes bloody, to what end? To collect taxes. Ethnographic study, to what end? To be able to carry out a policy better able to bring in taxes."[51]

Leiris did admit that the anti-colonialism of the young ethnologists could become "a bit convoluted," writing,

> What was going on was a rebellion against Western civilisation, plain and simple. I truly thought that so-called primitive societies were superior to ours. It was a kind of inverted racism. You might say that it took me a very long time to realize that within these splendid societies that ethnographers study there could be idiots and assholes exactly as in ours . . . But in the end, what matters and what is, I think, really important is that our first political position was an anti-colonialist position . . . we were concerned about the situation of colonized peoples well before we were concerned about the situation of the proletariat . . .

We were much more inclined to be solidary with "exotic" oppressed people than with oppressed people living here.[52]

Lévy-Bruhl, president of the Institute of Ethnology, encouraged ethnographers to emphasise the worth of African civilisations in order to promote a more tolerant colonial policy. This was, Leiris remarked, "given the time, an advanced idea."[53] Mauss advised his students not to comment on colonialism and certainly not to criticise colonial capitalism: "That can only reduce the scientific value of your work."[54] But in private he was scathing. French science had done nothing for "the Canaques of New Caledonia, whom it abandoned to alcoholism, syphilis, massacre, servitude, beastliness, in a word, Europeanisation, while offering only the attention of laboratory clinicians."[55]

In 1931, a colonial exhibition was held in the purpose-built Palais de la Port Dorée in the Parc de Vincennes in Paris.[56] Not all the presentations were authentic. A missionary anthropologist, Maurice Leenhardt, was surprised to discover that the war songs sung by a troop of Kanak dancers from the French territory of New Caledonia were actually Protestant hymns. (Some Kanak dancers jumped ship and remained behind in France.)

The Trocadéro Museum hosted a grand party in the West African pavilion. African soldiers mounted guard. Loudspeakers broadcast *"la musique nègre authentique."* André Schaeffner, acting as master of ceremonies, introduced acrobatic masked dancers from the Ivory Coast, a scene from the court of an African king and a Madagascan ritual. A galaxy of couturiers, writers, artists and composers were present, including George Bataille, Georges Braque, Manuel de Falla, Julien Green, Alberto Giacometti, Jacques Lipschitz, Henri Matisse, Pablo Picasso, Serge Prokofiev, Helena Rubinstein, Igor Stravinsky, Tristan Tzara and Ossip Zadkine.[57]

The surrealists called for a boycott—*"Ne visitez pas l'Exposition colonial"* ("Don't visit the colonial exhibition!"). They denounced the display of treasures seized from temples, which "completed the work of colonialism that began with massacres, continued by conversions, forced labour and disease." And they mounted a counter-exhibition at the headquarters of the Communist Party. Announced as "La Verité sur les colonies" ("The truth about the colonies"), it included an array of "fetishes" juxtaposed with an image of the Madonna and Child.[58] This was just a sideshow, however. Even party stalwarts didn't show up to see it.

When the colonial exhibition closed down, many of the exhibits were transferred to stock a new "Colonial Museum" in the Palais de la Port Dorée. Rivet saw to it that his protégé, Rivière, was put in charge, to ensure that it limited itself to colonial history and economic development. It should not aspire to be a museum of ethnography.[59] In 1935, the Colonial Museum was renamed the museum of France's Overseas Possessions (Musée de la France d'Outre-mer). In 1960, it became the Museum of African and Oceanian Art. In 2007 it was magically transmuted into a Museum of Immigration.

In 1937, the shabby old Trocadéro Palace was gutted and replaced by a new exhibition centre, the Palace of Chaillot, built to accommodate yet another colonial exhibition. It was here that Rivet rebranded the Museum of Ethnography as the Musée de l'Homme. On 20 June 1938 it was formally opened by Albert Lebrun, the last president of the Third Republic. Rivet arranged for a parade of colonial troops, because "our museum is first and foremost a colonial museum."[60] An ethnographic museum, he wrote, should be "an instrument of cultural and colonial propaganda," one of its functions being to serve as a "precious and indispensable centre" of documentation for colonial officials.[61]

Leiris remarked that the very name, Musée de l'Homme, appeared to be a contradiction in terms, so surprising was the conjunction of the word *homme* and the "dreary term" *museum*. Yet he maintained that the Musée de l'Homme was "the most modern, if not the most beautiful museum in the world."[62] Rivet was determined to give it a modernist scientific identity. Ethnographic objects were sorted into functional types. In an era of racist science, he introduced skeletons and skulls from the Natural History Museum in order to combat ideologies of racial identity and hierarchy. There were two deputy directors, one responsible for biology and prehistory, the other, Jacques Soustelle, for ethnography. In theory the two wings were integrated, though in practice there was some friction.

The collection of French folk crafts was moved to a new museum, the Musée national des Arts et Traditions Populaires. Once more, Rivet entrusted the direction of what might have been a rival institution to the hyperactive Rivière. (Rivière asked Lévi-Strauss to sketch a layout for exhibitions. "I had an exotic flower in my office, and that inspired the form," Lévi-Strauss recalled.)[63]

Benoît de L'Estoile notes that the two museums, one dedicated to the ethnography of primitive societies, the other to French folk traditions, were distinguished not only by their geographical coverage but also by their conceptions of time. The labels in the Museum of Arts and Popular Traditions described French folk artefacts in the past tense. In contrast, the natural history museum was "evolutionist" but ahistorical. "The conception of human 'cultures' on the model of natural species, defined by a fixed series of features produced a timeless display, with labels mostly written in the present tense."[64]

On 10 May 1940, German armies invaded France. Within a month, Paris fell. The Occupation began. The French government retreated to the resort town of Vichy in central France, where it set up a collaborationist regime under Marshall Pétain.

Rivet was president of a group of anti-fascist intellectuals. (Soustelle was secretary-general.) He arranged a programme of exhibits on the French colonial empire, to emphasise that many of the colonies allied themselves with de Gaulle and against Pétain and the collaborationist government in Vichy. On 14 July 1940, Rivet sent the first of four letters to Pétain, criticising the Vichy regime: "Marshall, the country is not with you, France is no longer with you." A collaborationist journal denounced him as leader of the "Jewish-Freemason Musée de l'Homme." On 19 November, Rivet was fired by the minister of education, along with other left-wing academics and civil servants. In February 1941, he fled to Colombia where he remained for the rest of the war years.[65]

Several ethnologists were active in the first resistance network in Paris. They published an underground newspaper, *Résistance*, from the basement of the Musée de l'Homme. A priest, Robert Alesch, infiltrated the network and betrayed them to the Gestapo. In 1942, Boris Vildé and Anatole Lewitzky, curators at the Musée de l'Homme, were executed by firing squad. Deborah Lifschitz, another curator and resistance figure, was deported to Auschwitz where she was immediately murdered. Her partner, Henri Lehmann, a German Jewish refugee who was also a curator at the museum, was smuggled out of the country and joined Rivet in Colombia, where they established an institute of ethnology.[66] Germaine Tillion, a student of Mauss, was deported to Ravensbrück concentration camp, together with her mother, also a *résistante*. Her mother was murdered in 1945, but Germaine was rescued by the Swedish Red Cross. During the Algerian War she gathered evidence of the torture of prisoners. In 1973 she published an ethnographic study of Ravensbrück, *An Eyewitness Account of a Women's Concentration Camp*. She is one of only five women to have been awarded the Grand-croix de la Légion d'honneur. In 2015, she was symbolically interred in the Panthéon.

Rivière kept his head down throughout the Occupation. He carried on with the development of the new museum of French arts and traditions, a field of study that was, however, compromised by the commitment of the Vichy regime to a nationalist and racist ethnology.[67] After the Liberation he was accused of collaboration, but cleared of all charges. A great French historian, Lucien Febvre, remarked that "*au fond*, he did not really give any more to Vichy than he had given to the Popular Front."[68]

Griaule became deputy director of the Musée de l'Homme after Rivet's escape from Occupied France. In 1941 he was appointed to the first chair in ethnology at the Sorbonne. After the Liberation, Schaeffner formally charged him with collaboration, in a letter co-signed by Leiris, but he was cleared by a commission of enquiry.

Soustelle escaped from France and joined de Gaulle's Free French forces in London. After the Liberation the former Marxist became a member of the post-war Constituent Assembly and secretary-general of the Gaullist political movement. In 1956, he was appointed governor of Algeria. In the turmoil of the Algerian revolution he sided with the terrorist wing of colonial extremists who were resisting the independence of the country. He went into exile in Switzerland in 1961.[69] In 1968, that very revolutionary year, Soustelle was officially rehabilitated. He returned to parliament, where he was given a succession of prestigious cultural and academic briefs. In 1983, with the support of Lévi-Strauss, he was elected to the most select of clubs, the Académie française.[70]

The survivors who were reunited in the Musée de l'Homme at the end of the war had lost their old élan. The new director was a biological anthropologist, Henri Vallois. The ethnologists were sidelined. Lévi-Strauss served briefly as deputy director of the museum and taught courses in the Institute of Ethnology, but in 1960 he set up his own laboratory at the Collège de France. Embracing the British term for his vocation, he named it the laboratory of "social anthropology."

The half-hidden fissures in the old Musée de l'Homme between the physical anthropology of Rivet, the ethnography of Mauss and the aestheticism of Rivière were clinically exposed half a century later when President Chirac established the Museum of the quai Branly. He ordered the transfer of all the ethnographic collections to his new museum, where they were rebranded as art. The Musée de l'Homme was closed for refurbishment in 2009. It reopened in October 2015, furnished with skulls, bones, busts and prehistoric artefacts, as a museum of human evolution.[71]

In 1962, as a young student, I spent several months in the Musée de l'Homme, studying in its reading room and exploring its musty lonely galleries. The atmosphere was redolent of atrophy and decline. Two years later the film *L'Homme de Rio*, starring Jean-Paul Belmondo, brought a reminder of more romantic times. A forerunner of *Raiders of the Lost Ark*, the plot hinged on the theft of an Amazonian statue from the Musée de l'Homme. In one haunting scene, Belmondo, on the run from shadowy enemies, finds himself in an obscure corridor of the museum that I recalled very well. Leading to a back entry, it was lined with an array of Amazonian shrunken heads.

AN AMERICAN IN PARIS

In 1889, the curator of ethnology at the U.S. National Museum, Otis T. Mason, made a three-month-long grand tour of Europe's centres of anthropology.[1] The high point was a visit to the Paris Exposition, where he attended the Congress of Anthropology. "I think that my visit to Paris has done me the greatest good on the side of acquaintance and personal contact," he informed the director of the National Museum, George Brown Goode.[2] To his wife he wrote: "How my heart rejoices when I see the men whose thoughts have moved the world. I ought to have taken this trip thirty years ago. My intellectual life has been in a bag."[3]

The Paris World's Fair in 1889 marked the centenary of the storming of the Bastille. It set a new record, attracting 32 million visitors.[4] The theme, as ever, was progress. The first issue of the *Bulletin de l'Exposition Universelle de Paris 1889* asserted that "the law of progress is immortal, as progress itself is infinite." Exhibits bore witness to technological advances made by the Third Republic at home and the cultural variety of the colonial empire abroad. At the entrance to the fairgrounds in the Champs de Mars the newly erected Eiffel Tower dominated an open-air gallery of ethnographic exhibits and cultural displays. The Beaux Arts architect, Charles Garnier, who designed the Paris Opera, was responsible for an outdoor spectacle, "The History of Human Habitation," a street of thirty-nine houses that ran from the Champ de Mars to the Trocadéro Palace, the large exhibition hall built specially for the exposition. Each house represented "a culture and a stage in world housing from prehistoric times to the present."[5] They were occupied by folk in native dress, busy making crafts, playing musical instruments and cooking.

Reporting back to the American Anthropological Association, Mason commended these stagey scenes of "native" life:

> It was possible to see there twelve types of Africans, besides Javanese, Tonkinese, Chinese, Japanese, and other oriental peoples, living in native houses, wearing native costumes, eating native food, practicing native arts and rites on the Esplanade des Invalides side by side with the latest inventions and with the whole civilized world as spectators . . . A portion of the space near the Invalides was set apart for the exhibition of African and Franco-Indian natives at their characteristic occupations, chief among the popular attractions of which were the Javanese theatre and the Annamite Buddhist temple. The members of the Congress, guided by the local committee, spent many hours in these savage enclosures and houses studying the people and their arts and listening to their rude music.[6]

But Mason was less enthusiastic about the European museums which he visited. Franks did not make himself available at the British Museum. Mason was looked after by his deputy, Charles H. Read. He wrote to Goode:

> After walking humbly around these great halls and feeling my poverty and littleness, you cannot imagine my delight on visiting their American department. My rooster could scarce refrain from crowing then and there. They are nowhere, and the specimens are way off in their labels. They frankly admitted that they knew little or nothing about the things. Half their American pottery belongs to the frauds exposed by Holmes.[7]

Goode had charged him with making connections with colleagues that might facilitate the exchange of specimens, but

Mason reported back that so far as the British Museum was concerned, "I have a fancy that they will be niggardly and smart." "The curators of this establishment are wisely called Keepers, for they keep all they get and get all they can."[8] Yet he noted approvingly that the ethnographic materials in the British Museum were so carefully arranged into divisions that "they have a pen for each and when they get a new specimen they turn it into the pen." At Oxford's Pitt Rivers Museum, the big men, E. B. Tylor and Henry Balfour, were absent, but, he wrote to Goode: "The museum is a gem. All the points are not fully worked out nor made out, but it is the most suggestive place I have seen. It shows thought at every fingertip."[9]

In Germany he was struck by the work ethic: "The activity of the Germans is prodigious." In Leipzig, however, Klemm's ethnological collection was still boxed up in store and inaccessible. In Berlin, Bastian and his colleagues were unavailable, but Mason was allowed to inspect the collections. He admitted that Berlin's North American holdings rivalled those in the Smithsonian, "and leaves us far, far in the shade in material from South America, Africa, Asia and Polynesia."

> What interests me most in this collection, however, is not its cases, nor its scientific treatment, it is its immensity. You will know, perhaps, that Bastian is not a scientific man. Nobody ever reads a word he writes. Every scholar in Germany will tell you the same. He is a . . . prince of good fellows, powerfully affected with what the Germans call chronic *Gedankenflucht* [a disorderly stream of ideas], with unlimited influence to get all the money he wants and, above all things, afflicted with the mania of collecting.[10]

From Germany, Mason went to Stockholm, where again he failed to make useful connections. Visiting Copenhagen, he was impressed by the museums of ethnology and Nordic antiquities. The Danish collections were strong on Greenland but "surprisingly, awfully poor in Alaskan material." "I have put in three good hours of hard work labelling some of their North American things and they are very grateful. There is nothing they will not do for us, if it lies in their power."[11]

Writing from Copenhagen, he warned Goode: "I was thinking today what a fine opportunity this summer had afforded me of sifting men and picking out the genuine friends . . . As a rule we shall waste our time following with the majority of European Museums for exchanges. They think it is more blessed to receive than to give." Now he was returning home fired with renewed purpose: "all Europe will ever know of [the American Indian] is what we tell her."[12] And he began to prepare for the next World's Fair, which was to be held in Chicago.

PART 2

NATIVE AMERICANS, MANIFEST DESTINY AND AMERICAN EXCEPTIONALISM

THE SMITHSONIAN INSTITUTION GOES WEST: OR, HOW THE WEST WAS SPUN

The saga of James Smithson and the legacy that established the Smithsonian Institution is as bizarre and as romantic as the story of Hans Sloane and the British Museum, or Pitt Rivers and Oxford's Pitt Rivers Museum. It was also, until very recently, enveloped in mystery. A fire at the Smithsonian Institution in 1865 destroyed Smithson's personal archive. Spencer Baird, secretary of the Smithsonian, commissioned a biographical essay, which was published in 1880, but he admitted that the materials were "exceedingly scanty," and that recent enquiries had yielded nothing new.[1] Some of the most tantalising puzzles were at last cleared up only in the twenty-first century, when Heather Ewing published a thoroughly researched biography of Smithson.[2]

Like Pitt Rivers, James Smithson went under another name for most of his life. This was because he was illegitimate. His mother, Elizabeth Macie, was a rich English widow with aristocratic connections. His father, Hugh Percy Smithson, was the second earl and later first duke of Northumberland. Elizabeth, a cousin of the duchess, was Smithson's long-term lover. In 1764 she became pregnant and moved to Paris to bear their child, whom she named Jacques Louis Macie. The duke recognised his illegitimate daughters but not his illegitimate sons, presumably in order to avoid problems over succession. Elizabeth took responsibility for the support of James and for a younger illegitimate son, also, apparently, fathered by the duke.

James was formally placed under the guardianship of a barrister at the Inner Temple, and educated at Charterhouse

School and Pembroke College, Oxford. At Oxford, according to a university friend, Davies Gilbert, who became president of the Royal Society, "Mr. Smithson, then called Macie, and an undergraduate, had the reputation of excelling all other resident members of the University in the knowledge of chemistry."[3] A well-off bachelor, Smithson travelled widely in continental Europe, collected minerals, published papers on chemistry, and became a fellow of the Royal Society. The French physicist and astronomer François Arago described him in middle age as "a distinguished foreigner, of great wealth, but in wretched health, whose life, save a few hours given to repose, was regularly divided between the most interesting scientific researches and gambling."[4]

Despite Heather Ewing's careful detective work, little is known about Smithson's personal life. What were his relations with women? Reminiscing about his friend at a meeting of the Royal Society, Gilbert recalled that Smithson had a favourite story "frequently repeated . . . with much pleasure and exultation, as exceeding anything that could be brought into competition with it." As Smithson told it, "happening to observe a tear gliding down a lady's cheek, he endeavoured to catch it on a crystal vessel; that one-half of the drop escaped, but having preserved the other half he submitted it to reagents, and detected what was then called microcosmic salt, with muriate of soda, and, I think, three or four more saline substances, held in solution."[5] He never married, and died childless, but his personal seal featured an image of Eros and Psyche embracing.[6]

Elizabeth had a substantial inheritance from her first husband, but she remarried after James's birth and her second husband fleeced her. She then squandered much of what remained in extravagant living and expensive law suits against various relatives.[7] On her death, in 1800, she left James £10,000. In those days this would have represented a comfortable capital settlement for a bachelor, but not riches. (Mr. Darcy, the eligible bachelor in Jane Austen's *Pride and Prejudice*, had an *income* of £10,000 a year.) James's illegitimate brother, Colonel Dickinson, died in 1820 and left him in control of a large capital sum. It remains unclear how much money was involved, how the colonel became so rich, and why he entrusted his capital to James rather than to his widow. The legacy was invested in French government bonds. James reserved much of the interest for the support of Dickinson's son.[8]

Within a month of his mother's death, James changed his name to Smithson. "Since her death," he explained in a letter to Sir Joseph Banks, "I make little mystery of my being brother to the present Duke of Northumberland."[9] In the summer of 1826, aged sixty-two, he wrote his will, primed by a do-it-yourself manual. It began very grandly: "I James Smithson Son to Hugh first Duke of Northumberland, & Elizabeth, heiress of the Hungerfords of Studley & niece to Charles the proud Duke of Somerset . . . ." He went on to specify that a large part of the estate was being held for his nephew, Dickinson's son, who would continue to enjoy the interest on it. If this nephew died and left a child or children, they should inherit the capital. Should there be no children, Smithson's estate would pass "to the United States of America, to found in Washington under the name of the Smithsonian Institution, an Establishment for the increase & diffusion of knowledge among men." Smithson died in 1829. His nephew died, childless, in 1835.[10]

In 1836, the United States Congress formally accepted Smithson's bequest. A diplomat was despatched to London to collect the funds. After a two-year battle in Chancery, the will was proved and the envoy returned to Washington with Smithson's archives, his scientific collections and 104,960 gold sovereigns packed in leather bags and sealed in eleven boxes. The sovereigns were melted down and coined into American currency, yielding $508,318.46. This was roughly equal to the endowment of Harvard University at the time. It was equivalent to one sixty-sixth of the U.S. federal budget for 1838.[11]

Smithson's reason for making this gift to the United States remains in doubt. (It was rumoured that he originally intended to leave his money to the Royal Society, but abandoned the plan when a paper of his was turned down for publication.)[12] As a young man, he had been stirred by the French Revolution, but his pride in his own aristocratic connections does not suggest that he held strongly republican views. Heather Ewing points out that he wrote his will just as the United States prepared to celebrate the fiftieth anniversary of the Declaration of Independence. By an astonishing chance, both John Adams and Thomas Jefferson, the second and third presidents of the United States, died on that same Fourth of July. They were both apostles of science and enlightenment, which may have moved Smithson.

While Congress was debating Smithson's legacy, the funds were invested by the U.S. Treasury in bonds issued by the State of Arkansas, which defaulted. This greatly upset John Quincy Adams. The son of John Adams, the second president of the U.S.A., John Quincy Adams, himself a former president, now a Massachusetts congressman, worried that Smithson's bequest would be "squandered upon cormorants or wasted in electioneering bribery." Determined to rescue it from "the fangs of the State of Arkansas,"[13] he persuaded Congress that the loss must be made good.

After a series of inconclusive debates, stretching over eight sessions, in 1846 Congress directed that Smithson's legacy should be used to fund an independent project, the Smithsonian Institution.[14]

Would the Smithsonian Institution take the form of a library, a college, a museum? John Quincy Adams, who chaired the congressional committee dealing with Smithson's bequest, fancied an astronomical observatory, and declared that he would "rather see the money of Smithson thrown into the Potomac than to have it devoted to the advance of education."[15] In the end, on the very last day of the session, Congress agreed to pay out the 6 per cent interest that was owing on the bonds to fund the institution in its first year. However, when it came to defining its mission, Congress settled on a fudge. ("The day, like all the last days of a Session of Congress was a Chaos of confusion," Adams wrote in his diary.)[16] "The legislation was a classic example of the art of congressional compromise," Heather Ewing writes. "It was bursting with programmatic directives; squabbles over the allocation of resources were inevitable."[17] The budget was clearly inadequate for all the activities that Congress wished the Smithsonian to take on, let alone to fund an architectural showcase to house a museum.

In 1846, President James K. Polk signed the legislation that established the Smithsonian Institution as a trust, to be administered by a board of regents and a secretary. A blue-ribbon board of regents was appointed, including the vice president of the United States, the chief justice, the mayor of Washington, and several members of Congress. But they were all busy men. It was clear that effective power would rest with the secretary. The regents appointed Joseph Henry to the post. A physicist and a pioneering figure in the field of electromagnetism, Henry held the first chair in natural history at the College of New Jersey (the forerunner of Princeton University) from 1832 to 1846. He served as secretary of the Smithsonian from 1846 to 1878, and in 1868 he was elected the second president of the National Academy of Sciences.

Joseph Henry hoped to make the Smithsonian Institution a centre of scientific research. However, Congress promised funding for a dedicated building that would house "objects of natural history, including a geological and mineralogical cabinet." This was perhaps appropriate, since geology and mineralogy were Smithson's own special love, and he was a dedicated collector. (Unfortunately, in 1865 Smithson's personal cabinet containing "a choice and beautiful collection of minerals, comprising probably eight or ten thousand specimens" was lost in a fire in the Smithsonian together with his personal archive.)[18] However, in one of his first annual reports, in 1857, Henry accepted that the Smithsonian should take responsibility for American antiquities and ethnology: "It is the sacred duty which this country owes to the civilized world to collect everything relative to the history, manners and customs, the physical peculiarities, and, in short, all that may tend to illustrate the character and history of the original inhabitants of North America."[19]

But Henry was reluctant to see the institute's reserves drain away to service disparate collections of uneven quality. In 1858, he negotiated a congressional grant specifically for the upkeep of the museum. It was agreed that $15,000 a year would go to the museum and library and $15,910 to research, publications and lectures.[20] Henry then effectively hived off responsibility for the direction of the museum to his assistant secretary, Spencer Fullerton Baird. A professor of natural history at Dickinson College in Pennsylvania, an ornithologist who had been taught to draw specimens by John Audubon himself, Baird arrived in Washington with his private natural history cabinets, which filled two railroad boxcars.[21]

When Congress voted to establish the Smithsonian Institution, Washington was still a small settlement with a handful of government buildings, the political leadership resident only while Congress was sitting. A southern gentleman who came to Washington for the inauguration of President Zachary Taylor in 1849 was unimpressed. "All that meets the gaze in Washington except the Capital and the Departments, seems temporary," he wrote. "The city appears like the site of an encampment."[22] Henry Adams—great-grandson of John Adams, and grandson of John Quincy Adams—visited the federal capital in May 1850 as a boy of twelve. This was just four years after the Smithsonian was founded, thanks largely to the determination of his own grandfather, and three years since it moved into its first building, the red sandstone "Castle," a short walk from Congress.

> Coming down in the early morning from his bedroom in his grandmother's house—still called the Adams Building—in F Street and venturing outside into the air reeking with the thick odour of the catalpa trees, he found himself on an earth-road, or village street, with wheel-tracks meandering

from the colonnade of the Treasury hard by, to the white marble columns and fronts of the Post Office and the Patent Office which faced each other in the distance, like white Greek temples in the abandoned gravel-pits of a deserted Syrian city.

This was all very different from the cultivated world of his own historic New England home, but "the boy liked it: distinctly it remained in his mind as an attraction . . . The want of barriers, of pavements, of forms; the looseness, the laziness; the indolent Southern drawl; the pigs in the streets; the negro babies and their mothers with bandanas; the freedom, openness, swagger of nature and man . . . "[23]

Everything changed after the Civil War. The population of Washington, DC, was 50,000 in 1850, including around 4,000 slaves. After the abolition of slavery in the District of Columbia, refugees and fugitives flooded in. By the end of the war Washington had 132,000 inhabitants, and by 1880, 178,000.[24] And now the federal government assumed huge new responsibilities. It undertook a costly, politically fraught "Reconstruction" of the South. In the West it launched one of the most momentous state projects of the nineteenth century, the exploration, appropriation and consolidation of the immense lands across the Mississippi.

At the time that the Smithsonian was founded, much of the trans-Mississippi was still, in the language of the age, "Indian country." In 1814, John Quincy Adams told a British plenipotentiary that this was rightfully the territory of the U.S.A.: "To condemn vast regions of territory to perpetual barrenness and solitude that a few hundred savages might find wild beasts to hunt upon it, was a species of game law that a nation descended from Britons would never endure," Adams insisted.[25]

The Indian Removal Act of 1830 prepared the way for the transportation of native peoples to territories west of the Mississippi River. Some 60,000 members of the five "Civilized Tribes" of the southeastern United States—Creeks, Cherokee, Choctaw,

Chickasaw and Seminole—were forcibly relocated to what is now eastern Oklahoma between 1830 and 1850. (The "Trail of Tears.") Resistance was hopeless. The Cherokee brought a court case against the State of Georgia, and won two judgments in their favour from the Supreme Court. In vain. President Andrew Jackson is said to have commented that "[Chief Justice] John Marshall has made his decision, now let him enforce it."

On Christmas Eve 1831, a young French traveller, Alexis de Tocqueville, came across a miserable procession of Choctaw trudging to Memphis on their way into exile. He wrote to his mother that Americans had discovered that one square kilometre could feed ten times more civilised men than savages, and so the savages should be booted out: "see what a fine thing logic is." The Choctaw had been sent on their way with gifts of "flasks of brandy, glass necklaces, earrings and mirrors." Tocqueville found one old man who could speak English and asked him why the Choctaw were leaving their lands. "To be free," the man replied.[26] Meanwhile, waves of settlers were moving westward. The frontier kept shifting further and further west as new territories were colonised. "Each was won by a series of Indian wars," wrote Frederick J. Turner, in his classic essay "The Significance of the Frontier in American History."[27]

In 1844, President Polk campaigned for the incorporation of the Mexican territory of Texas. In messianic vein, the popular *Democratic Review* prophesied that the annexation of Texas to the United States would mark "the fulfilment of our manifest destiny to overspread the continent allotted by Providence for the free development of our yearly multiplying millions." (This was the first appearance in print of the phrase "manifest destiny.") A war with Mexico followed in 1846–7. By the Treaty of Guadalupe Hidalgo, signed on 2 February 1848, Mexico recognised the independence of Texas and ceded 55 per cent of its territories to the United States, including most of what would become the modern states of Arizona, California, Colorado, Nevada, New Mexico and Utah. In 1867, Alaska was bought from Russia for $7.2 million: roughly two cents per acre.

The colonisation of the West accelerated after the Civil War. The Homestead Act of 1862 set aside 650 thousand square kilometres of public land—nearly 10 per cent of the total area of the United States—to be allocated, free of charge, in 160 acre lots, to men who had not taken up arms against the Federal government. Most of this land was beyond the Mississippi. Hundreds of thousands of new settlers trekked westwards. The U.S. army fought a series of local Indian wars. The Department of the Interior funded geographical and geological surveys. And the Smithsonian was now urgently required to document the Indian populations. As Frederick William True, the first head curator of biology (1897–1911) at the United States National Museum, observed: "the Museum is essentially a natural development springing from the activities of the government, growing with their growth, and expanding with their expansion."[28]

One of the most influential of the scientific explorers of the American West was John Wesley Powell, the fourth son of an English Methodist preacher who settled in the midwestern United States. Powell took college science courses, though he never completed a degree. In his holidays he liked to explore along the Mississippi and Ohio rivers, collecting fossils. He became a high school teacher in Illinois. And he married a cousin, the daughter of his mother's half-brother. This humdrum provincial life was upended by the Civil War. In the spring of 1861, five days after President Lincoln called for volunteers to fight rebellion in the South, Powell, twenty-seven years old, joined up. He was elected sergeant major, and within a couple of months commissioned a second lieutenant by General Ulysses S. Grant. In his very first engagement, in April 1862, at the Battle of Shiloh in Tennessee, he was wounded. The surgeon (a pharmacist in civilian life) hacked off his right arm just below the elbow. The wound would torment him for the rest of his life, but Powell returned to active duty and was promoted to the rank of major. From that day on he would be known as Major Powell.

After four years as a soldier, Powell became a teacher of

natural sciences at Illinois Wesleyan University in Blooming-
ton. He was soon back to exploring and collecting, and became
curator of the Museum of the Illinois Natural History Society.
In 1867, he led a ten-man unofficial "Colorado River Exploring
Expedition." (It ended badly. The party ran short of supplies.
Three men deserted. They came upon an Indian woman who
was gathering seeds, raped and murdered her, and were tracked
down and killed by Paiute Indians.)[29]

In the 1860s and 1870s, Congress funded four surveys of
the West to establish the prospects for mining, farming and
settlement. One was led by Powell: officially designated as the
"Geographical and Geological Survey of the Rocky Mountain
Region, J. W. Powell in charge."[30] Powell's survey, unusually, paid
particular attention to Indian populations. He shipped boxes
of artefacts to the Smithsonian from the Great Basin Tribes,
"including seed fans, winnowing trays, chipped arrowheads,
hafted stone knives, bullroarer 'whirrers,' parfleches, war clubs
and stone pipes."[31]

When Powell returned from the Rockies, he settled in Washington, DC. "In the decades following the war Powell became
one of the country's leading experts on the West—its topography,
geology and climate as well as indigenous peoples," according
to his biographer, Donald Worster. And he was a booster for the
trans-Mississippi. He "joined the cause of continental conquest,
and joined excitedly."[32] In the nation's capital Powell was the
right man, in the right place, at the right time. According to the
Dictionary of American Biography, he "was in appearance a somewhat rough and striking figure, with tumultuous hair and beard.
He was hearty and eminently magnetic, at times given to enforc-
ing his views with military arbitrariness. He had a remarkable
faculty for leadership and was likable in the extreme."

In 1878, the Cosmos Club was founded at a meeting held in
Powell's parlour. (Of course, Henry Adams was present.) The
prospectus stated that the club was open to "men devoted to
or interested in Science, professionally or otherwise."[33] The

Cosmos men, Washington's intelligentsia, were fascinated by the new ideas about "evolution" and "progress" coming over from England. "Never had the sun of progress shone so fair," Henry Adams remarked ironically, visiting London in 1870 after a nine-year absence. "Darwin was the greatest of prophets in the most evolutionary of worlds."[34] But Adams was a blue blood, an aesthete, no enthusiast. "Henry Adams was a Darwinist because it was easier than not," he wrote, in his wonderful third person memoirs. Indeed, "he really did not care whether truth was, or was not, true. He did not even care that it should be proved true, unless the process were new and amusing. He was a Darwinian for fun."[35] Adams developed his own idiosyncratic, even mystical, somewhat Hegelian notion of the better future that was coming, making much of a rather vaguely conceived dialectical relationship between human beings and Nature.[36]

In America, Herbert Spencer was an even more influential prophet of "evolution" than Darwin. He taught that common processes could be observed in the natural and the social world. A "struggle for survival" (Spencer's coinage) resulted in what Darwin preferred to call the selection of the fittest. The struggle might be hard, even bloody, Spencer conceded, but no-holds-barred competition between individuals, classes and races would bring about social, economic and political progress.

Many Americans revered Spencer as an apostle of progress and capitalism. Powell invited him to his office when he visited Washington. Afterwards, Spencer sent him a friendly note: "Take warning against doing too much, and by way of precaution abandon that telephone in your bed-room that you told me of."[37] It is unlikely that Powell followed this advice. In any case, raised as a Methodist, growing up in the atmosphere of midwestern individualism, Powell thought that Spencer was too much of a determinist. Nor was he in favour of letting capitalism rip, red in tooth and claw. He believed in the power of the state to improve things. Governments should impose moral responsibilities on corporations. In the ideal America of the future, men and women "will vie with one another to serve a maimed man."[38] Powell also had faith that the American West would be spared the worst features of Spencer's struggle for survival. Providentially, Nature smiled on settlers in those vast open territories. "Men are not crowded against plants, men are not crowded against beasts, and men are not crowded against one another. The land is yet broad enough for all."[39]

Powell's war record gave him an entry to political circles, and he was accepted into a special brotherhood of the war wounded, whichever side they had fought on. One of his cronies was David Bremner Henderson, a Unionist officer who had lost a leg in battle. A Republican and the first member of Congress from west of the Mississippi, Henderson became a member of the house appropriations committee and was then elected speaker. He would be helpful to Powell. Another friend, Charles Edward Hooker, a graduate of the Harvard Law School, had served as an officer in the Confederate Army and was elected to Congress as a Democrat from Mississippi. Hooker had lost his left arm in the Battle of Vicksburg. Since Powell had lost his right arm, the two men used to swap gloves.[40] Ulysses S. Grant, Powell's old commander, was president from 1869 to 1877. Powell also formed a special bond with President Garfield, a fellow mid-westerner and Civil War veteran.

These connections helped Powell to influence Washington's debates on the West. He was soon appointed to two key public posts. In 1879, Congress wound up the four western surveys and established the U.S. Geological Survey. Two years later, President Garfield appointed Powell its director. The congressional legislation that set up the Geological Survey provided funds for a Bureau of Ethnology (after 1897, the Bureau of American Ethnology) in the Smithsonian Institution, and transferred to it the government's archival records relating to "Indian" populations. This new agency was almost an afterthought. As Donald Worster explains:

At no point did Congress explicitly authorise a federally

funded Bureau of Ethnology. In the 1879 legislation abolishing the western surveys and establishing the Geological Survey, Powell had modestly asked for and received $20,000 to complete "the reports of the Geographical and Geological Survey of the Rocky Mountain Region with the necessary maps and illustrations." But a year later he was back, asking for $50,000 for his new "bureau" in the Smithsonian . . . He understood what Congress meant to do—or at least should have done—and held them to it.[41]

Powell became director of the Bureau of Ethnology. (He preferred the term "Anthropology" and complained about "the ill-named bureau in which I am placed.")[42] In 1882, he wrung a further $40,000 from Congress for his bureau, and this level of funding would be maintained for another decade.[43] Powell recruited a loyal staff, many of whom had a similar background in the federal army and the geological surveys, and he oversaw a network of agents in the West. E. B. Tylor, who had just been appointed to the first position in anthropology to be established in an English university, visited the Smithsonian Institution in 1884. Invited to address an anthropological meeting in Washington, he teased Major Powell about his spider's web of influence. "The energy with which the Bureau of ethnology works throughout its distant ramifications . . . is something like what one used to hear of the organization of the Jesuits, with their central authority in a room in a Roman palace, whence directions were sent out which there was some agent in every country town ready to carry out with skill and zeal."[44]

The bureau was, from the beginning, policy-oriented. Powell saw it as "the intelligence arm of the U.S. Army and the Indian Commissioner, as they tried to manage their wards."[45] The purpose of its research efforts, according to Powell, was "the discovery of the relations among the native American tribes to the end that amicable groups might be gathered on reservations." According to the Annual Report of the Bureau of Ethnology for 1892–3:

This demand for the practical researches conducted by the Bureau leads directly and unavoidably to an innovation in ethnic classification . . . So the initial work of the Bureau was the development of a practical system of classifying primitive peoples, and the conditions were such as to permit an actual test of the classification and to complete the rejection of unnatural, illogical, or incongruous systems.[46]

Powell wanted to escape the clutches of the department of the interior, and decided that his best option was to place the bureau in the Smithsonian under Baird. This arrangement would lead to tensions. The bureau was formally incorporated in the Smithsonian Institution, but Powell insisted on regarding it as autonomous. His relationship with Spencer Baird "was not cordial," according to Regna Darnell, and the bureau under Powell and the museum under Baird "often operated at cross-purposes." The department of the interior pressed the bureau to advance the classification of the Indians. Baird had different priorities. He wanted the bureau to concentrate its efforts on collecting specimens for the museum.[47] He told Powell

I have always found members of Congress very impatient in considering the question of pure philological work. Of my arguments before the appropriation committee, I have found the most potent to be the urgency of securing, at the earliest possible time, the archaeological and ethnological aboriginal matter which could be carried off to Europe, either by travellers sent out for the purpose, or by dealers in the U.S. collecting material for export.[48]

But Powell was not easily constrained. His views when it came to the economic development of the West and the future of Indian communities were decided and not always popular. His warnings against the risks of small-scale farming in what he called the Arid Lands of the West ran up against "the frenetic land-trading, farm-making, public-domain-settling economy of the entire West" and infuriated western politicians and settler lobbies.[49] In 1894, his congressional enemies forced his resignation from the Geological Survey. But while his ideas on "Indian policy" also challenged vested interests, Powell remained at the head of the Bureau of Ethnology, bringing in his side-kick, William McGee, to do the heavy lifting. ("McGee, I know what I want; you know what I want. Figure a way to do it before next March.")[50] The two had a bet as to who had the larger brain. Both men donated their brains to the Smithsonian. (Powell's won, though neither man's brain was especially large. When the Smithsonian had a launch party for the John Wesley Powell Library in 1979, Powell's brain was ceremonially wheeled in, to be welcomed by the two hundred guests.)[51]

Powell's scientific expertise was in geology. His direct experience of Native American life was limited to brief encounters during his western expeditions. For a deeper understanding of the Indians and their place in history, he drew on the theories of the only American who had won international recognition as an anthropologist, Lewis Henry Morgan. A lawyer in Rochester, New York, Morgan took a friendly interest in a nearby Iroquois reservation. He campaigned against a move to deport the Iroquois to Kansas and helped them to appeal a land claim. In 1851 he published an account of their institutions, *League of the Ho-de-no-sau-nee, or Iroquois*. With that, he wrote, "I laid aside the Indian subject to devote my time to my profession. My principal object in writing this work, which exhibits abundant evidence of hasty execution was to free myself of the subject . . . From the close of 1850 to the summer of 1857, Indian affairs were laid entirely aside."[52] But then he was elected to the American Academy of Sciences. This encouraged him to join in debates about the origins of the Indian population in North America and the affinities of their languages. He read up in philology, consulted speculative accounts by J. F. McLennan and Henry Maine of the origins of family and marriage, and arranged societies all over the world in a progressive series, according to their forms of marriage, from Native Americans (group marriage, no families, according to Morgan) to Africa, the Far East, and Europe. The evidence came from terminologies for kin, which supposedly encoded ancient marriage arrangements.

In 1887, Morgan published his masterpiece, *Ancient Society: Researches in the Lines of Progress from Savagery through Barbarism to Civilization.* "The great antiquity of mankind upon the earth has been conclusively established," he announced in the introduction. "It seems singular that the proofs should have been discovered as recently as within the last thirty years, and that the present generation should be the first called upon to recognize so important a fact."[53] And since that ancient beginning, human history had followed a clear path. "It can now be asserted upon convincing evidence that savagery preceded barbarism in all the tribes of mankind as barbarism is known to have preceded civilization . . . The history of the human race is one in source, one in experience, and one in progress."[54]

Powell was deeply impressed. He read *Ancient Society* "long into the night and planned to take it into the field with him."[55] "After reading your book," he wrote to Morgan in 1877, "I believe you have discovered the true system of social and governmental organization among the Indians."[56] He made it required reading for the staff of the Bureau of Ethnology.[57]

According to Morgan, North American Indians were mired in the middle or upper stages of savagery, with no effective leaders, no stable families and no conception of private property. Powell decided that Indian policy had to begin from this premise. In 1878, he wrote to the secretary of the interior that (following the war with Mexico and the huge accession of new territories to the U.S.A.):

The rapid spread of civilization since 1849 has placed the white man and the Indian in direct conflict throughout the whole area, and the "Indian problem" is thus thrust upon us, and it *must* be solved wisely, or unwisely. Many of the difficulties are inherent . . . but an equal number are unnecessary and caused by the lack of our knowledge relating to the Indians themselves. Savagery is not inchoate civilization; it is a distinct status of society with its own institutions, customs, philosophy, and religion.[58]

In 1880, in a letter to Senator Henry Teller of Colorado, a defender of Indian land rights, Powell sketched what he thought should be done:

All of our Indian troubles have arisen primarily and chiefly from two conditions inherent in savage society. The first is that the land belonging to an Indian clan or tribe is dear to it . . . chiefly because it is the locus of its religion. [In consequence] a removal of the Indians is the first step to be taken in their civilization . . . The great body of Indians of North America has been removed from their original homes. Only a few now remain to worship at the graves of their ancestors. This portion of the problem is almost solved, but the wisdom and patience of the American people must be exercised for a few years longer—demanding as they should on the one hand, that the progress of civilization and the establishment of homes for millions of civilized people should not be retarded because of the interests and superstitions of a small number of savages, but demanding on the other hand that strict justice and the widest charity be extended to the Indians.[59]

In short, as Morgan had explained, the Indians were stuck at a stage of primordial communism. If they were to progress, they had to sever their bond to the land of their ancestors. Then they would come to accept the principles of private property and so take the first step on the way to a civilised condition. Settled on reservations, they would learn to be farmers. Eventually, they might form part of the free yeomanry that would develop the West, thanks to the Homestead Act. According to Powell, "as soon as an Indian acquires property, he more thoroughly appreciates the rights of property, and becomes an advocate of law and order."[60] In the meantime, the Indians on the reservations should be protected from the new wave of settlers. As Powell explained to Congress, "Where the Indians are now scattered about the country, there seems to be no way in which justice can be secured to the Indians."[61]

The end point of Native American history was already fixed: "whether we desire it or not, the ancient inhabitants of the country must be lost; and we may comfort ourselves with the reflection that they are not destroyed, but are gradually absorbed, and become a part of more civilized communities."[62] Assimilation was both inevitable and desirable. "Civilization overwhelms Savagery, not so much by spilling blood as by mixing blood, but whether spilled or mixed, a greater homogeneity is secured."[63] These changes were well underway, and they were irreversible. "In a few years, it will be impossible to study our North American Indians in their primitive condition, except from recorded history."[64]

Morgan approved. He had been a Republican senator in the New York State Assembly. Once he had lobbied President Lincoln to make him secretary of Indian Affairs. Now he cheered Powell on. In November 1880, when Garfield was elected president, Morgan wrote to Powell: "I congratulate you and myself on our great Republican victory. It will give four years of steady encouragement to your work, and enable you to get it upon a solid foundation. This is something apart from the general good of the country which is now assured. Hurra for Garfield and the Ethnological Bureau."[65] (President Garfield's inaugural ball in 1881 was the first event to be held in the newly completed National Museum of Natural History. He was assassinated a few months later.)

At one of their first meetings, the regents of the Smithsonian called upon the commissioner of Indian Affairs to encourage his agents to collect materials "illustrating the natural history of the country, and more especially the physical history, manners, and customs of the American aborigines."[66] In 1873, Joseph

Henry suggested to General William Tecumseh Sherman that federal soldiers engaged in operations against Native peoples be instructed to collect "specimens illustrating life and warfare." As an example, he recalled that during the Battle of Ash Hollow against the Sioux in 1855, the opportunity was "embraced to secure from the bodies of the slain a very complete assortment of the articles referred to."[67]

At first, the anthropology collections were a jumble. Curtis Hinsley writes that the cases containing ethnographic objects "occupied the entire upper west gallery of the museum hall, one-fourth of total museum space," but the "contents of each display unit were determined by whatever items happened to have been collected, with haphazard results." Moreover, only one of the fifteen ethnology cases was devoted exclusively to North American Indian artefacts.[68]

Baird was charged with building up the collections, but his primary interest was in natural history. He married the daughter of a military man, Colonel Sylvester Churchill, a remote relative of the famous English Churchills. Churchill saw to it that military personnel should take every opportunity to collect specimens for the Smithsonian. As a result, Debra Lindsay writes, "the majority of the specimens deposited at the Smithsonian Institution during the 1850s were collected by employees of the War Department, the Department of the Interior, the army, the navy, the Topographical Bureau, and various state surveys."[69]

In 1858, Baird initiated an in-house exploration and collecting programme. He commissioned guidebooks to direct collectors, including *Instructions for Research Relative to the Ethnology and Philology of America*, written by George Gibbs, the first qualified linguist hired by the Smithsonian. With Baird's approval, the most successful of these expeditions, to the Mackenzie River district in the Canadian Arctic, branched out and collected ethnographic materials from Inuit and Athapaskan hunters who were trading with the Hudson's Bay Company at Fort Anderson. At this time, Debra Lindsay writes, "the Mackenzie River native population was suffering the worst effects of scarlatina, measles,

and influenza. When northern natives became too incapaci-
tated to hunt, they could trade their weapons, tools, household
effects, and other personal possessions for provisions and mer-
chandise from the company store. Many did."[70]

After the Civil War, stung by reports that foreign governments
were ransacking cultural treasures in the Southwest, Congress
pressured the Smithsonian and the Bureau of Ethnology to
step up the collection of Native American artefacts. In the early
1870s, Spencer Baird and Major Powell duly sent out regular
collecting expeditions, staffed by veterans of earlier geological surveys. Then came a new, grandiose federal initiative: the
blockbuster centennial exhibition mounted in Philadelphia in
1876 to mark the hundredth anniversary of the Declaration of
Independence.

An Act of Congress specified that the exhibition would
display "the natural resources of the country and their development, and . . . its progress in those arts which benefit mankind,
in comparison with those of older nations." As *The New York
Times* summed it up, the exhibition was "designed to carry the
spectator through the successive steps of human progress."[71]
Amazing new inventions were on display in Philadelphia, including telephones, refrigeration processes, and the Westinghouse
air brake for railway trains. The centrepiece of the machinery
hall was a massive electric generator that powered the exhibits.

The stands in the main building were organised by nation, or,
as one of the organisers explained, they represented "An installation by races." (The newly fashionable scientific terminology
elided national and "racial" identities.) "France and Colonies,
representing the Latin races, were given spaces adjacent to the
northeast central tower. England and Colonies, representing the
Anglo-Saxon races, were given spaces adjacent to the northwest
central tower. The German Empire, and Austria and Hungary,
representing the Teutonic races, were given spaces adjacent to
the southwest tower."[72]

The federal government's exhibits were masterminded by

William Phipps Blake. A chemist, geologist and mining engineer, Blake had taken part in the scientific mapping of the trans-Mississippi territories. He represented California at the Paris Exposition in 1867, and he was a prominent figure in the lobby for colonisation of the west, alongside Major Powell at the Smithsonian's Bureau of Ethnology.

Blake invited the Smithsonian to set up an exhibition of Indian archaeology and ethnology. Baird was happy to oblige. He extracted a special budget to fund collecting expeditions. These went to the Pacific Northwest, California, and (led by Major Powell himself) to the Rocky Mountain region. Mason commissioned agents of the Indian bureau to pitch in with local artefacts.[73]

Baird then recruited two young men to organise the haul of antiquities and ethnological items for the centennial exhibition: a reclusive German scholar, Charles Rau, and a seventeen-year-old Cornell student, Frank Cushing, who became the curator of the exhibits. (Both men would move on afterwards to posts at the National Museum.) The Smithsonian was granted a massive display area, matched only by that of the Department of the Interior.

The centennial exhibition won acres of coverage in national newspapers and magazines and brought in some 10 million visitors. Crowds packed the boisterous "Centennial City," with its food stores, bars and a privately run "museum" that showed, according to a contemporary witness, "the wild men of Borneo, and the wild children of Australia . . . and a collection of 'Feejees,' who were vouched for by the exhibitors as 'pure and unadulterated man-eaters.' "[74] This honky-tonk fringe may have been a crowd pleaser, but the scientific displays represented a public relations coup for Baird. He returned to Washington loaded with precious collections. Joseph Henry now accepted that the Smithsonian should pay attention to anthropology. In his annual report in 1877 he wrote: "Anthropology, or what may be considered the natural history of man is at present the most popular branch of science."[75]

Major John Wesley Powell with Tau-gu, a Paiute chief. Photographed by Jack Hillers for the U.S. Topographical and Geological Survey of the Colorado Valley, 1874. (By permission of the Smithsonian Institution.)

In 1878, Baird succeeded Joseph Henry as secretary of the Smithsonian. In 1881, at long last, a dedicated building was opened to house the National Museum. Baird explained that:

> The collections in the new building are intended to form an *Anthropological Museum*, organized upon the broadest and most liberal interpretation of the term "anthropology," and illustrating the characteristics of civilized as well as savage races of mankind and their attainments in civilization and culture. The central idea will be *man*, and the manner in which he adapts the products of the earth to his needs.[76]

In July 1883, Baird wrote a memo to Powell, reminding him that Congress still expected the Smithsonian to ramp up the American Indian collections.[77] The bureau was staffed largely by men like Powell himself: Civil War veterans who had taken part in the geological surveys. They had no background in ethnography or linguistics. Baird widened the pool. He recruited Frank Hamilton Cushing to help with the ethnological exhibits at the centennial exhibition and, in 1879, invited Cushing to take part in a collecting expedition to Hopi and Zuni pueblos in the Southwest. This was an inspired appointment. The frail, artistic, original, largely self-educated young man had been fascinated since his childhood by Native American artefacts. Now Cushing was captivated by his first exposure to the Pueblo way of life. He spent two and a half years among the Zuni, learned the language, adopted traditional dress and documented arts, techniques, rituals and beliefs.

"Cushing can think as myth-makers think," Powell said, "he can expound as priests expound, and his tales have the verisimilitude of ancient lore."[78] When Cushing required a scalp to take part in a Zuni initiation ceremony, Spencer Baird sent him one from the museum's holdings.[79] In the field he remained on full salary. Baird did sometimes worry that this was a very expensive way to collect ethnographic materials, and Cushing had to defend his methods. In March 1881, he wrote:

Mountain Chief, a South Piegan warrior of the Blackfoot
tribe, interpreting folksong recordings for ethnomusicologist
Frances Densmore at the Castle of the Smithsonian Institution,
1916. (By permission of the Smithsonian Institution.)

The Indians have only with the past few days consented
to my collecting any of the paraphernalia of their sacred
dances, or the ancient trophies of their tribes. They now
promise to *help* me get such things together, and I expect
as the result, one of the finest of ethnographic collections,
although time will be required for its completion, and additional stratagems and watchfulness.[80]

And a few months later, in response to a query from Baird,
he protested: "I have always made my paramount duty here
in Zuni that of collecting—not material, but data; yet always
when opportunity presented, I have gotten together what I
could toward filling up some of the gaps in our collection.
The costumes, primitive and modern—which I had once

despaired of securing, I have at last, through increased influence, obtained."

Cushing had less success when he tried to collect antiquities in Hopi pueblos, where he lacked local connections and did not speak the language. Sometimes his attempts to lay his hands on sacred objects put him in some peril. Even in Zuni, he had to be careful. Powell reported that Cushing had visited some old Zuni shrines, where war- and rain-gods and other sacred objects were to be found. "As, however, he was forced to visit these places either in company with Indians or by stealth, the objects could not be disturbed."[81] But in general, if he did not always get what he wanted, Cushing told Baird that it was because he did not have sufficient trade goods and cash to barter with.

> Now I can get in Zuni, anything for the price that a Zuni himself would have to pay; but just those things most needed by our collection are the very things which can be had only for a high price (comparatively) or things which they value—like plumes of the turkey, shell, and blue or green stones or imitations of the latter. Yet do not despair. I have some fine costumes. I can get a complete food, medicine, and to a lesser extent, industrial collection.[82]

Powell put Cushing on the payroll of the Bureau of Ethnology, yet even he could be thrown off his stride by the eccentric young man. On one occasion when Cushing turned up at a reception in Washington dressed in Zuni clothes, Powell "growled at him to 'go home and get dressed.' "[83] Not that Cushing's case was unique. Powell remarked "a curious tendency observable in students to overlook aboriginal vices and to exaggerate aboriginal virtues. It seems to be forgotten that after all the Indian is a savage,"[84] yet he allowed Cushing to return to the Zuni for another two years. In the interim, Cushing had married Emily Tennison of Washington, DC, and he returned to the field with his newly married wife, her sister and a cook. (It was suggested that he married Emily in order to get out of having to marry a Zuni woman.)[85]

In the end, politics was Cushing's undoing. He allied himself with conservative forces in Pueblo society and campaigned against the encroachments of missionaries and settlers. In 1884, he helped the local people resist a land grab by the son-in-law of a prominent national politician. This led to vituperative press attacks on his lifestyle and morals, and, eventually, to his recall to Washington.[86]

Franz Boas described Cushing as "a very able man," but, he added, "I'm afraid his work will have to be done all over again."[87] Certainly he was no plodding empiricist: Hinsley characterised his method as a matter of "intuitive insights and poetic impressions."[88] Yet his collections were remarkable. "Within a 25-year period the Smithsonian Institution alone collected at least 41,000 objects from the Southwest, of which more than 34,000 were accessioned into the permanent collections," Nancy Parezo writes. "Two-thirds of this extraordinary exercise . . . was completed in less than 6 years, primarily when Cushing was at Zuni."[89] And for the first time, ethnographic finds were carefully documented. Wherever possible,

> knowledgeable Zuni informants were asked to provide the native term for the object, describe its use and function, record its previous history, identify the design and its meaning, tell how it was made, discuss the history of the craft, state whether it was rare or common, and comment on the quality of the workmanship. Construction techniques were recorded in minute detail and raw materials identified.[90]

Baird wanted to make the collection of southwestern ethnography as exhaustive as possible, but he had a bias against anything that incorporated imported materials. "There was less emphasis on what American Indians were currently using than on what the grandparents of informants had made and used," Nancy Parezo writes.[91] Yet she points out that Cushing knew perfectly well that the Zuni were prepared to exchange traditional items for calico,

iron tools and so on. And he developed a sophisticated understanding of changes that followed the Spanish conquest and the
introduction of sheep and horses. Zuni were soon making fewer
baskets but more pots. As Cushing explained, this was because,
riding horses, they could acquire baskets from nomadic groups.
They made more pots because they could use sheep manure to
fire them, although this resulted in pots of lower quality than
those fired by brush wood or coal.[92]

These burgeoning collections of American Indian artefacts
were at once a source of pride and worry to Baird. Until the
National Museum building was ready, there had been no room
to exhibit or even to unpack all the booty from Philadelphia.
Still more concerning, many of the older specimens were in
poor condition and largely uncatalogued. Antiquities from east
of the Mississippi and ethnographic items from the west were
jumbled together. In 1876, fresh from his efforts at the centennial
exhibition, Charles Rau was put in charge of the antiquities. He
began to organise these on the established European model, by
materials—bone, stone, bronze, iron, glass, etc. However, the
ethnographic materials were in disarray.

In 1884, Baird appointed Otis Tufton Mason to become
the first curator of the division of ethnology in the National
Museum. Mason would go on to become a leading figure in the
American museum world, but at the time of his appointment
he was principal of a high school in Washington, and one of
Baird's devoted platoon of volunteer assistants. In his new post,
he had a huge job on his hands. He was told that the museum
held 200,000 ethnological artefacts, but he soon revised the
figure up to half a million. Most of these were uncatalogued.
Fragile items had not been looked after. "Between breakage and
the moths, things are fallen on evil times," Mason wrote to a
correspondent.[93]

Mason accepted the doctrine that artefacts should be considered more or less like natural organs. They had specific functions;
they served a need. But artefacts did not grow in bushes. They

were purpose-built. Mason liked to call them "inventions." So did Powell, who kept a notebook: "Evolution of Inventions."[94] The term "invention" had a special ring in the America of Alexander Graham Bell, who produced the first working telephone in 1876, and Thomas Edison, who announced his first famous invention, the phonograph, a year later, in 1877. Mason told the audience at a Saturday lecture at the National Museum:

> You cannot imagine the smile of satisfaction which stole over the face of a Patent Office friend when convinced that some of the most important materials of anthropology passed through his hands every day. He exclaimed, "I an anthropologist! I thought I was only an examiner. I am going to write a paper on anthropology." There is not a phase of civilization that has not had its tools, its edifices, its paraphernalia. There is not a tool, or building, or garment, that has not passed through a series of transformations most interesting to trace. These objects may be looked upon as species in natural history.[95]

This natural history perspective was shared by Baird's brilliant young deputy at the National Museum, George Brown Goode. He was, like the other leading figures in the Smithsonian, a natural scientist. His particular expertise was in marine life. In fact, he was offered the post of commissioner of fisheries by President Cleveland, but opted to stay on at the Smithsonian. In 1881, when the United States National Museum took possession of its new building, Goode, just thirty years old, was made assistant director. Soon after, he was appointed assistant secretary of the Smithsonian. In 1887 he became director of the museum.

Goode was an effective administrator. He was also a man of ideas. A public lecture he delivered at the Smithsonian, "The Museums of the Future," was packed with aphorisms that would be quoted by generations of museum folk. "A finished museum is a dead museum, and a dead museum is a useless museum." "The museum of the past must be set aside, reconstructed, transformed from a cemetery of bric-a-brac into a nursery of living thoughts. The museum of the future must stand side by side with the library and the laboratory." A museum should be designed for "teaching by means of object lessons." Above all, it should display a clearly classified universe of things. "The people's museum should be much more than a house full of specimens in glass cases. It should be a house full of ideas, arranged with the strictest attention to system . . . I once tried to express this thought by saying 'An efficient educational museum may be described as a collection of instructive labels each illustrated by a well-selected specimen.'" But perhaps his most characteristic aphorism was a solipsistic application of the doctrine of progress: "The degree of civilization to which any nation, city or province has attained, is best shown by the character of its Public Museums and the liberality with which they are maintained."[96]

Goode took special responsibility for the collections that came under the rubric of "arts and industries." These, he believed, were so closely related to "ethnographic" specimens "that it is impossible to make a definite division between them." This could be problematic. Goode complained that he had to deal with "all materials possessing anthropological significance, which are not elsewhere assigned."[97] (For his part, Mason protested that ethnology was understaffed and that the curators of the division of archaeology and the division of arts and industries dumped their unwanted material on him.)

Goode explained that when it came to the arrangement of artefacts, the Smithsonian was influenced by two European models. The British Museum and some of the leading German institutions favoured a geographical arrangement. The other model, which Goode himself preferred, was more in line with natural history museums. "Inventions" were classified by function—weapons, musical instruments, baskets and so on—and then arranged in an "evolutionary" series, which "should begin with the simplest types and close with the most perfect and elaborate objects of the same class which human effort has produced." Goode identified this approach with "the famous Pitt Rivers collection at Oxford," which arranged its exhibits "to show the evolution of culture and civilization without regard to race. This broader plan admits much material excluded by the advocates of ethnographic museums, who devote their attention almost exclusively to the primitive or non-European peoples."[98]

Working under the shadow of Goode, Mason did his best to combine these European models—essentially, a regional and a developmental arrangement. Mason's assistant—and successor—Walter Hough asserted that "Professor Mason was an expert in classification. He delighted in the problems involved in the schematic arrangement of the contents of the logos, and nothing was too difficult for his active mind, which grasped and marshalled multifarious relations with the suavity of a master." However, Mason himself conceded that the museum's ethnographic specimens were sometimes so poorly documented that "it is often begging the whole question to assign a specimen to a certain tribe."[99] He would say, insistently but rather hopefully, "put like with like, and tribes and localities will take care of themselves."[100]

When, in 1886, Mason mounted his first large display of the museum's Arctic holdings, he identified fifteen Arctic culture areas, and placed artefacts from a single region together. At the same time he insisted that "it must be distinctly understood that these areas are wholly secondary to types and material." And that wasn't all. He wanted to show that inventions were always being improved. Tools and instruments from all over the Arctic that served similar purposes should therefore be arranged in a series from the crudest to the most sophisticated and efficient. In order to respect these conflicting perspectives, visitors to the Arctic exhibition were confronted with daunting three-dimensional displays. "By walking along one axis of the checkerboard the visitor viewed a single cultural region in all its inventional variety," Hinsley writes, while "moving at right angles he could follow a single invention."[101] This seems remarkably like the rotunda imagined by Pitt Rivers.

It must have been a nightmare for the curators. Goode came up with a practical fix. "He carefully equipped his exhibit cases with casters and, in a matter of an hour or two, could have the entire display rearranged by either function or cultural association as the need required," G. Carroll Lindsay writes. "However, the triumph of scientific influence is apparent in the fact that he regarded the functional classification as the 'permanent' arrangement, and the cultural one as only temporary."[102]

Powell was struggling with a different, politically more urgent problem of classification at the Bureau of Ethnology. The Geological Survey was working on a series of physical maps of the American West. Congress expected the bureau to chart the distribution of Indian populations. This was not a straightforward matter. At the National Museum, Mason developed a card catalogue of Indian tribal names, eventually listing several thousand entities, but since the beginning of the nineteenth century there had been large-scale forced population removals. The reservations had to accommodate groups from different parts of the east. Most existing ethnic groups were amalgams, according to Powell. The "general progress toward unity" between different communities had "obscured primitive ethnic divisions, if such existed."[103] In consequence, "it was found absolutely necessary to abandon current systems of ethnic classification, and to devise and adopt a system based on purely human characteristics springing from intellectual activities."[104]

The first secretary of the Smithsonian, Joseph Henry, took the view that language provided the clearest and most reliable basis for classification. The German tradition of Indo-European studies inspired earlier Americanists, notably Albert Gallatin, who had published *A Table of Indian Languages of the United States* in 1826 and, ten years later, his more elaborate *Synopsis of the Indian Tribes of North America*. Samuel Haven's *Archaeology of the United States*, published by the Smithsonian in 1856, reviewed linguistic and archaeological evidence, and concluded, like Gallatin, that the natives of North and South America were linguistically and culturally related and that their common ancestors had migrated from Asia in prehistoric times. However, there was still no reliable account of North American Indian language families.[105]

The Smithsonian appealed for guidance to William Dwight Whitney, professor of linguistics at Yale. A Sanskrit scholar who had studied in Germany with Franz Bopp and Albrecht Weber, Whitney sketched out a method of phonetic notation for the collection of vocabularies. This proved too complicated for the bureau's field men. Powell applied his organisational talents to the task at hand and developed a simplified procedure. In 1885, the bureau produced a fifty-five-page booklet, "List of Linguistic Families of the Indian Tribes North of Mexico, with Provisional List of the Principal Tribal Names and Synonyms." In 1891, Powell was able to issue a map of North American Indian languages.

A ghoulish episode in the saga of the Smithsonian's collections has to do with the disposition of James Smithson's body.[106] Smithson's nephew buried his benefactor in Italy, in the old British cemetery of Genoa. The Smithsonian felt a certain responsibility for the maintenance of the founder's grave. The United States consul in Genoa was authorised "to put the monument in thorough repair and to arrange to have it kept in good condition at the expense of the Institution." In 1891, the secretary of the Smithsonian, Samuel Langley, made a grant "for the care, in perpetuity of the tomb." A new plaque was commissioned, honouring Smithson's legacy. In 1901, the Smithsonian was informed that due to the expansion of a stone quarry, the graves would be relocated. The inventor, Alexander Graham Bell, a trustee of the Smithsonian Institution, tried without success to persuade his colleagues that they should take possession of the remains of their founder and install them in a mausoleum in the National Museum. In the summer of 1903 he set off for Genoa to see to it himself.

As soon as he arrived, Bell came up against Italian bureaucracy. "There seemed to be no end to the red tape necessary to remove the body," Bell's wife Mabel wrote in her journal.

A permit to export the body beyond Italian limits, a permit to open the grave, a permit to purchase a coffin, permits from the National government, city government, the police, the officers, etc. etc. Alec felt very anxious that the whole matter should be kept very quiet and that we should leave with the body as soon as possible. He said that once we were on the ship, we were safe with the remains and it was necessary to be very sure that Washington would sustain him in any trouble that might arise.[107]

Relatives of Smithson objected to the removal of the body. Bell claimed that he was in Italy as the representative of President Theodore Roosevelt and told the local officials that since Smithson had bequeathed his estate to the U.S. government they owned his bones too.

At last the sarcophagus was opened. "I was surprised at the remarkable state in which the remains were found," Bell wrote.

The skeleton was complete. The bones have separated but they did not crumble when exposed to air as I had feared they would. As the stone slab covering the grave was removed, it looked as though the body was covered with a heavy blanket, under which the form was outlined. I could not explain this until the discovery was made that in the passage of time the casket had crumbled to dust. It was this dust which lay like a rug over the remains.[108]

Bell's son-in-law was the first editor of the *National Geographic Magazine*. He orchestrated a drumbeat of publicity. President Roosevelt sent a U.S. Navy ship to meet the party in New York Harbour. In Washington, a marine band escorted the body to the Smithsonian Castle. Draped in American and British flags, the coffin was laid in state in the old regent's room of the south tower. There was then the problem of a new tomb. The trustees commissioned a series of architectural plans, but Congress was not inclined to finance anything too grandiose. Eventually, in 1905, a room at the entrance of the castle was dedicated as a "mortuary chapel." Smithson's remains were interred there beneath the original marble sarcophagus brought from Genoa.

In 1974, the crypt was renovated and it was decided to disinter the bones once more. (According to one story, this was because there were rumours that Smithson's ghost had been seen wandering round the museum.) The curator of physical anthropology, Dr. J. Lawrence Angel, was invited to examine Smithson's remains. But there was an unfortunate accident. The workmen used a blowtorch to unseal the tomb. This set alight the velvet materials wrapping the bones. Fire extinguishers might have caused further damage. "Smithson was saved from absolute extinction only by the workmen racing down the hall to the water fountain, filling their mouths, and running back to put the fire out," writes Heather Ewing. "The casket was covered with a tablecloth borrowed from the dining room, and Smithson was discreetly, if unceremoniously, carted across the Mall to the laboratory."[109] Dr. Angel then found that the bones had been badly mishandled in Genoa, and were mixed in with nails and other debris, but he was able to establish that Smithson had been 5 feet 6 inches tall, was malnourished as a child, had bad teeth and smoked a pipe. Two days later the remains were sealed in the coffin and replaced in the tomb.[110] James Smithson was once again an exhibit in his own museum.

FRANZ BOAS CHALLENGES
THE SMITHSONIAN

A foundation myth of American anthropology has been handed down to generations of students. The hero of the story is Franz Boas. As late as the 1930s, many educated and influential Americans and Europeans took it for granted that biology was destiny. The European race was superior to all others. History was a record of racial conflict. Humanity progressed as the superior races subdued and even exterminated inferior races. Then, as Regna Darnell puts it, ironically, "Along came Boas."[1] He delivered a new and humane paradigm of cultural and historical analysis that swept away a racist social evolutionism.

A decisive battle was fought in 1887, or so the myth goes. The young foreigner, Boas, single-handedly challenged the Smithsonian behemoth, champion of the evolutionists. He accused the old guard of treating artefacts as though they were natural history specimens, to be arranged in an evolutionary sequence. Boas protested that masks, totems, musical instruments, even humble tools must be understood as cultural productions, imbued with meanings, only to be understood in their local context. This was the opening shot of the Boasian scientific revolution. Soon the evolutionists were vanquished. A relativist, anti-racist cultural anthropology emerged triumphant. And it moved out of the fusty old museums into the vibrant intellectual milieu of the new research universities.

Professor Darnell was brought up on this origin myth. However, as she delved into the history of the Smithsonian controversy she "discovered substantial continuities" between the

Smithsonian projects and the Boas agenda. "I found that Boas initially worked within the existing anthropological establishment and adopted many of its characteristic preoccupations," she wrote. "Moreover, it was closer to 1920 than 1900 before Boasian anthropology could be said to have exerted anything like hegemony over the discipline in North America."[2]

Nor were the Smithsonian ethnologists unwaveringly committed to an evolutionist paradigm.[3] According to the annual report of the National Museum for 1914: "The arrangements of the ethnological exhibits is geographical, the material belonging to each area being displayed as an assemblage or by classes of objects."[4]

Nor was Boas introducing a revolutionary new perspective. He was taking sides in a long-running argument, one that had been brought to Washington, DC, just three years earlier, in the autumn of 1884, in the course of a visit to the Smithsonian Institution by a distinguished English anthropologist, Edward Burnett Tylor.

Tylor's masterpiece, *Primitive Culture*, appeared in 1871. He was a fellow of the Royal Society but he had only just landed a real job in the field: a few months before visiting Washington he was appointed to the first academic post in anthropology at Oxford University, and, indeed, in the United Kingdom. When Tylor visited the Smithsonian, Major Powell took him on a tour of Native American reservations. And Tylor agreed to address the Anthropological Society of Washington.[5]

He began his talk with some impressions of America and American anthropology. In fact, he began with a tease. "Now one of the things that has struck me most in America, from the anthropological point of view," Tylor told his audience, "is a certain element of old-fashionedness." This particularly struck him when he toured Quaker and Mennonite settlements in rural Pennsylvania. "If I ever become possessed of a spinning-wheel, an article of furniture now scarce in England, I can hardly get a specimen better than in Pennsylvania, where 'my great-grandmother's spinning wheel' is shown—standing perhaps in the lumber-room, perhaps in an ornamental place in the drawing-room—oftener than in any other country that I ever visited."

Tylor remarked that although he himself had been brought up among Quakers, he was surprised to find that some American Mennonites were old-fashioned almost as a matter of religious principle. "Among them are those who dissent from modern alternation and changes by a fixed and unalterable resolution that they will not wear buttons, but will fasten their coats with hooks and eyes, as their forefathers did. And in this way they show with what tenacity custom holds when it has become matter of scruple and religious sanction."[6] His new Mennonite friends "thought it nothing strange that I should come to study them and their history," but they were astonished when Tylor let slip that he was about to go off to visit the Zunis with Major Powell:

> this confession on my part was received with a look of amazement, not quite unmingled with kindly reproof: it seemed so strange to my friends that any person travelling about of his own will should deliberately go to look at Indians. I found it hard to refrain from pointing out, that, after all, there is a community of purpose between studies of the course of civilization, whether carried out among the colonists of Pennsylvania or among the Indians of New Mexico.

Visiting reservations in the West with Major Powell, Tylor found that "things that one sees among the Indian tribes who have not become so 'white' as the Algonkins and Iroquois, but who present a more genuine picture of old American life, do often, and in the most vivid way, present traces of the same phenomena with which one is so familiar in old-world life." As with the Mennonites, so with the Zuni.

Imagine us sitting in a house just inside California, engaged in what appeared to be a fruitless endeavour on the part of Professor Moseley [an anthropologist at the Smithsonian] to obtain a lock of hair of a Mojave to add to his collection. The man objected utterly. He shook his head. When pressed, he gesticulated and talked. No: if he gave up that bit of hair, he would become deaf, dumb, grow mad; and when the medicine-man came to drive away the malady, it would be no use, he would have to die.

"Now this represents a perfectly old-world group of ideas," Tylor remarked. "If you tried to get a lock of hair in Italy or Spain, you might be met with precisely the same resistance; and you would find that the reason would be absolutely the same as that which the Mojave expressed."

So how did it come about that very similar customs, tools and ideas crop up in far removed parts of the world, in places with no shared history?

There is no day in my life, when I am able to occupy myself with anthropological work, in which my mind does not swing like a pendulum between the two great possible answers to this question. Have the descendants of a small group of mankind gone on teaching their children the same set of ideas, carrying them on from generation to generation, from age to age, so that when they are found in distant regions, among tribes which become different even in bodily formation, they represent the long-inherited traditions of a common ancestry? Or is it that all over the world, man, being substantially similar in mind, has again and again, under similar circumstances of life, developed similar groups of ideas and customs? I cannot, I think, use the opportunity of standing at this table more profitably than by insisting, in the strongest manner which I can find words to express, on the fundamental importance of directing attention to this great problem, the solution of which will alone bring the study of civilization into its full development as a science.

Tylor then gave an example from the U.S. National Museum itself. "This morning, being in the museum with Major Powell, Professor Moseley, and Mr. Holmes, looking at the products of Indian life in the far west, my attention was called to certain curious instruments hanging together in a case in which musical instruments are contained. These consisted simply of flat, oblong, or oval pieces of wood, fastened at the end to a thong, so as to be whirled round and round, causing a whirring or roaring noise." One of these came from the Ute Indians, the other from the Zuni. But, Tylor said, if an Australian aborigine had been with the party that morning, "he would stop with feelings not only of surprise, but probably of horror; for this is an instrument which to him represents, more intensely than anything else, a sense of mystery attached to his own most important religious ceremonies." Among the Xhosa of the eastern Cape in South Africa similar instruments were used to warn women to keep away when male initiation ceremonies were in progress. Often known as bullroarers, they cropped up in ancient Greek rites associated with Bacchus, and in German and English children's games.

What is more likely—that bullroarers turn up in widely separated locations as a result of trade and contact, or that they were independently invented? Independent invention was certainly possible. The mechanism was simple, and the loud noise was a convenient way of broadcasting a warning of some sort. "If we work it out as a mere question of probabilities," Tylor remarked, "the hypothesis of repeated re-invention under like circumstances can hold its own against the hypothesis of historical connection; but which explanation is the true one, or whether both are partly true, I have no sufficient means to decide."

Tylor did, however, suggest a test, which "may be called the argument from outlandishness." Could one readily imagine that this or that bizarre-seeming custom, or fanciful decoration, or cunning mechanism, had been dreamt up independently in widely separate locations? "When a circumstance is so uncommon as to excite surprise, and to lead one to think with wonder why it should have come into existence, and when that thing appears in two different districts, we have more ground for saying that there is a certain historical connection between the two cases of its appearance than in the comparison of more commonplace matters."[7]

When it came to museum displays, Tylor took a more decided line. Customs and tools might be borrowed, or inherited from a common source, or they might be independently invented. In any case, they could be arranged in a single progressive series. Tylor himself was engaged in the transfer of the Pitt Rivers collection to Oxford. This collection was "entirely devoted to the working-out of the development theory on a scale hardly attempted hitherto." As a young man, he had travelled in Mexico with Christy, whose anthropological collections had been installed a year earlier in the British Museum. Christy's collections were also arranged on "developmental," "evolutionist" principles. "The two principles which tend most to the successful work of anthropology—the systematic collection of the products of each stage of civilization, and the arrangements of their sequence in development—are thus the leading motives of our two great anthropological museums."[8]

Mason and Goode were probably in the audience when Tylor addressed that meeting of the Anthropological Society of Washington. I imagine them nodding in agreement. Like Tylor, they believed in science, evolution and progress. Yet when it came to museum displays, the Smithsonian curators were well aware that Europe's ethnologists were divided between two parties. One party went in for a geographical arrangement of their museum collections. Leaders of the other party, notably Pitt Rivers in England, regarded themselves as natural scientists. They organised their "specimens" by "type," and laid them out in an evolutionary sequence.

The Smithsonian men thought that there was something to

be said for both perspectives. "The ethnological collections in Washington are classified on a double system," Goode remarked. Mason explained that

> in a museum properly constructed it is possible to arrange the cases in the form of a checker-board, so that by going in a certain direction the parallels of cases represent races or tribes or locations. By inspecting the same cases in a direction at right angles to the former, the visitor may study all the products of human activity in classes according to human wants.[9]

Four years after Tylor delivered his Washington lecture, the twenty-nine-year-old Franz Boas issued a challenge to the Smithsonian anthropologists. Trained in Germany in the geographical, Lamarckian, anti-Darwinian tradition, he was dismissive of the functionalist, evolutionist displays in the National Museum. He was becoming an expert on North American ethnography, and he was out to make a name for himself in the U.S.A., if possible to make a career there.

In 1883, Boas carried out an intensive field study among Inuit communities in Baffin Island for his doctoral research in Germany. On his first visit to Washington, DC, in October 1884, he made contact at the Smithsonian with a German Arctic specialist, Emil Bessels. He also wangled an introduction to Powell, and he "'hunted up' the director of the Ethnographical division, Prof Mason, who was very friendly and cordial," Boas wrote to his fiancée. "He asked me right away whether I would like to have my things published by the [Smithsonian], which I neither rejected nor accepted." But Boas was not impressed by the National Museum, complaining of "the slowness that everything happens here, the wretched mix up in the museum." He and Mason "ran around all morning unpacking crates." "To hunt through the collection is hair-raising work, since everything is distributed around."[10]

In 1885, Boas spent a few months as an assistant to Adolf Bastian, the director of the Royal Ethnological Museum in Berlin, working on a large collection of ethnographic materials from British Columbia. In 1886, evidently inspired by this exposure to the region's remarkable arts and crafts, Boas spent three months doing fieldwork in the Pacific Northwest, the first of many expeditions he would make to the region.

In the summer of 1886 he was back at the Smithsonian, this time as an emissary of Bastian. After a decade in which the collections were closed to the public, Berlin's Museum für Völkerkunde was about to open in a grand purpose-built building, and Bastian wrote to the new secretary of the Smithsonian, Spencer Fullerton Baird, to propose a programme of exchanges. The Berlin museum wanted to add to its collection of American Indian artefacts. Bastian suggested that he would send casts of classical sculptures to Washington: or, as he put it, "exchange for the costly relics of the Red Man's past the relics of classical Greece."[11] Boas would act as his agent.

Boas was also conducting negotiations on his own account. He sent Bastian a catalogue of materials he had collected on the northwest coast. Would Berlin match the $600 offer he had from a buyer in the United States? "On principle, I'm not giving the Washington museum a single thing," he assured Bastian, complaining that in the Smithsonian they "tear asunder everything that has been grouped together according to origins and rearrange it according to object types."[12] And yet in May 1887, Boas was writing to offer Mason a selection of objects he had acquired in British Columbia.[13]

Just five days after posting his letter, Boas published a no-holds-barred critique of the ethnological displays in the U.S. National Museum. It appeared in *Science*, a newish, already prestigious journal, which was at the time largely funded by Alexander Graham Bell. Boas had recently been appointed assistant editor with a special responsibility for geography. Tylor's Washington lecture had also been published in *Science*, and Boas—though without mentioning Tylor—took up Tylor's central theme: "the occurrence of similar inventions in areas widely apart" (which was how Boas, ungrammatically, headlined his critique).[14] Like Tylor, Boas remarked that artefacts from distant parts of the world often appeared to be rather similar. And, again like Tylor, he asked whether they could have been independently invented. Or were they so apparently alike simply because wherever they happened to live, people were bound to work out similar solutions to similar challenges? Boas cited the opinion of the curator of ethnology in the National Museum, Otis T. Mason: "In human culture, as in nature elsewhere, like causes produce like effects. Under the same stress and resources the same inventions will arise."

Boas pointed out that while there might be superficial resemblances between Maori and Kwakiutl masks, or between the bows and arrows of Plains Indians and South African Bushmen, these could be misleading. Things that might appear much the same when put together in a museum showcase could have different functions and significance for the individuals who used them. Moreover, a variety of factors might lead to rather similar outcomes. Mason was guilty of an elementary mistake in logic. "In his enumeration of causes of similar inventions, one is omitted, which overthrows the whole system: unlike causes produce like effects." This proposition was central to a recent controversy in German geography. The point had been made that different environmental processes might have much the same consequences.[15]

Boas then broadened his critique, making no concessions to seniority or to the conventions of WASP politesse. "We cannot agree with the leading principles of Professor Mason's ethnological researches." Mason made deductions from theoretical assumptions. He, Boas, was an empiricist, as any proper scientist should be. Facts should come before theories. Not to put too fine a point on it, Mason was on completely the wrong track. "The leading idea of Otis T. Mason's writings on ethnology is his attempt to classify human inventions and other ethnological phenomena in the light of biological specimens."[16] That was bad enough in itself, but Mason had adopted an obsolete and false biological model. "In regarding the ethnological phenomenon as a biological specimen, and trying to classify it, he introduces the rigid abstractions species, genus, and family into ethnology." Finally, loftily, brutally: "Our objection to Mason's idea is, that classification is not explanation."[17]

Wrapping up his argument, Boas then told the curators of the National Museum precisely what they should be doing. They should follow the example of Adolf Bastian in the Royal Museum of Ethnology in Berlin, and classify artefacts with reference to what Bastian termed the "geographical province":

> we want a collection arranged according to tribes, in order to teach the peculiar style of each group. The art and characteristic style of a people can be understood only by studying its productions as a whole. In the collections of the national museum the marked character of the Northwest American tribes is almost lost, because the objects are scattered in different parts of the building, and are exhibited among those from other tribes.[18]

"I am very grateful for the candid spirit" of the critique, Mason wrote to Boas, "and with the permission of the distinguished editor [i.e., Boas] I will send my reply."[19] He began his response by restating what he considered to be first principles. Any classification had to be based on "certain notions, ideas, or characteristics . . . 'classific concepts.'" For curators of anthropological museums these would include "material, race, geographical areas, social organizations, environment, structure and function, and evolution or elaboration." So there were different ways in which artefacts could reasonably be classified. Curators would have their own ideas, "and I consider this the greatest blessing to science. If all the museums in the world were arranged upon the same plan, only one set of philosophic problems could be considered, and the study would be correspondingly circumscribed." In any case, ethnographic specimens were not of concern only to ethnologists. Musicians, artists, craftsmen, and students of war or religion visit museums to study objects that are of particular interest to them. No single arrangement will satisfy everyone.

Yet Mason agreed that an important question of theory was at issue. Artefacts from distant regions may indeed appear to be very alike. How was this to be explained? "The philosophical ethnologist is always in a 'double corner,' by reason of two interpretations of similarities," Mason judged. One interpretation put similarities down to "contact of some kind; the other, disconnected causes, whether similar or dissimilar it matters not." Mason himself was inclined to believe "that inventions of both customs and things spring from prior inventions, just as life springs from life." The "very ingenious" suggestion made by Boas that unlike causes may often lead to the same outcome "had nothing to do with the case." The sooner we "apply the methods and instrumentalities of the biologist, the sooner will our beloved science stand upon an immovable foundation."

Finally, Mason apologised for the fact that Boas had not been able to track down all the Northwest coast artefacts in the museum. This was not, however, on account of "any fault in my system," but simply because in the two years that Mason had been in charge of the ethnological collections "I have given no attention as yet to the west coast of America."[20]

Responding immediately, Boas stood his ground. There was little evidence to support the view that independent invention was commonplace. But in any case, that was the wrong question. It was often misleading to group tools and instruments according to their supposed functions. The ideas of local people gave particular artefacts meaning and significance. And then Boas offered an example. Tylor had illustrated his argument with the vibrato of the whirling howling bullroarer. Boas chose another simple mechanism that produces a loud sound:

The rattle, for instance, is not merely the outcome of the idea of making noise, and of the technical methods applied to reach this end: it is, besides this, the outcome of the religious conceptions, as any noise may be applied to invoke or drive away spirits; or it may be the outcome of the pleasure children have in noise of any kind; and its form may be characteristic of the art of the people. Thus the same implement belongs to very different departments of a psychological museum.[21]

At this point, Major Powell, the heavyweight, intervened. He pointed out that museum displays were necessarily selective. Arranging an exhibition, "the question is narrowed down to this: first, on what principles shall the selections be made? And, second, in what order shall they be arranged?" No arrangement was ever final. Indeed, the National Museum had gone for portable display cases precisely so that exhibits could easily be switched about to illustrate different relationships.

Powell remarked that Boas wanted to impose a fixed arrangement, by tribe. That was not possible. At the time of Columbus there were probably over 25,000 tribes in North America, "each a little band of people." Most were nomadic, and tribes would regularly die out or coalesce,

so that a hundred years after the discovery of America it is not probable that there existed any one tribe which could claim to be the pure and simple descendant, without loss, admixture, or change, of any tribe existing at the time of the discovery. These changes have been going on more and more rapidly until the present time, and they are still going on. Most of the tribes best known to history have been absorbed, consolidated, and re-divided again and again. Now, this means simply that under primitive and under modern conditions alike there has been no permanent tribal organization.[22]

What alternative was there to an arrangement by tribe? Biological classifications on the basis of skin colour, skull shape, and so on, were not a viable alternative: "no thorough classification of mankind on these characteristics has ever been established," Powell wrote. "Mankind cannot be classified into races thoroughly inclusive and exclusive." What else was there? Languages could be classified, "but this furnishes a very imperfect classification of peoples . . . The Paiutes of Utah, the Comanches of the plains, and six of the Pueblos of New Mexico . . . all belong to the same linguistic family; but their arts are most diverse." Powell concluded that there is "no science of ethnology, for the attempt to classify mankind in groups has failed on every hand . . . The unity of mankind is the greatest induction of anthropology."[23]

Powell did concede that a geographical arrangement of the type advocated by Bastian might yield interesting results. Environmental conditions were clearly relevant to cultural development. But he had a more fundamental objection to Boas's suggestions. Museums display artefacts. These represent only a very particular and limited aspect of a local way of life. "The human activities which characterise mankind may be classed as arts, institutions, languages, and opinions or philosophies. Of these activities, the arts only can be represented in a museum, and they but in part. An anthropological museum, therefore, is an impossibility."

Boas replied very briefly. There was "no difference of opinion between Major Powell and myself." It was all a misunderstanding. Powell was under the impression that Boas was referring to "archaeological collections of pre-Columbian peoples." This was not the case. He was concerned with ethnology, not with archaeology. "I fully agree with Major Powell's remarks," he wrote, "but venture to say that they do not belong to the question at issue."[24]

Mason was concerned that Powell's intervention might have bruised the young foreigner. He wrote to Boas to ask whether it would be helpful if he wrote another response for *Science*. "I do not wish to be tedious, but am willing to do all the good I can."[25] In fact Boas *was* feeling uncomfortable. Bastian sent a personal letter of support, but Boas told his parents that the whole affair

Franz Boas posing for a figure in a diorama in the U.S. National Museum. Entitled "Hamats'a coming out of secret room," this represents an incident in a "Kwakiutl Indian ceremony for expelling cannibals." The Smithsonian catalogue dates the photograph to "1895 or before." (By permission of the Smithsonian Institution.)

had given him a headache.[26] And yet, three days after his letter was published in *Science*, Boas wrote to Mason to accept his invitation to publish his ethnographic report with the Smithsonian. A few days later Mason offered to buy ethnographic artefacts that Boas had offered to the National Museum.[27]

In 1898, Boas was appointed assistant curator of ethnology and somatology at the American Museum of National History in New York City. He struggled to impose a regional and relativist perspective, but Morris K. Jesup, a Wall Street banker who chaired the Board of Trustees, a disciple of Herbert Spencer, was a gung-ho "evolutionist." When Boas resigned his position, in 1905, he explained that he felt he had a mission to impress on the general public "the fact that our people are not the only carriers of civilization, but that the human mind has been creative everywhere."[28]

HARVARD'S PEABODY MUSEUM
OF AMERICAN ARCHAEOLOGY
AND ETHNOLOGY

The Peabody Museum of American Archaeology and Ethnology was a not altogether welcome gift to Harvard University. The donor was a very rich self-made man, George Peabody. One of seven children, raised in an impoverished family in a small Massachusetts town, Peabody went into commodity trading in Baltimore, became a financier, and established himself as the leading American banker in London. There was some unpleasantness when the State of Maryland reneged on bonds that Peabody promoted. (He was blackballed by the Reform Club.) Later his firm nearly went under during a financial crisis. However, Peabody and his bank rode out all the storms. In 1864 he retired, withdrew his capital, and handed control to his associate, Junius S. Morgan, the father of J. P. Morgan, and the founder of what became the J. P. Morgan banking empire.

Haunted by childhood privations, Peabody was hardworking, hard driving, tight with money. He never married. In retirement he reinvented himself, becoming the first of the American tycoon philanthropists. He endowed housing projects for the poor, educational establishments in the southern states, and museums on the East Coast. He could afford it. When he died in 1869 his estate was worth $16 million, an astonishing sum at the time.

Founded in 1866, the Peabody museums at Harvard and Yale were entrusted with cutting-edge scientific missions. These were promoted by Peabody's nephew, Othniel Charles Marsh, a disciple of Lyell and Darwin who would become professor of palaeontology at Yale.[1] Marsh had two scientific passions: dinosaurs, and the prehistoric earthworks of the Midwest. The Yale Peabody Museum of Natural History would accommodate his dinosaur collection. Harvard was charged with the study and conservation of American prehistory.

"My own interest in American archaeology was mainly due to Sir Charles Lyell, who had just published his 'Antiquity of Man' and, when I saw him in London, urged me in the strongest terms to take up the subject in America as a new field for exploration," Marsh recalled. Back home he duly took up archaeology. And he had an epiphany. "The first idea of the Peabody Museum at Cambridge occurred to me in October 1865, while digging in an ancient mound near Newark, Ohio; and that evening I wrote to my uncle, Mr. Peabody, at London, urging him to establish such a museum."[2] Peabody obligingly came up with $150,000 to establish the Peabody Museum of American Archaeology and Ethnology at Harvard.

Harvard's president thought it best to accept the gift, though admitting that the subject matter "may not impress the College, or the community, at first sight, as one of the highest interest or importance."[3] Archaeology was regarded as a way of documenting, even appropriating, classical European civilisations. It had high status. On the other hand, a lack of interest in North America's pre-Columbian history, even a certain disdain for the subject, was not uncommon in cultivated circles in Boston and Cambridge (much as the establishment at the British Museum was dismissive of Anglo-Saxon and Celtic antiquities).

Washington and the Smithsonian Institution looked west, to America's new frontier. Boston and Harvard looked east, to Europe. The Archaeological Institute of America, formed in Boston in 1879, was dominated by classicists. Their first initiative was to set up the American School of Classical Studies in Athens. The founder-president of the Archaeological Institute, Charles

Eliot Norton, Harvard's professor of fine arts, was a disciple of John Ruskin, an expert on Dante's *Divine Comedy* and a devotee of Gothic art and architecture. He was, naturally, an associate of Henry Adams. Another friend, Henry James, said that Norton was America's "representative of culture" and credited him with a "civilising mission . . . that a young roaring and money-getting democracy . . . most needed to have brought home to it."[4]

Norton was described in rather different terms in a letter written by Frederic Putnam, the curator of the Peabody Museum of American Archaeology and Ethnology, to America's leading anthropologist, Lewis Henry Morgan. Norton, he wrote, was "a man of high social function" and "rich, with a fine house and large grounds here in Cambridge."

> So far as I know he has not taken an active interest in American antiquities or ethnology, but he is well up in all that relates to classic art. To my knowledge he has never been inside of the Peabody Museum, and he has not the slightest idea of what I have done or am trying to do there. If you can get him interested in the exploration of the ancient peoples of America you will be doing a good thing, for he is a man of considerable influence in Cambridge and Boston and he would be well backed up.[5]

But even Lewis Henry Morgan could not move Norton. "I don't care much for our American Archaeology (though as president of the society I must say this under my breath)," Norton wrote to Thomas Carlyle, "but I do care much for the Greeks, and believe that the more the influence of their sane thought and modes of life can be brought to bear on our modern youth the better will it be with the coming generation."[6]

Curtis Hinsley describes a telling debate at a meeting of the American Archaeological Institute in Boston in May 1880. Norton was in the chair. The Bostonian establishment was well represented. The guest speaker, the Smithsonian Institution's Major Powell, made a pitch for the collection and study of pre-Columbian antiquities. The audience was divided. What should take priority? The purchase of European classical antiquities—and they were becoming scarcer and pricier on the market—or digging up prehistoric American Indian settlements?

A prominent Bostonian intellectual, Charles Perkins, insisted that the priority should be Old World sites, so that "we may lay our hand upon something to be placed in our Museums."[7] One gentleman declared that "the knowledge which was useful to us was not that of barbarians but that of cultivated races which had preceded us." Some speakers were dismissive of "all the pottery ware, kitchen utensils and tomahawks" of the Native American peoples. As curator of the Peabody Museum, Putnam made the pragmatic case that the Archaeological Institute was, after all, in America, "where the study ought to begin . . . if *Ethnology* is the aim of the Institute, then America is the proper field." (On the other hand, he conceded, if the committee took the view that archaeology should concern itself rather with "*art* in its highest development," then they would look to Europe.)

It was left to Francis Parkman, a man of impeccable Bostonian lineage, and the author of several volumes on the history of colonial North America, to make a more considered argument for the study of American tribes. Not that Parkman had any sympathy for contemporary American Indians. He was a great believer in progress, especially, as one critic remarks, "the progress of Protestant Anglo-Saxon civilisation."[8] As a young man he published a best-selling travel book, *The Oregon Trail; Sketches of Prairie and Rocky-Mountain Life,* which was packed with aspersions on the American Indian way of life. Parkman did not claim that American Indians deserved study for their own sake. Rather, their very existence raised "questions of the greatest importance, the evolution of the human race, its civilization . . ."[9]

These were sensitive matters. Progress was just fine, but Darwinism was contentious, perhaps even anti-religious. Harvard itself was divided. Undergraduates had compulsory chapel twice daily, and the creationist holy writ, William Paley's *Natural*

Theology or Evidences of the Existence and Attributes of the Deity, was a staple of the curriculum. But the theological and classicist traditions of Harvard education were being challenged: the college had recently established a school of science. Three of America's leading natural scientists were Harvard professors, each with his own scientific collection. Asa Gray was professor of botany and head of the Harvard botanical garden. Louis Agassiz, Harvard's professor of zoology and geology, was the founder and director of the Museum of Comparative Zoology. Jeffries Wyman, the professor of anatomy, an expert on the gorilla, curated a Museum of Comparative Anatomy. All were men with solid international reputations in the scientific world. But even they could not agree on Darwin's theories.

Asa Gray was among the first American scientists to come out in support of Darwin. In 1861, shortly after the publication of *On the Origin of Species*, he wrote a paper headed "Natural Selection not Inconsistent with Natural Theology." Darwin published and distributed it in England at his own expense. "No one I think understands whole case better than Asa Gray, & he has been fighting nobly," he wrote to Charles Lyell.[10] But Darwin had to tread carefully with Gray when it came to the theological implications of evolution: "Certainly I agree with you that my views are not at all necessarily atheistical."[11] Despite Gray's prodding, however, he would not endorse the doctrine that the natural world conforms to a divine design.

Louis Agassiz rejected Darwinism. A descendant of seven generations of Swiss Protestant pastors, he had studied medicine in Munich, associated with Cuvier and Humboldt in Paris, and become a professor of natural history in Switzerland. In 1846, Agassiz delivered a course of lectures at the Lowell Institute in Boston entitled "The Plan of Creation as shown in the Animal Kingdom." This plan of creation, he explained, was "an intelligent plan, framed upon due consideration by the Omnipotent intelligence."[12] Five thousand people turned up to hear the good news. Each lecture had to be repeated for a second audience.

Harvard immediately created a chair for Agassiz. He

raised large sums of money from Boston Brahmins and even extracted a contribution from the Massachusetts legislature for his Museum of Comparative Zoology, which was modelled on Cuvier's Natural History Museum in the Jardin des Plantes in Paris. And he married an accomplished and very well-connected Bostonian, Elizabeth Cabot Cary, who gave him an entrée into New England's old money circles. (After Agassiz's death his widow became the first president of Radcliffe College.)

In January 1860, Gray informed Darwin that Agassiz "has been helping the circulation of your book by denouncing it as *atheistical* in a public lecture! I suspect, also, he means to attack it in the Atlantic Monthly. The book annoys him; and I suppose the contrast I run between his theories and yours will annoy him still more."[13] Faithful to the older orthodoxy, Agassiz believed in a young and stable universe that was populated by divinely created and unchanging species. He was a man of decided religious beliefs, but his stubborn opposition to Darwin probably had something to do with his irascible, authoritarian, inflexible personality.[14] Gray charged him with populism: "he is always writing and talking *ad populum*—fond of addressing himself to an incompetent tribunal." Relations between the two professors became poisonous. In 1864, they had a public row on a train from New Haven. Agassiz called Gray "no gentleman." There was even talk of a duel.[15]

Gray was, however, able to reassure Darwin that another Harvard natural scientist, Jeffries Wyman, had responded very differently to the new theories. "*Wyman*—the best of judges—& no convert, but much struck with it;—says your book is 'thundering able,'—'a thoroughly scientific & philosophical work.'"[16] A gentle and open-minded man, with a high reputation as a field biologist, Wyman was most impressed by the detailed observations that Darwin brought together.[17] For his part, Darwin had a high opinion of Wyman's expertise. When he began working on revisions to the *Origin* he asked Gray to solicit Wyman's assistance. A correspondence followed, Darwin quizzing Wyman on details of American fauna, and inviting his comments on the ways in which colour might play a role in natural selection. Wyman reported that among certain American pigs "only the black varieties could eat a particular plant, the paint-root, without their hooves falling off." Darwin added these observations to the third edition of *Origin*.[18]

Mulling over his donation to Harvard, George Peabody made an initial approach to Agassiz, but Agassiz turned him down. (He later claimed that this was because Peabody insisted on having his name on the museum.)[19] Peabody then announced that his Harvard museum would address "the great questions as to the order of development of the animal kingdom and of the human race, which have lately been so much discussed."[20] So it was to be a Darwinian museum. As the name proclaimed—the Peabody Museum of American Archaeology and Ethnology—it would specialise in American antiquities. The Harvard Darwinians, Gray and Wyman, were appointed trustees, alongside Robert Winthrop, a Massachusetts grandee and a former speaker of the House of Representatives, who chaired Peabody's educational foundation, two Peabody nephews, and John Quincy Adams, sixth president of the U.S.A., the grandfather of Henry Adams, and godfather of the Smithsonian Institution.

The new museum could not have been better timed. Remarkable prehistoric finds had been made in the Loire Valley and in Devon in England. *Geological Evidences of the Antiquity of Man* by Charles Lyell appeared in 1863, followed, in 1865, by John Lubbock's *Pre-historic Times*. Darwin himself was known to be preparing a radical statement on human evolution. (*The Descent of Man* was published in 1871.) Visiting London in the winter of 1867, Henry Adams found that "Darwin was convulsing society."[21]

The trustees of the embryonic Peabody Museum published a circular asking for donations, from any part of the world, of:

 1. *Lithics*: axes, gouges, chisels, clubs, pestles, sinkers, tomahawks, mortars, arrow-heads, spearheads

2. *Ceramics*: vases, pots, pipes, bowls, figurines
3. *Ethnographic*: bows, arrows, quivers, spears, rattles, drums, shields, snowshoes, knives, lodges, medicine bags, tobacco pouches, cooking utensils, articles of dress
4. *Somatology*: mummies, skeletons, particularly skulls and long bones
5. *Antiquities*: images, sculptures, casts from Peru, Mexico, Chile, Central America
6. Articles made by or relating to Eskimos, and the Fuegians or Patagonians.[22]

Wyman was appointed curator of the museum. In 1868, in his first annual report to the trustees, he wrote that "a collection of various objects pertaining to the purposes of this Museum was begun, and temporarily deposited in one of the cases of the Museum of Comparative Anatomy, 111 Boylston Hall." These "various objects" included "crania and bones of North-American Indians, a few casts of crania of other races, several kinds of stone implements, and a few articles of pottery." Donors soon added further items, including collections of skulls from Peru and from the Sandwich Islands. ("For the purposes of comparison, they are extremely suitable," Wyman assured the trustees.)[23]

Wyman organised digs in the Midwest, where he hoped to discover remains of Stone Age populations, and he bought European collections of prehistoric objects. The aim, he told the trustees, was "the gathering of means for making direct comparison between the implements of the Stone Age of the old world and the new."[24] But while his goals were ambitious, Wyman was a diffident man, in poor health, operating with a meagre budget. When he died, in 1874, Asa Gray could only say that he had done remarkably well "unaided, with feeble health and feebler means . . . without éclat . . . in silence and penury."[25]

Gray took over as interim director of the Harvard Peabody Museum after Wyman's death, and he began to scout for a successor. An obvious candidate was Frederic Putnam, the director of a museum of natural history and ethnography in nearby Salem, which was supported by Peabody funds. (This was the third Peabody museum, established on the recommendation of another Peabody nephew, George Peabody Russell, a native of Salem.)

A remote descendant of John Putnam, who had migrated from England in 1640, Frederic Ward Putnam was born in Salem in 1839. Like his near contemporary John Wesley Powell, he had only an informal education, but showed an early interest in natural history. At the age of seventeen he joined the Essex Institute, a local learned society which ran a library and a museum where he became curator of the bird collection. A few months later, Putnam moved to work with Agassiz at Harvard (where his father, grandfather and great-grandfather had studied before him). He stayed with Agassiz for seven formative but testing, arduous years.

Agassiz inspired his classes. "The only teaching that appealed to his imagination," wrote Henry Adams (as ever in the third person), recalling his own undergraduate years, "was a course of lectures by Louis Agassiz on the Glacial Period and Palaeontology, which had more influence on his curiosity than the rest of the college instruction altogether."[26] But Agassiz was a difficult colleague and a domineering chief. He was unimpressed by the collegial, anglophile, clubland habits of Harvard's humanist scholars. In his view, professors of the natural sciences should embrace the hierarchical style of German and French research universities. He ran his museum accordingly. He had no doubt that it would raise Harvard's scientific profile, but intended that it should also be a shrine to religion, insisting that the "great object of our museums should be to exhibit the whole animal kingdom as a manifestation of the Supreme Intellect."[27] Agassiz's student assistants were expected to devote themselves to the cause. They were prevented from publishing independently, expected to toe the anti-Darwinian line, and had to go along with Agassiz's view that the human races had been separately created and were inherently unequal. This was a particularly painful issue during the Civil War. In 1863 there was a revolt. Most of Agassiz's first cadre of student assistants walked out and were taken on by the newly established Salem Peabody Museum. Putnam, who had taken courses with Gray, and worked on archaeological digs with Whitney, was a leader of the secession.[28] Asa Gray was on the Salem board of trustees. In 1875, he would bring Putnam back from Salem to lead Harvard's Peabody Museum.

Putnam was keen to promote research in American prehistory, but he stumbled on to a false track. Impressed, like Wyman, by the dramatic discoveries of European prehistorians, he expected to find very ancient American Stone Age sites and to recover skeletons and skulls of pre-modern humans. Really old Stone Age settlements and burials were, however, hard to find in the Americas. Putnam funded a surgeon and self-taught antiquarian, Charles C. Abbott, who claimed that he had discovered Stone Age remains on his farm in New Jersey. This gamble ended badly when Abbott bought a fake collection from a local shoemaker on the museum's account.

Putnam supported excavations on the edge of glacial gravels in Trenton, New Jersey, for thirty years. "He lived and died with the firm conviction that man lived on this continent in glacial times," according to Alfred Tozzer, an American archaeologist who wrote a memoir of Putnam for the National Academy of Sciences.[29] But a Smithsonian archaeologist, William Henry Holmes, demonstrated that most of Putnam's finds were in fact modern, concluding that Putnam and Abbott took "a day's work of one Indian" and "made a scheme of culture evolution that spans ten thousand years."[30] Soon after Putnam's death an anthropologist at the Smithsonian Institution, Aleš Hrdlička, established that a high proportion of the human remains found by Putnam were associated with modern communities of Lenape Indians. Archaeological sites dating before 11,200 years ago, when a warm climatic interval began, are—to quote one authority—"rare to non-existent" anywhere in North America.[31]

Some antiquarians were intrigued by an alternative theory about America's ancient past. This had to do with mysterious earth mounds. Thomas Jefferson excavated ancient burial mounds near his homestead, Monticello, in 1770. There were similar earth mounds in the Ohio Valley: Peabody's nephew Othniel Marsh had been digging there when the idea came to him for a museum of American prehistory. They cropped up in Florida, in New Mexico, and in the Mississippi watershed. Excavations of the mounds turned up burials and a variety of striking craftworks. The very first volume of the "Smithsonian Contributions to Knowledge," a monograph series edited by Joseph Henry himself, was *Ancient Monuments of the Mississippi Valley*, a pioneering study of the mounds.

"These earthworks, which often contained elaborate artefacts made of pottery, shell, mica and native copper, challenged the belief that native American cultures were invariably primitive," a modern authority, Bruce Trigger, writes.[32] Were they the products of an advanced civilisation, associated, perhaps, with Toltec sites in Mexico? It might even be that these sites were really, *really* ancient, coeval with Britain's Brixham cave or the palaeolithic settlements in the Dordogne. And then a tantalising idea began to spread. Perhaps the mounds preserved the remains of prehistoric Viking settlements, or, why not, of yet more ancient European pioneers, who had been driven off by later waves of native peoples. Was it possible that Europeans were the first settlers of America's West?[33]

Putnam bought into a version of this fantasy. "For a long time I have insisted that the civilization of Mexico and Central America must have largely derived from foreign sources," he wrote to the French–American philanthropist and antiquarian, the Duke of Loubat, in 1900, and "I regard the builders of the great earthworks of the Ohio valley as an early offshoot of the Mexican element."[34] He excavated mounds in Ohio and encouraged a group of wealthy Boston ladies to buy the land on which the very dramatic "Serpent Mound" stood. (Donated to the Peabody Museum, it later became an Ohio state park.)

Lewis Henry Morgan had no truck with these speculations. "The tribes who constructed the earthworks of the Ohio Valley were American Indians," he wrote. "No other supposition is tenable."[35] Nevertheless, some congressmen urged the Bureau of Ethnology to investigate. In the summer of 1878, Putnam and Major Powell spent a fortnight supervising an excavation of earth mounds in Tennessee.[36] Powell soon came to agree with Morgan. He published a note in *Science* in 1885 headed, bluntly, "The Indians are the Mound-Builders."[37] "It is difficult to exaggerate the prevalence of this romantic fallacy, or the force with which the hypothetic 'lost races' had taken possession of the imaginations of men," Powell wrote in the 1890–91 annual report of the Bureau of Ethnology. "For more than a century the ghosts of a vanished nation have ambuscaded in the vast solitudes of the continent, and the forest-covered mounds have been usually regarded as the mysterious sepulchres of its kings and nobles. It was an alluring conjecture." Powell put a Smithsonian archaeologist, Cyrus Thomas, on the case, and he did a definitive demolition job.[38]

It has since been established that the mounds were associated with the American Indian Adena and Hopewell traditions. The earliest sites are dated to around 800 BCE.[39] Putnam later had better luck in interesting elite Bostonian donors in another, more respectable field: ancient Mayan civilisation.[40] But he stuck to his belief that this, too, was in origin European.

In 1877, the Peabody collections were installed in a newly constructed museum building and prepared for public display. According to a recent director of the museum, Rubie Watson, in those early days "the Peabody staff was keen to display the collections—all the collections—ordered primarily by regional-cultural origin (e.g., North America, Swiss Lakes, Pacific Islands) and secondarily by object type or function (e.g., mortars, stone axes, pottery)."[41] This suggests a compromise between a geographical arrangement, in line with the British Museum's displays under Franks, and a gesture in the direction of a functional, natural history style classification. However, visitors were not given clear directions. "Thousands of artefacts were displayed with minimal or no use of labels," Watson notes.

Around 1878 Putnam considered a rearrangement of the Peabody collection in order "to illustrate the development of Man toward civilization, as shown by his inventions, arts, and manufactures from remote times."[42] In January 1880 he wrote to Lewis Henry Morgan, urging him to visit the Peabody: "I have brought together at the Museum the *largest* and *most important* and in every way *authentic* collection relating the antiquities of America that has been made. This may seem a pretty strong statement for me to make, but *I know* the collections in other Museums."[43] In his annual report to the trustees, in 1891, he claimed that the Peabody Museum had "taken its full share in the work of introducing scientific methods of arrangement into the heterogeneous collections of antiquities and of curios from uncivilized peoples."[44] This was stretching things. There was no coherent theory behind the museum's arrangements. And Putnam did not reorganise the museum's displays on evolutionist lines.

In 1887, Harvard appointed Putnam to the Peabody professorship of American Archaeology and Ethnology. This chair had been endowed in the museum's original deed of trust, twenty years earlier, but the university was not convinced that Putnam was qualified to occupy it. "You know I don't believe in Putnam's capacity," Agassiz's son, Alexander, wrote to the president of Harvard, "but he is honest and industrious and an excellent *curator* . . . I only objected to his being made professor."[45] Nevertheless, once appointed Peabody professor, Putnam was the leading academic in a small but increasingly fashionable field. He soon accumulated positions, like a medieval bishop. In 1873, he became permanent secretary of the American Association for the Advancement of Science, an influential role that he retained for the next twenty-five years.[46] All the while refusing to relinquish his Harvard chair, Putnam snapped up professorships in Chicago, New York and at Berkeley, where he accepted a position at the Phoebe Hearst Museum which Boas thought he had a chance of landing for himself.

In 1889, the curator of ethnology at the U.S. National Museum, Otis T. Mason, wrote a teasing letter to Putnam from Paris, where he had met Ernest Théodore Hamy, the head of the Paris Museum of Ethnology:

> I was reminded of you a thousand times in Paris, by Dr. Hamy, who looks like you, talks like you, trots around like you, is general secretary of everything, and an indispensable man-of-affairs to the Paris Anthropologists.—in all our meetings nothing could go on until Dr. Hamy arrived; and to keep up the comparison, once in a while he came in a little late.[47]

Major Powell was less impressed by Putnam. "I think that he has a slip-shod method of writing and should distrust his judgment ... though he has a wide scientific acquaintance and pushes his way among scientific men."[48] One of his first students at Harvard, John Swanton, judged that Putnam's "fieldwork was limited in character, his primary contribution to American archaeology being in advertising the subject and building up the Peabody Museum."[49]

Putnam's reputation in American anthropology has come to rest largely on his role as the patron of Franz Boas. A myth developed according to which it was Putnam who championed the young German and his anti-evolutionist anthropology against the Smithsonian evolutionists and rescued his career after the crisis that ensued. In the early years of their relationship, Boas played up to this image, describing himself to Putnam as his "orphan boy," soliciting patronage and even borrowing money.[50]

Putnam was a more efficient careerist than Boas, but much less of a scholar, and he was no theoretician. He first encountered Boas—was buttonholed by Boas—at a meeting of the American Association for the Advancement of Science in 1886.

Putnam then helped him find a job as assistant editor of *Science* magazine.[51] When Boas had his spectacular row with the Smithsonian, Putnam did not, however, choose to get involved. There is no indication that he sympathised with Boas's critique of the evolutionists. The two men became collaborators a few years later, at the Columbian Exposition in Chicago, not because they shared a philosophy but because Putnam needed someone to do the hard work for him. Putnam was playing a long game. He expected that when the fair was over he would be made scientific director of the Chicago museum, with Boas to do the heavy lifting as head of anthropology. But the Smithsonian people had their own network in place in Chicago. In the event, it was no contest. The Smithsonian won on all fronts. Boas then followed Putnam to the American Museum of Natural History in New York, but their relationship did not end well.

THE WORLD'S COLUMBIAN
EXPOSITION, 1893

The 1893 World's Columbian Exposition in Chicago marked the four-hundredth anniversary of the voyage of Christopher Columbus to the Americas. Chicago had to beat off competition from New York to stage this ambitious, hugely expensive, patriotic blowout. Its benchmark was the Paris Fair of 1889, and Chicago was determined to surpass Paris. To fund the Exposition, the State of Illinois chartered a company with an initial $5 million stock issue. The federal government authorised $1.5 million for official exhibits.[1]

The centrepieces of both fairs were prodigies of industrial innovation. The Paris Fair had the brand-new Eiffel Tower, 324 metres (1,063 ft) high. Chicago had the first Ferris wheel. It was just 80.4 metres (264 ft) high, but it offered thirty-six passenger cars, each with forty revolving chairs. (Chief Standing Bear, a Ponca chief and a champion of Indian land rights, rode the Ferris wheel, wearing a full headdress.)[2] In Chicago, Edison's Kinetoscope showed the first moving pictures. Also on display were the first zip fastener; a new breakfast cereal, Shredded Wheat; and a flavoured chewing gum, Juicy Fruit.[3]

The Chicago Fair was housed in the purpose-built "White City." Leading architects were commissioned to design the pavilions; the landscape genius Frederick Law Olmsted laid out the park and gardens; Walt Disney's father was one of the building contractors. Set on the shore of Lake Michigan, the site came equipped with brand-new mod cons: electric street lights, public lavatories, and a day-care centre for the children of visitors.

But it was not all about technical wonders, civic boosterism, product placing, advertising and entertainment. There really had to be an educational purpose, some more elevated, world-historical theme, some *message*, if Chicago was to beat Paris at its own game. The planning committee approached George Brown Goode, the director of the U.S. National Museum, to draw up a blueprint. In his "First Draft of a System of Classification for the World's Columbian Exposition" Goode suggested that the fair should illustrate "the steps of progress of civilization and its arts in successive centuries, and in all lands up to the present time." It would be "in fact, *an illustrated encyclopedia of civilization*."[4] Back in Washington, Goode submitted a plan to Congress for the Smithsonian's ethnological display in Chicago. (This drew on Mason's enthusiastic reports of the 1889 Paris Exposition.)[5]

Putnam also had a plan. In a letter to the *Chicago Tribune* in May 1890, he advised that the theme of the Exposition should be "the stages of the development of man on the American continent."[6] He told a Chicago audience that it was necessary to show "the low cultural base" of the Americas at the time of Columbus in order to bring out, by contrast, "the material prosperity and the development of our race in the arts and in culture."[7] This approach would have further benefits. It would introduce the American public to the new science of anthropology and prepare the way for a future Chicago museum, which would be even better than New York's Museum of Natural History.

Serious people admitted that important lessons were on offer on the shores of Lake Michigan. An entire chapter of *The Education of Henry Adams* was devoted to the Chicago Exposition.[8] Adams visited the White City twice, spending every day there for a fortnight on the second occasion, "absorbed in it."

He found matter of study to fill a hundred years . . . educational game started like rabbits from every building . . .

Paris had never approached it . . . no such Babel of loose
and ill-joined, such vague and ill-defined and unrelated
thoughts and half-thoughts and experimental outcries
as the Exposition, had ever ruffled the surface of the
Lakes . . . That the Exposition should be a natural growth
and product of the Northwest offered a step in evolution to
startle Darwin . . . Chicago asked in 1893 for the first time
the question whether the American people knew where
they were driving . . . he decided that the American people
probably knew no more than he did . . . Chicago was the
first expression of American thought as a unity; one must
start there.[9]

A Congress on Evolution was organised at the fair, as part of a
World's Parliament of Religion. Providing an "Intellectual and
Moral Exposition of the Progress of Mankind," and bringing "all
the departments of human progress into harmonious relations
with each other," it aimed to reconcile evolution and Christianity. Herbert Spencer delivered the keynote address. Introduced
as "the Columbus of the new epoch," he urged Congress to
agree that egoism should be combined with altruism.[10]

So Chicago's message to the world was about evolution, progress
and civilisation. The same had been true in Paris. And in both
Paris and Chicago the civilised world was cast against its mirror
opposite: the uncivilised. A journalist remarked that in Chicago
the American Indian "is everywhere."[11] There were ethnographic
exhibits in provincial and national pavilions in the State Building.
American Indian crafts were displayed in the Shoe and Leather
Building, the Transportation Building, the Fisheries Building
and (curated by Otis Mason) in the Women's Building.[12] As in
Paris, there were live exhibits of native peoples in stagey villages.

National conferences of anthropologists and historians
hosted lectures on the past and future of "primitive peoples,"
with particular reference to North America. At a meeting of the
American Historical Association, a young historian, Frederick J.

Turner, presented a paper which would reverberate through American historiography for several generations: "The Significance of the Frontier in American History."[13] It offered a vision of the future of the West, Native Americans, and, indeed, the United States.

Turner began by quoting the superintendent of the census: "Up to and including 1880 the country had a frontier of settlement, but at present the unsettled area has been so broken into by isolated bodies of settlement that there can hardly be said to be a frontier line." For Turner, this marked a decisive historical break. Up to that point, the frontier had been "the meeting point between savagery and civilisation." Settlers raised in a European tradition adopted the native way of life. The frontier

> strips off the garments of civilization and arrays [the settler] in the hunting shirt and the moccasin. It puts him in the log cabin of the Cherokee and Iroquois and runs an Indian palisade around him. Before long he has gone to planting Indian corn and plowing with a sharp stick; he shouts the war cry and takes the scalp in orthodox Indian fashion. In short, at the frontier, the environment is at first too strong for the man.

But little by little the settler tamed the wilderness. There followed a process of "most rapid and effective Americanization." The settlers became models of American individualism and democratic sensibility.

So what happened to the American Indians? First of all, trade. "Long before the pioneer farmer appeared on the scene, primitive Indian life had passed away. The farmers met Indians armed with guns." As settlers moved West, "The Indian was a common danger, demanding united action." But once defeated, the future of the native peoples was settled: assimilation. The settler had once adopted an Indian way of life. Now the Indian would have to learn to live like an American. And, no longer a constant threat, their old way of life could be romanticised.

Native peoples from the Americas were not the only foil to American civilisation on show in Chicago. "It would not be too much to say that the World's Columbian Exposition was one vast anthropological revelation," Mason boasted. "Not all mankind were there, but either in persons or pictures their representatives were."[14] The fair's honky-tonk fringe, the vibrant, free-enterprise Midway, had a cosmopolitan cast of dancers, musicians and acrobats who put an alluring Orient on display.

Putnam was head of the department of ethnology. Boas was his right-hand man. They organised a large and eclectic exhibit in the anthropology building. Their Smithsonian rivals, led by Mason, had their own show on the ground floor of the government building. So the Harvard Peabody Museum was pitted against the Smithsonian Institution. Their rivalry was particularly sharp because it looked as though either Putnam or the Smithsonian party would take charge of ethnology in the new Chicago museum to be built after the fair.

The two parties delivered very different images of anthropology, but these did not fit the stereotype of Smithsonian generalists versus Boasian regionalists. On the contrary. The Smithsonian mounted a focused, regional presentation of North American ethnography. Putnam and Boas presided over a loosely arranged and opportunistically assembled sample of global ethnography, plus a display of skulls and skeletons and tables of measurements of the bodies of schoolchildren and American Indians.

The Smithsonian exhibition combined the resources of the Bureau of American Ethnology and the U.S. National Museum. Mason had spent three years making preparations. Powell's map of the distribution of native American languages, now unveiled at last, blown up to 16 × 12 feet (approximately 5 × 4 metres), was the centrepiece. Powell and his team had identified fifty-seven linguistic groupings in North America. Mason highlighted sixteen "great families." The original plan was to illustrate the map with vignettes of American Indian tribes, but the language groupings did not correspond with particular styles of material culture. The distribution of crafts and implements made a better fit with ecological regions identified in a biogeographic map of North America that had recently been published by the department of agriculture. Mason concluded that "the materialistic activities were controlled by the environment."[15]

This was in line with the approach of Boas's old professor, Adolf Bastian. Boas should, in principle, have been impressed. As usual, however, Mason hedged his bets. "I have arranged the costumes and art productions of these families in separate alcoves, so that the student taking his position in one of them may have before his eye a practical solution of some of the theoretical questions which have recently arisen concerning the connection between race and language and industries and philosophies." On the other hand, "In order to afford the student another point of view from which to look at the same set of phenomena, a few alcoves have been arranged upon another plan, in which a topical industry is made the primary classific concept, tribe or nationality the second concept, and linguistic affinities the third concept."[16]

The most successful exhibits were the "life groups," plaster mannequins, dressed in traditional costume, busily doing craftwork or performing rituals, an innovation that Mason had admired at the Paris Exposition. The groups were prepared by a rising star of the Bureau of American Ethnology, Powell's protégé, an artist turned archaeologist, William Henry Holmes. "Nothing draws the crowd like the groups," Mason commented. "No part of the Exposition is more frequented."[17]

Over at the Anthropological Building, Putnam claimed that he had brought to Chicago "the first scientific anthropological exhibit in this country." He inscribed his message in stone. "The Legend over the main entrance, 'Anthropological Building, Man and his Works,' is very comprehensive and indicates the scope of the department, which not only treats of the moral, mental and physical characteristics of man, but also shows the beginnings of his great achievements in art, in architecture and in manufactures."[18] The promise was grandiose, the plan poorly thought out, the execution chaotic.

Between 1891 and 1893, Putnam deployed fifty-five field assistants to collect materials for the exhibition, and he sent out a general call for materials. Too general. The response was overwhelming. Nancy Fagin writes that "mugs from Mesa Verde were shipped by the dozen, several cave-dried mummies arrived from Colorado, an entire model of a mesa village came from New Mexico, and the State Historical Society of Ohio contributed large plaster models of Fort Ancient and Serpent Mound. Room was allotted for the many miscellaneous donations from individuals who sent only a single artefact or case." Many objects were poorly documented. "The Department's informal method of receiving specimens made for a backlog of artefacts and curios . . . Putnam, Boas, and the staff faced crates of incoming specimens without an adequate acquisition form to produce descriptive labels, to catalogue, or to form meaningful groupings . . . Artefacts were stacked one on top of another and inside one another and hung from the ceiling by clotheslines."[19] In November 1892, Boas wrote to his parents: "in short, everything in a jumble and Putnam in despair."[20]

Since the aim was to represent American Indians as they were at the time of Columbus, the ethnographic artefacts came on the whole from the more isolated regions, particularly the Northwest and the West. "The Indians east of the Rocky mountains have been so much modified by contact with the white that, taken as a whole, a small amount of material only has been gathered," Boas noted.[21] As for the archaeological exhibits, they were designed to illustrate the unreliable theories of Putnam about the early appearance of Stone Age peoples in North America, and the supposedly European roots of the Aztec, Inca and Mayan civilisations. "The much-disputed paleolithic implements are fully represented," Boas remarked, evidently doing his best to be tactful. Models of earth mounds were on display, but "we must not imagine the mound-builders to have been a people very far in advance of the Indian tribes at the time of their discovery . . . their culture was on a similar level."[22] Reconstructions of Central American and Mayan monuments took pride of place in front of the anthropology building, but Boas did not mention Putnam's theory that these civilisations were diffused from Europe.

Boas was designated chief assistant in charge of physical anthropology. While Putnam's field assistants were busy collecting Indian arts and crafts for the exhibitions, Boas deployed some seventy university students to make measurements of 90,000 schoolchildren and 17,000 American Indians. There were three laboratories in the anthropology building. "A very full collection of crania and skeletons illustrates the anatomy of human races," Boas wrote in a special issue of *Cosmopolitan Magazine*.[23] Statues represented idealised young men of different races. Visitors could have their measurements taken by Boas and his assistants.[24]

There was no time to catalogue the materials pouring in, and the promised anthropology building was not ready when the fair opened on 1 May 1893. It did not become available until July. Meanwhile the collections were stored in a dairy barn, but at a critical moment they had to be moved to make way for a cheese exhibition.[25] Putnam himself was forced to move his office nine times. On one occasion

> without my knowledge or notice from anyone, a force of workmen was put into my office during my absence since Saturday; and partitions have been torn down and plastering removed without any care being taken of all the records and valuable property belonging to my department of the exposition. . . . disgraceful and arbitrary . . . a deep insult to me personally as well as to the position which I hold at the Exposition.[26]

The New York Times mocked "Prof. Putnam's Hard Luck" (*The New York Times*, 22 May 1893).

There is one very important section of the World's Fair which, because of its inaccessibility and distance from the main buildings, is likely to be overlooked by nine out of every ten visitors. And yet there are grouped in this territory sights which would repay even the long and tedious tramp in sand ankle deep to get to them . . . the Anthropological Building is the furthest in the rear, the most forlorn in its exterior and interior, and pre-eminently the one with the most promise of being a failure.

Though conceding that "no other chief of a department at the World's Fair has had so much to contend with and so much criticism to meet as Prof. F. W. Putnam, Chief of the Department of Ethnology," the reporter piled insult on injury. Putnam was

an active and an erudite little man, but he seems to be a sufferer from that great drawback of scientific and professional persons—lack of practicability . . . Consequently he has got into snarls and imbroglios and has been buffeted about by more worldly and self-assertive chiefs of departments, who got things done while Mr. Putnam had to wait, and as a consequence his building at this date is unfinished, his ethnological exhibits, many of them, are between here and Patagonia, and the poor scientist has to carry a load of detraction, criticism, and denunciation which culminated a few days ago in the expression of opinion by a Chicago newspaper that the anthropological department was a myth and Prof. Putnam as much an uncertainty as some of the archaeological problems he has been years in trying to solve.

This was over the top, but it could not be denied that Putnam's project was in bad shape and that he himself was responsible for many of its problems. His plans were overly ambitious, and he spent only part of his time in Chicago, since he was still very busy with the Harvard Museum and his work with the American

Association for the Advancement of Science. The fair's administrators were soon fed up with him. The director, Harlow N. Higginbotham, refused even to set foot in the anthropology building when it was, belatedly, completed.

Putnam himself was particularly interested in the exhibits on show in the courtyard in front of the anthropology building. Here were facsimile Mayan ruins, Inuit skin tents, Northwest coast plank houses, an Iroquois longhouse, a bark wigwam and a pioneer cabin.[27] The Smithsonian crowd had their plaster "live" groups. Putnam and Boas brought in flesh and blood American Indians to occupy the village. Putnam called it the "Sub-department for the representation of the Native Peoples of America." The pseudo villagers were dressed in ersatz traditional clothes. (It was impossible to find native dressmakers who could fabricate yucca fibre clothes.)[28] Occasionally they would perform dances and ceremonies. Unfortunately, the anthropology building was close to the noisy elevated railway, which, Putnam complained, "greatly mars the picturesque effect." When Boas presented a show of Kwakiutl dancers he had to use sheets to block out the Leather and Shoe Trades Building in the background.[29]

Boas directed his field assistant, George Hunt, to acquire a large Kwakiutl house and to commission artisans to carve a miniaturised village. Hunt also brought nine native men, five women and two children to Chicago. Putnam told the *Springfield Daily Republican* (20 August 1892):

> We have offered every possible inducement to native tribes in North, South, and Central America to make their own exhibits at the fair, that is, to come at their own expenses and depend upon the sale of their peculiar trinkets for sufficient revenue to meet the outlay. In some cases this will be done, in others we will have to bring the natives to Chicago ourselves, while in still other cases they will be sent by the governments of which they are subjects.

A Navaho contingent sponsored by the State of Colorado soon decamped to join the commercial strip on the Midway. Labrador Inuit families were imported to occupy an "Esquimaux Village" but most of them walked out, formed the Esquimaux Exhibition Company, and set up their own village just outside the fairgrounds, near Buffalo Bill's Wild West Show. (Excluded from the Midway, the Wild West Show was situated beyond the fringe of the fairgrounds, but it was immensely popular and profitable.)[30]

Boas later vowed "never again to play circus impresario."[31] Putnam, however, expressed pride in this "little colony of native people." It was "not intended for a side show for the amusement of the visitor, but for a scientific study of the first historic people of America," he wrote in an official history of the Columbian Exposition. "Moreover these people are treated with kindness and consideration and are allowed every opportunity for improvement by observations of the benefits of civilization and education. The Indian Schoolhouse nearby, which is conducted by the United States Government, shows to the world what the Indian is capable of when allowed such advantages."

In fact, nobody would make a serious study of "this little colony." And what sort of study did Putnam have in mind? What was the message? Thomas Jefferson Morgan, commissioner of Indian Affairs, had no doubt what was wanted. The Indian Schoolhouse should represent the promised assimilation of native peoples to the American way of life. Putnam explained that his displays represented the American Indian "in his primitive conditions," whereas the Bureau of Indian Affairs would show him "on his road to civilization."

Emma Sickles, head of the Indian committee of the Universal Peace Union, a political appointee in Putnam's anthropology section, and a former government teacher at the Pine Ridge reservation, denounced Putnam's stage village in *The New York Times*. The exhibition depicted "savagery in the most repulsive form, participated in by only the lowest specimens of the Indian race." Indeed, it represented "one of the darkest conspiracies ever conceived against the Indian race." It "has been used to work up sentiment against the Indian by showing that he is either savage or can be educated only by Government agencies." Putnam fired Sickles. The fair's administrators reinstated her.[32]

Putnam suffered another embarrassment. His "Department of Ethnology, Archaeology, History, Cartography, Latin-American Bureau, Collective and Isolated Exhibits" was initially given responsibility for the Midway. This outdoor entertainment hub, built around the Ferris wheel, operated by concessionaires, was billed by the organisers as an "open mart and caravansary of nations." There were "Egyptians and Sudanese, Indonesians in a Javanese village, fifty-eight Eskimos from Labrador, a party of bare-breasted Dahomeans in a West African setting, as well as Malays, Samoans, Fijians, Japanese, and Chinese."[33] A popular promenade, the "Street in Cairo," had won a gold prize at the Paris Fair. An Egyptian Temple and a Persian Temple of Eros had also featured at Paris. Other "Oriental" sideshows included Turkish, Algerian and Tunisian villages.[34] There were belly dancers. There were swimming races every Friday, featuring Zulus, Dahomeans, Turks and South American Indians. There was even a grand "Ball of the Midway Freaks" to which the leading officials of the fair were invited.[35]

This was not really Putnam's sort of thing. "What shall we say of the 'Street in Cairo,'" he wrote, "with its confusion of life: Arabs, Egyptians, Nubians and Soudanese in varying and characteristic costumes; jugglers, swordsmen, venders, donkey boys, and camel drivers?"[36] The fair's administrators had their own answer to this rhetorical question. They sidelined Putnam. Sol Bloom, a nineteen-year-old entrepreneur, took over the management of the Midway. He remarked that putting Professor Putnam in charge was like "making Albert Einstein manager of the Ringling Brothers and Barnum and Bailey Circus."[37] (Oddly enough, between 1883 and 1885 Barnum and Bailey had toured the country with a "Grand Ethnological Congress of Strange and Savage People.")[38]

The fair closed on the last day of October. Boas then spent nine months overseeing the transfer of the collections from the anthropology building to the Palace of Fine Arts, which was to house Chicago's new Columbian Museum. He and Putnam also bought ethnographic materials from exhibitors. Captain Jacobsen, on whose Northwest coast collection Boas had worked in his graduate student days in Berlin, was eager to sell off artefacts he had brought to Chicago. Boas and Putnam knew that he was desperate to save on transport costs, and coolly waited him out. Jacobson complained that "the Yankees" got "a brilliant collection for a pittance."[39]

Funding for the new museum had been in doubt, but a last-minute donation of $1 million from the department store mogul Marshall Field secured its future. Putnam and Boas expected to be given leadership roles, but they were outmanoeuvred by the Smithsonian people and their local allies.[40] Holmes was appointed to head the ethnology department in what became the Field Museum. "I immediately packed up and have left the Museum for good," Boas wrote to Putnam. "I am now, of course, adrift and shall appreciate whatever you may be able to do for me. You know I have nothing to fall back upon."[41] Putnam assured him that he was pursuing opportunities for them both in New York.

"All our Chicago ships have gone aground," Boas wrote to his parents.[42] In February 1894 he wrote to Putnam: "The delays in the completion of the Anthropological Building were used to best advantage against you and your administrative ability was assailed in every way. I was charged with lack of administrative ability again on account of the delay in getting the Anthropological Building into shape."[43]

Holmes and the Smithsonian men were left feeling rather awkward about the way in which Boas had his hopes dashed. Boas himself remarked that after the Chicago debacle he found the Smithsonian folk "surprisingly sympathetic." Even Holmes was conciliatory. "The Washington people felt uncomfortable," Boas reported to Putnam. "Therefore I know, they will be willing to do for me a good deal that they might otherwise not do."[44] McGee asked him to help catalogue Northwest coast material in the National Museum. Mason invited him to provide the National Museum with a "pretty complete collection illustrating the whole winter dance ceremonial of [the Northwest coast] tribes." (This commission led Boas to undertake what Ira Jacknis calls "the most intensive participant-observation work of his career.")[45] Powell offered Boas a position at the Bureau of American Ethnology for editorial work, with time for his own research. Boas was even contracted to take charge of the signature project of the bureau, the *Handbook of American Indian Languages*. He remade it to his own liking, eventually published two volumes, the first in 1911, the second only in 1922, and then let it drop, unfinished.

As for Holmes himself, he soon regretted his decision to remain in Chicago. He detested the commercial pressures in the Field Museum and as soon as he could, he returned to Washington and the Smithsonian. After Powell's death in 1902, he became director of the Bureau of American Ethnology, but this also did not go well. The new secretary of the Smithsonian, Langley, purged the bureau and brought it firmly under his control.[46]

On the last day of 1893, Boas looked back on the year: "A rushing rat-race, great uneasiness, and unsatisfactory work have been its watchwords."[47] To cap it all, the fair had an apocalyptic aftermath. The United States was in the middle of an economic depression. On 28 October, just days before the fair was dismantled, Chicago's mayor, Carter Harrison IV, was assassinated. Most of the buildings in the White City were then razed to the ground by rioting employees of the Pullman Palace Car Company.

But Putnam fell on his feet. Despite the bad publicity in *The New York Times*, he landed a position as director of anthropology at the American Museum of Natural History in New York, and he saw to it that Boas was appointed assistant curator of ethnology and somatology. (Putnam treated the position as part-time. He retained his chair in Harvard and was in New York only one week a month.)

Launched in 1869, the American Museum of Natural History was supported by New York's financial and political elite. Money was not a problem. Its trustees included the bankers J. P. Morgan and Morris K. Jesup and the father of President Teddy Roosevelt. A massive gothic pile backing on to Central Park was built to house the museum. Albert S. Bickmore, a former colleague of Putnam, a fellow rebel against Agassiz, was brought in to provide scientific leadership. However, the bankers and the curators did not always agree on priorities. Jesup chaired the board of trustees and micromanaged everything. Boas was soon complaining that Jesup was too keen on publicity, too fond of Herbert Spencer's evolutionist ideas, and too ready to impose his own ideas of museum displays. It particularly irked Boas that he occupied a rather lowly position in the hierarchy and could not deal directly with Jesup.

Boas did try to set up exhibits that would appeal to a broad public. Arranged on a functional, developmental plan, very much like the one he had criticised at the Smithsonian, they were designed to show "how the most primitive tribes depend entirely upon the products of their home, and how with the progress of civilisation wider and wider areas are made to contribute to the needs of man." Boas also claimed that the exhibits "would become of great interest to the tradesman . . . showing the development of the trades of the carpenter, the blacksmith, the weaver, etc. in different cultural areas."[48]

But Boas was a reluctant populariser. He irritated the administration by refusing to approve labels unless they were backed by monographic studies. And he rather disapproved of the visitors to the museum. Most "do not want anything beyond entertainment."[49] They required careful management. If there was a central aisle flanked with cases, visitors would "wander from right to left without order and it is impossible to compel them to see the collections in such a manner that they will have the greatest possible benefit from a short visit. . . . By dividing the Hall into two longitudinal halves . . . visitors are compelled to see the collections in their natural sequence, and even if they pass through only one half of the Hall will be more benefited than when seeing one alcove here, one there." Boas's English was still awkward, but his repeated use of "compel" is surely telling.[50]

While Boas was prepared to play along with Jesup to some extent, he was frustrated, and on the lookout for other opportunities. In 1901, there was an opening in the Hearst Museum at Berkeley. Boas had hopes but Putnam snaffled the position, again on a part-time basis. Boas wrote to Putnam that he had suffered "many sleepless nights," and that it would be a struggle "to regain our old harmonious relations."[51]

In fact, Boas was turning against museum anthropology. In 1899, he began to teach part-time at Columbia University. In 1902, he wrote in a letter to Langley, secretary of the Smithsonian, that the study of anthropology could not be confined to museums. It requires "that those lines of human activities that do *not* find expression in material objects—namely language, thought, customs, and I may add, anthropometric measurements—be investigated thoroughly and carefully."[52] In his final essay on museum anthropology, reflecting on two decades of work in Germany and America, he concluded that "the psychological as well as the historical relations of cultures, which are the only objects of anthropological inquiry, cannot be expressed by any arrangement based on so small a portion of the manifestation of ethnic life as is presented by specimens."[53] This was, ironically, precisely the argument Powell had made against Boas in 1887, concluding that "an anthropological museum, therefore, is an impossibility."[54]

Boas was not only turning away from the museum settings in which he had been working. He was breaking definitively with the American anthropological establishment, ensconced in its museum fortresses. In 1904, he delivered a lecture on the history of anthropology at an international conference. The theme was the struggle between three models of cultural development: one, which Boas associated with Tylor, postulated a universal course of cultural progress towards a civilised condition; a second, associated with Bastian, identified universal "elementary ideas," which found local expression, adapted to the environment; the third, promoted by the German geographer Friedrich Ratzel, emphasised migration and borrowing. But, as Joan Mark writes, the striking feature of this lecture was that it "dropped a whole generation of American anthropologists from the historical record. There was no mention of Lewis Henry Morgan, no mention of John Wesley Powell, William Henry Holmes, Frank Hamilton Cushing, Alice G. Fletcher . . . and no mention of the man to whom Boas owed so much, F. W. Putnam."[55]

William Sturtevant, long-serving curator of American ethnology at the U.S. National Museum dated what he called "the Museum Period of anthropology" from the 1840s to "about 1890."[56] The pioneer generation passed on. Goode died in 1896, Powell and Virchow in 1902, Bastian in 1905, Mason and Hamy in 1908. When, in 1905, Boas left the American Museum of Natural History to take up a full-time professorship at Columbia University, this coincided with a shift of the centre of gravity of anthropology from the museums to the universities.

The final episode of the Boas–Smithsonian relationship played out during the First World War. Boas and his circle opposed America's participation in what they saw as a quarrel between European empires. Holmes and the Smithsonian party supported the war. In 1919, Boas wrote a letter to *The Nation*, denouncing men who "have prostituted science by using it as a cover for their activities as spies."[57] He did not name names, but his main target was a well-known archaeologist, Sylvanus G. Morley, who collected information for U.S. Naval Intelligence while engaged in research in Mexico. Holmes was furious, complaining to an associate about "the traitorous article by Boas," blasting "Prussian control of Anthropology in this country," and demanding an end to "the Hun regime."[58] Boas was censured at the next meeting of the American Anthropological Association and narrowly escaped expulsion. But by then Boas and his students had begun to establish their hold on the emerging university departments of anthropology. At the same time, the influence of the museum anthropologists was waning. However, a simmering hostility between the two parties endured for a generation, and Boas remained a target for xenophobic and anti-Semitic slurs.[59]

PART 3

DIVESTING AND REINVENTING THE MUSEUM

BONES OF CONTENTION

As late as the seventeenth century Europe's apothecaries routinely stocked human body parts for medicinal purposes. Heads were supposed to have a particular potency.[1] Then the public dissection of corpses became a standard feature of medical education, immortalised in Rembrandt's "Anatomy Lesson," a group portrait of doctors and distinguished citizens in attendance at the annual public dissection laid on by the Amsterdam Guild of Surgeons. In January 1632, the demonstrator was Dr. Nicolaes Tulp, the official city anatomist. The body was that of a man recently hanged for armed robbery. Some of the doctors glance down at an atlas of anatomy that lies beside the body, probably one of the volumes of *De humani corporis fabrica*, published by Andreas Vesalius in 1543.

Schools of surgery multiplied in the eighteenth century. All required a steady supply of corpses for dissection. The Company of Surgeons in London could claim the bodies of six murderers a year from the public hangman. But the schools needed more. Wendy Moore writes that "surgeons flocked to Tyburn Tree on hanging days to beg, buy or steal the corpses of executed villains." The market was soon more reliably supplied by "unscrupulous undertakers, shifty gravediggers and, above all, the gangs of professional body-snatchers who scoured London's churchyards by night unearthing fresh bodies to deliver to dissecting rooms before dawn."[2] ("Resurrectionists" they were called.)

John Hunter, the most famous surgeon in Georgian England, "would dissect more bodies, and therefore require more bodies stolen from graves, than any other anatomist of the eighteenth century,"[3] according to his biographer, Wendy Moore. Rumours of collusion in grave robbery cast a shadow over his reputation, but Hunter built up Europe's premier private collection of skulls, bones, bottled body parts and freaks of nature, including the skeleton of an Irishman, Charles Byrne, who was 8 foot 4 inches (2.5 metres) tall.[4] The amiable Byrne allowed himself to be put on show. When he died, the *Morning Herald* reported: "The whole tribe of surgeons put in a claim for the poor departed Irish giant, and surround his house, just as Greenland harpooners would an enormous whale."[5] Byrne's friends kept watch over the body, allowing peeks at the corpse for a fee of 2s 6d. They then dropped the coffin into the sea, as Byrne had requested. But Hunter paid the undertaker a bribe of £500, a huge sum at the time. While the entourage stopped at an inn, the undertaker's assistants removed the body and filled the coffin with stones. Hunter boiled down the body and extracted the skeleton.[6] He kept it discreetly hidden away for many years, but when his friend Sir Joshua Reynolds painted Hunter's portrait in 1786 there were "curiously long feet, tantalisingly glimpsed in the top right-hand corner of the painting."[7]

Towards the end of his life Hunter opened his private museum to visitors twice a year—"in May to aristocrats and gentlemen, in October to fellow medical practitioners and natural philosophers."[8] On show, together with a stuffed giraffe and bones of an elephant and a whale, were the remains of quintuplets, a dwarf—and the Irish giant.[9] After Hunter's death the collection was transferred to the Royal College of Surgeons in Lincoln's Inn Fields. By the twentieth century the "Hunterian Museum," no longer used for teaching purposes, had become a tourist attraction. Eccentric, creepy, anachronistic, it was another of those museums that belong in a museum. In 2017, it was closed for "renovation." When the museum reopened, in May 2023, quirky human remains, including the skeleton of the Irish giant, were not exhibited (though they may be studied by researchers).

From the early nineteenth century, museums of medicine, natural history and anthropology exhibited skulls and skeletons and arrays of jars containing brains, foetuses and even entire human heads preserved in formalin. The U.S. National Museum of Natural History in the Smithsonian Institution had a collection of some 34,000 sets of bones and skulls. In 2001, a consortium of west European museums reported holdings of 131,562 skeletons. The bodies had been excavated by archaeologists, or discovered by chance on building sites, or in the course of roadworks or railway construction. Over 23,000 date from before Roman times, 12,772 from the era of the Roman Empire and 95,646 from the medieval period.[10]

By the nineteenth century, skulls, skeletons, brains and other organs were in demand for a variety of scientific research programmes. In 1805, Johann Friedrich Blumenbach, a professor of medicine in Göttingen, identified five races, largely on the basis of cranial measurements. Rival professors now produced accounts of skulls of the five (or four, or perhaps three) human races.

The pioneer of racial studies in North America was Samuel George Morton. Born in Philadelphia in 1799, raised as a Quaker, Morton studied at the University of Pennsylvania and then attended the prestigious medical school at Edinburgh University, where he was exposed to the latest developments in medical science and anatomy. Back in the U.S.A. he became one of the first professors at the Pennsylvania Medical College. Morton taught a class on "The different forms of the skull, as exhibited in the Five Races of Man." "Strange to say, I could neither buy nor borrow a cranium of each of these races," he recalled. "Forcibly impressed by this great deficiency in a most important branch of science, I at once resolved to make a collection for myself."[11] He built up an extensive private museum, mostly of human skulls, which his friends called the "American Golgotha." Louis Agassiz wrote home to his mother in Switzerland: "Imagine a series of 600 skulls, mostly Indian, of all the tribes who now inhabit or formerly inhabited America. Nothing else like it exists elsewhere. This collection alone is worth a journey to America."[12]

Morton documented these skulls in three lavishly illustrated monographs: *Crania Americana* (1839), on American Indian skulls; *Crania Aegypitiaca* (1844), which described skulls taken from ancient and more recent Egyptian tombs; and, in 1849, a final tabulation of all the 623 skulls in his collection. His researches were inspired by the new sciences of neurology, craniology and phrenology. Their common premise was materialist. Philosophical theories of "mind" were dismissed. The brain was the true embodiment of consciousness, intelligence and personality. The skull's shape and its protuberances revealed particular traits, such as fidelity, courageousness, criminality and sexual orientation.

Morton tried to establish whether the Native American populations constituted a single race. (All but the Polar Eskimos, he concluded.) But he was not content to identify racial types. He related race to intellectual capacity. "This, then, is the doctrine," reported Morton's colleague, Sanford B. Hunt. "Each of the pure, unmixed races has a cranial capacity and form, which is one of its most marked and permanent conditions. In a word, there is a permanent inequality in the size of the brain of different races of men, and also a variety of shape and contour of the braincase, which is almost equally marked and descriptive."[13] Morton claimed that one branch of the "Caucasoid Race"—the "Teutonic Family" (Germans, Anglo-Saxons, Anglo-Americans and Anglo-Irish)—had much the largest brains.

On Morton's death, friends bought his skull collection and donated it to the Philadelphia Academy of Natural Sciences, but by then his theories had fallen out of favour. One of his teachers at Edinburgh University, Robert Jameson, pointed out that Morton's statistical tables failed to distinguish male from female crania. Yet "it is impossible to compare national skulls with national skulls, in respect of their capacity, unless we compare male with male, female with female heads, or, at least, know how many of either sex go to make up the national complement."[14] In 1978, Stephen Jay Gould published a reanalysis of Morton's findings and concluded that "they are a patchwork of assumption and finagling, controlled, probably unconsciously, by his conventional a priori ranking (his folks on top, slaves on the bottom)."[15]

The Philadelphia Academy passed Morton's collection to the University of Pennsylvania's Museum of Archaeology and Anthropology in 1966. A recent posting on the museum's website reports that: "In July 2020, the Penn Museum relocated to storage the part of the Morton Collection that was inside a private classroom within its Center for the Analysis of Archaeological Materials . . . In August, we formed a committee to evaluate the next steps towards repatriation or reburial of the crania of enslaved individuals within this Collection."

In August 1862, at a critical juncture of the American Civil War, when Washington, DC, itself was in danger, the surgeon general, William A. Hammond, announced the establishment of an Army Medical Museum for "specimens of medical or surgical interest."[16] There would be more than 600,000 battlefield deaths in the course of the war. The first curator of the Army Medical Museum, Dr. John H. Brinton, took it upon himself to collect corpses and body parts from battlefields and military hospitals.

> Many and many a putrid heap have I had dug out of trenches where they had been buried, in the supposition of an everlasting rest, and ghoul-like work have I done, amid surrounding gatherings of wondering surgeons, and scarcely less wondering doctors. But all saw that I was in earnest and my example was infectious. By going thus from corps hospital to corps hospital, a real interest was excited as to the Museum work, and an active co-operation was eventually established.[17]

Soon after the Civil War came to an end, the Indian wars started up again. In April 1867, Surgeon General Barnes instructed medical officers to "collect crania together with the specimens of Indian weapons, dress, implements, diet, and medicines . . . To aid the progress of anthropological sciences by obtaining measurements of a large number of skulls of the aboriginal races of North America."[18] Acting Assistant Surgeon R. B. Hintz promptly sent in a Crow Indian war club, a set of elk antlers, and "two Indian Crania (perfect) which I exhumed myself. The one is a 'Spokane' and the other a 'Pagan' skull."[19] These were the first of many. Soon the museum could boast over 3,000 skulls and other body parts, including specimens from "the majority of the existing tribes of Indians, and of the extinct tribes of the historic period" and "skulls of the white and black races."[20]

In 1867, the collection was installed in Ford's Theatre on Tenth Street in Washington, DC, which had been shut following Lincoln's assassination there two years earlier. Dr. J. J. Woodward, one of the six doctors who performed the autopsy on Lincoln, approved: "what nobler monument could the nation erect to his memory than this somber treasure-house to the study of disease and injury, mutilation and death?"[21] By the 1880s the collection was attracting around 40,000 visitors a year.[22] However, army surgeons were losing interest in comparative anatomy. The Army Medical Museum turned over "a collection of 2,206 human crania, representing mainly the Indian tribes, ancient and modern, of North America" to the U.S. National Museum at the Smithsonian Institution.[23]

In 1903, the National Museum appointed its first curator of physical anthropology. Aleš Hrdlička had been a student of Paul Broca in Paris. He brought state-of-the-art measurement techniques to the museum and greatly expanded the already extensive collection of body parts.[24] "The anthropological collection as a whole is arranged on the basis of race and type, and further subdivided according to geographical distribution," he wrote.[25] This was thoroughly up to date, but Hrdlička's theories were eccentric. He believed that humanity first emerged in Europe, refused to accept the Asian origin of North American Indians, and rejected Darwin's theory of the primate ancestry of the first hominids.

The development of racial studies in the second half of the nineteenth century put a premium on the collection of racially diverse specimens. Anthropologists—Franz Boas, among others—began to collect human remains alongside ethnographic and archaeological artefacts for sale to museums.

Boas was warned by James Teit, a member of the Jesup expedition with long experience in British Columbia, that although collecting bones from prehistoric burial grounds "will be all right," the Indians "guard with very jealous (and religious) care any burial grounds in which they know for certain that their ancestors are buried."[26] So Boas took precautions. Visiting British Columbia in the summer of 1888 he was permitted to visit a prison to measure Indian inmates. He engaged a photographer who took pictures of prisoners, including "five beautifully tattooed Haidas." The photographer then took Boas to an island in the harbour where he said Indian skulls could be found. "We discovered that someone had stolen all the skulls, but we found a complete skeleton without [a] head," Boas wrote to his wife, Marie. "It is most unpleasant work to steal bones from a grave, but what is the use, someone has to do it . . . Besides having scientific value these skeletons are worth money." And again, "I dreamed of skulls and bones all last night. I dislike very much working with this stuff; i.e., collecting it, not having it." Visiting one remote community, Boas asked the photographer to "photograph the village while I tried to get a skull. I wanted him to do this in order to distract their attention . . . Of course I did not tell the photographer (a stuttering idiot) what I wanted until we were there. I took a skull and the entire lower portion of the man."[27] Boas later made contact with two brothers who had a business selling skeletal remains to scientists. Boas wrote to Marie that he "measured frantically all day long—about seventy-five skulls." The Smithsonian bought eighty-five crania and fourteen complete skeletons from him.[28]

Racial science remained the central preoccupation of physical anthropologists until the Second World War. After the Holocaust its premises were subjected to critical scrutiny.

Julian Huxley, the grandson of Thomas Henry Huxley, played a part in developing an "evolutionary synthesis" of the theories of Mendel and Darwin. Although once an advocate of eugenics, and despite his unselfconscious anti-Semitic prejudices, he was appalled by Nazi racism. "Races," he insisted, were social constructs rather than biological entities. Phenotypical features were a poor guide to psychological or intellectual traits. In 1936, he and the Cambridge professor of anthropology, Alfred Haddon, ridiculed the Nazi stereotype of the Aryan: "as blond as Hitler, as dolichocephalic as Rosenberg, as tall as Goebbels, as slender as Goering, and as manly as Streicher."[29]

When Huxley became the first director of UNESCO, he launched a series of short books on race, including essays by Michel Leiris and Claude Lévi-Strauss. The series was introduced in 1950 by an eleven-page pamphlet, *The Race Question*, written by Huxley himself. It concluded that:

> For all practical social purposes "race" is not so much a biological phenomenon as a social myth. The myth "race" has created an enormous amount of human and social damage. In recent years it has taken a heavy toll in human lives and caused untold suffering. It still prevents the normal development of millions of human beings and deprives civilization of the effective co-operation of productive minds. The biological differences between ethnic groups should be disregarded from the standpoint of social acceptance and social action. The unity of mankind from both the biological and social viewpoint is the main thing.

The old guard, however, insisted that biological race mattered, and science had nothing to do with politics, let alone genocide. In 1962, a professor at the University of Pennsylvania, Carleton Coon, published a massive study, *The Origin of Races*, which repeated old orthodoxies about racial typology and accorded Europeans a privileged evolutionary status (best adapted, most advanced, the first representatives of *Homo sapiens*). That year,

Sherwood Washburn, the dean of American physical anthropology, was due to deliver the presidential address at the annual meeting of the American Anthropological Association. The executive asked him to address the controversy which Coon's book had provoked. The auditorium was packed. Washburn dismissed Coon's ideas as "a reversion to nineteenth-century typological thinking" which was of "no use to the profession whatsoever."[30] Irven Devore, an up-and-coming young Harvard anthropologist, recalled that the speech received a standing ovation, but "as I looked around, some of the physical anthropologists had not even stood, and many were standing glumly and not even applauding, much less cheering."[31] Yet within a decade American physical anthropologists abandoned race studies. Typological thinking was out; a statistically based population genetics was in.

But not quite everywhere. In 1993, I visited the human evolution display in the Museum of Natural History in Vienna. A series of single skulls supposedly represented regional racial types. In the European display there was a "gypsy" skull, but for some reason Jews were not represented. In the small Asian section a case exhibited two skeletons: one was labelled "Japanese," the other "Indonesian." The exhibit culminated with an array of three skulls. These were labelled australopithecine, chimpanzee and "Bushman." The clear implication was that "Bushmen" were throwbacks to some more primitive species.

My colleagues in Vienna told me that they protested about this homage to Nazi science but were reprimanded for introducing political considerations into what was strictly scientific business. On their suggestion, I raised the matter in a letter in *Nature*.[32] Press reports followed in London and then in Vienna. The exhibition was closed. A few years later the museum unveiled an up-to-date presentation of human evolution.

As racial studies fell out of favour, anthropology museums were stuck with their collections of skulls and skeletons. Studies of human remains were increasingly governed by strict protocols, involving tedious bureaucratic processes. Some research carried on, particularly historical studies of diet, health, stature and migration. Like other branches of human biology, physical anthropology was revolutionised when Francis Crick and James Watson published the double-helix structure of DNA in *Nature*, on 25 April 1953. Minimally invasive techniques were quickly developed to study evolution, health, migration and the genetic make-up and relationships of human groups. But displays of human remains were now a very sensitive matter.

Testifying before the U.S. Senate's select committee on Indian affairs in 1987, Robert McCormick Adams, secretary of the Smithsonian Institution, revealed that the U.S. National Museum of Natural History held some 34,000 bones and skulls, approximately 42.5 per cent of which could be identified as North American Indian. A further 11.9 per cent were Inuit. (Remains of white people accounted for about 20 per cent of the collection. Just over 5 per cent were identified as remains of Black people. At least 20 per cent were unclassified.)[33]

"Tribal reaction to Secretary Adams' testimony was swift," the select committee reported, "and in the months which followed, Indian tribes around the country called for the repatriation of those human remains that could be identified as associated with a specific tribe or region."[34]

Senator Inouye of Alaska, chair of the Senate select committee on Indian affairs, proposed that the remains should be returned to tribal authorities for burial and a memorial erected in Washington, DC. In 1989, Congress mandated the creation of a National Museum of the American Indian within the Smithsonian system. The law also required the secretary of the Smithsonian Institution to inventory the U.S. National Museum's holdings of Indian and native Hawaiian human remains and "funerary objects." Unless the museum could demonstrate that an item had been freely traded, by someone who was authorised to transfer it, a claim for repatriation could be lodged by a federally recognised Indian tribe. The tribe would then have to demonstrate what Congress termed a relationship of "cultural affiliation." In 1990, the Native American Graves Protection and

Repatriation Act (NAGPRA) extended similar provisions to any museum in receipt of federal grants. And the range of objects that might be subject to restitution was expanded to include artefacts that qualified as "sacred" or as "cultural patrimony." (All these terms would soon be submitted to legal scrutiny in a series of court cases.)

Directors of leading museums wrote a joint letter to Congress warning that the legislation would set up "a ruinously expensive, adversarial, and lawyer-dominated process that would financially cripple the museums, remove uniquely valuable collections from the public domain, and deprive future generations, including Native Americans, of knowledge of an important part of human history."[35] Native American spokesmen countered that repatriation was justified on political, cultural, even spiritual grounds. "Repatriation is the most potent political metaphor for cultural revival that is going on at this time," according to Richard West, a Cheyenne Peace Chief and the first director of the National Museum of the American Indian.[36] The stakes were high, controversies sometimes heated.[37] Looking back, Jay Stowsky, the University of California's director of research and policy, was moved to remark: "I haven't seen this level of viciousness before—and you should remember that I was working in the Clinton White House."[38]

The legislation was shepherded through Congress by Senator John McCain, who was now chairman of the Senate committee on Indian Affairs. He remarked that its passage "marks the end of a long process for many Indian tribes and museums. The subject of repatriation is charged with high emotions in both the Native American community and the museum community. I believe this bill represents a true compromise."[39] Secretary Adams testified before the congressional select committee that "The case for the prior rights of descendants would appear to be very strong, even if the directness of their descent is only tentatively established. But there is also plausibility to the claims of science. Only the analysis of these specimens, with marvellous new laboratory techniques that are being introduced more and more rapidly, holds out the promise of tracing the exact derivation of recent groups from their more remote ancestors."[40] However, Adams soon conceded defeat. "When this came to the court of public opinion, we were going to lose." An opinion poll backed him up. Just 19 per cent of respondents opposed NAGPRA.[41]

As soon as the new regulations were mooted, American museum curators shuttered exhibits of skulls and bones. Then the hard slog began. The Smithsonian set out to identify and catalogue the thousands of body parts stored in its drawers and filing cabinets. These included bones collected by army surgeons during the Civil War and the Indian Wars to illustrate the effects of traumatic injuries; skulls assembled in the nineteenth century for research on race and evolution; mummies found in the American West and in Alaska from the 1870s, which were a big draw for museums; scalps and shrunken heads that were deemed to be of ethnographic interest; and among other curiosities, the pickled brain of Major John Wesley Powell, the first director of the Bureau of American Ethnology.

The museum directors were right about one thing at least: the process of repatriation would be extremely burdensome for all concerned. Tribal organisations grumbled about the bureaucracy involved, and the expense. The Navajo nation estimated that it would cost them $450,000 a year just to deal with all the paperwork that was required.[42] The Smithsonian Institution deployed ten scientists to work full-time on the return of human remains, in the meantime leaving some curatorial positions unfilled.

Even small university departments and museums had to review their collections. Margaret Bruchac recalls her experience between 2003 and 2010 as repatriation research liaison officer for Amherst and Smith Colleges:

> I found it necessary to track the collectors as much as the collections. This painstaking work entailed cross-referencing archaeological field notes, inventories, craniometric

records, faculty correspondence, and secretive departmen-
tal oral traditions (including stories of bones hidden in
faculty offices). The process also required considerable
inter-institutional diplomacy, to track materials that moved
through multiple institutions. I followed each piece of evidence forward, from the moment of excavation, through
processes of disarticulation, along various trajectories of
sale and circulation, to the end-point of curation. I also
compiled reports on "missing remains" that, despite being
well-documented on paper, were no longer physically
present in the collections.[43]

And yet the process of repatriation was slow. Diligent research
identified over 19,000 potentially relevant Native American
items in the holdings of the Smithsonian, but Samuel J. Redman
remarks that by 2016 fewer than 4,000 had been repatriated.[44]
Museums were sometimes charged with using delaying tactics.
According to one report, "some museums have responded to
the impending loss, potential illegality, and shifting cultural
interpretations of their native collections by restricting access
to information. Exhibits have been pulled from view, valuable
items have been placed under lock and key, and consultations
have been initiated in an often secretive manner."[45]

However, harassed curators must often wrestle with delicate, sometimes intractable problems. Documentation for
many specimens that were collected in the nineteenth century
is woefully incomplete. It is not always obvious whose ancestor's remains are in question, or who is the rightful owner of
particular artefacts, or whether certain ceremonial objects were
manufactured simply in order to be sold. The identification of
individual body parts is sometimes problematic, even impossible. Skeletons acquired from agents or dealers had often been
poorly sorted and labelled. "In some instances," writes Samuel J.
Redman, "bones were presumed to be similar enough to be
simply interchangeable within racial categories; if the jaw was
too broken or shattered for display, the museum could replace

the broken or missing bone with another similarly sized portion of a different Native American skeleton."[46] Some bones and skulls were collected from battlefields, but it was not always known on which side the dead man had fought. "Many tribes are also reluctant to claim unidentified remains because they do not want to risk burying enemies," according to Redman.

In 2010, new federal regulations made it easier for tribes to claim human remains of uncertain provenance. Nevertheless, Redman estimates that "only about 2.1 per cent of the culturally unidentifiable remains in museums have been claimed."[47] Even if body parts could be securely identified, it was not necessarily certain who had a rightful claim to them. Ben Nighthorse Campbell, a Cheyenne member of the U.S. Senate from Colorado, warned: "I know there are tribal conflicts within tribes on virtually every other subject, and I can perceive a tribal conflict on dealing with remains. I think it is a kind of big, unanswered area that we have to deal with before we *carte blanche* say we will give them all back."[48]

NAGPRA specified that ownership of human remains and "cultural artefacts" should be determined by "a preponderance of the evidence based upon geographical, kinship, biological, archaeological, linguistic, folkloric, oral tradition, historic, or other information or expert opinion." As David Hurst Thomas, curator of anthropology at the American Museum of Natural History, remarked: "No priority is given to one or other of these disparate sources of evidence."[49] Yet archaeological or historical sources sometimes contradicted oral traditions. "Making Native Americans the dominant power might make people feel better initially," a panel of museum curators complained, "but will do nothing in the long run for the heritage of the country or for Native Americans."[50]

There was also uncertainty as to who was entitled to lodge a claim. Old arguments started up again about who is an "Indian." The native North American population underwent huge demographic changes following European and African migration, and there was a significant level of population mixture.[51] Since 1960, the American census has permited respondents to self-identify as Indian. After 2000, a person could claim more than one racial or ethnic affiliation. However, in order to qualify for certain federal benefits, it is necessary to acquire a Certificate of Degree of Indian Blood from the Bureau of Indian Affairs. This involves submitting a genealogy, supported by birth certificates, to prove descent from a member of a federally recognised tribe, nation or pueblo. For official purposes, the actual proportion of Indian blood required varies from one benefit to another. Tribes have their own rules about the degree of blood required for membership. Most demand that a person must have one or sometimes two native grandparents in order to be recognised as a member, although the Cherokee, for example, have no such requirement.

Even more sensitive is the treatment of Black members of Indian communities. Before and after their forced removal to Oklahoma in 1830, the "Five Civilised Tribes" of the Southeastern U.S.A. were embroiled in an often unequal and conflict-ridden relationship with African Americans. Philip Deloria, a Harvard historian, quotes the hard-hitting summation of Buddy Cox, a twenty-first-century Creek, nephew of an important chief: "We owned some, we were some, and we slept with some."[52]

After the Civil War, descendants of African Americans were settled in Indian reservations, spoke local languages, adopted local customs. And then, between 1979 and 2007, several tribal authorities chose to exclude the descendants of freed persons from tribal citizenship. ("It might seem perverse," Deloria comments, "that in 1979, with the memory of the civil-rights movement still fresh, Indian tribes began to restrict citizenship on the basis of racial difference.")

David Hurst Thomas pointed out that the legislation "defines as 'Indian' anybody who belongs to an 'Indian tribe,' a definitional shift that places a tremendous burden on that deceptively simple word tribe (which itself has multiple definitions and shades of meaning)."[53] A Supreme Court decision in 1901, *Montoya v. United States*, which is still cited in recent court judgements, defined a tribe as "a body of [1] Indians of the same or similar race, united in [2] a community under [3] one leadership or government, and [4] inhabiting a particular, though sometimes ill-defined territory." Each of these criteria is highly problematic, and it remains unclear whether all conditions must be met—in full?—in order to gain federal recognition as a tribe.

Following years of intensive lobbying, the Indian Reorganization Act of 1934 granted federal recognition to over 500 American tribes. (There are now 562 federally recognised tribes plus certain Native Alaskan and Hawaiian organisations.) It is, however, often difficult, even impossible, to trace relationships between the communities that were officially recognised as "tribes" in 1934 and the sometimes nomadic, often loosely organised, sometimes ephemeral local associations whose members lived through the tragic wars and population movements of the second half of the nineteenth century, when so many Native American skulls, skeletons and ceremonial paraphernalia found their way into American museums.

Two decades after the passage of NAGPRA, museums were eager to clear out their remaining holdings of body parts. But unexpected problems cropped up. Some Christian communities confessed that they were not sure how to perform reburial rites.[54] When the Museum of the University of New Mexico informed local Zuni authorities that it held human remains and grave goods that came from Zuni settlements, they responded that since the clan identities of the dead were unknown the appropriate rituals could not be determined. "Some Native communities have had to construct new, often pan-Indian, traditions for the reburial of individuals who were never meant to be disturbed, in hopes of putting their spirits to rest," Michael Brown and Margaret Bruchac note.[55] Yet there have been some dramatic mass interments. In April 2006, the skeletal remains of 1,590 people were buried in the Mesa Verde National Park in the presence of representatives of the Hopi Nation and the Zuni, Zia and Acoma Pueblos.[56]

Rumours of grave-robbery still crop up from time to time. *The New York Times* reported in February 2009 that descendants of the Apache Chief Geronimo were suing Skull and Bones, a secret society at Yale University. They charged that in 1918: "Prescott Bush—father of President George H. W. Bush and grandfather of President George W. Bush—broke into the grave [of Geronimo] with some classmates during World War I and made off with the skull, two bones, a bridle and some stirrups, all of which were put on display at the group's clubhouse in New Haven, known as the Tomb."[57] That case was apparently dropped—or settled—before coming to court. In 1928, for some reason, the army concreted over Geronimo's unmarked grave and erected a tombstone.

A better documented case involved the revered anthropologist Franz Boas and a distinguished institution, the American Museum of Natural History. Six Greenland Eskimos—four adults and two boys—were brought to New York in 1897 by Robert Peary, an American naval officer and Arctic explorer. One of the original party soon returned to Greenland with Peary. According to Kirsten Hastrup, an ethnographer of the Thule region, "When he told his old compatriots about America, its buildings and trams, they took him for a liar, and he was forever known as the Big Liar. He hardly ever talked about it again, moved to a very remote headland—and lived comfortably hunting reindeer, until his longing for more company drove him back to new brawls. A long story."[58]

The remaining Greenlanders were accommodated in the American Museum of Natural History, where they were studied by Boas and his student, Alfred Kroeber. Three adults and one boy died of tuberculosis. One of the deceased, Qisuk, was survived by his son, Minik, who was then about five years old. The other Greenlanders suggested that Minik should be killed, which they said was customary in the circumstances. Kroeber was also told that according to Greenland custom, the bodies and personal belongings should be disposed of after death and not mentioned again. Kroeber nevertheless arranged a funeral for Qisuk. But it was faked. Technicians working in the museum's laboratory prepared a substitute corpse for the burial.[59]

Qisuk's body was whisked away for an autopsy, and the brain and skeleton were deposited in the museum. Hrdlička published a report on Qisuk's brain.

Years later, Minik discovered the truth. "I felt as though I must have died then and there," he said. "I prayed and wept. I went straight to the director and implored him to let me bury my father. He would not." Boas explained that the fake funeral had been performed "to appease the boy, and keep him from discovering that his father's body had been chopped up and the bones placed in the collection of the institution."[60]

The sad fate of this party came to wider attention in 1986 with the publication of *Give Me My Father's Body: The Life of Minik, the New York Eskimo,* by a Canadian writer, Kenn Harper. Stirred by Harper's account, Edmund Carpenter, an Arctic specialist in the American Museum of Natural History, and Jorgen Meldgaard, an archaeologist in the Danish National Museum, approached town officials at Qaanaaq, the village in Greenland from which Minik and his father had come. To their surprise, they found that the locals had little interest in bringing the skeletons back home. For one thing, the people who had gone away to New York—willingly, their townsfolk believed—were not Christians. Nevertheless, at the request of his bishop, the village pastor agreed to arrange a funeral. The Royal Danish Air Force flew the remains to Thule. Edmund Carpenter was present for the interment. He asked one participant how he felt about the return of the bones. "Embarrassment," the man replied. An elderly woman said that if the museum people wanted a burial, that was all right with her, but if the bones remained in New York that would be fine too.[61] (Kirsten Hastrup confirms that there is little local interest in the episode, and that people are reluctant to discuss the fate of the bodies.)

Another much-publicised case involved Kroeber again, by now a professor at the University of California at Berkeley and director of the university museum of anthropology. It had to do with the remains of a man who was known as Ishi. On 29 August

1911, a middle-aged American Indian was found scavenging near Oroville in California and taken into custody by the police. He had evidently spent three years on his own in the wilds after his family was killed in an encounter with a gang of cattlemen. The man spoke no English, or any of the major Californian Indian languages. Kroeber took him in, gave him the name of Ishi, which means "human" in the Yana language, and employed him at the university museum where he earned a small salary as a part-time janitor, and gave demonstrations of craft-making on Sundays. "He has been free to return to his old home and manner of living ever since being with us," Kroeber wrote to the Bureau of Indian Affairs in 1914, "but much prefers his present condition."[62]

In March 1916, Ishi died of tuberculosis. Kroeber was out of town, but he sent telegrams urging the medical school not to dissect the body. To Edward Gifford, the young acting director of the university museum, he wrote: "Please shut down on this. We propose to stand by our friends. If there is any talk of the interests of science, then say for me that science can go to hell."[63]

But it was too late. Ishi's body was cremated. His brain had been removed. Kroeber put it in a Pueblo Indian pottery jar which he wrapped in a deerskin and sent off to Aleš Hrdlička at the U.S. National Museum. Orin Starn, author of *Ishi in Two Worlds*, tracked down the accession entry, dated 1917. "Ishi's brain had been catalogued as Item 60884, just below 'Ivory charms' from Abyssinia and a 'Set of Current Postage Stamps of the Philippine Islands.'" It was added to Hrdlička's collection of some 225 human brains in Tank 6 in the Smithsonian's laboratory, alongside that of the founder of the Bureau of Ethnology, Major John Wesley Powell.[64]

Ishi had no surviving relatives. A book about him by Kroeber's wife, Theodora, was called *Ishi the Last of His Tribe*. When, eight decades after his death, activists identified Ishi as a candidate for repatriation, the Smithsonian Institution—after some obfuscation and delay—approached representatives of various

Californian tribes, before settling on one grouping whose language was related to Yana.[65] Ishi's remains were buried in August
2000.

Plans for burial sometimes raise tricky legal questions, left open
by the Native American Graves Protection and Repatriation Act
(NAGPRA). The category of "tribe" caused enough difficulties
on its own, but NAGPRA also laid it down that in order to qualify
as "Native American," human remains and artefacts must be
"of, or relating to, a tribe, people, or culture that is indigenous
to the United States" (NAGPRA, Section 2). This clause would
bedevil one of the most difficult tests of NAGPRA, the case of
Kennewick Man—"the Ancient One."

On 28 July 1996, two college students watching an annual
hydroplane race found a skull floating in a reservoir on the
Columbia River near Kennewick, Washington. The coroner
of Benton County called in a forensic anthropologist, James
Chatters, who was regularly consulted by the local coroner's
office.[66] Chatters recovered a further 350 bones from the site and
he reconstructed an almost complete skeleton. His first impression was that the man had died fairly recently and that he was
Caucasoid—that is to say, "European." Tests then revealed that
the skeleton was 8,900 to 9,000 years old, making this one of
the most remarkable finds of ancient human remains in North
America. Could it really be European? A report in *The New
Yorker* magazine had the tantalising lead: "Was someone here
before the Native Americans?"[67]

Since the skeleton had been discovered on federal property
it was the responsibility of the U.S. Army Corps of Engineers.
Representatives of American Indian tribes requested the right to
bury it. Eight anthropologists, including Dennis Stanford, director of the Paleoindian Program at the U.S. National Museum,
asked for permission to make a scientific study of the bones before
they were interred. "Our oral history goes back 10,000 years,"
responded Armand Minthorn, a leader of the Umatilla tribe,
whose ancestral home was in the Columbia Plateau region. "We

know how time began and how Indian people were created. They can say whatever they like, the scientists. They are being disrespectful."[68] Nudged by the White House, the Corps of Engineers agreed with the Indians. The anthropologists went to court. Their lawyer submitted that the "subtly implied message" of the Corps of Engineers "is that somehow Native Americans own the history of this country."[69] After five years of litigation the Oregon District Court ruled that it was impossible to determine the "cultural affiliation" of such an ancient skeleton, or even to identify Kennewick Man as "indigenous." The skeleton could therefore be studied by scientists (*Bonnichsen et al. v. United States et al.*, 2002). In 2004, the Ninth Circuit Court of Appeals confirmed the judgment.

NAGPRA admitted claims to bones or grave goods only from representatives of a "tribe, people, or culture that is indigenous to the United States." The key word here was "*is*." At one point Senator John McCain suggested that the difficulty could be finessed by changing the relevant clause to read "is or was indigenous."[70] This proposal was not followed through, perhaps because it would raise further complications. A commentator remarked: "The next debate may very well be over the meaning of *indigenous*, instead of the meaning of *is*."[71]

In the event, further scientific research settled the fate of Kennewick Man. In 2015, a team of physical anthropologists at the University of Copenhagen published a DNA study of a 0.2 gram flake of the Ancient One's finger bone and concluded that he was indeed closely related genetically to Indian populations now living in the Kennewick region.[72] In September 2016 Congress allowed a coalition of local tribes to take ownership of the skeleton. In February 2017, it was buried in the presence of some two hundred members of five Columbia Plateau tribes.

Despite these campaigns for reburial, the burial of the dead was by no means general practice in precolonial North America. "Among people of the Northwest Coast and Great Plains, the dead were placed above ground, in boxes on stilts or wrapped in blankets on tops of scaffolds," Chip Colwell writes. "Sometimes they were reverently laid in the branches of trees. Along the coasts, sometimes a canoe was simply placed over the body by the shore." In the eastern half of the continent bodies were cremated, or laid to rest in communal earth mounds. Some communities "buried their dead under the floors of their houses, in ceremonial chambers, or amid the debris and refuse piled outside their villages."[73]

But in the U.S.A. today, burial is widely agreed to be appropriate, even for old bones of uncertain origin. Perhaps this is because beliefs about the afterlife are widely shared. According to the Roper Center for Public Opinion Research at Cornell University, roughly three-quarters of Americans say that they believe in life after death. Puzzlingly, a slightly larger proportion, around 80 per cent, believe in heaven. On the other hand, only two-thirds believe in hell.[74]

Carl Sagan—astronomer, cosmologist and superstar science writer—visited the Musée de l'Homme in Paris at some time in the 1970s. "You had the sense of a museum of the second order," he wrote, "in which were stored not so much materials that might be of interest as materials that had once been of interest."[75] The affable director, Yves Coppens, led him into remote corners of the storerooms, where he was shown "more disturbing collections": "perfectly preserved human heads," Amazonian shrunken heads, jars of human embryos, and then "in a still more remote corner of this wing of the museum," shelf upon shelf of human brains, preserved in formalin.[76]

A few years later, Sagan's close friend, the brilliant writer and biologist Stephen Jay Gould, was given his own private tour of the stores of the Musée de l'Homme. Like Sagan, he was shown the skull of Descartes and the brain of Paul Broca. On the shelf above he noticed three jars that contained the dissected genitalia of three women. The jars were labelled *une négresse, une péruvienne*, and *la Venus Hottentotte*. Gould drily remarked that nineteenth-century scientists were fixated on the brains of great white men and the sexual organs of women of colour.[77]

The "Hottentot Venus" was a South African woman, Sara Baartman. On 6 March 2002, the president of France decreed that her skeleton and body cast should be returned to South Africa. (The jar that held her sexual organs was accidentally dropped and smashed in 1983.)[78] Documentation of Sara's early life is sparse. According to an authoritative historical study by Clifton Crais and Pamela Scully, she was born in the 1770s on the eastern frontier of the Dutch East India Company settlement on Africa's southern tip.[79] This was a violent, turbulent, rapidly changing land, ravaged by smallpox. Long-established populations of Xhosa and Khoi (whom the Dutch called "Hottentots") were subjected to the overlordship of immigrant Dutch "Boer" farmers. Yet Sara was brought up not far from the London missionary station of Bethelsdorp in what is now the Eastern Cape Province, where two radical missionaries, Johannes van der Kemp and James Read, preached a provocative mixture of evangelical Christian doctrine and French revolutionary egalitarianism. (One of Sara's sisters and two of her brothers would find refuge at the Bethelsdorp mission.)

Identities and affiliations were in flux in those remote borderlands. The Baartman family was probably associated with a Khoi community, the Ghonaqua, but *Baartman*—bearded man—is a Dutch name, and Sara spoke the local Dutch dialect, presumably alongside a Khoi language. When she and her siblings were born, the family were retainers of a Boer farmer. Sara's mother and the children were domestic servants. Her father tended livestock, sometimes driving cattle hundreds of miles to market in Cape Town. During one of these journeys he was killed by a Bushman band. Sara's mother died young. In the mid-1790s, aged about twenty, Sara moved to Cape Town, a lively, cosmopolitan port city. As Crais and Scully write, she left the frontier "at the very moment the Ghonaqua disappeared as an independent people."[80] This was also the era of the Napoleonic Wars, and in 1795 the Royal Navy seized the Cape for Britain.

Sara travelled to Cape Town with Pieter Cesars, a "free black," whose grandparents had been slaves. His employer, a rich German butcher, took Sara on as a servant. She had three children, all of whom died in infancy. After a few years she moved into the household of Hendrik Cesars, brother of Pieter, in a Free Black community on the outskirts of the city, where she was employed as a washerwoman and wet nurse.

In around 1809, a Scots army officer, Alexander Dunlop, a doctor at the Slave Lodge in Cape Town, entered Sara's life. The British had abolished the slave trade in 1807, the Slave Lodge was due to be closed, and Dunlop was desperate for money. Hendrik Cesars was heavily in debt. The two men agreed on a plan: Sara would be taken to London where she would be displayed in raunchy freak shows. Sara agreed, but only on condition that Hendrik came too.

By the time she left the Cape for England, "Sara Baartman had become a worldly woman in her thirties," Crais and Scully write. "She walked, and worked, and lived in the commercial mélange that was Cape Town. She wore skirts and tops and dresses, humble yes, but European clothing nonetheless. She was multilingual, knowing her own language, Dutch, and probably a smattering of English, and had heard the many other languages in the cacophonous Cape." Dunlop had promised her "Beads, clothes and support." "Who will give me anything here?" she had asked Cesar's wife, Anna.[81]

In London, Dunlop arranged for an exhibition—a performance, really—something between a freak show and a strip-tease—in the Egyptian Hall in Piccadilly. Posters represented Sara almost naked, with huge, monstrous buttocks. An advertisement in the London papers proclaimed that "the Venus" "has been seen already by the principal literati in this Metropolis who were all greatly astonished, as well as highly gratified with the sight of so wonderful a specimen of the human race."[82]

The anti-slavery African Association brought a law suit, alleging that Sara had been enslaved.[83] A leading ally of the abolitionist William Wilberforce, Zachary Macaulay, wrote in the *Morning Chronicle*: "This poor female is made to walk, to dance, to shew herself, not for own advantage but for the profit of her master, who, when she appeared tired, holds up a stick to her, like the wild beast keepers, to intimidate her into obedience."[84] However, Sara testified (in the presence of Cesars) that she had entered freely into a contract to exhibit herself. The case was dismissed, though the judge did suggest that a prosecution for indecency might have a chance of success.

In September 1814, Sara was taken to Paris, where an animal trainer exhibited her in aristocratic salons and on public stages in the Palais Royale. She was even the subject of a burlesque, *La Venus Hottentote*, by Théaulon de Lambert. As Zoë Strother sums up the plot, "Adolphe, a young naïf wounded by the fickleness of French women, and inspired by stories of the noble savage, vows to marry '*une femme sauvage*' . . . His cousin Amelie passes herself off as the 'Hottentot Venus' by dressing up in some brightly coloured clothing, and pretending not to know French." Adolph is charmed. But then he is confronted with a picture of Sara Baartman. Shocked, he falls into his cousin's arms.[85]

Sara also attracted the attention of the leading scientist in France, Georges Cuvier, director of the Museum of Natural History. He commissioned four artists to draw Sara in the nude and was particularly interested in the artificial elongation of the *labia minora* reputedly practised in the Cape, producing an effect that was known as the "Hottentot apron." "There is nothing more celebrated in natural history," Cuvier noted. However, Sara would not allow an examination. "She kept her apron concealed, either between her thighs or still more deeply," according to Cuvier.[86]

Sara died a year later, on 29 December 1815, perhaps of smallpox, perhaps pneumonia, perhaps syphilis. According to Cuvier, she died of drink. ("What flattered her taste more than anything else was brandy. I might even ascribe her death to an excess of drink to which she gave herself up during her last illness.")[87] Cuvier was granted permission to dissect the corpse. A body cast was made, the skeleton cleaned and articulated. Nine of the sixteen pages of Cuvier's report described Sara's genitalia, breasts, buttocks and pelvis. The external genitalia were removed and preserved in a bottle. Another bottle contained her brain, also carefully measured by Cuvier.[88] The question Cuvier posed was whether Sara was a member of the species *Homo sapiens*. His report did not reach a firm conclusion although he remarked on her quick understanding and linguistic skills, and praised *sa main charmante* (her charming hand).[89]

The "Hottentot Venus" became a fixture in the next generation's accounts of human "racial types." Sara's body cast was displayed at the Universal Exhibition in Paris in 1889, one of the last great European World's Fairs. In the first half of the twentieth century it was exhibited in the Museum of Natural History and then in the Musée de l'Homme. In 1994, the cast of Sara's body was a centrepiece of an exhibition at Paris's new art museum, the Musée d'Orsay. The title of the exhibition was: "nineteenth-century ethnographic sculpture from the Hottentot Venus to Gauguin's Tehura." Sara's body cast had been translated from scientific construct to work of art.

In 1994, South Africa held its first democratic elections. The African National Congress came to power nationally. Nelson Mandela became president. But the ANC did not win one of the key provinces in the country, the Western Cape. The majority of the so-called coloured population of the province, descendants of Khoisan and of slaves brought to the Cape from Dutch colonies in Asia, gave their votes to apartheid-era political parties.

Sara Baartman became an icon of a newly invoked ethnic identity, the Khoisan, which claimed a special Indigenous status, anterior to that of the Black majority population. Khoisan NGOs began to lobby for the return of Sara's remains. The South African government invited the country's leading physical anthropologist, Phillip Tobias, to begin negotiations with Henry de Lumley, director of the Musée de l'Homme. The official French view was that museum collections were inalienable, part of the national patrimony. There was also a reaction against the suggestion, made by some activists, that Cuvier was a monster of racism and colonial arrogance, and, moreover, a voyeur. But Mandela intervened. Assurances were given that this was a one-off, not the harbinger of a cascade of demands for restitution. It was agreed that France and the New South Africa shared a veneration for human rights. In February 2002, after six years of negotiation, the French National Assembly unanimously passed a law allowing Sara's skeleton and body cast to be removed from the museum and presented to the South African government.

The apotheosis of Sara Baartman now became a fraught polit-ical issue in South Africa. Rival Khoisan associations claimed her as their ancestress. Tobias suggested that DNA tests could sort that out, but activists responded that any further scientific studies of Sara's remains would be "invasive" and "neo-fascist." "Would Sara Baartman have wanted to have her body researched?" demanded Yvette Abrahams, a professor of women's and gender studies at the University of the Western Cape.[90]

South African government ministers proposed that Sara should be regarded as an icon of African womanhood, a mute witness to the humiliations experienced by generations of women under colonialism. Her remains, and her body cast, were buried on 9 August 2002, which was both International Indigenous Peoples' Day and South Africa's Women's Day. South Africa's second president, Thabo Mbeki, delivered a graveside oration. He said that Sara's life, a tragic epic of racism, oppres-sion and violence, epitomised the history of all South Africa's oppressed women. The villains of this story were the architects of the European Enlightenment: Montesquieu, Diderot and Voltaire. They and their heir, Cuvier, were the true barbarians, not the poor defenceless Sara Baartman.[91]

Within a few months of the state burial, Sara's grave, on a hilltop near the small town of Hankey, was marred by graffiti, vandalised by relic hunters, perhaps even subjected to thefts of body parts for use in *muti*, ritual infusions. To protect it, the grave was concreted over and surrounded by tall green metal bars. "Most everyone in South Africa knows about Sara Baartman and her history," Crais and Scully conclude. "Very few people voyage to this area to visit Sara Baartman's grave."[92]

A puzzling feature of these cases is the taken-for-granted dogma that body parts should be buried. In early modern Europe, graves were regularly turned over to make room for new burials, as in the gravedigger scene in *Hamlet*, where the skull of poor Yorick, the court jester, was dug up as a grave was prepared for Ophelia. (Hamlet asked the gravedigger how long it took before a corpse decomposed. "Faith, if he be not rotten before he die— as we have many pocky corses nowadays that will scarce hold the laying in—he will last you some eight year or nine year. A tanner will last you nine year.")

Not everyone was guaranteed even temporary tenure of a personal grave. In seventeenth- and eighteenth-century Europe, according to Michael Kammen, "only an estimated 5–7 per cent of the dead escaped the fate of a common trench."[93] The turn-over in graveyards accelerated as the population of Europe's cities expanded in the eighteenth century. Every now and then a graveyard would burst at the seams, spewing out skeletons, so skulls and bones were transferred to ossuaries. In the 1770s, Paris adapted a tunnel network associated with ancient stone quarries: the "Catacombs of Paris" would eventually store the remains of some 6 million people (among them Montesquieu, Racine and Robespierre). Opened to the public in 1874, it became a tourist attraction.

The heads of saints were on show, elaborately mounted, in many European cathedrals. Some could be touched, even kissed, by devotees. Skulls and skeletons also featured as memento mori. Baroque churches in Europe decorated whole chapels with hundreds of skeletons, mounted on the walls, hanging from the ceilings. This fashion began with the construction of the Church of Our Lady of the Conception of the Capuchins, commissioned by Pope Urban VIII in Rome in 1626. The bones of thousands of Capuchin friars line the walls of the crypt. Mark Twain visited in 1867, and he described the scene in *The Innocents Abroad:*

> We stopped a moment in a small chapel in the church . . . and then we descended into the vast vault underneath. Here was a spectacle for sensitive nerves! . . . There were six divisions in the apartment, and each division was ornamented with a style of decoration peculiar to itself—and these decorations were in every instance formed of human bones! There were shapely arches, built wholly of thigh bones; there were startling pyramids, built wholly of grinning skulls; there were quaint architectural structures of various kinds, built of shin bones and the bones of the arm; on the wall were elaborate frescoes, whose curving vines were made of knotted human vertebrae; whose delicate tendrils were made of sinews and tendons; whose flowers were formed of knee-caps and toe-nails.

The English Utilitarian philosopher, Jeremy Bentham, who died in 1832, invented an atheistic version of these saintly displays. Refusing burial, Bentham made his will with an alternative provision for the "disposal and preservation of the several parts of my bodily frame." His skeleton was to be "put together in such a manner as that the whole figure may be seated in a chair usually occupied by me when living, in the attitude in which I am sitting when engaged in thought in the course of time employed in writing." Then, "clad in one of the suits of black occasionally worn by me," it would be exhibited in a glass-fronted case.

Bentham himself termed this an "Auto Icon," and he sketched a ritual for it:

> If it should so happen that my personal friends and other disciples should be disposed to meet together on some day

or days of the year for the purpose of commemorating the founder of the greatest happiness system of morals and legislation my executor will from time to time cause to be conveyed to the room in which they meet the said box or case with the contents therein to be stationed in such part of the room as to the assembled company shall seem meet.[94]

The Auto Icon was furnished with a wax head. Bentham's brain was placed in a box beside it. This box was stolen in 1975 in a student prank, and is now in safekeeping in the stores of the Institute of Archaeology at the college. However, when I taught there in the early 1970s, the Senate of University College London—faithful to the college's Victorian reputation as "that godless place in Gower Street"—had the Auto Icon wheeled into meetings, a tradition allegedly maintained to this day. Bentham is minuted, the story goes, as "present but not voting."

TROPHIES OF EMPIRE, AFRICAN COURT ART, AND THE SLAVE TRADE

General Alfred-Amédée Dodds, the son of an Anglo-French father and an African mother, was born in 1842, in Senegal. A graduate of St. Cyr military academy (founded by Napoleon), he served in Réunion and in Vietnam, commanded French troops during the Boxer Rebellion, and saw action in the Franco-Prussian War in 1871. Later, he was based for more than two decades in French West Africa. In 1894, Dodds's troops crushed the ancient kingdom of Dahomey (which is in the present-day Republic of Bénin). The general donated royal Dahomean thrones and regalia, four intricately worked relief doors from the palace, three large statues of past kings (one in the form of a man-lion) and an iron statue of a god of war to the Trocadéro Museum of Ethnography in Paris.[1] In the early twenty-first century this booty was passed on to the Museum of the quai Branly–Jacques Chirac.

In August 2016, the newly elected president of the Republic of Bénin, Patrice Talon, demanded that France restore General Dodds's trophies to his country. The French Foreign Ministry responded that objects deposited in French museums are part of the national patrimony of France. They may not be alienated. A year later, however, another newly elected president, Emmanuel Macron of France, tweeted: "African heritage cannot be held prisoner by European museums."

President Macron was more circumspect in a speech at the University of Ouagadougou in Burkina Faso in November 2017: "I hope that within five years arrangements will have been put in place to permit the *temporary or definitive* restitution of African patrimony to Africa." (My emphasis.) A statement issued by the Élysée in 2020 was still more guarded:

> This is not a matter of the restitution of all African works that are held in French public and private collections. It is not about putting in question the constitutive principle of the French conception of museums, the inalienability of national collections. Africa's patrimony should continue to be exhibited in Paris just as in Dakar or Cotonou. Restitution should . . . encompass all forms of circulation: restitution, but also exhibitions, exchanges, loans, deposits, cooperative projects, etc.[2]

President Macron commissioned a report from a Senegalese economist, Felwine Sarr, and an art historian, Bénédicte Savoy. A specialist in the provenance of works of art, Savoy is now head of the department of art and cultural history at the Technical University in Berlin and a professor at the very prestigious Collège de France. But neither Sarr nor Savoy is known as an expert on African history or African art. Stéphane Martin, director of the Museum of the quai Branly, protested that they were *personnes engagées*, partisans. Parodying Macron's tweet, he added that "museums should not be held hostage to the painful history of colonialism."[3]

The Sarr/Savoy report, "The Restitution of African Cultural Heritage: Toward a New Relational Ethics," was published in November 2018, precisely a year after Macron's speech in Ouagadougou.[4] It placed the issue of restitution in the post-colonial context: "The crux of the problem: a system of appropriation and alienation—the colonial system—for which certain European Museums, unwillingly, have become the public archives."[5]

The report identified four categories of acquisitions made by French public museums during the colonial period (1885–1960) that should be repatriated to African countries:

(i)   spoils or trophies obtained during military operations;

(ii) objects collected in colonial times by military personnel or government officials;

(iii) collections made by scientific expeditions prior to 1960 ("only to be excused where there is evidence of consent");

(iv) objects on loan from African institutions.[6]

In addition, objects acquired after the colonial period "under proven conditions of illicit trade" should be restored.[7]

In November 2019, the French prime minister presented to the president of Senegal a ceremonial sword, made in France, that had belonged to a nineteenth-century local grandee, El Hadj Omar Tall. As Sally Price noted, however, "the sword, which was returned for a period of five years (what Macron apparently meant by 'temporary restitution') had, in fact, already been on display in the Museum of Black Civilisations in Dakar, on loan from France."[8] Then, in September 2020, the French parliament approved the despatch to the Republic of Bénin of twenty-six items appropriated by General Dodds from the Abomey palace.

The Republic of Bénin's President Talon came up with an ambitious plan for investment in tourism under the banner "Bénin revealed." Tourist resorts modelled on Club Med will be developed. At least four museums are planned. But Didier Houénoudé, director of the National Institute of Art, Archaeology and Culture, is concerned. "The authorities advertise the restitution of these objects to develop mass tourism," he says. "They risk being put to use to serve a purely commercial project."[9] Didier N'Dah, lecturer in archaeology and prehistory at the University of Abomey-Calavi in Cotonou, remarks that successive Bénin governments failed to invest in local archaeological projects. No provision is made for salvage archaeology when large building projects are undertaken by the World Bank or the Chinese government.[10]

Romuald Hazoumé is a Bénin artist, whose multimedia work *La Bouche du Roi*, "the king's mouth," was exhibited in the United Kingdom as part of the bicentenary of Britain's abolition of the slave trade and is now in the British Museum. The title invokes a port in the Bight of Benin from which slaves were transported to the Americas. In Hazoumé's work, inspired by an eighteenth-century print illustrating a slave ship, slaves are represented by hundreds of masks made from black plastic petrol cans. Their names are broadcast in a loop, mixed with sounds of chains and the creak of ships' timbers. Two masks on the ship's prow represent a white and a black king, the scales of justice placed ironically between them. Both are implicated in this crime.

Hazoumé complains that the rulers of the Republic of Bénin neglected the arts for half a century after independence. And he dismisses the promised return of the twenty-six royal Dahomean items as "a phony good idea," pointing to a large, empty display case in the Historical Museum of Abomey that once held a very special sword, symbol of the magical power of Dahomean kings. Stolen in 2001, the sword has not been recovered. "I have no desire to lose these things for a second time," Hazoumé comments.[11]

Concerns about security are shared by some museum directors. Silvie Memel-Kassi, director of the Musée des civilisations in Abidjan, told *The Art Newspaper* that there are some 4,000 objects from the Ivory Coast in the quai Branly and a similar number in the Metropolitan Museum in New York. She hoped that it would be possible to reach a negotiated settlement with France with respect to loans and returns, but sounded a note of caution. "Africa has to update its museums if it wants some of its heritage back," she said.[12] Dr. Memel-Kassi cited Léopold Sédar Senghor's praise of the museum in Abidjan, in 1971, as "one of the richest museums of *art nègre* in the world" and then noted that 120 pieces in that collection were stolen in 2010.[13]

The kingdoms of Asante, Dahomey and Edo border a roughly 400-mile-long stretch of coastline in the Gulf of Guinea in West

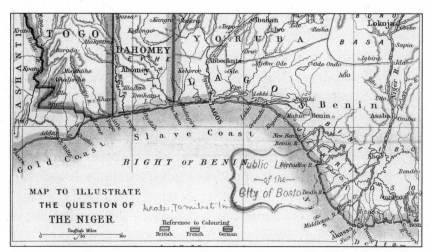

Map by W. and A. K. Johnston, showing the "Slave Coast" in
West Africa, 1898. Note Ashanti; Abomey, ancient capital of
the kingdom of Dahomey; and Benin. (By permission of the
Norman B. Leventhal Map Center, Boston Public Library.)

Africa. Known to geographers as the Bight of Benin, it was once
notorious as the Slave Coast. Some 12 million Africans were
transported from here to the Americas between the sixteenth
and nineteenth centuries.

Beginning in the late fifteenth century, Portuguese merchants pioneered trade between Europe, West Africa and the
Americas. They found willing partners in local kingdoms,
notably Dahomey (now in the Republic of Bénin), Edo (known,
confusingly, as Benin, and now in Nigeria), and later in Asante
(now in Ghana). These kingdoms sold slaves to European traders
who shipped them to the Americas. In return they received firearms, cannons and trade goods. Portuguese trading firms were
soon placing wholesale orders for brass bracelets with German
producers. These were melted down by African craft guilds and
reworked into brass busts and ornamental plaques to decorate
the royal courts. At the same time, the guilds began to tailor
products for European markets. In Europe, ivory was valued
more highly than brass, and artefacts carved from ivory were

now produced for export, including such very particular items as salt cellars and hunting horns featuring Portuguese knights and sailors and incorporating Portuguese coats of arms.

The Portuguese monopoly was gradually eroded by British, French, Dutch and Danish trading companies. Exports of slaves soared in the second half of the eighteenth century. Alongside the slave trade, a market for natural resources developed. African kings took control of local supply chains and rates of exchange were established. Cowrie shells brought from the Indian Ocean became a form of currency. "Cowries were essential, the smaller the more esteem'd," according to Captain Thomas Phillips, a slave trader in the employ of the Royal African Company. "The next in demand are brass neptunes or basons [i.e., basins], very large, thin and flat. Certain textiles were also acceptable, but only to a limited extent; near half the cargo value must be cowries and brass basons to set off the other goods."[14]

Britain and France banned the Atlantic slave trade in the first decade of the nineteenth century but some local rulers pushed back against the restrictions. Joseph Dupuis, a British envoy, visited the Asante court in 1824 and reported the Asantahene ("King of all the Asante") boasting:

> If I fight a king, and kill him when he is insolent, then cer-
> tainly I must have his gold, and his slaves, and the people are
> mine too. Do not the white kings act like this? . . . When I
> fought Gaman, I did not make war for slaves, but because
> Dinkera [the king] sent me an arrogant message and killed
> my people, and refused to pay me gold as his father did.
> Then my fetische made me strong like my ancestors, and I
> killed Dinkera, and took his gold, and brought more than
> 20,000 slaves to Coomassy. Some of these people being bad
> men, I washed my stool in their blood for the fetische. But
> then some were good people, and these I sold or gave to
> my captains.

The Asantehene asked Dupuis to tell King George III "that these slaves can work for him, and if he wants 10,000 he can have them. And if he wants fine handsome girls and women to give his captains, I can send him great numbers."[15]

Slavery continued in West African kingdoms (as it did in the Americas), even after the ban on the Atlantic slave trade. Herbert S. Klein estimates that "by 1850 there were more slaves in Africa than there were in America—probably numbering close to 10 million."[16] Slaves provided labour for commercial operations in natural resources: gold, ivory, wild peppers and palm kernels (used in the production of soap and lubricants).

In 1883, the French set up a "protectorate" in the region, in Porto-Novo, which began to compete with Dahomey for trade revenues. Facing insolvency, the king of Dahomey, Behanzin, upped his slave-raiding activities.[17] This provided the French with a reason—or a cover—for intervention. By now the "Scramble for Africa" was in full swing. The Berlin Conference of 1884–5 designated the spheres of influence of Europe's maritime powers in Africa. The regulation of trade became a matter for governments. General Dodds opened negotiations with King Béhanzin, making an offer of joint sovereignty, but this was refused. In January 1894, a French force commanded by Dodds seized the royal capital of Abomey. Béhanzin was sent into exile.

The French press was fascinated by the all-woman palace guard at the Dahomey king's court. The women were legally married to the king and were known as *mino* (our mothers) or *ahosi* (royal wives). Female regiments saw action in military conflicts between France and Dahomey and they impressed French officers. Some claimed that they were more effective than most male soldiers. The women chanted: "As the blacksmith takes an iron bar and by fire changes its fashion so have we changed our nature. We are no longer women, we are men." After the defeat of King Béhanzin a few (possibly not authentic) Dahomian "Amazons" were included in an ethnographic spectacle in the Jardin d'Acclimatation in Paris.[18]

As the French troops entered the palace grounds, the buildings were set on fire by order of the king. Only portions of two nineteenth-century palaces survived. These were occupied for some years by members of the royal family, but they did not have the means to maintain them. In 1911, the buildings were restored by the French colonial government, and in 1943 were converted to house an Abomey historical museum. Eva Meyerowitz, an ethnographer of West Africa, visited soon after. Writing for the *Burlington Magazine for Connoisseurs*, she praised the museum's collection of brilliantly coloured embroidered hangings and the array of royal accoutrements—carved stools of kings, silver amulets, sceptres, armour—though she insisted that the most impressive example was in a private museum in Paris. Also on display, she noted, were "presents given to the kings by the Portuguese slave traders, like a set of liqueur glasses and other articles of European origin." In passing, Meyerowitz remarked: "I was shown jewellery which the French Government had bought from the impoverished royal family for the Trocadéro Museum in Paris," which she was able to photograph before it was sent off to France.[19]

The palace complex of Abomey was listed as a world heritage site by UNESCO in 1985. Following a fire, the complex was inscribed in UNESCO's List of World Heritage in Danger. An international consortium, led by the Getty Foundation, undertook a major project of reconstruction and conservation. In 2007, the palaces were removed from UNESCO's "in danger" list.[20] In November 2021, the Dahomean royal treasures taken by General Dobbs were transferred to the Abomey Palace Museum, which had been restored at a cost of €20 million, funded by the *Agence Française du Développement*.

In January 2018, *The Washington Post* published a report by Kevin Sieff, headlined "An African country reckons with its history of selling slaves."[21] This was precisely the moment when international campaigns were targeting statues of men who profited from the slave trade. And yet in the town of Ouidah, in Bénin, once the largest slave port in West Africa, there is a

Royal stool from Abomey. The king, sitting beneath a parasol, is surrounded by ten wives. At a lower level, beneath the seat, are two soldiers with seven prisoners who are bound by their necks to a wooden board. They are destined to be enslaved or sacrificed. In 2021 the stool was transferred from the Museum of the quai Branly in Paris to the Abomey Historical Museum in the Republic of Bénin.

statue of Francisco Félix de Souza, a Brazilian who, Sieff points out, became "one of the biggest slave merchants in the history of the transatlantic slave trade." Not only is there a statue: there is a museum devoted to his family and a plaza is named after him. And the de Souza family is still one of the most influential in the country.

Sieff describes the annual pilgrimage made by the patriarch

of the de Souza family, accompanied by a retinue of relatives, to Abomey to meet the king. "The ceremony was about celebrating a relationship between two families that was originally forged over slaves," Sieff comments. He witnessed the ritual in 2017.

> On that humid morning, Moise de Souza stepped out of an SUV wearing a gold-trimmed shawl and cap. He walked to the front of a dimly lighted meeting room . . . A group of American anthropology students, almost all of them white, had been allowed inside to watch. Finally, the king arrived, surrounded by several wives wearing matching yellow-and-orange dresses. He shook de Souza's hand. Glasses of champagne were poured.

The ceremony was filmed for the national TV news.

The Republic of Dahomey, taking the name of the ancient kingdom, was established in 1960, when French West Africa was divided into independent states. There followed a series of military coups, the fifth of which, in 1972, was led by a colonel in the army, Mathieu Kérékou. Two years later Kérékou (by then a general) adopted a Marxist–Leninist platform, nationalised the country's oil companies and banks, and changed the name of the country to the People's Republic of Bénin.

Things did not go smoothly for the new people's republic. The radical political programme and a series of corruption scandals led donors to cut back on aid. Kérékou—who was known locally as "the chameleon"—swiftly adopted more moderate policies and embarked on an international PR campaign. In 1999, on a tour of the United States, he fell to his knees in an African American church in Baltimore, apologised for the role that precolonial African states had played in the slave trade, invoked the Christian doctrine of forgiveness and made a plea for reconciliation. He then convened an international leaders' conference on reconciliation and development. A global cast of speakers, including two American congressmen, apologised for slavery.[22] Kérékou also made a personal apology to the local Catholic arch-bishop for his political errors, abandoned Marxist–Leninism, and in 2005 retired from politics.

The current government of what is now the Republic of Bénin, *tout court*, is constructing an international museum of memory and slavery. Largely funded by the World Bank, it will feature a tourist complex of 130 rooms, "places of reflection" and a reconstruction of a slave ship. This initiative was inspired by Ghana's successful introduction of tours of slave sites to attract African American visitors.[23] And slavery now crops up as an issue in domestic politics. In a TV debate during the 2016 presidential election campaign, one candidate, Lionel Zinsou, pointed out that his opponent, Patrice Talon, an entrepreneur known as the "King of Cotton," was descended from slave merchants. But Talon won the presidency. In April 2021, after imprisoning the leader of the opposition and appointing his personal lawyer chief justice, he was re-elected with 86 per cent of the vote on a very small turnout. *Foreign Policy* magazine head-lined its pre-election coverage: "Bénin's 'King of Cotton' makes its democracy a sham." It was President Talon who elicited a promise from President Macron to return the symbols of the old Dahomey monarchy. In February 2022 he gave them a grand ceremonial welcome.

When British colonies were established in West Africa, the local African kingdoms were soon "pacified," their ruling families forced to submit to foreign overrule. In 1873, a large British force under General Garnet Wolseley attacked the Asante kingdom. The following year, British troops briefly occupied the Asante capital and ransacked the "stone palace," the *Aban*, which had been built for the Asantehene in 1822. A *Daily Telegraph* reporter described the palace as "the museum, for museum it should be called."[24] A colleague from the London *Times* reported that each of the Aban's upstairs rooms "was a perfect Old Curiosity Shop. Books in many languages, Bohemian glass, clocks, silver plate, old furniture, Persian rugs, Kidderminster carpets, pictures and engravings, numberless chests and coffers . . . With these were many specimens of Moorish and Ashantee handicraft." According to the historian Ivor Wilks, the Aban was "one of the most cherished projects of Osei Bonsu, who had been interested to learn of the functions of its distinguished and older counterpart, the British Museum."[25] After removing the more valuable items, British soldiers blew up the palace.

The Treaty of Formena, signed in July 1874, obliged the Asantehene to pay Britain an indemnity of 50,000 gold ounces, to put a stop to human sacrifice and to guarantee freedom of trade. But the treaty did not hold. In January 1896, the British invaded once more and deported the Asantehene. (He would spend most of his long exile in the Seychelles, in the company of two kings exiled from Uganda, the Kabaka of Buganda and the Kabagarega of Toro.) In March 1900, Sir Frederick Hodgson, governor of the Gold Coast colony, demanded the surrender of the Asante golden stool that symbolised royal power. Another war broke out. It ended a year later with the annexation of the kingdom to the British colony.[26] The golden stool remained hidden in the forest for two decades. In 1921, it was discovered by road workers and stripped of some of its gold ornaments. The thieves were sentenced to death by an Asante court, then reprieved and sent into exile by the British authorities. In 1995, a Manhyia Palace Museum was established in Kumasi, the capital of the Asante kingdom. The museum exhibits furniture, memorabilia, photographs and fibreglass mannequins representing past Asante royals, and has a rotating display of royal regalia. However, there is no acknowledgement of the kingdom's involvement in the slave trade.

The most notorious instance of the plunder of African antiquities is the case of the Benin Bronzes. The designation is doubly misleading: they were mostly cast from brass or carved from ivory. And they were taken from the kingdom of Edo in what is now southwestern Nigeria. "Benin" is the Portuguese version of a vernacular term, *itsekiri Ubinu*, meaning royal capital. Europeans began to call Edo "Benin," and the term was applied more widely to the region bordering a bay on the Gulf of Guinea in West Africa, which became known as the Bight of Benin.

The sacking of Benin city is in some ways depressingly similar to the raids on the royal seats of Dahomey and Asante. Resistance was quickly put down. Even by the standards of colonial campaigns of the day, however, the scale of pillage was remarkable. There is no way of knowing precisely how many brass plaques, busts and ivory carvings were seized in 1897, or how many found their way into museums from later excavations, but there must have been several thousand.[27] The British Museum alone holds around 950 although just a hundred are usually on display. The quality of these artefacts astonished and impressed connoisseurs, and transformed European ideas about Africa.

The saga began when the British Foreign Office established a "protectorate" in the Niger delta in 1885. In 1888, a new Oba came to power in Edo after one of the bruising phases of factional strife that erupted periodically in the ruling family. He then set about repairing the royal finances. In November 1896, James Phillips, an English lawyer who had just been appointed deputy commissioner and consul-general for the Niger coast protectorate, reported to the Foreign Secretary that the Oba had "placed a Juju on (Palm) Kernels, the most profitable product of the country, and the penalty for trading in this produce is death."

> I am certain [he continued] that there is only one remedy, that is to depose the king of Benin from his stool. I am convinced from information which leaves no room for doubt as well as from experience of native character, that pacific means are now quite useless, and that the time has now come to remove the obstruction. I therefore ask his Lordship's permission to visit Benin City in February next to depose and remove the king of Benin and to establish a native council in his place and take such further steps for

the opening up of the country as the occasion may require . . . I would add that I have reason to hope that sufficient ivory may be found in the King's house to pay the expenses in removing the King from his stool.[28]

Phillips did not wait for the Foreign Office to respond. He also ignored a message from the Oba who said he was in seclusion, busy with a ritual honouring his ancestors, and that Phillips should postpone his visit. Phillips set off in December 1896, accompanied by seven British officials, two traders and some two hundred carriers (though the military band that had marched off with them was sent home before they arrived at their destination). The column was ambushed. Phillips and another six of the nine British men and an unknown number of African bearers were killed.

In February 1897, a punitive expedition was sent in under the command of Rear Admiral Harry Rawson of the Cape Town squadron of the Royal Navy. The Oba knew what to expect: the British had recently got rid of several uncooperative chiefs in the region. In 1887, a merchant chief, Jaja of Opobo, was deposed by a tricky manoeuvre that a local British official confessed was "not cricket" and "contrary to our ideas of fair play." (Lured on board a British ship with a promise of negotiations, Jaja was detained and sent into exile.)[29] Nana Oluma, chief of another merchant community which traded with Edo, was deported in 1894. So the Oba took precautions. He readied the city's old Portuguese cannons, mobilised his troops and sacrificed hundreds of slaves and captives to his ancestors. To no avail: the British easily took the town. Battle-hardened marines were appalled by what they found. In a letter to the first sea lord, Rawson wrote: "this place reeks of sacrifices and human blood, bodies in every state of decay, wells full of newly killed, crucified men on the fetish trees (which we have blown up), one sees men retching everywhere."[30]

Rawson had taken part in the sacking of the imperial summer palace in Beijing as a sixteen-year-old ensign and complained

Members of the British military force that occupied Benin City in
1897, photographed in the Oba's palace compound, surrounded
by bronzes and ivories. The photographer, Dr. Robert Allman,
accompanied the Benin expedition. He became principal medical
officer in Southern Nigeria. (By permission of The British
Museum, London © The Trustees of the British Museum.)

that he had then not been present for the looting of treasures
"of which there were a tremendous lot taken, one officer getting
£1,000 worth in the shape of a solid gold picture-frame."[31] He
would not lose out this time, as the Oba's palace and sanctuaries
were ransacked.

British soldiers found brass plaques depicting heroic exploits
of Obas and scenes of life at court lying covered in dust on the
floor of a palace courtyard. (The palace roof was about to be
replaced with brass sheeting, and the plaques were evidently
laid aside until they could be installed again.)[32] The soldiers also

plundered memorial brass busts from the shrines of dead kings and scooped up intricately carved ivories and wooden sculptures, some of which may date from the fifteenth century. All were produced by guilds operating under the patronage of the divine king: brass-casters—the senior guild—and guilds of wood and ivory carvers, iron smiths, weavers, and leather workers.[33]

The British set up a makeshift headquarters and hospital in the Oba's palace. A golf course was laid out. ("The chief drawback," an officer reported to *Golf Magazine*, "was the huge quantity of human skulls and bones which littered the course; and sad as it is to state, our best green happens to have been made on the turf immediately beneath a tree known as the 'crucifixion tree,' on which many a poor slave breathed his last.")[34]

Meanwhile, Ralph Moor, consul-general of the newly proclaimed Niger coast protectorate, struggled to keep control of the looting. Stacks of elephant tusks and hundreds of brass plaques were set aside for the British government to cover the costs of the sortie. Two ivory statues of leopards were reserved for Queen Victoria. The distribution was briefly interrupted by a fire that consumed most of the palace buildings. Officers and gentlemen then had their pick. Henry Charles Seppings Wright, who covered the punitive expedition for the *Illustrated London News*, scored several masterpieces, including a life-size brass commemorative head of Idia, the mother of a sixteenth-century Oba, which was donated to the British Museum by the paper's managing director, Sir William James Ingram.[35] Even lowly seamen came away with keepsakes.

The Oba was captured and exiled to Calabar, where he died in 1914. Slavery was abolished in the colony in 1915, and thousands of former slaves converged on Benin City to celebrate.[36]

Back in London, the crown agents auctioned off a large batch of ivories (in those days, more expensive than anything made of brass). Most of the brass heads and plaques were deposited on loan in the British Museum. Officers placed their swag with London's curio dealers and auction houses.[37]

A pendant mask, carved from ivory with iron and brass inlays, possibly sixteenth century, thought to represent Idia, a Queen Mother of the Edo [Benin] kingdom. Note the heads of Portuguese men on the tiara. There are two almost identical masks, one in the British Museum, the other in the Metropolitan Museum of Art in New York. Two similar items are in the Seattle Art Museum and the Linden Museum in Stuttgart. (By permission of The British Museum, London © The Trustees of the British Museum.)

Consul Ralph Moor kept for himself an ivory box decorated with an image of two Portuguese men trying to throttle one another, alongside a tethered pangolin; two ivory amulets; and a pair of sixteenth-century ivory masks, twenty-three centimetres long, representing a commanding woman who had also been identified as Idia, the subject of the brass head donated to the museum by the *Illustrated London News*. The extraordinary detailing in Idia's necklace and tiara includes miniature carved heads of Portuguese men. The masks were bought by Charles Seligman, professor of ethnology at the London School of Economics, who sold one to the British Museum in 1910 at a knock-down price. His widow sold the other to Nelson Rockefeller in 1957 for £20,000. She donated the proceeds to the Royal Anthropological Institute, which put an image of the mask on the institute's Christmas card. William Fagg, curator of African ethnography in the British Museum, described it at the time as "the finest and most valuable Benin—or indeed West African—antiquity still in private hands in the world."[38] (It is now in New York's Metropolitan Museum.)

General Pitt Rivers began to buy Benin Bronzes for his Oxford museum at the first public auction in May 1897. Ethnographic museums in Berlin, Leipzig and Vienna were also eager customers. Prices soared. Felix von Luschan, who succeeded Bastian as director of the Africa and Oceania department at Berlin's Ethnological Museum, was soon complaining about the asking prices. One of the main London dealers, W. D. Webster, a "Collector of Ethnological Specimens, European and Eastern Arms and Armour," replied, in April 1898, that he was "perfectly aware that Benin specimens are expensive but everyone wants them so prices have gone up considerably." Indeed, he would himself "give nearly double the money for specimens I sold soon after they were brought over [since] it is quite impossible to get any more as Benin was cleared out and everything brought to this country."[39]

Von Luschan assembled 580 Benin pieces for the Berlin

Museum of Ethnology and published an authoritative study of the crafts of Edo.[40] Hans Meyer, a wealthy businessman and a geographer, put together a collection of fifty-three Benin pieces, which went to the Ethnological Museum in Leipzig. "It is actually a riddle to me, that the English let such things go," Meyer wrote to von Luschan. "Either they have too many of them already or they have no idea what these things mean for ethnology, cultural history, and art history . . . whatever the case may be, the main thing remains, that *we* have these magnificent specimens."[41] Some English scholars did grumble. Deaf to irony, H. Ling Roth, author of the first English monograph on Benin, wrote that "it is especially annoying to Englishmen to think that such articles, which for every reason should be retained in this country, have been allowed to go abroad."[42]

But the British authorities recognised the propaganda value of their haul. The Oba's palace was sacked just a few months before the celebration of Queen Victoria's Diamond Jubilee. At the suggestion of the colonial secretary, Joseph Chamberlain, the jubilee celebrations broadened into a "Festival of the British Empire." In September 1897, doing its bit for the empress, the British Museum mounted a show of trophies from the Benin expedition. Three hundred Benin plaques were exhibited in the Assyrian saloon in the basement of the museum. Carved ivories and brass memorial heads were exhibited in the ethnological gallery. (Ivory still had top billing.) The press floated fanciful theories of the origin of the art. (China, Egypt, Italy? Surely not Africa!) When the exhibition closed in January 1898, the Foreign Office allowed the British Museum to keep the plaques and some brass heads.[43]

Nigerian museums hold some five hundred Benin Bronzes. Most were accessioned during the colonial period by three eccentric Englishmen: Kenneth Murray, the grandson of Sir James Murray, first editor of the *Oxford English Dictionary*, and two brothers, William and Bernard Fagg, sons of an antiquarian bookseller. (Dictionaries and antiquarian bookshops have a lot in common with museums.) The three men were all art lovers, and they treated Nigerian antiquities as works of art.

Kenneth Murray dropped out of Balliol College, Oxford, to study art. In 1927 he went to Nigeria as an art teacher. In 1943, he was appointed Nigeria's first surveyor of antiquities. "Practically single-handed, he set out to locate, photograph and catalogue all the works of art in the country," recalled Frank Willett, who had himself been a museum curator in colonial Nigeria. Willett added that Murray "saved a great many masterpieces from destruction by purchasing them out of his own pocket, and eventually presented his collection to form the core of the Nigerian Museum in Lagos which was opened in 1957."[44] That museum became a popular venue during Nigeria's independence celebrations in October 1960, attracting 30,000 visitors in a single day. "The crowds were so great," Murray wrote, "that no one could get in or out and all the flowers were trampled and the stairs almost broken."[45]

Bernard Fagg, a Cambridge-trained archaeologist, was appointed government archaeologist in Nigeria in 1947 and became a friend and ally of Murray. In 1952 Fagg set up the first public museum in British West Africa, in Jos, and in 1957 he succeeded Murray as director of antiquities in Nigeria and established several new museums. By 1958, Murray and Fagg had accessioned ninety Benin artefacts to the recently established National Museum in Lagos, including twenty-three Benin plaques donated or sold to the Nigerian antiquities service in 1950 and 1951 by the British Museum.[46] His successor, the first Nigerian director of the department of antiquities, Professor Ekpo Eyo, was, like Fagg himself, a product of the department of archaeology and anthropology at Cambridge University. He said that Fagg "was sent out to Nigeria to project the image and power of the British empire but reversed all expectations and projected the image and past of the Africans."[47]

After the independence of Nigeria, Bernard Fagg became a curator at Oxford's Pitt Rivers Museum. His older brother, William Fagg, joined the British Museum in 1938 and remained there until his retirement. Like his brother, William became an Africanist. (In 1946, he recalled, the British Museum's curators of antiquities and ethnography "decided as a matter of policy to specialise, by continents, and I as the junior was 'left with' Africa.")[48] A friend of notable English artists, including Jacob Epstein, Henry Moore and Roland Penrose, Fagg published textbooks on African sculptures, and worked up a schema for the dating of Benin works of art. Following his retirement from the British Museum he became a consultant to Christie's, a role that some of his colleagues thought not quite proper. He persuaded the firm to change the name of the "primitive art" department to "tribal art."

After the country's independence celebrations, despite initial popular enthusiasm, Nigeria's museums fell into disrepair, as the country went through bouts of economic and political crisis, interspersed with periods of military government under Muslim generals from the north of the country who were not all disposed to respect pagan antiquities. Museums were starved of funds. Conservation was neglected, security lax, thefts not uncommon. The journalist Barnaby Phillips reports that in recent years the National Museum in Lagos can only exhibit some three hundred objects, while tens of thousands are in storage, "poorly labelled and often chaotically crammed together." The curator, Mrs. Omotayo Adeboye, told him that the museum has only about thirty visitors a day, mostly parties of schoolchildren.[49]

In 2020, Transparency International published its latest corruption ranking of 180 of the world's "nations and territories." Denmark and New Zealand were in a tie at number one as the least corrupt nations. Somalia and South Sudan were tied in last place, at 179th. Nigeria was in 149th place, in a tie with Cameroon, Guatemala, Iran, Lebanon, Madagascar, Mozambique and Tajikistan. (See the recent scathing satire on Nigeria's corrupt political elite, *Chronicles from the Land of the Happiest People on Earth*, by Wole Soyinka, Nigeria's Nobel Prize–winning poet and novelist, which Ben Okri describes as "a vast danse macabre . . . a tale about all that is rotten in the state of Nigeria.")[50]

Then there is the epidemic of criminal violence. Kidnapping is rife. Travellers along the road between Benin City and Lagos are terrified. Train travel is also dangerous. On 28 March 2022, explosives placed on the track derailed a train from Kaduna to the federal capital, Abuja. Waiting gunmen then killed eight passengers, injured twenty-five and kidnapped an unknown number. "The attack was the most brazen yet by the kidnapping gangs locally known as bandits that terrorise the region," *The Economist* commented. "This lawlessness, in addition to a long-running insurgency in the north-east by jihadists affiliated with Islamic State and regular clashes between farmers and herders, are rendering large parts of Africa's most populous country ungovernable."[51]

Nigeria's museums have not been immune from graft, and even armed robbery. "Hundreds of millions of dollars worth of art has been stolen from the museums of Nigeria," writes Kwame Anthony Appiah, "almost always with the complicity of insiders."[52] Leading politicians routinely visited the national museum to choose gifts for foreign heads of state. In 1961, Prime Minister Balewa took a Benin carved ivory tusk from the national museum and gave it to President John Kennedy. (It is in the JFK Presidential Library in Boston.) Barnaby Phillips, author of an excellent book on the politics of the Benin Bronzes, was told about another egregious instance by Ekpo Eyo, successor to Bernard Fagg as director of Nigeria's federal department of antiquities. Professor Eyo was telephoned at home one Saturday morning in 1973 by the head of state, General Yakubu Gowan. (The professor's phone had been out of order for months, but it was suddenly, miraculously, in working order.) The general told him that he was on his way to the national museum to choose a present to give to Queen Elizabeth on his coming state visit to Britain. Eyo rushed to the museum to hide irreplaceable objects. He was relieved when Gowan selected a relatively minor piece, a mid-period Benin head, although he felt that this would undermine the Nigerian case for repatriation; and indeed the British Foreign Office would soon be raising the matter of the gift when Nigerian diplomats tried to negotiate the return of looted Benin artefacts.

Ironically, as the Foreign Office was aware, this particular head had once been stolen from the Nigerian National Museum. It found its way to the British Museum, and was returned to Kenneth Murray in Lagos in 1950 thanks to the good offices of William Fagg. The head is now in the royal collection in Windsor Castle.[53]

When Nigeria hosted the World Black and African Festival of Art and Culture in 1977, the British Museum's carved ivory image of Idia was chosen to be the official symbol. The Foreign Office tried to persuade the museum to lend its mask for the occasion, but was turned down on the grounds that the ivory was cracked and might not withstand the move and exposure to heat. The Nigerian press judged this excuse cynical and insulting. In truth, the condition of the mask may not have been decisive. Privately, British Museum curators were not confident that it would be returned. After all, three of the bronze plaques sent to Lagos in 1950 by the British Museum had somehow ended up in American collections. In 1980, during a brief oil boom, the Nigerian government bought some brass heads at auction. Several soon turned up again on the international market.

Professor Eyo's son recalled his father saying that he "had to be careful of his colleagues, there were ones that needed to be watched."[54] And Eyo was not alone in his concerns. "We are losing our cultural heritage at such an alarming rate," the Nigerian minister of culture, Walter Ofonagoro, warned in 1996, "we may have no cultural artefacts to bequeath to our progeny."[55] In 2000, John Picton, an authority on Nigerian antiquities, told a conference of museum curators that recent thefts from Nigerian museums and archaeological excavations "constitute at least as serious a tragedy as the looting of the art of Benin City by British forces in 1897."[56]

The low point came when Professor Edo and the Nigerian National Museum arranged a touring exhibition, "Treasures of Ancient Nigeria."[57] When it was first shown, in Detroit, in 1980, the press revealed the huge insurance value of the exhibits. This so impressed an employee of the National Museum in Lagos that he ransacked the reserve collection of Benin antiquities. "That exhibition has continued to travel in one form or another ever since, as a means of keeping safe some part of the national heritage by lending it to responsible institutions elsewhere in the world," Frank Willett, a former museum curator in Nigeria, told an international conference on museums in 2000.[58]

Since 2007 a "Benin dialogue group" of European, American and Nigerian curators and officials has held regular meetings to discuss the accession of Benin Bronzes from abroad to an "Edo Museum of West African Art." This museum is being planned by a local not-for-profit organisation, the Legacy Restoration Trust. Headed by a local entrepreneur and supported by the governor of Edo State it has raised around $4 million with the assistance of the British Museum. A design for the new museum has been prepared by Sir David Adjaye, architect of the National Museum of African American History and Culture in Washington, DC.

But in a statement issued in July 2021, the Oba of Benin rejected these plans. "I do not believe that the move by a privately registered company, the Legacy Restoration Trust Ltd., and the purported establishment of Edo Museum of West African Arts are in consonance with the wishes of the people of Benin kingdom," his spokesman said. The Oba proposed that all Benin bronzes should be given to the Benin royal museum that he was planning to establish.[59]

This royal interest in antiquities was new. For some time, antiquities in the possession of the Benin royal family had been neglected. When Eva Meyerowitz visited Benin City in the 1940s she reported that "valuable bronzes, some still encrusted with earth, those which were found buried in the ground, are kept carelessly, one on top of the other in an open room, and are carried into a courtyard when shown to visitors and afterwards left lying about, as nobody in particular seems to be in charge of them."[60] Bernard Fagg was so concerned about the condition of the Benin royal collections that he supervised their removal from the palace to the more secure premises of the city post office.

Some donors questioned whether it would in any case be appropriate, or democratic, to put the Oba in control. And it is not clear what the local population thinks about the Oba's plans, or indeed whether there is much local enthusiasm for the return of ancient royal memorials. In Benin City, now the fourth largest city in Nigeria with a population of 1,782,000, there is limited evidence of a strong civic pride in the heritage of the precolonial kingdom. The city is ringed by an earth wall, eleven kilometres long, dating from the thirteenth century. This is a Nigerian national monument, but Phillips reports that some stretches of the wall are fronted by privately erected billboards advertising evangelical churches. The moat is clogged with rubbish and plastic bags. Local builders dig it for clay.[61]

One obvious reason is that the modern Benin City has a diverse and strongly Christian population. Immediately after the British banished the Oba, the Church Missionary Society launched an evangelical mission in Edo. (A leading missionary was Bishop James "Holy" Johnson, son of a Yoruba man who had been enslaved by Edo, sold to European traders, and rescued by a Royal Navy patrol.)[62] In other ways, too, the region has been transformed. Schools and universities were established in the colonial period, and modern media has now penetrated even the most isolated villages. A significant and relevant index sign of the times is, perhaps paradoxically, the recent revival of urban shrines in Benin City. These are notably syncretic. An ethnographer, Charles Gore, reports: "The contemporary urban shrine configurations are developed by charismatic *ohens* through their individual skill and compete against each other and a range of other religions, most notably the orthodox and

Pentecostal churches . . . but also Hare Krishna, Rosicrucian and other denominations."[63] It is in this post-modern milieu that the current Oba is attempting to maintain control of the craft guilds and to restore the pomp of his inherited position.

The call for the restitution of Benin Bronzes resonated in Britain and in Germany. The British Museum is home to the largest collection of Benin antiquities in the world. Museums in Berlin, Dresden, Hamburg and Leipzig have substantial collections of Benin brass heads, plaques and ivory carvings, largely acquired from London dealers and auctioneers in the early twentieth century. In both countries the disputed ownership of Benin antiquities fuelled a reassessment of the colonial past.

In Britain, the Brexit campaign whipped up imperial nostalgia. The German debate was very different. After the First World War, Germany was stripped of its colonies. A generation later, after Hitler's defeat, the German public struggled, painfully, to come to terms with the true nature of the Nazi regime and the Holocaust. In the meantime, memories of the colonial period faded. A reconsideration began in the twenty-first century, when some younger historians suggested that a straight line might be drawn from colonial ideologies and policies to the Nazi Reich. The brutal suppression of Herero and Khoi rebellions between 1904 and 1908 in what is now Namibia has been characterised as a genocide, even a trial run for the Holocaust (though some historians dispute this).[64] Demands for compensation and for the restitution of stolen goods followed.

As the restitution movement gained momentum, symbolically laden items, some not of African origin, were presented by German institutions to the government of Namibia. A bible and a whip, collected in the 1890s, came from the Linden Museum in Stuttgart. A fifteenth-century Portuguese stone landmark collected from the coast of what is now Namibia in 1893 was donated by Berlin's Museum of History. These were haphazard initiatives. The return of these colonial artefacts had not been requested by Namibian authorities, and indeed the

Portuguese landmark apparently still has to find an appropriate new home.

German activists now represented art collections drawn from colonial encounters as the equivalent of the *Raubkunst* (looted art) of the Nazis. A member of the Benin dialogue group told me that some Nigerian counterparts argue bluntly: "You gave stolen goods back to the Jews, why not to us?" "The spread of demands for reparations in the more recent past follows from the fact that the Holocaust has come to comprise the 'true emblem' of our age," writes John Torpey, director of the Ralph Bunche Institute for International Studies at the Graduate Center, City University of New York.

> The perfidy of the Nazi assault on European Jewry has emerged as a kind of gold standard against which to judge other cases of injustice and to which advocates seek to assimilate those instances of human cruelty and oppression for which they seek reparations . . . the Holocaust has become the central metaphor for all politics concerned with "making whole what has been smashed."[65]

Couched in these terms, the case for restitution has particular force in Germany.

In early 2019, the ministers of culture of Germany's federal states declared that objects in German museums which had been stolen from their countries of origin should be returned. Complex bureaucratic formalities are still to be completed, but there seems little doubt that at least a substantial proportion of the Benin Bronzes presently held in museums in Berlin, Hamburg, Leipzig, Stuttgart, Cologne and Dresden will soon be handed over.

But handed over to whom? The competing claims of the Oba of Benin and the local association backed by the governor of Edo State put foreign museums in a difficult situation. In January 2022, Nigeria's National Commission for Museums announced that it would handle all negotiations for the Benin treasures.

Foreign governments and museums may have been relieved. Here at last was an apparently authoritative interlocutor.

But suddenly the situation was transformed. On 28 March 2023, the outgoing President of Nigeria, Muhammadu Buhari, proclaimed the Oba of Benin the outright owner of all Benin bronzes: "to the exclusion of any other person or persons and or institutions." With immediate effect, "custody of the repatriated artefacts shall, from wherever and whenever they are brought into Nigeria, be handed over to the Oba."[66]

"We were blindsided," an official at Nigeria's National Commission for Museums and Monuments told the BBC. Moreover, they added, the order was "not practical nor compatible with existing Nigerian law [and] it was written by someone who doesn't understand how museums work."[67]

"There is no more talk of travelling exhibitions, loans, public access, international scientific cooperation and exchange," noted Brigitta Hauser-Schäublin of Göttingen University. "A public good has become private property."[68]

Meanwhile, an African American non-profit, the Restitution Study Group (RSG), sued to stop the Smithsonian Institution from sending its Benin bronzes to Nigeria. The RSG pointed out that Benin had sold many thousands of slaves to European traders in exchange for brass bracelets—some of which were melted down to cast the famous "bronzes." Surely descendants of those slaves had a moral interest in Benin's treasures, now worth billions of dollars.[69] In any case, "there is no reason why we should be obligated to travel to Nigeria to see them," declared the director of the RSG, Deadria Farmer-Paellmann. "I don't want to get kidnapped" she added, citing U.S. government travel warnings.[70]

BUT IS IT ART?

In the 1890s, anthropologists began to study arts and crafts from Africa, Oceania and the Americas. Henry Balfour, curator at the Pitt Rivers Museum in Oxford, published *The Evolution of Decorative Art* in 1893. At Cambridge University, Alfred Cort Haddon followed with a monograph, *Decorative Art in New Guinea*, in 1894, and a theoretical treatise, *Evolution in Art: As Illustrated by the Life-Histories of Designs*, in 1895. In the idiom of the day, they spun theories about the evolution of decorative styles (naturalistic to abstract, or perhaps the other way round), and compared contemporary "primitive" art from the South Seas with prehistoric cave paintings that were being discovered in France.

A very different take on exotic art swept the art world in the first decades of the twentieth century. Collectors and post-impressionist painters embraced an aesthetic—even an ideology—of *primitivisme*. For the next century the construct of primitive art would be contested between ethnographers, who knew about the societies that produced these wood and ivory carvings and bronzes, and the artists, curators, dealers and collectors who found their own uses for them.

In his recent two-volume history, *Primitivismes*, a French historian of art, Philippe Dagen, argues that artists born around 1880, like Braque, Derain and Picasso, needed to distinguish themselves from the Impressionists. To scandalise, to *épater la bourgeoisie*, they came out as wild men, primitives.[1] Paradoxically, artefacts from Africa and Oceania strewn casually around the studios of young artists signalled hyper-modernity. At the same time they conveyed contempt for the Western tradition

Picasso in his Montmartre studio, with African carvings, 1908. Photograph by an American artist and writer, Franck Gelett Burgess. (Public domain.)

of fine art. The masks and carvings that Picasso collected were "signifiers of a rupture," according to Dagen. Picasso himself said, "The African sculptures that hang around my studios are more witnesses than models."[2] To what did they bear witness? "They affirmed that Picasso was freeing himself from the lessons of the European *beaux-arts*," Dagen claims. Picasso himself said something similar: "When I discovered *l'art nègre*, it was a way for me to oppose what was termed 'beauty' in the museums."[3]

Earlier generations had had their flings with exotic arts and crafts. In the late eighteenth century there was a fashion for chinoiserie. In the early nineteenth century, as France began its colonial occupation of Algeria and Tunisia, Islamic carpets and paintings of ladies and eunuchs in harems came into fashion. There was even a French Orientalist Painters Society. After Japan opened up to foreign trade in 1858, there was *japonisme*. These modes were mostly to do with the decorative arts. Primitivism was something else: a movement in modern art. Moreover, as Dagen remarks, "Primitive and exotic are not synonyms."[4]

The Paris World's Fair of 1889 was among many other things a celebration of arts and crafts from faraway countries. Vincent van Gogh visited the mock-up of a Mexican village, which he judged "primitive and very beautiful."[5] Paul Gauguin wandered happily around the "native villages" and bought two Loango spirit figures *(minkisi)* from the French Congo, which he modified and repainted.[6] But a full-blown *primitivisme* emerged in Paris only in 1905—or perhaps as early as 1904, or, in some accounts, in 1906. It was then that avant-garde artists came to value the Ethnographic Museum at the Trocadéro Palace in Paris as a gallery of primitive art. And they began to put together their own collections.

In 1905 (or was it 1906?), at the end of a day spent painting near the Seine at Argenteuil, Maurice de Vlaminck visited a bistro. As Vlaminck told the story, "Sailors and coal-stevedores were gathered round the counter. While sipping my white wine and seltzer water, I noticed, on the shelf behind the bar, between the bottles of Pernod, anisette and curaçao, three Negro sculptures.

Two were statuettes from Dahomey, daubed in yellow ochre, and white, and the third, from the Ivory Coast, was completely black."[7] After some haggling he acquired them in exchange for a round of drinks. When his friend André Derain saw these African pieces in Vlaminck's studio he insisted on buying one for himself.[8] It was the start of a passionate engagement with African art. In 1910, reporting on a visit to the British Museum, Derain wrote to Vlaminck that he found the African sculptures there "amazingly, frighteningly expressive."[9]

Another iconic, and better documented, encounter is dated to 1906. Henri Matisse bought an African wood carving from a shop in the Rue de Rennes called "chez le Père Sauvage." (So dealers in "primitive art" were already operating in fashionable commercial districts.) As Matisse recalled

> There was a whole corner of little wooden statues, of Negro origin. I was astonished to see how they were conceived from the point of view of sculptural language; how it was close to the Egyptians . . . compared to European sculpture, which always took its point of departure from musculature and started from the description of the object, these Negro statues were made in terms of their material, according to invented planes and proportions.[10]

Matisse took the piece to show the American writer Gertrude Stein, "and then Picasso came by, and we chatted," Matisse recalled. "That was when Picasso became aware of African sculpture."[11] Picasso dined afterwards with Matisse and his wife, "refusing to be parted all evening from the statue," writes Hilary Spurling, "and staying up afterwards in his studio at the Bateau Lavoir where the poet Max Jacob found him next morning, surrounded by drawings of a one-eyed, four-eared, square-mouthed monstress which he claimed was the image of his mistress."[12] Picasso had been struggling with a portrait of Gertrude Stein. After ninety sittings he put it aside, unable to represent her face.

Now he found a solution. "He completed it in the sitter's absence by painting in the mask-like features which, as he rightly said, she soon came to resemble."[13]

Picasso claimed that he experienced an epiphany in the Museum of Ethnography.

> When I went to the Trocadéro it was disgusting. The flea market. The smell. I was alone. I wanted to get away. But I didn't leave. I stayed. I stayed. I understood something very important: something was happening to me, wasn't it?
>
> The masks weren't like other kinds of sculpture. Not at all. They were magical things . . . I understood what the purpose of the sculpture was for the Negroes . . . all the fetishes were used for the same thing. They were weapons. To help people stop being dominated by spirits, to become independent. Tools. If we give form to the spirits, we become independent of them. The spirits, the unconscious (which wasn't yet much spoken of then), emotion, it's the same thing. I understood why I was a painter. All alone in that awful museum, the masks, the Red Indian dolls, the dusty mannequins. *Les Demoiselles d'Avignon* must have come to me that day, but not at all because of the forms; but because it was my first canvas of exorcism—yes, absolutely![14]

Les Demoiselles d'Avignon, painted in 1907, featured five stylised, angular nude prostitutes, two with African masks for faces. Suzanne Preston Blier suggests that Picasso adapted illustrations from a book on masks in African secret societies by Leo Frobenius.[15] But Picasso denied that the *Demoiselles* borrowed from African models. "There is nothing of *art nègre* in the *Demoiselles d'Avignon*," he insisted. Rather, he claimed, the painting owed a great deal to reliefs uncovered in the ancient Iberian city of Osuna which he had seen in the Louvre.[16] According to his biographer John Richardson, Picasso was inspired by Gauguin's statue of a Tahitian goddess, entitled *Oviri* ("savage"). Intended by the artist to stand over his grave, it was displayed at the *Salon d'Automne* in 1906.[17]

German expressionist painters took up primitivism at roughly the same time as the French post-impressionists. Wassily Kandinsky, a leading light in the Blaue Reiter circle, began to sketch African and Oceanian artefacts in the Bavarian State Museum of Ethnology in Munich. Emil Ernst Ludwig Kirchner, one of the founders of Die Brücke (The Bridge—a bridge to the future, of course), was fascinated by exotic carvings in the Dresden Museum für Volkerkunde. The young men printed batik curtains and carved wooden stools for their studios. And they were nothing if not eclectic. The Blaue Reiter manifesto, edited by Kandinsky and Franz Marc, published in 1912, was illustrated by examples of their own work, those of sympathetic French artists, and also (as a historian of art, Robert Goldwater, remarked in wonder),

> figures from New Caledonia, the Malay Peninsula, Easter Island, and the Cameroons; a Brazilian mask, and a stone sculpture from Mexico; a Russian folk statuette and Russian folk prints; Egyptian puppets and an archaic Greek relief: Japanese woodcuts, Bavarian glass painting of the fifteenth and sixteenth centuries, and German nineteenth-century folk pictures; a thirteenth-century head of a stone cutter, fourteenth-century tapestries, and a Baldung-Grien woodcut . . . children's drawings and popular votive images.[18]

In the first flush of post-impressionist success, fauves (the wild ones) and cubists exhibited together with their counterparts in Die Brücke in Dresden in September 1908. Works by Picasso were shown along with African sculptures in Berlin's Neue Galerie in December 1913 and in Dresden in January 1914. Galleries began to attach modernist labels to works from Africa and Oceania. A Dogon sculpture might be identified as "cubist," a piece from the Sepik as "expressionist" or "surrealist," a Samoan work as "minimalist."[19]

Offshoots of primitivism appeared in Scandinavia, Austria, Belgium and England. Roger Fry, a member of the Bloomsbury Group who organised a landmark exhibition, "Manet and the Post-Impressionists," in London between November 1910 and January 1911, wrote essays on "negro sculpture" and "Bushman art." Henry Moore said, "Once you'd read Roger Fry the whole thing was there," but in fact he and other English sculptors, including Barbara Hepworth and Jacob Epstein, were more interested in matters of technique than in high-flown continental ideas about primitivism.[20]

Pissarro and Seurat began to talk about the "primitive-modern." Soon a search was on for home-grown European primitives. Henri Rousseau, a naïve Sunday painter, nicknamed the douanier (customs officer) for his day job as a toll collector, was feted by Picasso, Braque, Apollinaire and the absurdist playwright Alfred Jarry for his apparently unschooled—artless—technique. (They also appreciated his penchant for painting lions and tigers in jungle settings—or, in point of fact, imagined in hot-houses in the *jardin des plantes*.) In 1908, Picasso threw a legendary banquet for Rousseau.

A German counterpart to Rousseau was Emile Nolde. Born Hans Emil Hansen, he was brought up on a farm in the Danish–German region of Schleswig-Holstein. Trained as a woodcarver, he began in his early thirties to make his way as an artist. He changed his name to Nolde, after his native village, and married a Danish actress. In 1906, he was picked up by the Brücke group and later by the Blaue Reiter. With his rustic North German background, Nolde was valued by the more conventionally urban, middle-class expressionists as a natural primitive.[21] Shortly before the outbreak of the First World War, Nolde and a rare fellow artist from a working-class background, Max Pechstein, made a pilgrimage to German colonies in the South Seas.[22]

The political trajectories of the two men later diverged, though each was, in his way, representative of vanguard artists in the 1920s and 1930s. Pechstein became a member of revolutionary left-wing groups. Nolde joined the Danish section of the Nazi Party. (He then denounced Pechstein as a Jew, which he wasn't, and claimed that "the art dealers are all Jews.")[23] Despite the fact that Goebbels was an enthusiastic collector of Nolde's work, both Nolde and Pechstein were included in the degenerate art exhibition that the Nazi regime put on in Munich in 1937. In the purge that followed, over a thousand works by Nolde were removed from German museums, more than those of any other artist.

But the very epitome of the primitive artist in rebellion against bourgeois Europe was Paul Gauguin. Although Gauguin was almost unknown until after his death in May 1903, 227 of his paintings and carvings were included in the Salon d'Automne in 1906, where they were shown alongside the latest works of Cézanne, Derain, van Dongen and Matisse. As much as his art, Gauguin's legend entranced the post-impressionists. Here was a married stockbroker who gave it all up to live a primitive life and make primitive art.

"For my part, my resolution is made, in a while I will go to Tahiti, a little island in Oceania where life can be managed without money," Gauguin wrote to his Danish wife, Mette, in March 1887. "A terrible epoch is coming for the next generation in Europe: the kingdom of gold. Everything is spoilt, the people and art."[24] In 1891, he walked away from his day job, abandoned his family and spent two years in Tahiti, living with a Tahitian woman and painting works that incorporated both Polynesian and Western motifs and styles.

Gauguin also had a theory—or at least some ideas—about the wickedness of civilisation and the superiority of the primitive condition. August Strindberg said that Gauguin was "the savage who hates a whimpering civilization." (Strindberg, a Swedish playwright and novelist, had published an experimental ethnography, *Among French Peasants: Subjective Travel Notes*, in 1889.)[25] "Civilization from which you suffer," Gauguin responded, "barbarism which has been a rejuvenation for me." He told his daughter: "You will always find nourishing milk in the primitive arts, but I doubt if you will find it in the arts of ripe civilizations."[26]

Yet Gauguin was disillusioned by the reality of the South Seas. Soon after his arrival in Polynesia, he wrote to Mette: "The soil of Tahiti is becoming totally French, and bit by bit the old state of things is disappearing. Our missionaries have already brought in Protestant hypocrisy and removed some of the poetry, not to mention the pox that has weakened the whole race." It was still possible to find a few authentic and interesting carvings, but they were mostly imported from another French colony, the Marquesas Islands. (Policemen were the main dealers.) Gauguin complained that "the Administration has not considered for a single moment, something which would have been easy for them to do, to make a museum of Oceanian art in Tahiti."[27]

"We lack a convenient word to designate the art of faraway countries," a critic noted in the *Bulletin de la vie artistique*, in 1923.

> The Museum of Decorative Arts calls them "indigenous." Do we have to accept this designation? Should we say exotic? But this term has taken on a pejorative sense; it makes one think of "attractions" that lack seriousness: belly dancing and opium dens . . . *L'art nègre*: again a scandalous word. One must excuse oneself for using it. But there is no equivalent. The art of faraway countries? In ordinary talk it is insufferable to use such a long phrase. Indigenous is too loose, exotic too louche. Who can rescue us from this embarrassment?[28]

Whatever they were to be called, avant-garde young artists took it for granted that these African and Oceanian carvings were inspired by religious and magical ideas. They called these very disparate objects "fetishes." For the rest, their ideas about primitivism and civilisation were anything but informed or coherent. Historians of art would attempt to pin down formal affinities between post-impressionist and "primitive" artworks, but these are also elusive. Picasso insisted that he saw African masks very differently from Matisse, Braque and Derain. He understood that these were magical or religious icons, Picasso said, while his colleagues regarded them as "just like any other kind of sculpture." As for Braque, he "wasn't even frightened of them. Exorcism didn't interest him . . . He doesn't understand these things at all: he isn't superstitious!" Gertrude Stein put it another way. "The effect of this African art upon Matisse and Picasso was entirely different. Matisse through it was affected more in his imagination than in his vision. Picasso more in his vision than in his imagination."[29] In any case, Picasso kept changing his story. In April 1920, a short-lived avant-garde review of the arts, *Action*, quizzed artists about *"l'art nègre."* Picasso responded, *"L'art nègre? Connais pas!"* (Don't know it!)[30] "Everyone always talks about the influence of the Negroes on me," he protested in a conversation with André Malraux in 1937. "What can I do? We all loved fetishes."[31]

Not all the experimental young European artists were converted to primitivism. "Unfortunately all kinds of primitive races have impressed some of the young German painters and nothing seems more important to them than Bushman painting and Aztec sculpture," the dissident Expressionist painter Max Beckmann complained in 1912. "But let's be honest! Let's admit that we are not negroes or Christians of the early Middle Ages! . . . Are those crude and shabby figures we now see in all the exhibits really an expression of the complicated spirit of modern times?"[32]

And yet the primitivists were winning articulate and sophisticated advocates. In 1912, Guillaume Apollinaire, a charismatic poet, playwright, novelist, journalist and occasional art dealer, called for "a grand museum of exotic art, which will be to this art what the Louvre is to European art."[33] Apollinaire bought Benin Bronzes. (He called Picasso "the Benin Bird.") And he became a leading theorist of what he dubbed *l'art nègre*, an airy term for art from Africa and Oceania. (Maureen Murphy dubs this unlikely combo *A'O Art*.)[34] Apollinaire's views were widely shared in the Paris avant-garde. In 1920, the *Bulletin de la vie artistique* posed the question "Will arts from remote places be admitted into the Louvre?"[35] Artists and writers who responded were overwhelmingly in favour.

Primitivism took more coherent form in the 1920s. The surrealists, the new pace-makers in the Parisian avant-garde, venerated "fetishes" from Africa and Oceania and became fans of African American music and dance.[36] In the 1920s, the surrealists' commissar, André Breton, developed a potent mix of conceptions about instinct, the unconscious, sexuality and the primitive (all good), and civilisation (rotten, artificial). He charged that scientists knew everything about their objects except what mattered most, the fusion of the heart and spirit with the work and pleaded that something of the enigmatic should not be disturbed, the last veil should not be lifted.[37]

For reasons that remain unclear, some surrealists now pretended that Oceania was even better than Africa. A "Surrealist Map of the World" was published in 1929 in a special issue of *Variétés*, a Belgian surrealist magazine. At the centre of this world was a gigantic Polynesia. Africa and India were tiny. Alaska and Labrador loomed over a diminished North America. A miniaturised Europe, smaller than Easter Island, was dominated by Germany. Hanging on the very edge of this tiny Europe was Paris.

The primitive was identified with the civilised child. He was also racially marked. French artists and intellectuals now talked freely of *l'art nègre*. This term was applied in a vague sort of way to music or arts and crafts from the South Seas or Africa, perhaps even native America, but the most popular living practitioners of *l'art nègre* in Paris were African American jazz musicians and dancers. The enthusiasm was real enough, and yet there was a distinct element of anti-racist racism in all this. Apollinaire punned about a new cult, *"le Melanophilie ou Melanomanie."*[38]

Then there were the dealers. They made the market, and invented a doctrine of authenticity that ensured scarcity. "Real

African art, the argument goes, consists of old objects which were manufactured in the pre-contact or precolonial era for indigenous use," Christopher Steiner explained in his valuable account of the market in African art. Contact was equated with contagion and decay.[39] The dealers and the well-to-do collectors who were their customers embraced the authenticity doctrine. It was good for business.

Dealers pounced as soon as avant-garde artists showed an interest in *primitivisme*. In November 1912, Frank Burty Haviland, a wealthy French-American, whose grandfather coined the term *japonisme*, gave Picasso an African mask in exchange for one of his drawings. In retrospect, this deal was a symbolic marker of a new market that included classical African and post-impressionist art on an equal footing.

Also in 1912, Apollinaire became a business associate of an up-and-coming art dealer, Paul Guillaume.[40] Twenty years old, from Pigalle, then a poor quarter of Paris, Guillaume had a job as a salesman in a garage near the Place de l'Étoile. Tyres were sourced from rubber factories in French West Africa, and local suppliers were ready to include other stuff in their shipments. Guillaume got his hands on some masks and carvings, which he put in the window of the garage among the car tyres and bicycles. Passing by one day, Apollinaire (an early car buff) noticed a striking African carving. Soon he was introducing the young Guillaume to artists and dealers. Guillaume put up a sign in a Paris café frequented by colonial officers on home leave: "Paul Guillaume pays high prices for all pieces and collections of African origin."[41] Within a year he had his own gallery and was representing up-and-coming artists, including Francis Picabia, a cubist, and the surrealist painters Giacomo De Chirico and Pierre Roy, featuring their work alongside carvings from Africa and Oceania.

When Germany and France went to war in 1914, Apollinaire volunteered for the cavalry. Wounded in 1916, he returned to the front. On 9 November 1918, two days before the Armistice, he died of influenza. Guillaume remained behind in Paris, and he flourished. He mastered the latest publicity techniques, including exhibitions, modish receptions and publications, among them *Sculptures Nègres*, which featured Apollinaire's essay "Concerning the art of the blacks." He moved his gallery to an aristocratic quarter of Paris, the Faubourg Saint-Honoré. In 1918, he arranged a *fête nègre* in the théâtre des Champs-Élysées.

Apollinaire had introduced Guillaume to Marius de Zayas, a Mexican artist and dealer, who was in Paris as the representative of "291," the avant-garde Fifth Avenue gallery of Alfred Stieglitz. Stieglitz had mounted a show of Rodin and Matisse in 1908, Cézanne in 1910, and Picasso in 1911. De Zayas was an enthusiast for *l'art nègre*. He reported back to Stieglitz that Guillaume "knows everything there is to be known of this movement, who works for his own pleasure, who is well known for his honesty and rectitude and respected by all the different bands of the modern artists in Paris." In October 1915, Stieglitz staked de Zayas to a new showroom, the "Modern Gallery," a branch of "291." According to the publicity material, it would be dedicated to "the sale of paintings of the most advanced character of the modern art movement, negro sculptures, pre-conquest Mexican art and photography."[42]

In 1922, Guillaume made a connection with Alfred Barnes, a business tycoon who was building up a collection of modernist and primitive art in Philadelphia. Writing in *Opportunity Magazine*, a forum for the Harlem Renaissance, Barnes named Guillaume's gallery "The Temple" and Guillaume himself the "High Priest":

> because in no other rendezvous have I witnessed so much devotion by so many of the painters, sculptors, composers, writers, connoisseurs, who have made the art history of our time . . . His little gallery and museum of ancient Negro sculpture is now the Mecca not only of the important creators in France, but in America, Japan, England, and every continental country. I have seen six chiefs of African tribes there at the same time with four principals of the Russian ballet.[43]

Guillaume put together a catalogue of "Primitive Negro Sculpture" for Barnes. The text, written by Thomas Munro, Barnes foundation professor of modern art at the University of Pennsylvania, argued for a purely artistic take on the exhibits, concentrating on "the plastic qualities of the figures—their effects of line, plane, mass and color—apart from all associated facts." Ethnology, Munro opined, "tends to confuse one's appreciation of the plastic qualities in themselves. From the artistic point of view the important question is not what subjects the sculptor chose, but how he executed them, with what distinctive uses of his medium."[44]

After the First World War, American collectors beat a path to Paris to buy modernist paintings and primitivist carvings and statues. Nelson Rockefeller was a regular visitor to the gallery of Hélène Leloup on the Boulevard Raspail. "These people knew nothing," she recalled, "they were wild for novelties, for French wine, French couture and, why not, *d'art nègre*." (Leloup noted that demand was met with the help of African entrepreneurs, who delivered truckloads of artefacts to warehouses in Paris.)[45]

French dealers of primitive art soon set up shop in New York. Guillaume and Leloup were regular visitors. "Negro art is fashionable!" Guillaume exulted.[46] Apollinaire's friend Joseph Brummer had moved there in 1914 and he and his brother dealt in Paris modernists and *l'art nègre*, providing competition to Stieglitz and de Zayas. In 1923, the Brooklyn Museum became the first U.S. institution to exhibit African carvings and sculptures as art ("Primitive Negro Art, Chiefly from the Belgian Congo"). In 1933, an exhibition at the Museum of Modern Art in New York, "American Sources of Modern Art (Aztec, Mayan, Incan)," brought together American modernist art with pre-Columbian masterpieces from Central America. The scarcely disguised subtext was that American modernists were the equals of those Europeans. Moreover, the Americans found inspiration in American, *not* African, primitives. (Ironically, the show was largely dependent on French loans.)[47] The Museum of Modern

Art followed up in 1935 with a hugely popular exhibition of "African Negro Art."

In 1938, Robert Goldwater, a young American historian of art, published his doctoral dissertation, *Primitivism in Modern Art*. Goldwater did not buy into the myth that post-impressionist artists—including Gauguin—learned much from African or Oceanian models. Exotic masks and carvings may turn up in their paintings, but "there is little that is not allusion and suggestion rather than immediate borrowing." The reception of "primitive art" "widened our concept of what 'art' is, has made us realize the many shapes art can assume," Goldwater wrote. Nevertheless, "both the social purposes and the aesthetic achievements of primitive art—its forms and its functions—are widely different from those of modern art." In the preface to the revised edition of his book, published in 1968, Goldwater summed up his thesis: "although modern artists admired primitive art they neither copied it nor, despite what they themselves sometimes thought, ever really had the same ends in view."

Goldwater's most important move was to distinguish between "primitivism"—a modern Western idea—and the "primitive." The primitive was the business of anthropologists. "It is primitivism in which we are interested; but this presupposes the knowledge of some kind of primitive." Yet Goldwater had to admit that neither the primitive nor primitivism could be clearly defined. Some anthropologists were sceptical about the very idea of a primitive condition, or primitive peoples. "Our definition of primitivism must, in consequence, be discursive," Goldwater conceded.[48] *Primitivism in Modern Art* gave scholarly support to anyone with a stake in primitive art. It became a minor classic of art history. And yet Goldwater is perhaps best remembered for a riddle. Question: What is primitive art? Answer: It is the stuff that isn't in the Metropolitan.[49] (That didn't work for long. After 1982, primitive art *was* in the Met.)

A year after Goldwater made the aesthetic case for primitivism—and against anthropology—Claude Lévi-Strauss, arguably the leading European anthropologist of the second half of the twentieth century, arrived in New York as a refugee from German-occupied France. The son and nephew of professional artists, as an adolescent Lévi-Strauss imagined that he would be a composer, like his grandfather, who was the leader of the court orchestra of Napoleon III. However, he studied philosophy at the Sorbonne and found his vocation as an anthropologist by chance. A recent philosophy graduate, newly married, teaching in a provincial *lycée*, Lévi-Strauss took a phone call at nine o'clock one Sunday morning in the autumn of 1934 from the director of the École normale supérieure. "Do you still want to study anthropology?"—"Most certainly"—"Then apply for a post as a teacher of sociology at the University of São Paulo. The suburbs are full of Indians, whom you can study at the weekends. But you must give a firm answer before midday." Lévi-Strauss had only idly considered learning anthropology, but he accepted at once, joining a small group of young French scholars—including Fernand Braudel—sent out to join the faculty of the new Brazilian university.[50]

He knew little about sociology, which he was expected to teach, or ethnology, which he hoped to practise. But his imagination was fired. "I felt I was reliving the adventures of the first travellers of the sixteenth century," he confessed. He and his wife made brief expeditions to the Caduveo and Bororo tribes of the Mato Grosso and, a year later, a more extensive visit to the Nambikwara in the Amazon region. Funded by the Musée de l'Homme in Paris, the couple spent much of their time collecting thousands of material objects to be dispatched to Paris, where Lévi-Strauss would curate a well-received exhibition; but he published only short accounts on face painting, decorative arts and social organisation. Castro Faria, a young Brazilian scholar who accompanied them in the field, remarked that (in contrast to his wife) Lévi-Strauss had no vocation for ethnographic fieldwork. He was "a philosopher among the Indians."[51]

Lévi-Strauss returned to France a few months before the German invasion in 1939 and served briefly in the army. After the fall of France he escaped to the United States in one of the last ships carrying refugees. (André Breton was a fellow passenger.) His wife refused to join him. In his early thirties, he arrived in New York alone, exiled, an anthropologist without formal training or qualifications, his country occupied, his wife and parents in hiding from the Vichy authorities. Yet he was oddly happy in America. He became fluent in English, and Americanised his name, presenting himself as Claude L. Strauss. (A colleague told him that his real name would make students laugh, "because of the blue jeans.") He got to know Franz Boas, the dean of American anthropology, and developed collegial relations with Boas's lieutenants, Robert Lowie and Alfred Kroeber, but his close friends were drawn from among the exiled French surrealists. His biographer, Emmanuelle Loyer, remarks that they shared his curiosity about unconscious thought processes and his passion for exotic art, and that he liked their aristocratic dandyism. He considered taking lodgings near the Boasian base at Columbia University but decided rather to rent an apartment in Greenwich Village, where the surrealists were concentrated.

The village reminded him of Montparnasse. There, he recalled, "one could still lodge, as in Paris in the time of Balzac, in a duplex on two or three floors with a back garden."[52] Once an habitué of Parisian flea markets, in New York Lévi-Strauss scoured antique shops for African and American masks and sculptures together with André Breton, Max Ernst and Marcel Duchamp, "sharing among ourselves, according to the funds available, the pieces for sale at New York antique dealers. It was a time when these works did not arouse any interest, which, in itself, seems like a myth today. In 1951, I had to sell my collection."[53]

In 1943, in an essay for a little magazine that Breton had started, Lévi-Strauss described "a magic place [that] may be seen daily from ten to five o'clock at the American Museum of Natural History. It is the vast ground-floor gallery devoted to the Indians of the Pacific Northwest Coast, an area extending from Alaska to British Columbia." This was the collection that Boas had installed.

Lévi-Strauss appreciated Boas's regional comparisons, but instead of a series of chance local interactions and borrowings he discerned a creative ferment. The Northwest coast had been occupied by Europeans for a century and a half. This period "saw the birth and flowering of not one but ten different forms . . . This unceasing renewal, this inventive assuredness that guarantees success wherever it is applied, this scorn for the beaten track, bring about ever new improvisations which infallibly lead to dazzling results—to get any idea of them, our times had to await the exceptional destiny of a Picasso."[54]

Lévi-Strauss regarded these Northwest coast artefacts as works of high art. In an essay published in 1943, he echoed Apollinaire's prophecy: "Surely it will not be long before we see the collections from this part of the world moved from ethnographic to fine arts museums to take their just place amidst the antiquities of Egypt and Persia and the works of medieval Europe."[55]

After the liberation of France, Lévi-Strauss returned to the United States as cultural counsellor at the French Embassy. "I had the opportunity of acquiring for France a famous collection [of native American art], which is now in a museum on the West Coast of the United States; in payment, the seller wanted a few Matisse and Picasso canvases instead of taxable dollars. But despite all my efforts, I failed to convince the officials responsible for our artistic policy who happened to be visiting New York."[56] This was a sign of the times. The market in primitive art had moved from Paris to New York. And it found a new patron, a politician, plutocrat and obsessional collector, Nelson Aldrich Rockefeller.

Nelson's grandfather, John D. Rockefeller, was the founder of Standard Oil. Nelson's mother, Abby Aldrich Rockefeller, collected twentieth-century art. In 1929, nine days after the Wall Street crash, she founded the Museum of Modern Art—known cosily as MoMA—together with two friends, Lillie Bliss and Mary Quinn Sullivan (a formidable trio, the "adamantine ladies").

Nelson would make his career in politics, but his lifelong hobby—and passion—was collecting. On his honeymoon, a world cruise funded by his parents, managed by the global representatives of the family firm, he began to collect Oceanian carvings and Asian sculptures. Back in New York, he branched out into African and pre-Columbian American art.

Soon after graduating from Dartmouth College in 1930, Nelson became a trustee, then, in swift succession, treasurer and president of the council of MoMA. He was also a trustee of the Metropolitan Museum of Art. Nelson was young, but these were caste entitlements. MoMA was virtually a family business. However, the Met was even more prestigious. In 1942 he offered the Met choice items from his collection of primitive art. The director, Herbert Winlock, was dismissive. That sort of thing did not belong in a museum of great art. In 1914, the Met had transferred its own pre-Columbian holdings to the Museum of Natural History, which occupied another corner of Central Park. Perhaps Rockefeller should consider placing his own collection there.[57]

Nelson had different ideas. He acquired his own mentor in primitive art: René d'Harnoncourt. Born into a decaying, provincial aristocratic family in Austria, d'Harnoncourt turned up, penniless, in Mexico City in 1925. He was twenty-four years old, with no particular qualifications. After a year of drift he was taken on by an Austrian antique dealer who, d'Harnoncourt recalled, "had received a large shipment of antique furniture from the Palace of Schönbrun, or so he said, which he wanted to dispose of. I had learned enough Spanish and English to help him sell this, and other things he had, to Mexicans and Americans."[58] D'Harnoncourt went on to manage the art business of an American entrepreneur in Mexico City. He was now mixing with Mexican and North American collectors, including the U.S. ambassador. An invitation soon came to curate an exhibition of Mexican arts and crafts at the Met. Moving to the U.S. in 1933, d'Harnoncourt became Nelson's indispensable advisor on art purchases.

Nelson was in need of help. He had just suffered a very public embarrassment at the hands of the radical Mexican artist, trickster and fabulist, Diego Rivera. In 1933, Nelson commissioned a painting from Rivera to decorate the lobby of the main building of the Rockefeller Center. ("Although I do not personally care much for his work," Nelson told the management of the centre, "Rivera seems to have become very popular just now and will probably be a good drawing card.")[59] The artist insisted on a huge mural, to be fixed to the walls.

Rivera was not entirely frank about his plans, but it soon became apparent that he was painting a celebration of revolutionary communism, done in social realist style, featuring muscular female gymnasts leaping over hurdles, a large and handsome working man controlling a futuristic machine— and . . . Surely not! But yes . . . "I noticed that in the most recent portion of the painting you had included a portrait of Lenin," Nelson wrote to Rivera. "The piece is beautiful but it seems to me that his portrait appearing in the mural might very seriously offend a great many people . . . As much as I dislike to do so, I am afraid we must ask you to substitute the face of some unknown man where Lenin's face now appears." Rivera refused to paint over his Soviet icon, but offered to add a portrait of Abraham Lincoln. Rivera's wife, Frida Kahlo, "was peeking in and out of the door to keep check on developments," Nelson recalled. "When I went out, she came in."[60] There were demonstrations in support of Rivera on Rockefeller Plaza. But Nelson's father was not happy. The mural was peeled from the wall. Rivera said that this act of censorship would "advance the cause of the labour revolution."[61]

D'Harnoncourt's first job in the U.S. was as general manager of a New Deal project, the Indian Arts and Crafts Board. In 1941 he curated a successful show at MoMA, *Indian Art of the United States*. Nelson was soon paying part of d'Harnoncourt's salary so that he could moonlight as his advisor. In 1949, he installed d'Harnoncourt as director of MoMA, where he remained until 1967.

D'Harnoncourt impressed, even awed, Manhattanites. Under the title "Imperturbable Noble," *The New Yorker* magazine ran a profile that reads like a celebrity puff piece:

> Like a good many of his ancestors, René d'Harnoncourt, the agile, gigantic, genial, hard-working, courtly, confident, aristocratic, wildly conversational Vienna-born director and champion *installateur* of the Museum of Modern Art, who is a descendant, direct and collateral, of a cloud of Middle European noblemen who flourished as chamberlains and provosts to a cloud of Dukes of Luxembourg, and Hapsburg emperors, has exhibited a gift for making himself indispensable to a succession—and quite often an overlapping—of patrons.[62]

In 1957, guided by d'Harnoncourt, Rockefeller set up a private Museum of Primitive Art in a beaux-arts town house next door to his childhood home. According to the official brochure, it was "the only museum devoted entirely to the rich and dynamic native arts of Africa, Oceania and the Americas." This art was "as important to our cultural heritage as the arts of the more advanced civilization of the Orient and the West."

Rockefeller was, of course, president of his Museum of Primitive Art. D'Harnoncourt was vice-president. Robert Goldwater, author of *Primitivism in Modern Art*, was director. A young Englishman, Douglas Newton, was taken on as assistant curator. He had no expertise in art or in museum work, but evidently showed a talent for installation. He would succeed Goldwater as the museum's director.

Everything was in place, but how was this sort of art to be branded? In November 1956, Rockefeller was writing to a donor: "One thing that has been preoccupying us is the name 'indigenous.' It doesn't seem to convey anything to anybody except a few professionals."[63] So he switched to "primitive," explaining to *Life* magazine that this was a generally accepted designation. "Like 'gothic,' long ago, and 'modern' more recently, it was once a term of disapproval, and like them, it has become a term of historical description and praise."[64]

All this while, Rockefeller had his hands full with politics. He was governor of New York State from 1959 to 1973, and vice-president to President Gerald Ford from 1974 to 1977. He also ran three campaigns for the Republican presidential nomination. (Coming from the liberal wing of the party, he lost in 1960 to Richard Nixon, to Barry Goldwater in 1964 and to Ronald Reagan in 1968.) Yet he always found time for his primitive art collection. "More than once during the contentious Eisenhower years, a jaded Rockefeller picked up the phone and cajoled MoMA director René d'Harnoncourt into flying down to Washington with a suitcase full of Peruvian gold work or pre-Columbian figures," writes Richard Norton Smith, Rockefeller's biographer. Nelson would then spend a restorative half-hour selecting the "stuff" he wanted to buy. "I think I inherit my weakness for shopping from the Aldrich family," he confessed to his mother's sister, Lucy. "There's nothing in the world I'd rather do."[65]

The Rockefellers were among the great American dynasties of the twentieth century. Nelson expected his son Michael to succeed to the leadership of MoMA.[66] Michael shared his father's passion for primitive art. And like Nelson he was a risk taker—reckless on ski slopes, regularly ticketed for speeding in his car. In 1961, when he was twenty-three years old, a student at Harvard, Michael joined an expedition to New Guinea organised by Harvard's Peabody Museum. Travelling between two offshore islands on a dugout canoe, he and a young Dutch anthropologist found themselves in difficulties. Michael opted to strike out for land through shark-infested waters. He disappeared. Rockefeller set up a memorial exhibition in the Abby Aldrich Rockefeller garden at MoMA. On display were hundreds

Michael Rockefeller among the Asmat in New Guinea, shortly before
his disappearance aged twenty-three, in 1961. Photograph by Jan
Broekhuijse. (By permission of the President and Fellows of Harvard
College, Peabody Museum of Archaeology and Ethnology.)

of Asmat carvings that Michael had collected. The only picture
Nelson kept on his desk was one of Michael.[67]

And then, in 1968, Nelson's mentor, d'Harnoncourt, was run
down and killed by a drunk driver. Nelson closed the Museum
of Primitive Art. In 1969, he offered its collection to the Met.
This time there was no resistance. The trustees undertook to
build a whole new wing for primitive art. It was to be named
for Michael. A department of primitive art was established. Nelson's team moved in. Robert Goldwater became consultative
chairman. Douglas Newton became department head.

Nelson pledged $4 million to fund the new wing, but he did
not deliver. The director of the Met, Thomas Hoving, publicly
called him a "grifter." According to Nelson's biographer the sum
was "eventually cobbled together with help from Brooke Astor

and the estate of Nelson's stepmother."[68] The Michael C. Rockefeller wing of the Met opened in January 1982, showing artworks
from sub-Saharan Africa, the Pacific Islands and the Americas.
Susan Vogel, one of the curators involved in the installation,
recalls that the Met wanted the galleries to look like other galleries in the museum. "This immediately meant that installation
techniques used in museums of natural history were out. No
mannequins, no photo-murals, no music."[69] And no ethnography—indeed, very little in the way of contextual information.

The lead-up to the Met's new wing of primitive art spawned
a surge of competitive exhibitions. MoMA reacted quickly.
In 1984 it put on "'Primitivism' in 20th Century Art: Affinity
of the Tribal and the Modern,'" curated by William Rubin of
MoMA and a historian of art, Kurt Varnedoe. Rubin more or
less accepted Goldwater's thesis that what mattered was not the
primitive (whatever that might be), but rather "primitivism,"
which was a movement in modern art. "We owe to the voyag-
ers, colonials, and ethnologists the arrival of these objects in the
West. But we owe primarily to the convictions of the pioneer
modern artists their promotion from the rank of curiosities and
artifacts to that of major art, indeed, to the status of art at all."[70]
So let anthropologists worry about the context in which these
African and Oceanian objects were made: "I have quite different
aims; I want to understand the Primitive sculptures in terms of
the Western context in which modern artists 'discovered' them.
The ethnologists' primary concern—the specific function and
significance of each of these objects—is irrelevant to my topic,
except insofar as these facts might have been known to the
modern artists in question."[71]

Rubin argued that the post-impressionist artists picked up
on primitive masks and carvings only once they had made an
aesthetic breakthrough, a paradigm change, that he characterised (rather allusively) as the "shift from the perceptual to the
conceptual." The point was that primitivism logically followed
on from cubism. "The 'discovery' of African art . . . took place

when, in terms of contemporary developments, it was needed." But it did not *cause* a revolution in modern Western art.[72]

Although he had no interest in the views of anthropologists, Rubin did not hesitate to make his own large claims about the meaning of what he called "tribal" art. "Like all great art, the finest tribal sculptures show images of man that transcend the particular lives and times of their makers."[73] Goldwater had written of "allusion and suggestion." Rubin judged that Goldwater underestimated the impact of the psychological and even stylistic affinity of some modernist works and "tribal" exemplars. He, Rubin, knew better. How was that? "Apart from the testimony of a few artists, the answer lies in my sense of how the artistic mind operates, by what byways and indirect paths it achieves its goals."[74]

In 1984, Susan Mullin Vogel, an associate curator in the department of primitive art at the Met, set up the "Center for African Art" in a pair of converted town houses on Manhattan's Upper East Side. In 1988 she curated an exhibition "Art/Artifact: African Art in Anthropology Collections." This confronted a nagging old problem. "Virtually all of the African art works we now know were once classified as artifacts," Vogel wrote in her introduction to the catalogue. "The problem of distinguishing between the two categories has proven remarkably resistant to clear-cut solutions, and continues to bedevil those who collect and exhibit African and other 'Primitive' arts." Vogel took the line that the difference between art and artefact is no longer as salient as it once had been. Art historians and anthropologists had moved on. Anthropologists are now more aware of aesthetics, art historians increasingly concerned with the broader social context of artistic activity. In consequence, installations in art and ethnographic museums now resemble each other. Or rather, both employ a similar, elegant, minimalist gallery style.

Yet difficult choices still have to be made. Might a hunting net of the Zande people of Sudan be regarded as a work of art? Vogel showed a photograph of a net, collected in 1910, to her mentor, Arthur Danto, a philosopher of aesthetics at Columbia University. Danto was a stern judge. He had described the primitivism exhibition at MoMA as "stupendously misconceived," a case of "museological manipulation."[75] So did he consider the hunting net to be a work of art or an artefact? "It is in one sense a matter for experts to decide," Danto wrote in his contribution to the exhibition catalogue. But then again, he mused, perhaps not. "Because of their striking resemblances, even a highly trained anthropologist is incapable of distinguishing between an artwork and an artifact from the region."

Whether art or artefact, this particular net had languished in the store of the American Museum of Natural History, never exhibited, for a century. When it was retrieved by Enid Schildkraut, curator of the African collection, and loaned to the Center for African Art, the net was still bound—as it had been for almost a century—with a rope wound around it by the original collector, Herbert Lang, a photographer with the American Museum Congo Expedition (1909–15). Susan Vogel decided to exhibit it just as Lang had prepared it for transport and storage, tied in a bundle. So if this was now to be regarded as a work of art, should it be credited to the weaver of the net, to the collector, Herbert Lang, or to the curator, Susan Vogel? Or was it a matter for the viewer to decide, all in the eye of the beholder? Vogel suggested that Manhattan sophisticates would immediately associate the coiled net with contemporary artworks, for instance Jacqueline Winsor's wood and twine piece, *Bound Square*, in the Museum of Modern Art. Alfred Gell, a specialist in the anthropology of art, praised her for making a curatorial breakthrough and compared what he called "Vogel's Net" to Marcel Duchamp's *Fountain*, a readymade sculpture from 1917 featuring a porcelain urinal signed "R. Mutt."[76]

But Danto was, after all, an idealist philosopher. He wanted to set universal, perhaps even eternal standards. After invoking Socrates, Hegel and Wittgenstein, he concluded that there was no such thing as primitive art: "the fact that some . . . [African] artifacts should have come, through the restless drives of

Western art, to resemble artworks of considerable sophistication no more makes those artifacts into works of art than it confers upon them that sophistication. When it came to "knives or nets or hairpins, the objects' meaning is exhausted in their utility," Danto pronounced. "They are what they are used for, but artworks have some higher role, putting us in touch with higher realities: they are defined through the possession of meaning. They are to be explained through what they express."[77]

This was perhaps the last moment when high priests of the art world felt free to pontificate about which "non-European" carvings, bronzes, ceramics, fabrics, totems, cult objects, decorated furnishings and weapons might be labelled works of art. By the early twenty-first century even posing the question—but is it art?—was a sure sign of philistinism. In the run up to the 2004 Turner Prize (the UK's premier award for contemporary art), five hundred experts were asked to name the most influential work of modern art. Andy Warhol's 1962 silkscreen painting of Marilyn Monroe came third. Picasso's *Les Demoiselles d'Avignon* (1907) was second. In first place was Marcel Duchamp's urinal, *Fountain*, first put on display in 1917.

The English press delivered predictable verdicts. The left-wing *Guardian* hailed a "direct link" between Duchamp's urinal and Tracey Emin's notorious unmade bed, which was nominated for the Turner Prize in 1998. (It did not win, but sold at Christie's in 2014 for $4.2 million.) The right-wing *Daily Telegraph* sniffed that the vote "explains an awful lot about today's art," but didn't explain precisely what it explained. "The choice of Duchamp's Fountain as the most influential work of modern art ahead of works by Picasso and Matisse comes as a bit of a shock," one expert told the BBC. "But it reflects the dynamic nature of art today . . . The work itself can be made of anything and can take any form."[78] The *New Statesman* suggested that Duchamp was "just taking the piss."

The dichotomy between "authentic" primitive art and stuff churned out for tourists was also crumbling. In 1989, "Magiciens de la Terre" (magicians of the earth), an ambitious exhibition at the Pompidou Centre in Paris, set out to make the Paris Biennale more inclusive. It gave equal space to contemporary Western and non-Western artists and featured tourist art and outright kitsch alongside fine art. But it was still in thrall to the old primitivist creed. The curators favoured ritualistic or mystical subject matter. Western artists were selected for their supposed rapport with the primitive.[79]

The museums of Paris struggled to keep pace with New York, while New York kept looking over its shoulder at Paris. But the dynamic of the two centres is very different. Museums in Manhattan are philanthropic foundations, endowed by tycoons and their wives or widows. In Paris the great museums and monuments have always been the playthings of successive rulers: kings, emperors and presidents of the republic.

Following the Liberation, as the French economy began to recover, successive presidents of the Fifth Republic created a series of cultural landmarks in Paris. France's first minister of culture, André Malraux, persuaded President de Gaulle to approve an ambitious, hybrid project that would unite a museum of modern art, a library and a musical archive. De Gaulle's successor, Georges Pompidou, brought it to completion. A later president, Jacques Chirac, named it the Pompidou Centre. President Giscard d'Estaing built an art museum, the Musée d'Orsay. Dedicated to the nineteenth-century artists who were eclipsed by the post-impressionists, it expressed a nostalgia for the neoclassical conventions of the Académie des Beaux-Arts. Giscard's successor, François Mitterrand, the first Socialist president of the Fifth Republic, commissioned a large pyramid of glass and metal at the entrance to the Louvre in the Cour Napoléon. He also chose the (controversial) design for a new opera house and directed the modernisation of the Bibliotheque nationale de France ("the largest and most modern library in the world," he proclaimed).

Jacques Chirac, president of France from 1995 to 2007, had been a collector of African art since doing his military service as an officer in Algeria. For his *grand projet* he decided on a museum of "primitive art."[80] This may seem a surprising choice. Previous presidents had built monuments to modernity, to civilisation and to France. (And to themselves.) But Paris had been left behind by New York. What answer did it have to the Rockefeller wing of the Met? And besides, this was, surely, a matter of human rights. Chirac claimed that his museum was intended to be a tribute to the Enlightenment ideals of fraternity and equality. "There is no hierarchy among the arts just as there is no hierarchy among peoples," he asserted in his address at the opening of the quai Branly museum on 20 June 2006, in the presence of Kofi Annan, secretary-general of the UN, and Lévi-Strauss. "Every people has a particular message to deliver to the world which can enrich humanity and contribute its portion to beauty and to truth."

Chirac had the backing of Jacques Kerchache, a shady dealer who had been detained in prison in Gabon in 1965 for the illegal export of some twenty sacred reliquaries. Chirac described him as a "global specialist in *des arts premiers* . . . probably, even certainly, the man who has seen most of the loveliest things in the world . . . whose eye can distinguish, almost within a millimetre, the vulgar from the work of genius."[81] Kerchache himself invoked Rousseau: the *"chefs-d'oeuvre* of the whole world were born free and equal."[82] In March 1990, he orchestrated a manifesto in the progressive newspaper *Libération*, demanding "instantly" the establishment of a new section of the Louvre, to be devoted to "objects issuing from African, American, Arctic, Asiatic and Oceanian cultures." Among the signatories were some of the leading anthropologists in Paris, but not Claude Lévi-Strauss. "The Louvre Museum is not at all a universal museum," Lévi-Strauss said. "The role of the Louvre is to bring together all that has formed the traditions of France and the Western world."[83]

In 2000, as his new project was taking form, President Chirac invited the Louvre to mount a temporary exhibit of primitive art. Kerchache would loan 120 African, Asian, American and Oceanic masterpieces from his own inventory. Some curators

objected that the Louvre was dedicated to the highest achievements of civilisation. It was not the place for primitive crafts.
And should a dealer really be invited to show his personal stock
at the Louvre? The president insisted. He and Kerchache got
their way. The exhibition was mounted in an interstitial, notion-
ally temporary venue, the Pavillon des Sessions. It is still there.[84]

Then Chirac announced that nothing less than a whole new
museum would suffice. Lévi-Strauss now came out in favour of
the presidential project. Writing in *Le Monde* in 1996, he observed:

> an ethnographic museum can no longer offer an authentic
> image of the life of societies that are most different from
> our own. With a few exceptions, which will not long con-
> tinue, these societies are being progressively integrated in
> global politics and economics. When I look again at the
> objects that I collected in the field between 1935 and 1938,
> and this is also true of others, I know well that their interest
> has become either documentary or—and above all—aes-
> thetic. In the former aspect they belong in a laboratory;
> in the latter, in a grand museum of arts and civilisations.[85]

This was a hugely significant concession, even a surrender to
the art world. But not all Lévi-Strauss's fellow anthropologists were on board with Chirac's project. They pointed out
that Paris already had significant collections of non-European
art, in the Musée de l'Homme and the Musée des Arts Africains et Océaniens. Chirac promptly closed them down and
appropriated 280,000 pieces from the Musée de l'Homme and
nearly 30,000 from the Musée des Arts Africains et Océaniens
for the new museum.[86] That, incidentally, helped to solve a
more mundane problem. Chirac secured an initial $300 million
government grant for the quai Branly, but the market for primitive art exploded as soon as plans for the new museum were
published. Sotheby's put on a sale in Paris to coincide with the
opening of the museum. Fifteen pieces went for more than half
a million euros each. It was quite a piece of luck, then, that the

masterpieces of the old museums would cost the quai Branly nothing.

But anthropologists raised vexing objections to the very conception of a museum of primitive art. Both terms, "primitive," and "art," were problematic. Chirac countered by invoking the authority of André Malraux, France's very first minister of culture (whose corpse Chirac ordered to be disinterred and then installed in the Pantheon). Malraux's imaginary "museum without walls" reserved a special place for *l'art nègre*, together with the art of children and the insane. According to Malraux, they shared a crucial Hegelian feature: "all are arts outside history and chronology."[87]

Well, perhaps, but what on earth did Malraux mean by "savage" or Chirac by "primitive"? Germain Viatte, a career museum curator who became the first director of museology at the quai Branly, proposed a less contentious formula. The museum would be dedicated to "exotic art," or "the art and cultures of non-western civilisations."[88] There was talk of including objects from "traditional" enclaves in Europe, though excluding France, but this idea was soon dropped. The new museum would be dedicated to the art and artefacts of "indigenous" peoples in Oceania, the Arctic, the Americas and Africa. But what did these far-flung peoples have in common, apart from their experience of European colonisation? Kerchache floated an alternative name for Chirac's museum—the Musée des Arts Premières. The *first arts*? *Really?* Did hunter-gatherers from the Arctic to the Amazon all belong to the same school of art? And was the rock art of the South African Bushmen or the Australian aborigines simply a contemporary version of 20,000-year-old cave paintings at Lascaux?

A Canadian museologist, Élise Dubuc, amused, bemused, summed up the succession of names proposed: "Museum of Primitive Arts (a term used by journalists), Museum of Primordial Arts (Malraux), Museum of First Arts (suggested by Chirac, since it would be the First Nations that would be represented), the Museum of Civilisations and First Arts (November 1996),

Museum of Mankind, Arts and Civilisations (February 1998) and then the Museum of Arts and Civilisations . . ."[89]

In 1997, France's mid-term elections returned a Socialist parliamentary majority. Chirac was forced into an uncomfortable "cohabitation" with the opposition. The new prime minister appointed a left-wing anthropologist, Maurice Godelier, to the planning team for the president's museum. Godelier wanted a "post-colonial" museum that set artefacts in the context of their creation and use and which would explore similarities and differences between local understandings of universal themes (invisible beings, power, the life cycle, sex, representations of nature). Kerchache wanted none of that. "Works of art are not reducible to a discourse of the conditions of their production," he claimed, "they have an intrinsic plastic value which only the cultivated eye can discern."[90] Kerchache died, aged fifty-eight, in August 2001, but the majority in the planning team shared his views. Ethnologists had ruled at the Musée de l'Homme ("a museum of anthropology created by a staff of art lovers").[91] Art historians were soon in command in the new museum. The ethnologists were backroom technicians.

And now, at last, a name had to be chosen. Construction of the museum was about to begin on the banks of the Seine, at the quai Branly. It was formally opened in June 2006 with a provisional name, the Musée du quai Branly. Chirac let it be known that should a future occupant of the Élysée wish to change the name to the Jacques Chirac Museum, he would consider it a great honour. This honour was conferred after his death. It is now the Musée du quai Branly–Jacques Chirac.

Whatever the museum might be called, the architect, Jean Nouvel, had a very definite idea of its mission. Indeed, he set it in stone. His building invites the visitor to explore a pristine tropical paradise, home to a prelapsarian civilisation. In the spirit of another Paris-based institution, UNESCO, the museum was dedicated to cultural diversity, which was conceived, as Benoît de l'Estoile remarks, on the model of biodiversity.[92] The garden in which it is set gestures to a tropical forest. Within the building is a stunning but intellectually incoherent collection of anonymous masterpieces from Europe's former tropical colonies. These are presented, without qualification, as works of art.

Emmanuel Désveaux, a disciple of Claude Lévi-Strauss, was the scientific director of the quai Branly museum between 2001 and 2006. In an interview with *Le Monde* he was asked about the difference between the new museum and the Musée de l'Homme. He responded that the Musée de l'Homme, established under the umbrella of the Museum of Natural History, was a museum of human evolution. It associated exotic ethnographic materials with the findings of prehistory, and more or less explicitly distinguished all that from the productions of modern European civilisation. The quai Branly museum, in contrast, insisted on cultural diversity. Pushed to explain why, nevertheless, European civilisation was absent from the new museum, Désveaux fell back on a pragmatic excuse: Europe was simply so richly documented and represented that its presence would overwhelm the rest.

Why then, his interviewer demanded, did the new museum "privilege the aesthetic"? Désveaux gave two answers. First, "it has been accepted since the early twentieth century that there is no progress in art. Emphasising this theme—and that is the project of the quai Branly—firmly establishes the equality of all societies. This approach has a significant moral benefit." Second, "art is a good entry point for the presentation of the diversity of cultures. The value of art is widely appreciated today in our own culture. And that is because art has become a substitute for the religious, it is sacralised."[93]

Benoît de L'Estoile pointed out that as it became more and more evidently an art museum, the quai Branly might be described as "post-ethnographic."[94] "While the Musée de l'Homme presented a realist fiction, pretended to give an account of the world as it is," he writes, "the quai Branly museum offers an initiation into a universe that is atemporal and dreamlike."[95] And where the Musée de l'Homme was "evolutionist," the quai Branly proclaimed that it was post-Darwinian. (*Le Monde* ran the disconcerting headline: "The quai Branly museum rejects Darwin.")[96]

Maurice Godelier may have wanted the quai Branly museum to be "post-colonial,"[97] but a former minister of culture in Mali, Aminata Traoré, noted that just as the museum was about to open its doors to the public, the French government introduced strict controls on immigration: "our works of art are protected by copyright where we . . . are forbidden to stay."[98] Nevertheless, the museum proved to be hugely popular, and not least among French people of immigrant origin. This may be due in part to the fact that the budget of the quai Branly was about a third higher than that of President Giscard d'Estaing's Musée d'Orsay. French citizens represent 81 per cent of all visitors.

Berlin was perhaps just a little piqued by the enormous publicity garnered by the plans for Chirac's glamorous museum. In 2002, the German chancellor, Gerhard Schröder, launched an ambitious and very expensive federal project. But, of course, it had its pragmatic side. It was, among many other things, the solution to a city planning problem: what was to be done about the Stalinist monstrosity erected by the East German regime on the site of the Kaiser's palace in Berlin?

The fifteenth-century Stadtschloss (city castle) was expanded and restored in baroque style by Frederick the Great in 1713. It was bombed by the Allies in February 1945. When the city was divided, the central Mitte district, with the Museum Island and the palace, became part of East Germany. The Communist authorities bulldozed what remained of Frederick's palace and replaced it with a concrete Stalinist pile, the Palace of the Republic. Here the People's Chamber of the East German Democratic Republic rubber-stamped the decrees of the regime. When East and West Germany were united in 1989, the whole edifice was closed for health reasons. (It was heavily contaminated with asbestos.) Left vacant for many years, the German parliament decided in 2002 that it should be demolished and the old Stadtschloss restored in its place.

The building project took a very long time. The German chancellor, Angela Merkel, thought that it was much too expensive. Construction was delayed by the financial crisis. And the plans for the new building were controversial. The façade of the old palace was reconstructed on three sides, but the interior was designed to serve as a modernist display space. Edwin Heathcote, architecture critic for the *Financial Times*, remarked that "a building which awkwardly combines Prussian Baroque and stark rationalism with undertones of fascist architecture is a curious statement in a country that, having come to terms with its history, sees itself as modern, industrial, technocratic and cosmopolitan."[99]

The planners confronted equally controversial political problems. Social Democratic politicians worried that rebuilding the Schloss would feed nostalgia for an assertive and militarist state. Some East Germans had fond memories of cultural events, even discos, at the People's Palace, and anyway they resented the condescension of westerners. So the future function of the building was a sensitive issue.

The royal Schloss was situated at the heart of Berlin's "Museum Island," where five museums were constructed and stocked between 1830 and 1930. In 1999, Museum Island was designated a World Heritage Site by UNESCO. So the federal parliament decided to dedicate the new building to a museum project. This was named the Humboldt Forum, after Germany's world-famous and largely apolitical scientific hero who had flourished conveniently long ago. A suitably international mandarin, the former director of the British Museum, Neil MacGregor, was put in charge.

But what would it be a museum of? An international committee of experts was consulted. They advised that the Humboldt Forum should make a statement about the reunited Germany's place in the world: peaceful, cosmopolitan, multicultural. Now was the time to bring Berlin's non-western collections back from their long exile in suburban Dahlen.

The immediate point of reference for the Humboldt Forum was Jacques Chirac's museum in Paris. The quai Branly was stocked with the collections of two established Paris museums: the Musée de l'Homme and the Museum of African and Oceanic Art. The Humboldt Forum took over the collections of Berlin's Ethnological Museum and the (much smaller) Museum of Asian Art. Exiled to suburban Dahlen at the beginning of the First World War, these museums suffered war damage during the Second World War. At the start of the Cold War, important ethnographic collections were removed to the Soviet Union. Even after the reunification of Berlin the Dahlen museums found it hard to lure visitors away from Museum Island. Boosters of the Humboldt Forum promised that moving the exotic materials to Berlin Mitte would stimulate interest. The curators of the ethnological museum were cautiously optimistic, but they were soon disabused. As in the quai Branly museum, so in the Humboldt Forum: art historians would run the show.

Fritz Kramer, ethnologist and art historian, delivered a damning verdict. "The Humboldt Forum has a tragicomic birth defect: the intention was to display cosmopolitanism, to reflect globalization, to promote a dialogue of cultures—and the idea was to rely for this on ethnographic collections, of all things." The intrinsic problem, the birth defect, was that ethnological collections are made up of "objects from small, marginalized societies without writing, on the edges of [past] colonial empires." They had nothing to do with globalisation. "To put it bluntly: in the Humboldt Forum, Australia would be represented by the boomerang, America by feather headdresses—an obvious absurdity." Kramer concluded that "those responsible are now trying to extricate themselves from this dilemma. That is why, in my opinion, the ethnologists are being shut out."[100]

In fact there was an even more urgent problem. Among the transfers from Berlin's Museum of Ethnography was a large collection of Benin Bronzes that had been bought at London auctions a century earlier, so to all the other controversies surrounding the Humboldt Forum there was added the complicated, sensitive, emotive issue of restitution. In 2017, Bénédicte Savoy, one of the two authors of the official French report on restitution, resigned from the Humboldt's panel of international experts. She protested that provenance research was taking too long. "I want to know how much blood is dripping from a work of art," she told the *Süddeutsche Zeitung*. "Without such research, the Humboldt Forum should not open."[101] When it did finally open, virtually, in December 2020, in the middle of the Covid pandemic, the Benin Bronzes were nowhere to be seen.

And yet, despite their caution, the Humboldt management tripped up. In May 2018, a press release headlined "South Seas boat floats into the Humboldt Forum" announced that "The reconstruction of the Berlin Palace as the Humboldt Forum has successfully reached a key milestone: right on schedule, on 29 May, the unique Luf boat from Oceania moved into the exhibition hall on the first floor as the first large object from the *Staatliche Museen zu Berlin*."

A historian, Götz Aly, immediately claimed that this prize exhibit was imperial war booty.[102] In 1881, Hernsheim & Co., a Hamburg trading company, established an outpost on Luf Island off Papua New Guinea. The following year, several traders were murdered. The company appealed for help. Two German gunships were sent in. They bombarded Luf and launched a ground attack, destroying boats and homes. At the time Luf had between four and five hundred inhabitants. Perhaps fifty islanders were killed. Some men were abducted to serve as labourers on plantations. In 1903, two decades after the punitive action, an agent of Hernsheim & Co. acquired the Luf Boat. Constructed in 1890, it had been kept in a ceremonial men's house on the island. Jacob Anderhandt, a historian of Hernsheim & Co., judges that the acquisition was consensual. The company donated the boat to Berlin's Museum of Ethnology. In September 1906, an ethnologist at the Berlin Museum visited Luf Island and over several days he interviewed the headman and the two craftsmen who built the boat. They readily gave him a technical account of the construction and explicated the symbolic decorations. There was evidently no lingering local resentment over the fate of the Luf Boat.[103]

Meanwhile New York was preparing to counter the new developments in Paris and Berlin. In November 2018, the Metropolitan Museum announced that the Michael Rockefeller wing was to be completely rebuilt. "By ushering artistic traditions of three-quarters of the globe into the Met, the building of the Rockefeller Wing helped define us as an encyclopedic fine arts museum," the press release boasted. "The galleries—40,000 square feet on the Museum's south side—will be overhauled and reimagined to reintroduce each of the three major world traditions [Africa, Oceania and the Americas] represented in the department's collection, displaying them as discrete elements in an overarching wing that is in dialogue with the Museum's collections as a whole."[104]

This is the latest sign that the long-running competition between the art world and the anthropologists may be headed for a decisive victory on the part of the big battalions. The anthropologists have the better of the argument, but the art world gives out the prizes. Some ethnologists have followed Lévi-Strauss and given up the struggle. When the National Museum of Denmark reinstalled its ethnographic collection in the early 1990s, "the ethnographic exhibition became an art exhibition," said the former director, Ulf Dahne. "Everyone felt guilty about telling other people's stories, so they decided not to tell them at all."[105]

The people who ran the Met, the quai Branly and the Humboldt Forum might not be able to explain what kind of art they are promoting, but they agree on one big thing. This stuff is the business of art historians, not anthropologists. It is art, at least in the sense that it is not science. Nigeria's Nobel-winning writer, Wole Soyinka, is delighted. Even as a boy, he recalls, "one's attitude to these works, even where they had never left their home of origin, has been anything but anthropological. History, yes; anthropology, out!"

No wonder it was a deep, euphoric exhalation and sense of vindication that emerged from the throat—"At long last!"—when I visited the Musée du quai Branly, after that prodigious institution embarked on its new policy of taking African art away from anthropology. At the old Musée de l'Homme, the arts of a continent had been press-ganged, by habit, into a cohabitation that did not remotely reflect the value of African creativity, an aesthetic denial that merely catered to the determined agenda of exclusionism and artistic downgrading.[106]

So what is primitive art? The stuff that isn't in a museum of anthropology.

NATIONAL MUSEUMS AND
IDENTITY MUSEUMS

In April 2017, just as I was getting into the research for this book, I gave a talk at the National Museum of Anthropology in Mexico City. I began by saying that anthropology museums were in crisis. That was true enough, but, I thought, of concern mainly to anthropologists. It turned out that in Mexico the future of anthropology museums was a matter of national interest. To my astonishment I was asked to explain myself on state television. I had known, of course, that Mexico City is rightly proud of the National Museum of Anthropology, one of the most famous anthropology museums in the world and a must-see tourist attraction, but, shamefully, I was not aware of its pivotal and contentious role in the nation's consciousness.

National museums all over the world tell patriotic stories, but national museums in the Americas (and Australia and New Zealand) are a special case. Alongside a majority who are descended from European immigrants, these countries have Indigenous communities that trace their ancestry from pre-colonial populations. In the U.S.A. and Brazil there are also many descendants of African slaves. Can this diversity be accommodated in a national museum?

One solution is to make a division between history and pre-history. History is then all about European empires, nationalist revolutions and independent republics. Relics of the age before colonialism were displayed separately, often in a museum of natural history. This division was gradually abandoned in the course of the twentieth century. Indigenous populations were repositioned in the national mythology, but in very different ways. Each country developed its own narrative and projected a particular image of its precolonial condition. And as I should have known, Mexico was a special case.

When Spanish conquistadores vanquished the Aztec Empire it was with the support of tributary city states whose leaders bitterly resented Aztec domination. After the fall of Tenochtitlán in August 1521, Cortés destroyed the Aztec capital and built a colonial city on its ruins. Aztec temples were razed to the ground, a cathedral and churches built on the rubble. For two centuries, records of the pre-Columbian past were systematically suppressed. And then, in 1790, repair work in the central plaza of Mexico City uncovered two extraordinary monuments: the Stone of the Sun, the Aztec calendar with elaborate symbolic markings, and a sculpture of a goddess, usually identified as Coatlicue, mother of the god of war, who had prophesied the end of the Aztec Empire. By this time, Enlightenment ideas had taken root in Mexico. The finds were celebrated. The Stone of the Sun was put on display in front of the cathedral. The statue of Coatlicue was given into the care of the national university, although when visitors began to pray in front of it, holding candles and making offerings, it was reburied.[1]

In 1810, just as the Mexican War of Independence against Spain began, Alexander von Humboldt published his great work on pre-Columbian monuments in Mexico and the Andes. He remarked that the true value of these relics of ancient empires could now be appreciated at last, despite the fact that they were so very different from the classical European ideal. Within Mexico, however, interest in the country's precolonial heritage was limited throughout the nineteenth century. In 1865, the Hapsburg Emperor Maximilian, installed by Napoleon III, created a national museum of natural history and promoted pre-Columbian archaeology. However, republican politicians were committed to the assimilation of the Native population. They were not inclined to support the study of the Aztec, Inca or Toltec past.

In 1909, in the final phase of the long presidency of Porfirio Diaz, the national museum was divided in two: a natural history museum, and a museum of archaeology, history and ethnography that soon established itself as a centre of research and teaching. In 1910, celebrating the centenary of the declaration of Mexico's independence, the new museum presented a review of national history that, at last, incorporated the pre-Columbian age. Its centrepiece, the "Hall of Monoliths," included the Stone of the Sun, the Coatlicue statue, and monuments from Yucatán. This signalled the beginning of a new intellectual movement, *Indigenismo*, which drew upon pre-conquest mythology and art to reimagine Mexican identity. A central theme in the ideology of the Mexican revolution (roughly 1910–20), Indigenismo became an integral part of the national mythology for the rest of the twentieth century.

The archaeologist and anthropologist Manuel Gamio was one of the architects of Indigenismo. He was closely associated with Franz Boas, with whom he studied at Columbia University in 1909–10. In 1910, Boas was appointed a visiting professor in the National University in Mexico City, where he helped develop a research programme. Under his direction, Gamio undertook the first systematic archaeological study of Teotihuacán, established a preliminary stratigraphic analysis of the ancient settlement and reconstructed the pyramids. He also directed an ethnographic survey of the local peasant population, arguing that although just 5 per cent of the inhabitants spoke the Aztec language, Nahuatl, they retained elements of the old culture.

But Gamio was a moderniser. The grand aim, he declared, should be "a powerful patria and a coherent, defined nationality" based on "racial approximation, cultural fusion, linguistic unification and economic equilibrium." By racial approximation, Gamio meant *mestizaje*, the long process by which a Spanish-speaking population of mixed ancestry became the majority element in Mexico.[2] As a historian of modern Mexico, Alan Knight, writes: "according to the emerging orthodoxy of the

Revolution, the old Indian/European thesis/antithesis had now given rise to a higher synthesis, the mestizo, who was neither Indian nor European, but quintessentially Mexican."[3]

Gamio wanted traditional crafts to be fostered by national institutions and he argued that contemporary Mexican artists should take inspiration from the Aztecs. In 1922, a group of painters and sculptors, including Diego Rivera and José Clemente Orozco, published a *Declaration of Social, Political and Aesthetic Principles*. They proclaimed that the "noble work of the race, down to its most insignificant spiritual and physical expressions, is native (and essentially Indian) in origin. With their admirable and extraordinary talent to create beauty, peculiar to themselves, the art of the Mexican people is the most wholesome spiritual expression in the world and this tradition is our greatest treasure."[4]

Riviera went on to assemble the largest private collection of pre-Columbian art in Mexico. His wife, Frida Kahlo, complained that he spent so much money on his pursuit of antiquities that he neglected the financial needs of his own household. (He eventually donated his collection to the state.) Rivera incorporated Aztec motifs in some of his murals, and even identified martyrs of the Mexican revolution with the Aztec myth of the warrior sun god who dies each night and is reborn in battle next morning.[5]

These anthropological, artistic and political perspectives became part of the orthodox legacy of the Mexican revolution and the spirit of Indigenismo informed the Museo Nacional de Antropología that opened in 1964 in Chapultepec Park (once a retreat for Aztec rulers). Nearby is the National History Museum, which tells a conventional story of colonialism, revolution, and a post-revolutionary republicanism. But it is the anthropology museum that became the most potent expression of a national myth. A magnificent building was commissioned for the museum. Expeditions were financed to assemble new archaeological and ethnographic collections. Some 3,500 archaeological specimens were added to the museum's holdings, more than doubling their size. Ninety-five per cent of the ethnographic collection was assembled in the two years before the new building was opened. A 168-ton stone statue of Tlaloc, the Aztec rain god, was brought from Texcoco and placed at the entrance to the driveway.[6]

The ground floor of the museum is devoted to archaeology, and the floor above to ethnographic displays of more or less contemporary populations in modern Mexico but including examples from former Mexican territories annexed by the United States in 1848. The Aztec empire is represented as the apotheosis of pre-Columbian Mexico: the heart of the museum is the grand hall devoted to the Mexica of Tenochtitlán. Here is the Aztec calendar stone, mounted on a wall of Italian marble.

Four years after the new museum opened, in 1968, student demonstrators were mown down by soldiers in the Plaza of the Three Cultures in Tlatelocolco, precisely where, 450 years earlier, a Spanish captain rounded up and butchered Aztec priests and dancers. Octavio Paz, a Mexican diplomat and poet, soon to be awarded the Nobel Prize for Literature, resigned in protest from the foreign service and published *The Other Mexico: Critique of the Pyramid*, which analysed the ideological foundations of a repressive centralisation that (he argued) had persisted throughout the history of Mexico.

Paz noted that Mexico is shaped like a pyramid, and he suggested that the same is true of its enduring political structure. The truncated summit of the country and its politics is the capital city of Mexico-Tenochtitlán, where in Aztec times the divine king, the Tloatoani, presided and received periodic tributes of human sacrifice. The Aztecs themselves were intruders into an established civilisation, and Paz cites approvingly the insight of an anthropologist, Laurette Séjournée, that they were able to hold on to power only by taking control of the old symbolic system and using it to dominate their subjects. The Spaniards then repeated the same trick: "when Cortés decided that the capital of the new kingdom would be built on the ruins of México-Tenochtitlán, he became the heir and successor of the

Aztecs," Paz wrote. "Although the Conquest destroyed the indigenous world and built another and different one on its remains, there is an invisible thread of continuity between the ancient society and the new Spanish order: the thread of domination. That thread has not been broken: the Spanish viceroys and the Mexican presidents are the successor of the Aztec rulers."[7]

Why, Paz asks, did the Aztecs become the mythical ancestors of modern Mexico rather than the older Inca, Mayan and Toltec dynasties? He finds an answer in the Museum of Anthropology: here "anthropology and history have been made to serve an idea about Mexico's history, and that idea is the foundation, the buried and immovable base, that sustains our conceptions of the state, of political power, and of social order." The very layout of the museum suggests that the epitome of Mexican history and identity is the Aztec capital. "This exaltation and glorification of México-Tenochtitlán transforms the Museum of Anthropology into a temple," Paz concludes. "The cult propagated within its walls is the same one that inspires our school-books on Mexican history and the speeches of our leaders: the stepped pyramid and the sacrificial platform." This glorification of the Aztec model of power "condemns the museum." It is "an exaltation of the image of the Aztec pyramid, now guaranteed, so to speak, by science."[8]

When I was taken through the museum by the sophisticated and erudite director, Antonio Saborit, we came across a party of neo-Aztec devotees chanting before the statue of Coatlicue, just as their predecessors, two centuries earlier, had danced and prayed before it in the old university museum. They were welcome, Dr. Saborit told me. Did they perform sacrifices? He smiled.

The Royal Natural History Museum was established in Rio de Janeiro in 1818. In 1889 the royal family was exiled, and three years later the museum was moved into one of the former royal palaces. It was now beautifully housed but kept very short of funds. In the twentieth century, the Museum of Natural History gradually developed a programme of anthropological teaching and research. When the military dictatorship of 1964–85 finally came to an end, the museum became the most important postgraduate centre for anthropology in Latin America.

But could it be a museum of modern Brazil? A leading Brazilian anthropologist, Carlos Fausto, points out one difficulty. Unlike Mexico or Peru or Colombia, Brazil could not refer back to its own pre-Columbian empires, to a past furnished with magnificent buildings and statues, comparable to Europe's Graeco-Roman monuments. The Tupi-Guaran of the Atlantic coast and the hunter-gatherers of the Amazon rainforest were represented by the early missionaries as lacking even the trappings of statehood. They left behind not great stone monuments but only skulls and bones and some simple artefacts made of "fragile materials—feathers, wood, and pottery."[9] Professor Fausto notes that while some Brazilian intellectuals imagined a connection between themselves and the sixteenth-century Tupi-Guaran, they tended to suppress uncomfortable elements of the national past, notably the seizure of lands from Indigenous peoples and the importation of African slaves.

On the night of 2 September 2018, the museum burned down, destroying 80 per cent of the millions of items in its collections and its world-class library. Perhaps Brazil's institutional amnesia allowed successive governments to neglect urgent requests to shore up the old palace and protect it from fire. Fortunately, scholarly curators had documented a large proportion of the collections, and the museum had established close ties with a number of *indios* communities, encouraging local crafts by bringing examples of traditional work to the attention of new generations.[10] These long-standing networks now mobilised to help restore what was lost, as far as this is possible. It had become their museum too.

Museums of Indigenous peoples in the U.S.A. and Canada followed a different trajectory. A romantic conception of identity was revived in the 1960s. This suggested a way of thinking about a development that greatly surprised many social scientists: far from melting away, ethnic identities were reasserted, and they were now viewed positively. Identity had become a political issue again.

The term multiculturalism was coined, first, in the mid-1960s, in Canada. In the U.S.A., the idea of multiculturalism was absorbed into a modern radical tradition that runs through the civil rights struggle, the resistance to the war in Vietnam, the women's movement and the gay rights movement. Very much like Polish or Czech intellectuals in the last days of the Austro-Hungarian Empire, the New Left argued that the state behaves like an imperial power, not only in its foreign policy but also at home. On this argument, the U.S.A. is run by a culturally hegemonic community of straight WASP men, who recognise only one set of standards and treat any form of difference from themselves as a sign of inferiority. The remedy is that the U.S.A. must learn to celebrate difference. African Americans, Native Americans, Spanish-speakers, women, gay people, all demand recognition of an authentic and credit-worthy cultural identity. Difference is itself a fundamental value.

In reaction, conservative intellectuals adopted the classic Enlightenment belief in a universal civilisation, its standard bearer the most advanced nation, which was now, of course, the U.S.A. Western civilisation—and college courses in "Western Civ"—are good for everyone. Samuel Huntington, theorist of the "clash of civilisations," predicted that recent hostilities between Western and Islamic forces were no more than a preliminary skirmish, a stage on the way to the climactic struggle to come, "the greater clash, the global '*real* clash,' between Civilization and barbarism." Huntington argued that any civilisation or empire (which he represented as one and the same thing) will be fatally weakened if it does not sustain its particular values. The U.S.A. should reassert its Anglo-Protestant identity. Immigrant values dilute this identity and must be resisted.[11]

Reverberations of the culture wars penetrated the staid museum world. Two identity museums opened on the National

Mall in Washington, DC, in the first decades of the twenty-first century: the National Museum of the American Indian (NMAI) and the National Museum of African American History and Culture. In December 2020, Congress gave the go-ahead for a National Museum of the American Latino (though funding has not yet been allocated). These identity museums represent a potent challenge to the Museum of Other People.

In the autumn of 2016, I spent four months as a visiting scholar in the U.S. National Museum of Natural History in Washington, DC. The original flagship of the Smithsonian Institution, the national museum was responsible (among many other things) for the world's greatest collection of Native American antiquities and ethnographic materials. But I was astonished to discover that this precious hoard was hidden away in a depository in Maryland.

In 1986, the National Congress of American Indians complained that some Native American exhibits were "highly offensive, in part due to the display of several hundred Indian skeletal remains, a practice ceased by most museums several decades ago . . . We would prefer to see the Indian exhibit hall empty, with an accompanying explanation of why the exhibit has been removed."[12] The responsible curator, William Merrill, reported at the time that "the ethnology halls are replete with inaccuracies and tend to portray American Indians as 'frozen in time,' usually at the point in their histories at which they became stereotyped in the non-Indian mind."[13] He drew up a plan to renew the displays, but it was too late. In 1989, the U.S. Congress mandated the creation of a National Museum of the American Indian (NMAI) as "a living memorial to Native Americans and their traditions."

Robert McCormick Adams Jr., secretary of the Smithsonian Institution, was concerned that the NMAI would be run by cultural activists. The director and the majority of the curators were Native Americans. Congress mandated that a third of the trustees should be Native Americans, rising to half after the first few years. An insider told me that Adams thought the

U.S. National Museum would come under pressure to surrender its American Indian collections to the new institution. So he negotiated to purchase the collections of the Museum of the American Indian in New York City. This was the personal project of an investment banker, George Gustav Heye, who died in 1957, leaving his museum in disarray. Bought for $219 million, half the money provided by the federal government, the rest by private donors, including $30 million from three American Indian tribes with very profitable casino operations, the Heye collection of over 8,000 artefacts and 125,000 photographs was donated to the NMAI in 1990. This accounts for 85 per cent of its holdings.[14]

In May 2004, the Native American exhibits in the Museum of Natural History were taken away and deposited in the basement of that storage facility in Maryland. In September 2004, the National Museum of the American Indian was opened, a short walk down the Washington Mall from the Museum of Natural History.

For the time being the American Indian collections of the Natural History Museum are safe, though out of sight. But for how long? And to what purpose? Setting up a National Museum of the American Indian, lamented one veteran Smithsonian curator, signalled "the end of our dream of a Smithsonian Museum of Anthropology, or of Man."[15] Sidney Dillon Ripley, secretary of the Smithsonian Institution from 1964 to 1984, had promised to house this museum of mankind on the last available slot on the National Mall. The eminently desirable site was now allocated to the NMAI. From his office perch the museum's director looks directly across at the Capitol building.

On 21 September 2004, members of over five hundred tribes from all over the Americas, many in traditional dress, sporting feathered headdresses, drumming and singing, paraded down the Mall in Washington, DC, from the National Museum of Natural History to the newly opened National Museum of the American Indian (NMAI). "This Native Nations Procession, organized by the museum and forming, perhaps, the largest assembly of America's native peoples in modern times, will also be a self-celebration," wrote the arts correspondent of *The New York Times*, Edward Rothstein.[16] James Lujan, a filmmaker and playwright from Taos Pueblo, New Mexico, a member of the faculty at the Institute of American Indian Arts in Santa Fe, was there. For the marchers, he wrote, "it was a celebratory, emotional, long-delayed, long-awaited symbol of national recognition and vindication for Indian culture (I was in the thick of it, and it was an awe-inspiring spectacle)."[17]

This grand opening was the culmination of more than a decade of planning. Consultations began in 1990, just a year after Congress passed a law establishing the NMAI. Native experts on ritual, crafts and traditions were invited to share their views. NMAI curators travelled the country to meet with them. A select few became long-term collaborators, known as "community curators." A young curator at the NMAI, Chavez Lamar, found herself mediating between community curators and NMAI administrators. "As a Native person at the NMAI," she remarked, "I occasionally felt anxiety and disappointment at how budget, time, and upper management priorities conflicted with the needs and desires of the community curators. At the same time, I felt dismay over the limited availability of some co-curators to the project due to lack of interest and commitment, but also due to their multiple project, committee, job, and family responsibilities."[18]

Dr. Lamar was regularly called on to smooth over delicate issues. There were complaints that this or that tribe was excluded. Agonising questions were raised about who is an Indian. At one meeting Indians of mixed ancestry complained that they were discriminated against because they did not look Indian, but they did not want this to be discussed in public. A Yakama co-curator instructed Lamar that "we as a people, the Yakamas, we have to decide how much we can tell and how much we [don't] tell. There are certain things we can't talk about."[19] So from the start, editing, even censorship, was part of the deal.

James Lujan, the Pueblo intellectual, was sceptical:

the result of filtering and processing the exhibits through the eyes and agendas of the Native community curators is, quite naturally, an exercise in cultural propaganda that emphasizes the positive, glosses over the negative, and is generally very cryptic about what really makes Indians tick. Ultimately, the depth of understanding we come away with is little more than what we would get from stopping at a tribal community centre or gift shop.[20]

Marc Fisher, a senior editor of *The Washington Post*, made much the same point: "The museum feels like a trade show in which each group of Indians gets space for its founding myth and favourite anecdotes of survival. Each room is a sales booth of its own, separate, out of context."[21] "The notion that tribal voices should 'be heard' becomes a problem when the selected voices have so little to say," Rothstein commented. Sometimes the voices became a babble. There were *lots* of labels, all individually signed. This was apparently in itself a statement of something, perhaps a sophisticated post-modern uncertainty. But it was not easy for the visitor to make sense of it all. Rothstein remarked that objects were glossed differently on labels posted by professional curators and community curators. A caption for a display from the Santa Clara Pueblo of New Mexico explains: "We are made up of two major clans, Summer and Winter people." But a Pueblo co-curator wrote: "There is no dividing line. There is just a sense." Labels offer platitudes, homilies, bromides. "Respect and sharing of yourself is very important." "Everything has a spirit and everything is interconnected." Invited to list ten crucial historical moments, the Tohono Oodham in Arizona chose as their first "Birds teach people to call for rain." The tenth, marking the year 2000, was "desert walk for health."

Amanda Cobb, editor of the *American Indian Quarterly*, urged the museum not to water down its multivocal presentations "in spite of the confusion that has resulted . . . Instead the NMAI should find ways to prepare visitors, to let them know how they will be asked to respond, and to 'teach them to read.' "[22] Leslie

Marmon Silko, a Laguna Pueblo Indian woman, a writer and teacher, offered guidance to the disoriented visitor:

> For those of you accustomed to a structure that moves from point A to point B to point C, this presentation may be somewhat difficult to follow because the structure of Pueblo expression resembles something like a spider's web—with many little threads radiating from a center, criss-crossing each other. As with the web, the structure will emerge as it is made and you must simply listen and trust, as the Pueblo people do, that meaning will be made.[23]

The premise of the National Museum of the American Indian is that Native peoples should speak (if not necessarily with one voice). Anthropologists, archaeologists and historians should not presume to butt in on their conversations. The insistence on the privileged knowledge of insiders—even if they disagree among themselves—may require the silencing of scholarly expertise.

"Instead of the objective, anonymous third-person voice of the 'expert,' in this museum individuals tell their stories, some more fluently than others," explained two sympathetic art historians, Aldona Jonaitis and Janet Catherine Berlo. "The NMAI deliberately denies the grand narrative of Euro-American historical representation. In its place, the museum offers eloquent fragments of various realities, leaving to the history and anthropology museums the tasks of more conventional interpretations of Indian culture."[24] Lujan put this more bluntly. The NMAI "did away with conventional, third-person presentations of Indian history, particularly the ones that depicted Indians as victims of broken treaties and genocide, and took the initiative to recruit Native communities themselves to tell their own histories and explain their culture in their own way, in the process deliberately thumbing their noses at the dusty, academic conventions of anthropological science."[25]

The secretary of the Smithsonian Institution warned that

conceding unquestioned authority to local spokespeople would "challenge the traditional stance of the museum as the singular voice of authority on excellence and cultural meaning."[26] But no such "singular voice of authority" was on offer. Jolene Rickard, a citizen of the Tuscarora nation (Turtle clan) teaches about Indigenous peoples at Cornell University. Co-curator of two of the four permanent exhibitions at the NMAI, she remarks that "there is no single curatorial perspective at play at NMAI. Multiple curatorial styles bump up against each other, often within the same gallery."[27] Nor is there "agreement among the Native scholars on what is the official narrative of Native history," nor even a consensus on "such central concepts as sovereignty, the use of the term genocide to describe contact with the West, the notion of autonomous Native nationhood (not citizenship), and more." Dr. Rickard concluded that this "made the task of creating take-away messages nearly impossible."[28]

Richard West, a member of the Cheyenne and Arapaho tribes of Oklahoma, and the first director of the NMAI, rejected these criticisms: "I believe that these distinct ways of understanding are stated most articulately and are discerned by museum visitors most clearly when the Native voice is permitted, from an interpretive standpoint, to speak for itself."[29] This did not persuade James Lujan. The NMAI "bills itself as a museum," he commented, but "simply doesn't deliver on the minimum standards of scientific and academic vetting I've come to take for granted, especially from a brand name like Smithsonian . . . as a cynical Native person, my cynical reaction was, 'Who are they trying to kid?'"[30]

Then there is the problem of what the NMAI is about. A historian, Ira Jacknis, suggested that it may be understood as "a kind of national tribal museum." Tribal museums have been founded in over two hundred territories in the U.S. and Canada since the 1960s. But situated as it is on the National Mall in Washington, DC, the NMAI has a more global remit. So does it represent the variety of native peoples from Alaska to Tierra del Fuego, or a generic conception of the American Indian?

"Here's the contention it continually asserts: Indians are all different; overarching Indianness makes them all alike," wrote Paul Richard, art critic of *The Washington Post*. "Well, which is it? The museum can't make up its mind." Nor can it decide what kind of museum it sets out to be. "This is not an art museum, that's clear," Richard concluded. "It's not a history museum, either. Its whole thrust is ahistorical. What it is, instead, is a unity museum."[31] Lujan felt the same way. The only message that he took away from his visit to the museum was—*we are still here.*[32]

But really, did it have to come to this, another slew of vapid New Age platitudes? Paul Richard cited a dismal selection: "Native people believe that unseen powers and creative forces formed the Earth." "Native Americans of the past and present consider many places holy." "They manifested their beliefs through ceremony and ritual." For all tribes, the circle is "a symbol of unity."[33] Lujan remarked that "in its efforts to shatter stereotypes, the NMAI may, in fact, be perpetuating them, particularly the romantic, New Age notion of 'Indian as great spiritual warrior.'"[34] That did not bother Lloyd Kiva New, a Cherokee artist. "We will probably come out with the daddy of stereotypy regarding who American Indians are and what they stand for, but at least it can be a more or less updated version—espoused by Indians themselves."[35]

The NMAI took a principled decision not to emphasise the terrible experiences of the nineteenth century: the deportation of tens of thousands of Indians from the eastern United States to new territories in the West (the Trail of Tears), the Indian Wars, the epidemics, the loss of hunting grounds and the extinction of buffalo herds on the Plains. Native consultants who advised the museum "did not want to dwell on the history of extermination and discrimination but instead to look positively toward the future," explained the art historians Aldona Jonaitis and Janet Berlo.[36] Speaking at the opening ceremony, the first director of the NMAI, Richard West, insisted that Indians should not see themselves as victims of their history. ("As the Mohawks have counselled us, 'It is hard to see the future with tears in your eyes.'") But there is little looking toward the future here, despite exhibits that mix in contemporary tack to convey—I don't know, perhaps something post-modern. Paul Richard wrote of "totem poles and T-shirts, headdresses and masks, toys and woven baskets, projectile points and gym shoes . . . all stirred decoratively together in no important order that the viewer can discern."[37] The NMAI started with a wonderful flourish, but the critics were damning, and the public seemed to agree with them. Whenever I visited the museum I found myself wandering its corridors almost alone.

The muddled messaging of the NMAI is in marked contrast to the clear narrative line delivered by the National Museum of African American History and Culture, which was opened by President Obama on the grounds of the Washington Monument in September 2016. This museum tells a straightforward, moving story. A dimly lit hall at basement level documents the transportation of slaves from West Africa to the Americas on European ships. (It does not mention that those slaves were captured by soldiers of African kingdoms who then marched them to the ports to be sold.) Moving up through the five levels of the museum the visitor sees exhibits documenting American slavery and emancipation; segregation and the civil rights movement; the place of churches in the African American experience (though, for whatever reason, Black Muslims are granted equal time with the Christian churches, which are attended by the great majority of Afro-Americans). Finally, heroic figures in music, sports and politics are celebrated. There are state-of-the-art audio-visual effects. The museum had over 600,000 visitors in the first three months, and it remains very popular.

So is this the future? Will Museums of Other People be turned into identity museums? It is certainly apparent that anthropology museums are in danger of losing their authority. Assertions of expertise are challenged. Appeals are made to a more authentic insider authority. An alternative, primordial, mystical source of knowledge is invoked, Indigenous folk its anointed guardians.

Any objections from alien scientists and scholars may then be condemned as inappropriate, even sacrilegious.

In 1978, the U.S. Congress passed the American Indian Religious Freedom Act. It was uncertain whether, or in what way, this bestowed any religious rights on Native Americans over and above those guaranteed to all citizens by the First Amendment to the U.S. Constitution. Nevertheless the publicity around the law encouraged some Indian tribes to request the return of sacred objects held by museums. A striking case in point is the Willamette meteorite. The largest meteorite found in North America, it was acquired by the American Museum of Natural History in 1906. In 2000 it was installed as the centrepiece of a new exhibition hall. In 2005, the Confederated Tribes of the Grand Ronde Community of Oregon sued for its return, claiming that it was sacred tribal property.

The parties eventually agreed that the meteorite would remain in New York, but that it would be exhibited in a way that satisfied the Grand Ronde Community, whose members would have the right to celebrate it in annual rituals. The exhibit was furnished with two sets of explanatory labels. One describes the meteorite from the point of view of astrophysics. Another gives the Grand Ronde version. "The label states that the meteorite is a representative of the sky people sent to earth to assist its living descendants," writes Enid Schildkraut, who was a curator at the museum at the time. She notes that some curators were not pleased with this resolution. "Following this logic, some ask, will museums have to give equal weight to 'intelligent design' along with the theory of evolution?"[38]

One possible reading of the American Indian Religious Freedom Act is that anything which may be associated with a religion has a privileged status. It was once and always will be *sacred*. To expose it for all to see in a public museum is sacrilegious. Zuni political authorities accordingly demanded the deaccession of *Ahayu:da*, Zuni war gods, which have long been prized possessions of American museums. Stylised figures carved from cylindrical pieces of cottonwood or pine, some 50 to 75 cm long, their base adorned with prayer sticks, the twin war gods influence the weather, confer prosperity or withhold it, and give protection against enemies.[39] Every year, at the time of the winter solstice, Bow Priests bring two new *Ahayu:da* to shrines around Zuni Pueblo. The old *Ahayu:da* are retired and left to disintegrate into dust. They must not be removed: to do so would be to risk great harm. "The disruption of Zuni religion by the Spanish and U.S. governments and the removal of sacred objects from Zuni lands has created a spiritual imbalance in the world which has had 'adverse effects,'" Zuni negotiators argued. "To restore harmony, the objects must be returned to their proper place on Zuni lands."[40]

Zuni politicians identified *Ahayu:da* in the National Museum of Natural History in the Smithsonian Institution as a strategic target. Concessions there would soon be followed by museums up and down the country. Negotiations began in 1978. These covered two *Ahayu:da* and also eighteenth-century statues of Saint Michael and Saint Gabriel taken from a Spanish mission church at the Zuni Pueblo. Collected in the late nineteenth century by anthropologists working for the Smithsonian, they were all finally transferred to Pueblo authorities in 1987.[41] In 1989, Congress passed the National Museum of the American Indian Act, followed by the Native American Graves Protection and Repatriation Act (NAGPRA) in 1990, which gave further support for the return of sacred objects. In the following decade some sixty more *Ahayu:da* were transferred to Zuni priests by state and university museums.

Zuni negotiators also asked the Smithsonian to withdraw sacred Zuni objects from public display. According to William Merrill, who led the Smithsonian team, there followed long discussions "on the very complicated issue of how to determine whether a particular object is sacred or not." An anthropologist representing the Zuni claimed that almost all Zuni objects may be considered sacred, but he conceded that Zuni were still working on a clearer formulation.[42] That was never delivered.

The Smithsonian initially asked for guarantees that the
Ahayu:da would be conserved for study and for future generations. This provision was dropped in later negotiations. Chip
Colwell, senior curator of anthropology at the Denver Museum
of Nature and Science, went to see what had been done with war
gods that his museum had handed over to a Zuni community.
He was taken to a specially constructed shrine. It was securely
locked, but open to the sky. Inside were 106 statues. They were
in various stages of disintegration, as a result of exposure to the
elements. "As a museum curator, I am supposed to be incensed
to see these precious artifacts—these gods—dissolving into
literal dust," Colwell writes. But he was assured that this is what
the Zuni wanted. The statues were meant to return to nature.
Colwell recalls that he looked into the eyes of his guide and
experienced an epiphany. He now felt that allowing the *Ahayu:da*
to disintegrate in "this holy site" was somehow essential to the
very survival of the Zuni as a people. "I can imagine no better
place for them," he concluded. Yet he does acknowledge that
colleagues at the Denver museum had reservations. Some challenged "the positioning of Indian religious rights above scientific
rights." Others were concerned about "the museum's responsibilities to the objects, donors, audiences, and public trust."[43]

Zuni negotiators persuaded the Smithsonian and other
museums that they should also surrender copies of sacred
objects that had been commissioned from local craftsmen, made
by the ethnographers themselves, or, in one instance, copied by
a troop of boy scouts. Edmund J. Ladd—a Coyote clan member,
a National Park Service archaeologist, and a delegate for the
Zuni religious council—remarked that this raised two difficult
issues: "What is real? and Whose belief system is to be applied?
These questions and others will take time to answer."[44] In the
meantime, who, if anyone, might claim to speak with authority
about sacred objects? And what should museums do with them?

In September 2020, the director of the Pitt Rivers Museum withdrew its most famous exhibition case: "The Treatment of Dead

Enemies." This displayed heads taken as war trophies in Nagaland, scalps from North America, carved boards for the display
of skulls from New Guinea and shrunken heads collected from
the Amazonian Jivaro people and accessioned by the museum
between 1884 and 1936. (As it turns out, only six of the ten
shrunken heads held by the museum were in fact human. Two
were sloth and two monkey heads.)

Trophies were manufactured from the bodies of dead
enemies in a number of regions bordering the Amazon. Heads,
sometimes mummified shrunken heads, were of particular
importance but there were also drinking cups manufactured
from scalps, wind instruments made from arm and leg bones,
and necklaces decorated with teeth. Some instances of ritual
cannibalism were reported. All these uses of body parts were
supposed to promote success in hunting and gardening, to
strengthen young men and to make women fertile.[45]

The Jivaro and Canoa peoples of eastern Ecuador and northern Peru were specialists in shrunken heads. The corpse of a
newly slain enemy was decapitated. When the warriors came
home the bones in the head were removed, but the hair, the seat
of the soul, was carefully preserved. Hot sand was placed inside
the skin, which was boiled, dried, and then modelled by hand
to restore a semblance of human features. The lips and eyes
were sewn up to keep the spirit trapped in the head. The hair
was carefully dressed and decorated. The finished artefact was
known as a *tsantsa*. When the warrior made a triumphant entry
to his home village, rooster blood was applied to his thighs,
symbolising menstruation. The head was then ritually reborn,
given a new name, and introduced to his adoptive country. A
year later, Carlos Fausto writes,

> a large celebration was organized in which the head,
> after being renewed and introduced three times into the
> house, was fastened to the central pillar. The hosts then
> offered beer to the invitees and served them the meat of
> pigs specially raised and killed for the ceremony . . . This

extinguished the head's special powers, turning it into an ornamental souvenir, kept at home by its owner until finally buried at his death.[46]

After the ritual had been completed, however, some warriors were willing to sell their tsantsas to traders.[47]

The two main divisions of the Jivaro were the Shuar and the Achuar. They were culturally and linguistically identical, but hereditary enemies. And each was, for the other, the ideal source of a tsantsa suitable for incorporation (as a relative by marriage) into the community of the killers.

Headhunting raids by the Shuar on the Achuar became more frequent in the last decades of the nineteenth century. At their peak, they occurred roughly once a month. This acceleration was stimulated by the development of a trading system in which heads were exchanged for guns (and later often marketed to tourists, some ending up in museums). This trade flourished well into the twentieth century.[48] Headhunting finally stopped among the Jivaro, Anne Christine Taylor writes,

> not because people decided collectively to forget past offences and desist from raiding for trophies: it stopped because of increasing missionary control over individuals' lives and choices, because of the threat of army intervention, because the kin of victims gradually grew old and died, taking with them the memory of their rage, and because fewer and fewer men are left who retain the practical and ritual knowledge associated with taking and shrinking heads.[49]

In the early 1950s, Salesian missionaries drew on graduates of their Shuar boarding schools to develop a network of Catholic chapels. In 1964, this evolved into a government recognised "Shuar Federation." One of its very first cultural initiatives was the publication of a book on the manufacture and ritual uses of tsantsas. In October 1995, the Smithsonian's National Museum of the American Indian handed twelve tsantsas over to what was now, conveniently, though as it turned out only temporarily, a more ecumenical Shuar-Achuar federation. Since the Shuar and Achuar were now apparently united, the museum was not obliged to decide whether tsantsas rightly belonged to the Achuar, whose ancestors had been beheaded, or to the Shuar, whose ancestors had taken the heads.

What, then, is the modern Shuar attitude to tsantsa? The educated and devoutly Catholic officials of the federation refused to look at the tsantsas when they made an official visit to the National Museum of the American Indian in Washington, DC, to negotiate their return. An ethnographer of the Shuar, Steven Rubenstein, remarks that this gesture expressed "a sentiment not highlighted in the ethnography of pre-Federation Shuar . . . respect for the dead."[50] In 1998, however, the president of what was now once more just the Shuar Federation showed Rubenstein the tsantsas that had been presented by the NMAI. "These are sacred," he declared. He added that the Federation should build a museum in which to place them.[51]

As for the common people, Steven Rubenstein remarks that they are often ambivalent about the elite leaders of the Federation, whom they associate with the state, but they respect their warrior ancestors and are not inclined to disown the tsantsa. Rubenstein writes,

> I have yet to meet a Shuar who expressed any shame or embarrassment concerning tsantsa. Everyone with whom I have talked about this has expressed a solemn pride and sense of admiration and awe. But whereas some Shuar were eager to see tsantsas turned over to the Federation, others seemed not to care. When I accompanied a few Shuar to the American Museum of Natural History in New York [in 2003], they were pleased to see tsantsas on display for others to admire (while noting that few museumgoers looked at the heads).[52]

In 2011 the Pitt Rivers Museum published a booklet, *Shrunken Heads*, written by Laura Peers, curator for the Americas collections at the Pitt Rivers Museum and professor of museum anthropology. The introduction begins:

> One of the most fascinating displays in the Pitt Rivers Museum is labelled "Treatment of Dead Enemies." The case includes a number of shrunken heads, or tsantsas, from South America. Each of these is about the size of a large orange. Some are suspended from cords, some have the iridescent wing-covers of beetles as hair decorations. Their mouths and eyes are sewn shut. To visitors today they may appear gruesome, but also compelling. As the curator responsible for the Museums' collections from the Americas, I want to explain why the shrunken heads were made and what they meant in the societies they come from. I also want to discuss the issues that are raised by their exhibition, and some of the questions that museum staff and visitors have asked about the display. The tsantsas have much to teach us, about how human beings understand themselves, and about why humans treat each other like this—both within the societies that the tsantsas come from and in the societies that display tsantsas in museums.

According to Professor Peers, the most common question that visitors asked at the front desk of the museum was, "Where are the shrunken heads?" They featured in a scene in a Harry Potter film. "Leading artists regularly ask to photograph and draw them," Professor Peers reported. "They are iconic objects that are often associated by the public and the media with the essence of the Pitt Rivers Museum." Certainly they had to be carefully handled, but Professor Peers assured her readers that all was well. "The Pitt Rivers Museum knows of no ethical problems in the way that the tsantsas in its collection were acquired, nor has the museum ever had a repatriation request for them."[53]

It therefore came as a shock when Laura van Broekhoven,

A Shuar warrior returns to his village with a tsantsa (shrunken head). Note the rifles. Photograph by Rafael Karsten, a Finnish ethnographer and philosopher of religion, 1921. (By permission of the World Culture Museum, Gothenburg. Negative 2435.)

newly appointed director of the Pitt Rivers Museum, announced in 2020 that the "Treatment of Dead Enemies" exhibit was to be withdrawn. When it was first reported that the museum planned to remove the collection of shrunken heads, a spokesman for the Friends of the Museum protested that they were a particular favourite with the children.[54] The clincher for the director was apparently that a number of visitors seemed to find the exhibits barbaric: the things themselves, not the fact that they were on show, which they generally appreciated. In September 2020 the museum withdrew the Jivaro shrunken heads, South Asian Naga trophy heads and an Egyptian mummy of a child. The director announced that many of the 2,800 sets of human remains held by the museum would be deaccessioned and passed on to appropriate institutions in what were now described as "communities of origin."

Several reasons were given for taking down the exhibition. "Little is known about the reasons tsantsa were made or the method of making them," an official statement pronounced, waving away a century of first-rate ethnographic research that documented in remarkable detail precisely how and why tsantsa were made, and which had been referenced by Professor Peers in her Pitt Rivers pamphlet.[55] Displays of human remains are now generally "felt to be unethical or inappropriate," the statement continued, although it goes on to cite the UK government's Guidance for the Care of Human Remains in Museums (DCMS 2005), which permits displays if "the museum believes that it makes a material contribution to a particular interpretation" (*sic*); the exhibits are "accompanied by sufficient explanatory material"; and are "displayed in such a way as to avoid people coming across them unawares."

In place of the famous old showcase, the museum has erected a large poster that explains why visitors can no longer view skulls and tsantsas: "Indigenous people have long argued against the public display of the ancestors' remains." An anonymous Navaho is quoted as saying: "We too have the human right to get buried and stay buried." No evidence is adduced for either proposition, and quite a lot could be cited to contradict them. And, by the way, why would the Shuar Federation bury the tsantsas from the Pitt Rivers Museum? There is no traditional or recent precedent for doing so.

Professor Peers had noted that the Pitt Rivers was considering whether to permit photographs of the tsantsa to appear in the media in future. "The Museum often receives requests for photographs," she wrote, "but we find that people only want to use the images because of the stereotypes associated with shrunken heads: they want to use these stereotypes of exoticism."[56] And yet her own pamphlet included a photograph of the old display case with its skulls, scalps and tsantsa. Similar photographs are easily accessed on the internet.

I applied to the Pitt Rivers for permission to use their photograph to illustrate my discussion of the exhibit. I had no intention of promoting the "stereotypes of exoticism" that concerned Professor Peers. It is unusual for a university museum to censor a scholarly publication, but I received a cold note from the museum's marketing and media officer. She said she had consulted Dr. van Broekhoven, the director, and the answer was no. "The image you suggest is of the display which was removed last summer out of respect for the people involved. Because this display is no longer in place, we would prefer other images to be used and Laura [van Broekhoven] has suggested some of the newer photos showing the replacement display explaining why the changes have been made."

The people involved! Who were they, who consulted them, what in fact did "they" believe, and why were they (whoever they were) given the right to determine the policy of a famous and long-established university museum?

SHOW AND TELL

Backstage at the museum, curators look after artefacts, make acquisitions, weed out fakes, set aside surplus stock for possible loans or exchanges. They update catalogues, establish the identity of objects, determine their provenance, rewrite labels. All this activity is usually invisible to the public (although the BBC series *Secrets of the Museum* mesmerised viewers who were taken behind the scenes at the Victoria and Albert Museum).

Exhibition halls are the public face of the museum. In large museums, exhibitions are highly selective. Only between 1 and 3 per cent of the collection may be on show. Sooner or later permanent (read long-term) exhibitions become dated, but since it can cost millions of dollars, even tens of millions, to refurbish galleries in a major museum they often remain more or less unchanged for a generation or even two. At least one hall is generally set aside for temporary themed exhibitions that will often include loan objects.

The selection and arrangement of artefacts for display make a statement, or, as curators now prefer to say, they tell a story. These stories are highly constrained—by what the museum has in store or can borrow, by the expertise and enterprise of curators, by the physical limitations of a museum building, and by money and politics and pressure groups. Every exhibition is the product of a tug of war between curators, designers, administrators, donors, dealers, outside experts and activists, each with their own agenda.

Museum folk hope that an exhibition will attract publicity, but fear that somebody somewhere will raise a stink about it.

Exhibitions in a Museum of Other People are especially likely to be controversial because they make statements—tell stories—about kinds of person, about relationships between peoples, about their differences and what they may have in common: all this in multicultural cities in a globalised world. Identity politics—on the left and on the right—has led to new challenges, constraints and controversy. And since the late twentieth century, governments have pushed museums to look for private sponsorship.

Sponsors expect to influence, if not dictate, the subject matter of exhibits and the type of thing selected for show. They assume that the exhibition will tie in with their corporate interests. At the very least it should not cause them embarrassment. They hope that the exhibition will foster optimism and goodwill (ideally, the message should be that creativity, spiritual uplift, love of children, are everywhere part of the human experience, and that we're all in it together). Every sponsor introduces bias, if only in the choice of themes. Occasionally a hubristic billionaire tries to impose a more particular agenda. Left unsaid, but taken for granted by modern museum directors and sponsors, is the conviction that ethnographic or archaeological or historical scholarship can be discounted.

In 1970 the British Museum made an experiment. The impetus was a space crunch. There were long-standing plans for the Library to vacate the large, circular reading room, once the legendary haunt of scholars, exiled revolutionaries and Grub Street scribblers. In the meantime, the department of ethnography was shunted out to a rented building in Burlington Gardens in Piccadilly. It was given a grand title: the Museum of Mankind. (The name, taken from the venerable Musée de l'Homme in Paris, was suggested by a trustee of the British Museum and director of the National Gallery, Kenneth Clark, who fronted a popular TV series, *Civilisation*.)

When Malcolm McLeod became keeper of ethnology in 1974, he insisted that curators should have an advanced degree in anthropology, carry out regular field studies and engage with the latest ideas in the field. Anthropologists in the late twentieth century made a cult of ethnography. It became an article of faith that the only reliable way to reach an understanding of how other people live their lives and make sense of the world is by way of a long and intimate involvement in their daily routines. Context is all. Old-school exercises in promiscuous comparison and speculative sweeps of history were now regarded with scepticism, even suspicion, so exhibitions in the Museum of Mankind typically focused on a particular people in a specific place and time. Consider the roster of exhibitions put on in its last year in Burlington Gardens: African Hairdressers' Signs; Mexican Textiles; Central Asian Nomad Felts from Kyrgyzstan; Malaita: A Pacific Island; Mancala Game-Boards; Patagonia: The Uttermost End of the Earth; South African Beadwork.[1] (A single exhibition that took a global perspective, "World Ceramic Traditions," was an outlier.) Usually the visitor could expect to be confronted with some (aesthetically striking) craftworks and to come away with a sense of how they were used and what they meant to people in a particular locale.

The Museum of Mankind carried on for a quarter of a century. At last the Library moved from the neoclassical edifice of the British Museum to its new home, a modernist building next to St. Pancras station, which then Prince Charles described as "more like the assembly hall of an academy for secret police." Exhibitions ceased at the Burlington Gardens site in 1997. The collections were put in store and in 2004 the department of ethnography moved back to the British Museum in Bloomsbury. A week later the newly appointed director of the British Museum, Neil MacGregor, turned up at a staff meeting to announce that he was closing down the department of ethnography. The curators would be redeployed to a new department of Africa, Oceania and the Americas.

Like many directors of metropolitan museums, MacGregor was an art historian. But he did not intend to turn the British

Museum into an art museum. He thought the museum should remain a universal, encyclopaedic institution, true to its Enlightenment roots. He liked to talk about its collection, in the singular. The implication was that no disciplinary cabal should exercise seigneurial rights over any part of it.

And yet this particular administrative ploy was hard to understand. *What on earth did Africa, Oceania and the Americas have in common?* MacGregor did not explain in which ways Tahitians were like Zulus or Navaho Indians, and what they might share with Australian Aborigines or with the Inuit of Alaska—apart, of course, from a century or more of conflict-ridden, sporadically violent colonial encounters. Was the British Museum stuck with a Victorian vision of supposedly primitive aboriginal peoples who lived in different continents and yet were very like one another and completely different from everyone else?

Of course not! The museum was, very respectfully, reordering its ethnographic materials by geographical region, just as antiquities were now being divided between Asia, the Middle East and Europe. So Africa, America and Oceania were what was left over when Europe, the Middle East and East Asia were taken out. But monuments from pre-Columbian empires in Central America were kept under the control of a well-organised clique of archaeologists. One curator recalls that "Asia was a department of art historians and the one anthropologist employed as a middle-ranking curator to look after its new acquisitions from Ethnography eventually left in frustration at the new department's lack of interest in cultures which did not produce Oriental art."[2] Was the idea to separate the primitive from the civilised? Or, looked at in a different light, were anthropologists (thought of as specialists in primitive societies) being opposed to classicists and orientalists (connoisseurs of ancient civilisations)? It would take a seminar room of highly trained structuralists to work out the logic here.

The curators in the Museum of Mankind were my contemporaries. We shared the same intellectual formation. I sympathised with their frustration at being messed about by high-and-mighty mandarins. Like them, I was baffled by the very idea of a department of Africa, Oceania and the Americas. And it did seem a great pity that the experiments of the Museum of Mankind had come to an end.

When they returned to the British Museum, in 2004, the anthropology curators expected—had been promised—a good showing for their African, American and Pacific collections, but the museum's new director, Neil MacGregor, was not persuaded that everyday crafts made some time ago by marginal populations in faraway countries would prove much of a draw. And money was tight. The Treasury kept squeezing the budget. Sponsors and donors increasingly called the shots.

In July 1993, the president of Mexico, Carlos Salinas de Gortari, made a state visit to Britain. He spent time in the British Museum—presumably not on the off-chance—and then complained that although the museum owns perhaps the most important collection of Mexican antiquities outside of Mexico itself, very few examples were on permanent exhibition. A substantial donation from the Mexican authorities persuaded the British Museum to dedicate a large space to a Mexico gallery. (There was accordingly less room for other South American exhibits.)

Donors also sponsored temporary exhibitions. One highly publicised example, "Living with gods: peoples, places and worlds beyond," was on show in the British Museum from November 2017 to April 2018. It was curated by Jill Cook, keeper of Britain, Europe and Prehistory, and Neil MacGregor. (An art historian by training, MacGregor was director of the National Gallery in London from 1987 to 2002, and director of the British Museum from 2002 to 2015. He returned to the British Museum as a guest curator for this exhibition.)

The exhibition was funded by the Genesis Foundation. The creation of an investment banker, John Studzinski, this foundation is dedicated to "the theme of art and faith." Studzinski is a Catholic, but he explained to the *Financial Times* that "spiritual doesn't have to mean religious."[3] The booklet issued by the museum to accompany the exhibition reads like a New Age manifesto:

> There is no known human society without beliefs in invisible spiritual powers. While the nature of these beliefs and the rituals that accompany them are diverse and vary according to their environmental and cultural background, what underlies them is a natural human inclination for transcendent worlds and beings. Living with gods tries to explore this tendency by looking at how beliefs expressed in stories, objects, images and rituals unite believers, decrease anxieties and promote the formation of strong social bonds that help to make our worlds well-ordered and understandable. This starts with the human mind.

The centrepiece of the exhibition was the 40,000-year-old "Lion Man" sculpture. In the summer of 1939, Robert Wetzel, a German anatomist, prehistorian and Nazi intellectual, was engaged in the excavation of an Upper Palaeolithic site, Stadel Cave, near Ulm in Baden-Württemberg, in southwest Germany. Financed by a "scientific" organisation of the Nazi SS under the direction of Heinrich Himmler, the excavation had to be abandoned on 25 August 1939, a week before Hitler's armies invaded Poland and the Second World War began. On that very last working day, intriguing fragments of worked ivory were uncovered in a small chamber at the rear of the cave.

After Wetzel's death in 1962, the fragments of the ivory sculpture were deposited in the Ulm museum. In 1982 a Swiss palaeontologist, Elisabeth Schmid, discovered further fragments that evidently belonged to the same object. In 1988, the pieces were reassembled and restored. It now appeared that the 31.1 cm-high sculpture represented a figure with the head and forelegs of a great cat—perhaps a cave lion—and the lower body of a human being: it was named the *Löwenmensch*, the Lion Man. Further excavations between 2008 and 2013 uncovered 575

Standing just over one foot (31 cm) tall, carved from mammoth ivory, this 35,000–40,000 years old sculpture was discovered in a cave in the Jura mountains in Germany in 1939. Known as the *Löwenmensch*, or Lion Man, it has a human body and the head of a cave lion or perhaps a cave bear. Photograph, Yvonne Mühleis. (By permission of the Landesamt für Denkmalpflege im RP Stuttgart und Museum Ulm.)

more fragments of the same object. Radiocarbon dating established that it was between 35–40,000 years old. It is therefore one of the oldest figurative carvings yet discovered. A meticulous restoration was then undertaken, in the course of which it became evident that something like a third of the figure was missing.[4]

Jill Cook and Neil MacGregor did not, however, express any doubts about what the sculpture represents. The Lion Man, they explained, has the "head of a cave lion with a human lower body. He stands upright, perhaps on tiptoes, with well-shaped human legs and narrow manly hips . . . His gaze, like his stance, is powerful and directed at the viewer. The details of his ears and eyes show he is alert. He is watching, and he is listening." This "powerful, mysterious predator . . . is a being that does not exist in physical form but symbolises the thoughts, concerns and curiosity of the maker about the relationship between humans and the rest of nature."[5]

An authoritative scientific analysis published three years before the British Museum exhibition had, however, raised questions that were ignored by Cook and MacGregor. Is the Lion Man indeed alert, poised to leap into action? Possibly, but the archaeologists suggest that the sculpture "might equally also depict a floating state and not a realistic behaviour at all."[6] Is it a religious image? The archaeologists thought that it might represent a shaman who is wearing a lion head. Perhaps it had been placed deliberately in the alcove at the rear of the cave because this was a sort of shrine.[7] These speculations hardly amount to a definitive identification. The website of the Ulm museum is wisely agnostic: "We cannot know precisely the intentions of its creators. Even though this unique relic is a fantastical creature, which draws us intuitively towards the spiritual world of early humans living in the grip of the last ice age, we will never be able to decipher their clearly highly complex world view."

And is the Lion Man really male? The genital region of the statue is fractured. An Upper Palaeolithic expert, Joachim Hahn, interpreted the small plate on the abdomen as a flaccid penis. Elisabeth Schmid, who supervised the reconstruction in 1982, identified it as a pubic triangle.[8] She suggested that the statue represents a woman with the head of a *Höhlenlöwin* (a female cave lion), or perhaps a cat.[9] Kurt Wehrberger, deputy director of the Ulm museum, told *Der Spiegel* in 2011 that as the Lion Woman it had become an "icon of the feminist movement." The latest scientific assessment leans towards a male identity. The small plate in the genital area is separated from the groin, and this may indicate that a fragment—perhaps a penis—is missing. Perhaps the striations on the side of the plate "may be interpreted then as the stylized genital of a male."[10] It would seem that all these questions are still unsettled. The British Museum exhibition should have made that clear.

Permanent exhibitions are more problematic than even the most quirky temporary exhibition, because they will remain in place for many years. When ethnography came back home to the British Museum, two galleries were set aside for ethnographic materials. A medical charity, the Wellcome Trust, sponsored one gallery, "Living and Dying," which opened in 2003. In accordance with the charity's mission, this exhibition is about health issues, broadly defined. It adopts the functionalism of mid-twentieth-century anthropology. The fundamental principle is that people everywhere confront many of the same problems, but need to find solutions that fit in with the constraints of the local power structure and religious beliefs, and which can be managed with the available resources. So, to quote the British Museum website, "Living and Dying" "explores how people everywhere deal with the tough realities of life and death . . . These challenges are shared by all, but strategies to deal with them vary from place to place, people to people."

The Wellcome gallery, formerly the museum's north library, is enormous: 870 square metres. The lofty ceiling is 6.3 metres high. The hall is dominated by huge glass display cases over 5 metres in height, each of which shows how people in one or another (exotic) part of the world deal with a particular existential problem: "relating to spirits" (Nicobar Islands), "sustaining one another" (Pacific islands), "living with the earth" (American Indians). And so on.

The most popular exhibit comes closer to home. It is contained in a 14-metres-long glass-topped trestle table in the middle of the hall. Evoking a gigantic showcase in an upmarket luxury goods shop, labelled "Cradle to Grave," this installation, designed by two artists and a family doctor, invites the viewer to reflect on the place of medication in everyday Western lives. The exhibition guide explains: "Two lengths of knitted fabric, one for a man and one for a woman, lie side by side. Knitted into each piece of fabric are examples of all the prescribed pills that this man and woman might take in their lifetime. Lying alongside are family photographs, documents and other medical interventions such as a hearing aid, which mark the progress of their lives."

This exhibit certainly gets the attention of visitors. It can be inspected more comfortably than the ethnographic artefacts arrayed in their high cases. It is also much easier to comprehend. Goodness, so many pills! Apparently an average English person will take 14,000 prescription pills in a lifetime, more than half of which are swallowed in the last ten years of life. This does not include over-the-counter remedies, food supplements and antioxidants. Syringes, x-ray images, a mammogram and a blood donor collection bag represent medical technologies. Family photographs evoke the stages of life. A selection of objects—a condom, an ashtray filled with stubs, a glass of red wine—suggest the sort of health-related concerns that crop up in everyday conversation. I suppose that if a visitor then glances up at a display case showing magical remedies in use in other parts of the world, a moral might pop into her head, perhaps something to do with the "medicalisation" of anxieties in the West. Some may consider giving magic a try.

In 2004 the Wellcome gallery was awarded the Museum and Heritage Show Award for the best permanent exhibition in a UK museum. Was there really no better candidate for this prize in all the museums in Britain?

The Sainsbury Trust is dedicated to the support of the visual arts, and to African arts in particular. When the Sainsbury galleries in the British Museum first opened in 2001 (and they are much the same twenty years on), visitors entering from the main staircase immediately confronted elaborately carved coffins from Ghana that imagine the progress of the deceased in the afterlife, and banners made for the "Free Nelson Mandela" concert held at Wembley in 1988. According to the curators, the installations and displays of contemporary art, ceramics, carnival outfits and weapons are intended to make the visitor question "what we understand to be Africa and African art in the globalizing world of the twenty-first century."[11] So, for example, although Magdalene Odundo, a potter born in Kenya but resident in Britain, is placed by the curators "in the tradition of potting in sub-Saharan Africa," they note that she is inspired by Cycladic figurines and by the modernist masters Arp, Gaudier-Brzeska and Brancusi.[12]

The adjacent hall presents some of the museum's most famous holdings of West African court arts, including a selection of Benin brass plaques and busts. There is little by way of commentary or explanation. Some artefacts are arranged according to the materials used in their manufacture. "This is less arbitrary than it might at first seem," the curators insist, "as a whole philosophy often underlies each different material and technology, and this can be used as a means of shedding light on African history and social life." Well, perhaps it could be used in that way, but that is not evident here. The visitor is given little guidance about anything at all. "Rather than suggesting some sort of distillation of 'African-ness' in the galleries," the curators explained, "our aim was to highlight the continent's extraordinary diversity—cultural, geographical, ethnic, and artistic—and its immense impact on the rest of the world."[13] Yet what the visitor actually sees is a roomful of uncontextualised precolonial court art, juxtaposed with another exhibition space that shows contemporary craft productions from here and there in sub-Saharan Africa.

Two decades later, an exhibition curated by Philippe Dagen, "Ex Africa," that ran from February to July 2021 at the quai Branly museum in Paris, presented a more radical and more interesting perspective on the relationship between classical and contemporary African art. Dagen, an art historian, is the author of a two-volume study, *Primitivismes*, that tells the story of the post-impressionist infatuation with the arts of Oceania and Africa, an affair that degenerated into what he considers the commercialisation of "primitive art" in the second half of the twentieth century. A pivotal moment was the 1984 exhibition "'Primitivism' in 20th Century Art: Affinity of the Tribal and the Modern" in New York's Museum of Modern Art. Here African masks and court art were shown with little consideration for the meaning these works had for the people who commissioned or created them. And MoMA did not provide any space for post-colonial African art. Only European art could be modern.

Dagen pitched "Ex Africa" against the MoMA exhibition. The first room was devoted to "The Chapman Family Collection." At first sight this appeared to be an elegantly presented but otherwise conventional enough display of precolonial African ritual and court art. A closer look revealed that these were clever fakes, some tagged with Ronald McDonald logos. The exhibit was the work of artistic tricksters, the brothers Dinos and Jake Chapman. The next, much larger room showed twenty-first-century works of art, some produced expressly for this exhibition, that address painful features of the contemporary African experience—dictatorship, corruption, illegal migration, sexual trafficking and unresolved legacies of colonialism. Several artworks referred directly or obliquely, and often irreverently, to the classical African canon or to iconic French primitivist art of the early twentieth century.[14]

In the late twentieth-century exhibitions of African history, ethnography and art in the U.S.A. and Canada began to attract political attention, particularly from African American organisations. They were now seen through the prism of debates about race and colonialism.

In November 1989 a temporary exhibition, "In the Heart of Africa," curated by Jeanne Cannizzo, an anthropologist at the

University of Toronto, opened at the Royal Ontario Museum (the ROM). The history of Canada's brief and rather peripheral engagement with colonial Africa, not well known in the country, was presented in the first three rooms in the exhibition: "The Imperial Connection" explained the link with the British Empire; the "Military Hall" featured engagements during the Zulu and Boer wars in South Africa, in which Canadian troops participated; and the "Missionary Room" drew on the experience of Canadian missionaries in Africa.

Dr. Cannizzo chose to present the colonial period as it had been experienced by Canadian participants. There were triumphalist images of white soldiers battling black warriors. A lantern slide presentation was re-created, one of those well-meaning missionary productions designed to show stay-at-home congregants that Canadians were confronting Satan in faraway mission stations and instructing young African Christians in Western craft skills.

The final two rooms were supposed to give an impression of African life in colonial times. They were not very interesting. (The ROM did not have a serious collection of African ethnography.) The "Ovimbundu Compound" re-created, a village homestead in Namibia, where Canadian missionaries had been active in colonial times. There was also a rather conventional collection of African crafts.

To the astonishment and dismay of the curator and the museum, this rather worthy exhibition created a furore. "Just about everything that could go wrong with an exhibition seems to have gone wrong," commented Enid Schildkraut, curator of African ethnography at the American Museum of Natural History. "The controversy that erupted was quite extraordinary, and made many of us working in the field of ethnographic exhibitions, particularly African exhibitions, tremble with a sense of 'there but for the grace of God go I.' How could an exhibition have gone so wrong? How could an exhibition offend so many people from different sides of the political spectrum?"[15]

Well, for one thing, presenting the colonial experience from the viewpoint of Canadian missionaries and soldiers was liable to create misunderstandings. Was this how a major Canadian museum understood Africa? Even some missionary families felt uneasy. "It was too subtle for some of the public, too ironic . . . too intellectual," commented Simon Ottenburg, an anthropologist who devoted a long career to African ethnography. "It raised the question of how subtle it is possible to be in an exhibit designed for the general public."[16]

Irony is not easy to pull off in a museum setting. Who is supposed to be talking? Dr. Schildkraut commented that "the ROM and the curator must have assumed, and hoped, that the audience would understand that this was intended as irony or tongue-in-cheek—something like an off-color joke told with a knowing wink." But visitors to a museum may not pay careful attention to labels, or recognise that some quotes may be selected for ironic effect. Here they were confronted with patronising, ethnocentric observations about Africa and Africans, read them literally, and reacted with shock. "Predictably," Schildkraut notes, "many critics asked whether an exhibition on the Holocaust from the point of view of the Nazis would be acceptable."[17] No African voices were introduced to challenge colonial attitudes. Nor were contemporary Zulu or Boer accounts of the wars cited.

The *Toronto Globe and Mail* commented: "One had to be very literate and sophisticated to appreciate the show as the curator intended, which then raised the broader question: whose museum is this anyway?"[18] A very good question. Toronto had recently become a global immigrant destination. It was home to a substantial Afro-Caribbean population. There were local tensions, including allegations of police brutality. All this was against the background of a bland official "multiculturalist" discourse.

A loose alliance of Caribbean immigrant organisations came together under the banner of "Coalition for the Truth about Africa." They made the ROM exhibition a rallying point.

Complaining that the exhibition ignored Africa's rich history,[19] campaigners demanded that the museum withdraw the exhibition, and apologise to the African community. In future any museum exhibition on Africa should be curated by Africans.

The campaign was a success in its own terms. Dr. Cannizzo left her job at the University of Toronto. Four Canadian museums which had contracted to take the exhibition withdrew. "The one party that had the grace not to express dismay with Jeanne Cannizzo was the ROM itself," Dr. Schildkraut noted. The museum authorities argued that they had to respect the curator's right to free speech. However, in November 2016 (twenty-seven years after the exhibition closed), the ROM's deputy director of collections and research, Dr. Mark Engstrom, delivered an official apology: "The ROM expresses its deep regret for having contributed to anti-African racism. The ROM also officially apologizes for the suffering endured by members of the African-Canadian community as a result of 'Into the Heart of Africa.'"

The Ontario debacle put curators of African collections in Canada and the United States on notice. Exhibitions of African art, history and ethnography were politically very, very sensitive. Even the most august institutions had to pay attention.

The natural history building of the U.S. National Museum (now the Smithsonian Museum of Natural History) opened to the public in 1911. Its ethnographic collections were, of course, dominated by American materials. However, there was a "Hall of African Cultures." This was arranged to illustrate a supposed hierarchy of civilisations from primitive to civilised.

Accessions to the Smithsonian's African collection came in at first through anti-slavery contacts. There were donations from Christian pastors in Liberia, a settlement established in 1821 by freed slaves from the United States. Another early donor was Commodore Matthew Perry, who mounted anti-slavery patrols off the coast of Liberia from 1819 to 1820 and then led sorties against pirates and slave traders in the West Indies. Later acquisitions came from world fairs or were passed on by European museums in exchange for American Indian artefacts. But the collection was patchy, assembled opportunistically and very small scale. By 1920 it held just over 2,800 African artefacts, most of them acquired in parcels of fewer than ten objects.

In 1922 a British artist, Herbert Ward, donated 2,700 Congolese artefacts together with his own sculptures of African men and women, doubling the size of the Smithsonian's African holdings. Recommended by Henry Morton Stanley, Ward had served for two years in the Congo, where he befriended the anti-colonial activist Roger Casement and financed the publication of Edmund Morel's tract, *The Congo Slave State*. Back in Europe he became an established figure in the Paris art scene.

The Ward collection in the Africa hall was exhibited in a separate niche, the display modelled on Ward's romantic installation in his studio in Paris: weapons and carvings organised in decorative patterns, backed by fabrics, deer and elephant heads ranged above, all dimly lit. The Belgian authorities may well have had a hand in the Ward donation. They were engaged at the time in promoting exhibitions of Congolese art in American museums in order to counter the unfortunate image left over from King Leopold's Congo Free State.

In 1962 the African displays were removed. A new Hall of African Cultures, curated by Dr. Gordon Gibson, the Smithsonian's first Africanist curator, opened in 1969.[20] The presentation was regional, informed by the environmental determinism that was current in American anthropology at the time. Artefacts were grouped according to their "function," a term of art in the anthropology of the day. Mary Jo Arnoldi, curator for African arts and ethnology, notes that at this stage the collection was in any case largely made up of utilitarian objects—tools for metalworking, weaving, animal husbandry, hunting and fishing; furniture, pottery and baskets; textiles, costumes and jewellery. And there were lots of weapons: the Ward collection alone added over 1,700 spears, knives and arrows.

More than half the displays represented ethnic groups— "The Herero and Himba," "The Bushmen," and so on—brought to seeming life in dioramas. Artefacts were not dated. The image was of a traditional, rural Africa, apparently untouched by outside influences. There were remarkably few masks and statues, although a clumsy gesture was made towards recognition of the aesthetic value of some African artefacts. The label for one showcase—"Native Fetiches and Wood Carvings"— read: "The African native displays much skill in carving wood. He does not hesitate to boldly attempt the fashioning of the human form in his fetiches and this barbaric sculpture achieves what to him are satisfying works of art and which convey their interest to civilized man. Stools, headrest, and domestic utensils are worked with a view to pleasing forms and decorations."[21]

By the 1980s, the curators were thoroughly fed up with the dated, unrepresentative and occasionally downright obnoxious exhibits and labels. The Smithsonian authorities conceded that the hall was in urgent need of renewal. But work on the gallery had to take its place in the queue. Perhaps 2017 . . . ? However, complaints began to come in from African diplomats and African American politicians in Washington. In September 1992, during Congressional hearings on the funding of the Smithsonian, representative Gus Savage, head of the Congressional Black Caucus, confronted the secretary of the Smithsonian Institution about "offensive and racist" labels in the Hall of African Cultures. Mr. Savage drew particular attention to a label on the exhibit case "Control of the Supernatural." It read: "SECRET SOCIETIES of prophets, diviners, medicine men and others are politically powerful in Zaire. Members, sometimes in costume, assemble in clubhouses where they chant, dance, and participate in secret rites such as orgies, cannibalism, and the eating of exhumed corpses—all to acquire supernatural powers."[22] The Smithsonian could offer no defence. In December the exhibition was closed.[23] The makeover began at once.

The Smithsonian authorities set up a consultative body of curators and designers, specialists on African ethnography, art and history, and Africans, African Americans and members of the Smithsonian African American Association. A hundred and twenty members were tapped, but over the following seven years regular attendance averaged at around sixty.

What was the target audience? For people of African descent this exhibit might be a primary destination, but the bulk of visitors to the Smithsonian museums come in family groups from around the U.S.A. and spend on average an hour in the National Museum of Natural History. This might include at the most fifteen minutes in the Africa hall. And research confirmed that most visitors to the museum are not at all familiar with life and conditions in today's Africa. They tend to believe that Africa was and remains backward, cut off from the modern world.

The advisory board quickly agreed that "the exhibition needed to highlight Africa's history, diversity, and dynamism; African's connections to the wider world; and African agency both historically and in the present."[24] Artefacts from Africa and the African diaspora were sourced, including modern West African textiles, Candomblé ritual apparatus from Bahia, Brazil, and works by contemporary African artists.[25] It was agreed that the hall would be renamed "African Voices" and that the exhibition would privilege the perspectives of Africans and African Americans.

Predictably, there were disagreements in that sixty-strong advisory group. "Moving from these generally agreed upon abstract objectives and goals to fashioning an exhibition script and design was difficult to achieve," Dr. Arnoldi concedes.[26] African Americans and African immigrants living in Washington sometimes had very different ideas about how Africa should be represented. On the whole, African Americans wanted the exhibition to present a modern, urban Africa, while Africans hoped to see a respectful treatment of African traditions. After years of discussion a decision was made to set up four galleries: Living in Africa, Wealth in Africa, Work in Africa and Global Africa. Cities, rural areas and the diaspora would all be represented.

The framework of an *aqal*, a Somali nomadic house which had been collected in northern Somalia in the early 1980s and later donated to the museum, was installed in the "Living in

An *aqal*, a Somali nomad's dwelling, collected in northern
Somalia in the early 1980s, installed in 1999 in the African
Voices hall in the U.S. National Museum of Natural History.
(By permission of the Smithsonian Institution.)

Africa" section of the exhibition. "As the idea for the story took
shape, a number of our American and African advisors became
uneasy about using the house," Dr. Arnoldi recalls.[27] Might it
strike the casual visitor as somewhat . . . primitive?

A Somali resident in Washington, a member of the advisory
team, had grown up as a nomadic herder. He explained that the
aqal is a central symbol of Somali identity. Committee members
were persuaded. Somali women from the Washington area
were then invited to select traditional domestic objects from
the museum stores—carved wooden headrests, water and milk
containers woven from grass. They insisted on adding a short-
wave radio and a brass tray and coffee pot. They also wished
to display a spear and shield, but "other Somali scholars and
members of the community" insisted that a modern automatic
rifle should be added. On a video screen, Somali Americans,
dressed in Western clothes, reminisce about life in an *aqal*.[28]

A "history pathway" that runs through the hall is intended to provide a point of reference for the other galleries. Perhaps a good idea in principle, it was difficult to implement in practice. "A major problem was how to help visitors appreciate the fact of Africa's long history while physically moving them only several hundred feet through the hall," Dr. Arnoldi writes. A decision was made to concentrate on ten pivotal "moments," but even so, the first half of the section called "Walk Through Time" covers more than 230,000 years, beginning with the first humans in the Rift Valley and ending in the eleventh century with an exhibit entitled, provocatively and inexactly, "African Muslims Rule Spain."

The gallery "Living in Africa" is linked to the history pathway by transitional exhibits. A history "moment" about the ancient city of Jene-Jeno in Mali is placed near an exhibit that evokes a modern urban market in Ghana. Displays illustrating Kongo rituals in Africa and in the African diaspora tie in with showcases displaying aspects of "Global Africa."

Because the exhibition space could be entered from either end of the hall it was difficult to lay down a narrative with a definite beginning and end. The limitations of the museum's African collection were a further constraint. And then there were technical problems. "We spent an enormous amount of time carefully choosing photographs, but they unfortunately are often blocked by the object displays," the curators recalled. "The designers tended to treat the photographs as contextual wallpaper."[29]

Labels and more extensive texts were also tricky. Posters near each entry point provided an initial orientation. Each section was introduced by a poster that set out its main themes. Each item had its individual label. "Though the text hierarchy helped us organize our thinking on the different topics and prioritize the information for each text, its impact on the audience appears to be minimal," Dr. Arnoldi discovered. "Anecdotal evidence suggests that most of our visitors are not aware of the different kinds of texts in the exhibition, and most do not seek out the gallery text to get the main messages of any particular section. Similarly our efforts to develop way-finding aids and to distinguish between thematic galleries by color-coding the labels goes relatively unnoticed."[30] The first labels that were drafted offered brief poetic leads to particular exhibits, but visitors found them confusing and said they felt that they were being manipulated. When some exhibits were tested six months before the exhibition opened to the public, visitors complained about clutter. They wanted labels to be placed closer to the objects that they were looking at.

The difficulty of encapsulating complex histories and the clash of agendas was perhaps most troubling when it came to the representation of slavery in Africa. An attempt was made to draw attention to connections between the West African slave trade and the wealth of some precolonial African courts: gold-encrusted Akan royal regalia were juxtaposed with replica shackles and a branding iron. However, Dr. Arnoldi reports, "testing showed that visitors did not understand the point we were trying to make."[31] A new section was introduced in the history path, "Money Drives the Slave Trade." The accompanying text explains: "Soon after Europeans began colonizing the Americas, they turned to enslaved labor to work their plantations and mines. European slave traders negotiated with African elites to procure captives. Most were taken as prisoners in African wars, others were captured by European-led expeditions. From the moment of captivity, millions of Africans fought for freedom."

European museums of anthropology and "non-European art" possess large colonial-era collections. Curators are now challenged to give an accounting of their museum's relationship to empire and the slave trade. They must also consider the interests and sensitivities of an international public, including immigrants and visitors from formerly colonial counties.

In 1885, as European powers divided up spheres of influence in Africa, King Leopold II of Belgium made off with a personal fiefdom, the "Congo Free State." This feudal estate swiftly became an international byword for brutal exploitation. A PR campaign was launched. The Brussels International Exposition in 1897 featured a colonial exhibition in the suburb of Tervuren. Congolese coffee, cacao and tobacco were promoted in the "Hall of the Great Cultures." Congolese villages were built in the park, with 267 Africans in residence. The following year, the Royal Museum of Central Africa was established on the exposition site in Tervuren. It was dedicated to the natural history and ethnography of the Congo.

Despite all that investment in public relations, the Congo Free State remained a pariah. Under considerable pressure, Leopold sold it to the Belgian government in 1908. The colonial administration instituted reforms. Rebranded the Belgian Congo, it gradually became a standard issue colony, not obviously much worse governed than British, French and Portuguese colonies in Africa. In 1960, following a massive anti-colonial campaign, Belgium abruptly granted the country independence. Meanwhile, the Africa museum in Tervuren remained virtually unchanged. In 2005, it launched a radical makeover with a major exhibition, "Memory of Congo: The Colonial Era."

This exhibition presented a revisionist take on the history of the Belgian Congo, addressed primarily to a domestic audience which was, apparently, still under the impression that the colony had been a paragon of enlightened imperialism, and that decolonisation had been an act of generosity. This was to brush aside unofficial but decisive Belgian support for the secession of the resource-rich Katanga region immediately after Congolese independence, and the collusion of Belgian and U.S. secret agents in the assassination of the country's first prime minister, Patrice Lumumba. The sad state of the country's politics and economy in the late twentieth and early twenty-first century was blamed on the greed and inexperience of homegrown politicians.

The immediate impulse for the exhibition may have been the publication of Adam Hochschild's *King Leopold's Ghost: A Story of Greed, Terror and Heroism in Colonial Africa*, which appeared in English and French editions in 1998. The subtitle of the French edition was "The Forgotten Holocaust." The Tervuren exhibition was clearly designed to counter some of Hochschild's most damaging claims. It promised a nuanced and scholarly perspective that would respect competing perspectives and leave judgements to the museum's visitors. "This is a shared history, charged with emotion," explained the official booklet, "and as such the voices of those who experienced it or who interpret it today need to be heard. The exhibition therefore features interviews through which Belgians and Congolese relate their experiences."

The most controversial message was that early twentieth-century critics of Leopold's regime exaggerated the number of lives lost to starvation, epidemics and forced labour in his Congo Free State. (Hochschild adopted an extreme estimate of around 10 million victims.) The brutality of Leopold's regime was now relativised by invoking the slave-trading and warfare that characterised the precolonial kingdoms. But to the surprise, apparently, of many Belgians, the exhibition did document the persistence of a colour bar in the Belgian Congo, in living areas, employment and the legal system. Exhibits covered anti-colonial political movements and grassroots cultural activity, including contemporary art and the new urban music, the "Congolese rumba," that emerged in the 1940s, partly in response to popular Cuban music, and which would produce a booming music industry and an international vogue for Congolese music and dance. Finally, a reflexive section, "Representation," explored the ways in which images of colonists and colonised were deployed for purposes of propaganda. Included here was the Tervuren museum itself. Although admittedly "a propaganda tool," the official guidebook explained that the museum "was also a scientific establishment dedicated to the study of the colony."

Adam Hochschild denounced the exhibition in the New York Review of Books (his review, inevitably, was headlined "In the Heart of Darkness"). The museum's director, Jean-Luc Vellut, responded that the exhibition was balanced, and that it left viewers to draw their own conclusions. "Hochschild believes that this approach betrays lack in moral commitment," Vellut wrote, "and yet the formula adopted by Tervuren introduced colonial history into the social consciousness of Belgium on a wide scale. It was appreciated by 140,000 visitors . . . Furthermore the Congo government showed its welcome appreciation by inviting the show to come to Africa."[32]

It is not easy to achieve balance, or even the appearance of balance. Who selects the historical narratives that have to be weighed against one another? And what has been left out? Tellingly, the Tervuren exhibition was reticent about current political conditions in the Congo. However, *The New York Times* remarked that the experience of post-colonial ethnic and militia violence "has led some Congolese to view the colonial period more positively." It quoted Ndaywel è Nziem, a Congolese historian who advised the Tervuren museum on the exhibition: "In the eyes of many Congolese, the colonial era now looks like a golden age, while Belgian opinion is going in the opposite direction and recognizing the crimes of the past." Some older inhabitants of Katanga recall the colonial era as *la belle époque*.[33] One can see why the Tervuren curators did not want to tread there.

Curators may hesitate to take on popular prejudices or special interests. Let them be bold. They should be ready to imagine exhibitions that are at once scholarly, historically informed but innovative, even challenging. Special exhibitions may also be the most effective way to attract a broader, younger public. In 2011 Anna Schmid, director of the "Museum of Cultures: European and non-European Ethnology" in Basel, began a radical refashioning of what had become a distinctly old-fashioned institution. Half of the museum is now dedicated to short-term exhibitions. There are no permanent displays. Long-term exhibits are turned over every five years, and so they are installed with an eye to flexibility. There are no display cases, no bulky installations. As far as possible, exhibits are not shown under glass. Storerooms are opened to visitors under the supervision of a curator.

Basel City is a prosperous Swiss canton. It has 200,000 well-off, well-educated and famously well-behaved inhabitants, and thirty-six very well-funded public museums. No doubt Dr. Schmid's situation is unusually cushy. And she is apparently immune from political pressures. When I asked about "restitution," she responded that nobody has asked her museum to give up artefacts in its collection.

Perhaps Basel's innovations would not work so well in larger, busier museums in more diverse cities, but it must often be possible to set more space aside for temporary exhibitions. And rather than ducking controversy, museums should make it clear that original, challenging exhibitions will be commissioned, presenting a variety of perspectives, drawing on collections from a number of collaborating museums.

From the archives:

> The questions investigated in this study were whether the casual Sunday-afternoon visitor followed the sequence of exhibits at the Peabody Museum of Natural History (Yale University) in the order intended, how much time he spent studying the exhibits, how often he read the labels, and especially, whether this arrangement prevented or even delayed "museum-fatigue." When the individual records were examined, it was found that the route taken by the average visitor was the reverse of that planned in the Guide Book; 24.4 per cent of the exhibits were examined; 10.9 per cent of the labels were read; and the average time taken by the visitors for reviewing the history of life on the earth during the past 500,000,000 years was 21.40 minutes. Conclusions arising from a behavior inventory of visitors and from a leaflet experiment were: (1) that mere juxtaposition of exhibits in a logical sequence does not, by itself, guarantee their examination by the casual Sunday-afternoon visitor

in the order intended; and (2) that the visitors benefited from the use of the leaflets to an extent that was
statistically significant.

Mildred C. B. Porter, 1938, *Behavior of the Average Visitor in
the Peabody Museum of Natural History, Yale University*. Publications of the American Association of Museums, New
Series, Number 16, Washington, DC, p. 15.

THE COSMOPOLITAN MUSEUM

The number of museums worldwide grew from 23,000 to 55,000 in the four decades to 2018. Some 4,000 opened in China alone.[1] The Louvre, the most popular museum in the world, had 10.2 million visitors in 2018, an increase of 25 per cent over 2017. In London, the British Museum and Tate Modern each recorded some 6 million visitors, about three-quarters of whom were tourists. Attendance at the twenty most-visited museums in the United States peaked at almost 50 million in 2019. In 2020, at the height of the COVID-19 pandemic, attendance at the hundred most popular art museums in the world fell by 77 per cent, but visitor numbers picked up once restrictions were lifted.[2] In 2021 the museum industry in the United States turned over $15.4 billion, a 19 per cent increase over the previous year.[3]

But despite the boom, all is not well. The great metropolitan museums, situated at the heart of multicultural, globalised, tourist-ridden cities, have been slow to reassess their role in a post-colonial world. Most troubled of all, the Museum of Other People confronts existential challenges. Topping the list are demands for the return of world-famous treasures seized in imperialist campaigns in the nineteenth century. More broadly, almost any colonial-era acquisitions in European and North American museums may be viewed with suspicion.

"It is still commonly presumed in the media that ethnographic artefacts were mostly looted," writes Nicholas Thomas, director of the Museum of Archaeology and Anthropology at Cambridge University. "While some objects, including famous ones such as the Benin Bronzes were indeed seized in the aftermath of violence, the bulk of what is in anthropological collections was obtained through purchase or exchange."[4]

Blanket claims are nevertheless lodged to furnishings, regalia, weapons and armour, carvings and masks that were collected more than a century ago from kingdoms and empires that have since vanished from the map. Who is making these claims, and in whose name? Do the remote descendants of pre-colonial African rulers—whose ancestors were in many cases local imperialists, slave owners and slave traders—really have an overriding claim to ancient sites and to artefacts now held in foreign museums? The alternative may be to transfer disputed property to national museums, but account must be taken of local circumstances, including smuggling, political upheavals, civil wars, authoritarian rule and the current sad state of many historical monuments and collections.

More nuanced, less confrontational perspectives are being explored. As part of its settlement with the movement for the independence of New Caledonia, a colonial archipelago in the South Pacific, the French government endowed the Tjibaou Cultural Centre, named after the independence leader, Jean Marie Tjibaou. When the centre opened in June 1998, Jean Marie's widow, Marie Claude Tjibaou, described it as "a powerful gesture of restitution by the government of France." Addressing a symposium in Paris at the quai Branly museum in July 2007, she said: "In the end, and contrary to the idea that prevailed until recently, according to which the patrimony that has been dispersed should be repatriated to New Caledonia, the Tjibaou Cultural Centre proposes an alternative. In fact we consider that the presence of Kanak objects in great European and American museums constitutes today a new form of representation for our culture. These objects become, in a way, our ambassadors to the wider world."[5]

In 2013, Emmanuel Kasarhérou, formerly head of the Museum of New Caledonia, curated an exhibition of Kanak artefacts in the quai Branly museum. He presented the objects as silent witnesses to a colonial encounter, products of a complex process of unequal, often contentious but sometimes creative interaction. He added that, as the son of a French mother and a Kanak father, "I feel as much the descendant of people who were colonizers of a certain place as of people who were colonized."[6] In 2020, Kasarhérou was appointed director of the quai Branly museum.

Claims for the restitution of artefacts shade into another controversy. The crux is competing claims to expertise: scholarship vs. insider knowledge. Who gets to select items for exhibition, to make up and tell the story of an object or a display, to compose a descriptive label for a mask or a ritual artefact, to write a guide to a gallery?

Can only the Native speak with authority about the Native? And if so, which Native should be elected to speak? Conceptions of native expertise take various forms. It is an article of faith in the international Indigenous peoples movement that shamans have a special insight into the origin, ownership and powers of certain artefacts. Some museums do their best to accommodate this special knowledge.

Between 1905 and 1907 Konrad Theodor Preuss, a curator at the Museum of Ethnography in Berlin, carried out extensive ethnographic fieldwork in the western Sierra Madre in Mexico and collected materials for the museum. Some he bought directly from craftsmen, even commissioning replicas of specialised artefacts. Occasionally he filched ritual objects from shrines.

Margarita Valdovinos of the Universidad Nacional Autónoma de México, an expert on the Cora people of the region, explains that objects used in ritual are constructed in the course of a ceremony. The culminating act is their dedication to particular deities. They then belong to the gods and must be left to decay. And so restitution is problematic. Did the gods reject the gift? Can an ordinary person take possession of the property of a divinity? How might museums manage such sacred artefacts?[7]

In 2005, a group of Huichol shamans from the Sierra Madre visited the Berlin ethnographic museum. They were sponsored by German activists campaigning for the return of ethnographic materials (although no Mexican claim had been made to the Preuss collections). Dr. Valdovinos was present when the shamans inspected Huichol artefacts in the museum stores. She noticed that the curator who was passing items to the shamans for inspection unwittingly included Cora and other materials. The shamans did not hesitate to identify and interpret these non-Huichol pieces. "I knew the collection pretty well, and I knew the logic of the catalogue numbers, so I rapidly realized their mistake," Dr. Valdovinos recalls. Later she warned the director against using the responses of the shamans for cataloguing purposes. That was her responsibility as an ethnographer. She is the expert, after all.[8]

In February 2020 a Maasai *laibon*, a medicine man and diviner, was invited to give guidance on provenance at the Pitt Rivers Museum in Oxford. *The Economist* described the climax of his visit: "In the oak-panelled Bookbinders Ale House, a group of Maasai tribespeople gathers the day before returning to Tanzania and Kenya, to sip cappuccinos and bitter and to chew over the results of a two-week visit to Oxford. Despite the vile February weather, they are satisfied with their trip for they are closer to getting back sacred objects that are held by Oxford's Pitt Rivers Museum."

"The Maasai have come," the *Economist* explained, "at the invitation of Laura van Broekhoven, director of the Pitt Rivers, and InsightShare, an NGO, to establish where and when the objects were taken. To that end, they have brought Lemaron ole Parit, a *laibon*—a spiritual leader—with mystical powers. His family has been providing spiritual leadership for generations . . . Nick Lunch, InsightShare's organiser, is impressed that Mr. ole Parit has been talking with his father, Mokompo ole Simel, who holds ultimate spiritual power in the tribe but stayed at home, 'not just on WhatsApp but also through his dreams.'

"Sitting on the floor of Mrs. van Broekhoven's office, Mr. ole Parit breathes into an *enkidong* vessel packed with stones and snuff tobacco. He then shakes out the stones, whose patterns reveal the artefact's history to him. 'I've identified the circumstances under which objects were taken,' he explains. 'The times when they were taken, and how many hands they went through.'"

Mr. ole Parit viewed 188 artefacts and picked out five that should be handed back to . . . well, to some still to be designated Tanzanian institution. A year before Mr. ole Parit's intervention, these same five artefacts had in fact been identified by a visiting Tanzanian civil rights activist, Samwel Nangiria, an associate of the Oxford-based activist group InsightShare. Mr. Nangiria was not troubled by the museum's holdings of Maasai spears, arrow heads, necklaces, gourds, and so on, but he claimed that five bracelets were personal possessions, which typically pass from father to son. He insisted that they could not therefore have been legitimately acquired by the missionaries and colonial officers who donated them to the Pitt Rivers Museum more than a century ago.[9]

Dr. van Broekhoven accepted the diviner's verdict and agreed to surrender the five bracelets. Explaining her reasoning, she endorsed what is sometimes called epistemic relativism, the doctrine that claims to knowledge should be assessed with reference to local cultural premises rather than supposedly universal scientific and scholarly tests and standards. (Some relativists also insist on equal time for what President Trump's spokesperson famously called "alternative facts.") "Real decoloniality is to see each other's knowledge systems as equal," said Dr. van Broekhoven. After all, the museum's own documentation is not infallible. "It would be quite disingenuous to say, 'Your knowledge system is inferior to ours.'"[10]

This particular form of epistemic relativism is often associated with a call for the "decolonisation" of scholarship. Edward Said's *Orientalism*, published in 1978, made the case that all "colonial sciences" have a common structure: they divide the peoples of the world into two: ourselves and others, we and they. Natives of the tropics and the antipodes are cast as our oppo-site numbers. They are superstitious, emotional, violent. Their very otherness justifies colonialism: Said claimed that Oriental-ism is "a kind of Western projection onto and will to govern over the Orient."[11] Yet he respected scholarly studies of other kinds of people, dismissing the presumption that "only women can understand feminine experience, only Jews can understand Jewish suffering, only formerly colonial subjects can understand colonial experience."[12] Nevertheless, it was soon widely accepted in the growing field of post-colonial studies that only the native can understand the native. Foreign "experts" (always referenced in scare quotes) are suspect, scholarship discounted. This is apparently now the official view at the Pitt Rivers Museum.

And yet Dr. van Broekhoven may be rather too quick to tell us what "the Maasai" think, based, apparently, on conversations with an NGO activist and a shaman. Two ethnographers, Paola Ivanov, of the Berlin Ethnographic Museum, and Jonas Bens, of the Free University in Berlin, arranged a field study in northern Tanzania to find out what local people might in fact think about the Maasai artefacts in the Pitt Rivers Museum. Shown photo-graphs of the exhibits, respondents expressed surprise that they should be displayed in a faraway museum, but hardly anybody suggested that the artefacts had been seized by colonialists. They assumed that family treasures were sold off during an unpopular period of economic liberalisation in the 1980s. Told that the transfers occurred a century or more ago, a number of respondents reasoned that the objects must have been taken by force. Their great-grandparents would not have given up such personal belongings of their own free will.[13] Yet they were aware that precolonial Maasai country was no Arcadia. The region was stalked by Arab slave traders. Nor was it closed off from foreign influences. Their great-grandparents were familiar with curren-cies and trade, as they were with Islam and Christianity.[14]

Resort to the wisdom of shamans is the *reductio ad absur-dum* of the indigenist credo. There cannot be many curators in

Europe who would support the invigilation of an exhibition of Islamic art by fundamentalist mullahs. Do any Oxford museums insist that only a clergyman may curate a display of medieval Christian art and artefacts? And yet some respectable institutions go along with the equally questionable doctrine that only people with an ancestral relationship to a particular precolonial cult are entitled to say what it is all about.

Are certain kinds of knowledge encoded in racial memory? More plausibly, claims of insight based on identity may be understood as a power play. It follows, surely, that if a person has no ancestral relationship to a particular tradition then whatever they say about it should be dismissed as the product of personal (inherited, status-related) prejudices. Why bother to consider their arguments? Just ask—demand—where they are coming from.

Shamans are not a good substitute for curators, but nor are government spin doctors. In March 2022 it was announced that the Smithsonian Institution would hand over thirty-nine Benin artworks to Nigeria's National Commission for Museums and Monuments. (This decision must still be endorsed by the trustees.) Some of the pieces are then to be returned to Washington for an exhibition that Nigerians will curate. "This exhibition will be from the perspective of Nigeria and how we want them to be displayed," Abba Isa Tijani, director general of the Nigerian Museum Commission told the *Washington Post*. "What is more important than being in control of how your heritage, your artifacts, are displayed?"[15] The *Washington Post* really should have asked Mr. Tijani why, in that case, Nigeria's museums are unable to display the five hundred Benin Bronzes in their collections.

In any case, the logic of Mr. Tijani's claim is dubious. He demands an exhibition of Benin art in Washington "from the perspective of Nigeria." Nigeria is a complex society, riven with religious, political, class and ethnic rivalries. In July 2022, Nigeria's population was estimated at 217 million. According to the *World Factbook* produced by the CIA, there are over 370 ethnic groups, and more than 500 languages. The country is divided roughly equally between Muslims and various Christian denominations. A small minority identifies with other religious traditions, including precolonial cults. However, reliable numbers are hard to come by. As Afe Adogame, professor of Christianity and society at Princeton, explains:

> In the past, the politicisation of the census on religious and ethnic grounds resulted in unreliable religio-ethnic demographic data in Nigeria, as population statistics were (and still are) often manipulated for political, economic, and religious ends, not least because such figures constitute one basis for the sharing of national revenue and other resources. That partly explains why religious indices were excluded from the recent national census.[16]

So who are the rightful owners of the looted Benin antiquities? The Oba of Benin claims they belong to his family. The German Foreign Minister said they should go to the "Nigerian people."

But as Kwame Anthony Appiah asks:

> what does it mean, exactly, for something to belong to a people? Most of Nigeria's cultural patrimony was produced before the modern Nigerian state existed. We don't know whether the terracotta Nok sculptures, made sometime between about 800 BC and AD 200, were commissioned by kings or commoners; we don't know whether the people who made them and the people who paid for them thought of them as belonging to the kingdom, to a man, to a lineage, or to the gods. One thing we know for sure, however, is they didn't make them for Nigeria.[17]

Attacks on the right of Museums of Other People to own, display and interpret their collections may be over-generalised and over-simplified. There are, however, good grounds for more informed and sober criticisms. These museums are sitting on a huge reserve of the world's treasures. The bulk of their holdings have never been publicly exhibited. The rest are in store, often far from the prime location of the museum itself; accessible, if at all, only to scholars. Museums should set up lending libraries to service other museums. A programme of rotating loans, expertly curated, would foster the development of local expertise. Alliances of museums could set up collaborative travelling exhibitions.

Above all, these museums have been slow to adapt their thinking. Battered by a decade of controversy, curators are shellshocked, defensive, secretive. And yet collections of everyday artefacts, cult objects, musical instruments, masterpieces of craftwork, relics of ancient civilisations, beginning with pieces acquired by Captain Cook and his companions, built up generation after generation by missionaries, scholars, collectors and dealers, still fascinate connoisseurs and captivate museumgoers. They open a door to other lives, even other worlds.

But is a Museum of Other People viable in the twenty-first century? Should it be made over as an identity museum, or repurposed as a museum of art, specialising in . . . whatever . . . "primitive," "tribal" or "non-European," or, more expansively but in no way logically or defensibly, that colonial ensemble "African, American and Oceanian Art"? Art museums appropriate masks, busts, representations of gods and demons and rebrand them as sculpture, or reimagine ethnographic assemblages as art installations. These may be admired, even wondered at, by visitors. But art museums do not explore what these artefacts mean to the people who make and use them.

Unfortunately the Museum of Other People does not always do much better. Caution, even timidity, inhibits innovation. Curators sometimes buckle and allow activists to dictate terms. But if they are to take the initiative, museums really must undertake a renewal of sclerotic permanent exhibitions and put a stop to bland temporary exhibitions that pander to sponsors or sell out to collectors and dealers.

Above all, the ultimate challenge must be confronted. *What are they museums of?* Might there be a place for a cosmopolitan museum that is not a simple propaganda tool, and does not lapse into empty generalities about the human condition?

Between 2014 and 2018, funded by the European Union's "Creative European Programme," leaders of ten European ethnographic museums met to discuss a new kind of Museum of Other People, one that would come to terms with the legacy of colonialism and take account of large-scale immigration into Europe from Africa and Asia. Pioneered in Sweden, the Netherlands, Austria and Germany, this came to be known as the World Culture Museum. It is not a Museum of Other People because it includes Europe on equal terms, at least in principle, though in practice Europe is present, if at all, only in the form of folk traditions. In fact, disappointingly but unsurprisingly, most World Culture Museums simply bring together established ethnographic museums and museums of Asian art. So what makes a World Culture Museum different from a Museum of Other People? ("It is all about people" is the feeble formula of Vienna's *Weltmuseum*.)[18]

The project of a World Culture Museum was pursued most seriously in Sweden. The government wanted to shake up the nation's museums and encourage them to take account of the diversity of what had once been a remarkably homogeneous population. In 2016, a plan was floated to merge three Stockholm museums to form a World Culture Museum. An acrimonious public debate erupted about what was meant by World Culture. The official government gloss was "cultures originating outside Sweden."[19] Si Han, curator of Chinese art at the Museum of Far Eastern Antiquities, protested: "To gather all the non-European museums under one roof is real us-and-them thinking, pretend-multiculturalism."[20]

Drawing on local resources, a Museum of World Culture was established in Gothenburg, Sweden's second city. When an American sociologist, Peggy Levitt, paid a visit, she found that "the staff constantly debated what *world culture* meant." The director of the museum, Jette Sandahl, was struggling to combine cultural relativism with the Declaration of Human Rights. She explained to Levitt:

> When you heard Swedes talking about cultural diversity, they meant ethnicity or religion [particularly Islam]. I took all that off the table. I went straight to the UNESCO positions on cultural diversity and to the United Nations Universal Declaration of Human Rights and used them to build the mission statement for the museum . . . UNESCO says that all cultures are equal and make [an] equal contribution, but I cheated on this. There are cultural practices that I don't like, that I don't value equally, such as female-genital cutting. The UNESCO statement is valueless, but we corrected this by coupling it with the UN definition, which speaks to another basic core human value. If you just have the UNESCO statement, you are a cultural relativist, but if you add the Declaration of Human Rights, there are certain things that are unacceptable.[21]

So the Gothenburg World Culture Museum is relativist, except when it comes to stuff the curators don't like. This is not a cosmopolitan programme. It smacks rather of old-style "development" projects that take for granted the superiority of Western (read, "civilised") values.

The classical Museum of Other People featured a kind of people who, it was imagined, lived as their ancestors had done, enclosed in an unchanging ethnically pure province, unaware of other ways of life or a wider world. And yet even people living in remote islands are familiar with other ways of doing things. So were their ancestors. In a number of cases, studies of material culture can trace these connections back for tens of thousands of years. Imitation, reaction, adaptation, all the forms of what is sometimes disapprovingly described as cultural appropriation, are far more common than successful resistance to foreign influences, however heavily policed. The myth of one person, one tribe, never made much sense. The local cannot be curtained off from the global. Every human society is hybrid, a dynamic amalgam of traditions and populations. Although some nativists may deny it, we are all multicultural even cosmopolitan.

If a modern society had a bird totem, as do many more traditional societies, it would surely be the magpie. We borrow music, fashions, technologies, ideas. Virtually every African is at least bilingual, and usually at home in several languages. Yet even stubbornly monolingual Brits and Americans are tempted to try fusion cuisine, to listen to "world music," to dabble in Chinese medicine or Tibetan mysticism. Most people in the world depend on the World Wide Web, attend the temples, churches or mosques of world religions, and from time to time consider making a move—from a village to the city, from one city to another, to another country, to another continent.

There is, of course, a difference between an insider's experience of a way of life and the understanding that an immigrant—or an ethnographer—might achieve. And yet few insiders are objective or even well informed about local cults and political arrangements. Most natives struggle to recognise the significance of unspoken conventions and taken-for-granted prejudices. It would be absurd to suppose that your average Londoner understands more about her city, its history, its ethnic complexity, its informal customs, than a qualified researcher, who might come from Paris, or Bombay, or Singapore, and whose findings are tested by scholarly criticism of sources, methods and logic. So we do need experts. A sense of history, a comparative perspective, a broader angle of vision enrich the appreciation of human interconnections. An exhibition of Benin arts and crafts, for instance, might trace connections between Edo and other West African traditions, and examine the response of local guilds to European markets, materials, techniques and forms. Loans from the teeming storerooms of the great museums could support exhibitions of early Venetian glass in Shanghai; of European Gypsies or Lapland reindeer herders in museums in Nairobi or Lagos; of West African textiles in the Museum of the quai Branly; and, virtually anywhere, displays of non-fungible tokens

Carved wooden funerary screen, showing the leader of a Kalabari trading house dressed in his masquerade outfit. Known as *Bekinarusibi* ("white man's ship on head"), it celebrates the wealth that comes from trade. Nineteenth-century, eastern Niger Delta Region, Nigeria. (By permission of The British Museum, London © The Trustees of the British Museum.)

(NFTs) and Bitcoins might be set off against the cowry shell currencies of nineteenth-century Africa, or the *soulava*, long red shell necklaces, and *mwali*, white shell bracelets, that were exchanged by *Kula* expeditions sailing between the islands of the Massim archipelago.

In 1995–6, the British Museum mounted a special exhibition of nineteenth-century Kalabari funerary screens under the title "Play and Display: Masquerades of Southern Nigeria." Middlemen in the slave trade and later in the trade in palm oil and ivory, the Kalabari adopted techniques and styles from their European trading partners. According to the exhibition's curator, Nigel Barley, the funeral screens were inspired by reproductions of Western paintings and "were created at the end of a protracted process of burial that involved the speaking of English, European foods and Western dress."[22] One particularly flamboyant screen in the exhibition depicts the leader of a trading house wearing his masquerade outfit: *Bekinarusibi* ("white man's ship on head"). According to the curatorial note for the exhibition, this "celebrates the wealth that came from trade." Work by contemporary artists was included in the exhibition, offering fresh reflections. Sokari Douglas Camp, born in Nigeria and educated at art school in the UK, modelled masquerade figures. Her nephew was filmed participating in a modern Kalabari masquerade. A Scottish artist, Eduardo Paolozzi, introduced playful variations on the funeral screens.

The great metropolitan and university museums should be out there, confident of their mission, playing to their strengths, offering a global perspective.

We must imagine a Cosmopolitan Museum, one that transcends ethnic and national identities, makes comparisons, draws out connections, tracks exchanges across political frontiers, challenges boundaries: a museum set in the shifting sands of the past and the present but which is informed by rigorous, critical, independent scholarship.

The Cosmopolitan Museum will make room for challenging

perspectives and contrasting points of view, so long as these are backed by research rather than appeals to mystical insight or to the authority of identity. Visitors to the Museum will be invited to cast off the blinders of solipsism. Free to enjoy the prizes and surprises of unexpected juxtapositions, they may hope to experience what Herman Melville called the shock of recognition: "For genius, all over the world, stands hand in hand, and one shock of recognition runs the whole circle round."[23]

NOTES

Chapter 1

1. Chang Wan-Chen, 2012, "A cross-cultural perspective on musealization: the museum's reception by China and Japan in the second half of the nineteenth century," *Museum and Society*, 10(1), 15–27. See pp. 16–17.

2. See Benoît de L'Estoile, 2007, *Le Goût des Autres. De l'exposition coloniale aux arts premiers*, Flammarion. *Les musées des Autres* is now an established meme in France.

3. In a letter to a social reformer, Edwin Chadwick. Cited in D. Eastwood, 1994, "Rethinking the debates on the Poor Law in early nineteenth-century England," *Utilitas* 6(1), 97–116. Citation, p. 99.

4. Michel Foucault, [1966] 1970, *The Order of Things: An Archaeology of the Human Sciences*, Routledge, p. 375.

5. Ian Hacking, 2002, *Historical Ontology*, Harvard University Press, chapter 6.

6. Nélia Dias, 1991, *Le Musée d'ethnographie du Trocadéro (1878–1908)*, Editions du CNRS, p. 23.

7. James Cowles Prichard, 1843, *The Natural History of Man: Comprising inquiries into the modifying influence of physical and moral agencies on the different tribes of the human family*, H. Ballière.

8. Francis Schiller, 1979, *Paul Broca, Founder of French Anthropology, Explorer of the Brain*, University of California Press, pp. 133–5.

9. Anon. 1881, M. Paul Broca, *Popular Science Monthly*, volume 20, December.

10. George W. Stocking Jr., 1991, *Victorian Anthropology*, The Free Press, p. 252.

11. Stocking, 1987, *Victorian Anthropology*, p. 252.

12. George W. Stocking Jr., 1971, "What's in a name? The origins of

the Royal Anthropological Institute (1837–71)," *Man* (n.s.), 6(3), 369–90. Citation, p. 379.

13. Anthropological News 1868, *The Anthropological Review* 6, 324.

14. Anon. 1864. "Anthropology at the British Association," *The Anthropological Review*, 2(7) (November 1864), 294–335.

15. Stocking, "What's in a name?"

16. Gavin de Beer (ed.), 1960, *Darwin's Notebooks on Transmutation of Species* (4th Notebook, October 1838–July 1839), British Museum, pp. 69–70.

17. Charles Darwin, 1871, *The Descent of Man*, p. 145.

18. Letter from Darwin to Kingsley, 6 February 1862, Darwin Correspondence Project, letter 3439, University of Cambridge.

19. E. B. Tylor, 1871, *Primitive Culture: Researches into the Development of Mythology, Philosophy, Religion, Art, and Custom*, J. Murray, volume 1, p. 26.

20. Michael C. Carhart, 2007, *The Science of Culture in Enlightenment Germany*, Harvard University Press.

21. Han Vermeulen, 2015, *Before Boas*, University of Nebraska Press. Citation, pp. 322–3.

22. J. R. Seeley, 1883, *The Expansion of England*, Macmillan, pp. 4 and 12.

23. Franz Boas, 1928, *Primitive Art*, Harvard University Press, p. 2.

24. William C. Sturtevant, 1969, "Does anthropology need museums?," *Proceedings of the Biological Society of Washington* 82, 619–49. Citation, p. 619.

25. Roland Barthes, [1957] 1972, "The Great Family of Man," in *Mythologies*, translated by Annette Lavers, Jonathan Cape, pp. 100–101.

26. Dalya Alberge, 2019, "British Museum Is World's Largest Receiver of Stolen Goods, says QC," *Guardian*, 4 November 2019.

27. Dan Hicks, 2020, *The Brutish Museum: The Benin Bronzes, Colonial Violence and Cultural Restitution*, Pluto Press, p. 4.

28. https://www.britishmuseum.org/collection/term/x94302.

29. William St. Clair, 1967, *Lord Elgin and the Marbles*, Oxford University Press, p. 100, n 6.

30. Louise Tythacott, 2018, "The Yuanmingyuan and Its Objects," in Louise Tythacott (ed.), *Collecting and Displaying China's "Summer Palace" in the West: The Yuanmingyuan in Britain and France*, Routledge.

31. Victor Hugo, 1875, *Actes et Paroles. Pendant l'exil: 1852–1870*, Lévy, p. 201.

32. Richard J. Evans, 2010, "Looted art and its restitution," The Third Lee Seng Tee Distinguished Lecture. https://www.richardjevans.com/lectures/looted-art-restitution/ p. 1.

33. Hugo Grotius, 1625, *De Jure Belli ac Pacis*, Book III.

34. Andres McClellan, 1994, *Inventing the Louvre: Art, Politics, and the Origins of the Modern Museum in Eighteenth-Century Paris*, University of California Press, pp. 122–3.

35. Lieut. Colonel Gurwood, 1838, *The Dispatches of Field Marshall the Duke of Wellington*, John Murray, volume 8, p. 266.

36. Evans, "Looted art," p. 2.

37. Evans, "Looted art," p. 8.

38. Matthieu Aikins, 2021, "How one looted artefact tells the story of modern Afghanistan," *The New York Times*, 4 March 2021.

39. John Henry Merryman, 1986, "Two Ways of Thinking About Cultural Property," *The American Journal of International Law*, 80(4), 831–53.

40. James Cuno, 2008, *Who Owns Antiquity? Museums and the Battle over Our Ancient Heritage*, Princeton University Press, p. 49.

41. Larry Buchanan, Quoctrung Bui and Jugal K. Patel, 2020, "Black Lives Matter May Be the Largest Movement in U.S. History," *The New York Times*, 3 July 2020.

42. Nicolas Truong, in dialogue with Julien Volper and Yves-Bernard Debie, 2018, "Restitutions d'art africain," *Le Monde*, 28 November 2018.

43. *Le Monde*, 20 February 2020, "L'ex-patron du Quai Branly dénonce un rapport prônant des restitutions massives d'oeuvres à l'Afrique."

44. Alison Abbott, 2020, "Confronting the colonial legacy of museum collections," *Sapiens*, 7 May 2020, https://www.sapiens.org/culture/museum-restitution/

45. Craig Simpson, 2020, "British Museum removes bust of slave-owner founder Sir Hans Sloane," *Daily Telegraph*, 24 August 2020.

46. Farah Nayeri, 2018, "Return of African artifacts sets a tricky precedent for Europe's museums," *The New York Times*, 27 November 2018.

47. Brent Hayes Edwards, 2017, Introduction to the English translation, Michel Leiris, *Phantom Africa*, Seagull Books, p. 63.

48. Marja Warehime, 1986, "'Vision sauvage' and Images of Culture: Georges Bataille, Editor of Documents," *The French Review*, 60(1), 39–45. See p. 43.

49. J. Newell, 2005, "Exotic possessions: Polynesians and their eighteenth-century collecting," *Journal of Museum Ethnography*, 17, 75–88.

50. *Boswell's Life of Johnson*, Aetat. 67, Wednesday, 3 April 1776.

51. Newell, "Exotic possessions," 80.

52. Neil Chambers, 2007, *Joseph Banks and the British Museum: The World of Collecting, 1770–1830*, Pickering & Chatto, p. 12.

53. Newell, "Exotic possessions," 85–6.

54. J. Ita, 1972, "Frobenius in West African History," *The Journal of African History*, 13(4), 673–88.

55. Enid Schildkraut, 2018, "The Frobenius Effect: Frederick Starr in the Congo," *Critical Interventions*, 12(1), 71–83.

56. Schildkraut, "The Frobenius Effect," 81.

57. Johannes Fabian, 1998, "Curios and curiosity: Notes on reading Torday and Frobenius," in Enid Schildkraut and Curtis A. Keim (eds.), *The Scramble for Art in Central Africa*, Cambridge University Press, p. 91.

58. Fabian, "Curios and curiosity," p. 93.

59. Gregory Bateson, 1946, "Arts of the South Seas," *The Art Bulletin*, 28(2), 119–23. Citation, p. 119.

60. Melville J. Herskovits, 1959, "Art and Value," in Robert Redfield and Melville Jean Herskovits (eds.), *Primitive Art*, Museum of Primitive Art, New York, pp. 41–68. Citation, p. 42.

61. Maureen Murphy, 30 November 2019, "Les non-dits du débat sur la restitution du patrimoine africain," *Le Monde*.

62. J. Picton, 2010, "To See or Not to See! That Is the Question," *African Arts*, 43(4), 1–6.

63. Z. S. Strother, 2020, "Iconoclasms in Africa: Implications for the debate on restitution of cultural heritage," *HAU Journal of Ethnographic Theory*, 10(3), https://www.haujournal.org/index.php/hau/article/view/1501

64. Kwame Anthony Appiah, 2009, "Whose Culture Is It?," in James Cuno (ed.) *Whose Culture? The Promise of Museums and the Debate over Antiquities*, Princeton University Press, pp. 80–82.

65. Azadeh Moaveni, 2021, "The Caviar Club," *London Review of Books*, 9 September 2021.

66. Jytte Klausen, 2009, *The Cartoons that Shook the World*, Yale University Press.

67. Peter Walkman and Golnar Motevalli, 2015, "Iran has been hiding one of the world's great collections of modern art," *Bloomberg News*, 17 November 2015.

68. Mary Beard, 2002, *The Parthenon*, Profile Books, p. 21.

69. Sarah Baxter, 2022, "Why the Elgin Marbles may finally return to Greece," *Sunday Times*, 30 July 2022.

Chapter 2

1. Andrew McClellan, 1994, *Inventing the Louvre: Art, Politics, and the Origins of the Modern Museum in Eighteenth-Century Paris*, Cambridge University Press, p. 91.

2. Irène Aghion, n.d., "Le Cabinet des médailles et antiques," https://journals.openedition.org/inha/2774

3. A. L. Cointreau, 1800, *État succinct des acquisitions et augmentations qui ont eu lieu, à dater de l'année 1754 jusqu'à la fin du siècle (an 8 de la République Française)*, Pugens et Bouquet.

4. E-T. Hamy, 1890, *Les Origines du Musée d'Ethnographie: Histoire et Documents*, Ernest Leroux, pp. 18–19.

5. Jean Copans and Jean Jamin, 1978, *Aux origines de l'anthropologie française*, Le Sycomore, pp. 153–8.

6. Hamy, *Les Origines du Musée d'Ethnographie*, pp. 23–4.

7. Hamy, *Les Origines du Musée d'Ethnographie*, p. 33, n. 1.

8. Hamy, *Les Origines du Musée d'Ethnographie*, p. 39, n. 1.

9. Hamy, *Les Origines du Musée d'Ethnographie*, p. 38.

10. Hamy, *Les Origines du Musée d'Ethnographie*, p. 136.

11. Hamy, *Les Origines du Musée d'Ethnographie*, p. 38, n. 2.

12. Hamy, *Les Origines du Musée d'Ethnographie*, p. 40.

13. Hamy, *Les Origines du Musée d'Ethnographie*, pp. 41–2.

14. Hamy, *Les Origines du Musée d'Ethnographie*, p. 45.

15. E-F. Jomard, 1831, *Sur le but et l'utilité d'une collection ethnographique, et les moyens de la former. Réponse de Férussac.* This was printed as an appendix (pp. 63–92) to a brochure written by Jomard, *Considérations sur l'objet et les avantages d'une collection spéciale consacrée aux cartes géographiques diverses et aux branches de la géographie*, Duverger. It is reprinted in full in Hamy, *Les Origines du Musée d'Ethnographie*, pp. 125–44.

16. Hamy, *Les Origines du Musée d'Ethnographie*, pp. 40–41.

17. Hamy, *Les Origines du Musée d'Ethnographie*, pp. 145–62.
18. Hamy, *Les Origines du Musée d'Ethnographie*, p. 133.
19. Hamy, *Les Origines du Musée d'Ethnographie*, p. 129.
20. Hamy, *Les Origines du Musée d'Ethnographie*, p. 129.
21. See Michel Foucault, 1970, "La situation de Cuvier dans l'histoire de la biologie," *Revue d'histoire des sciences et de leurs applications*, 23(1) (janvier–mars 1970, pp. 63–92). The essay has been translated by Lynne Huffer, 2017, "Cuvier's Situation in the History of Biology," *Foucault Studies* 22, 208–37.
22. Philippe Taquet, 2007, "Establishing the paradigmatic museum: Georges Cuvier's Cabinet d'anatomie comparée in Paris," in Simon Knell et al. (eds.), *Museum Revolutions: How Museums Change and Are Changed*, Routledge, pp. 3–14.
23. Toby A. Appel, 1987, *The Cuvier-Geoffrey debate: French biology in the decades before Darwin*, Oxford University Press; Marjorie Grene, 2001, "Darwin, Cuvier and Geoffroy: Comments and Questions," *History and Philosophy of the Life Sciences*, 187–211.
24. Hamy, *Les Origines du Musée d'Ethnographie*, p. 133.
25. On Siebold's career, see Rudolf Effert, 2008, *Royal Cabinets and Auxiliary Branches: Origins of the National Museum of Ethnology, 1816–1883*, CNWS Publications; Ken Vos, 2001, "The composition of the Siebold collection in the National Museum of Ethnology," in Leiden, *Senri Ethnological Studies* 54, 39–48.
26. Effert, *Royal Cabinets*, p. 119.
27. Akira Yoshimura, [1979] 2016, *Siebold's Daughter*, Merwin Asia Press.
28. Effert, *Royal Cabinets*, p. 124.
29. Vos, "The composition of the Siebold collection," 45.
30. Philipp Franz Balthasar von Siebold, 1832–52, *Nippon. Archiv zur Beschreibung von Japan und dessen Neben-und Schutzländern: Jezo mit den Südlichen Kurilen, Krafto, Koorai und den Liukiu-Inseln*, Seven volumes, Leiden.
31. Rudolf Effert, personal communication.
32. Effert, *Royal Cabinets*, pp. 16–17.
33. Effert, *Royal Cabinets*, p. 19
34. Effert, *Royal Cabinets*, p. 60, n. 189.
35. Philipp von Siebold, 1837, "Kort begrip en ontwikkeling van de doelmatigheid en van het nut van een ethnographisch museum in Nederland." Reprinted in C. C. F. M. le Roux, 1937, *Overzicht van de*

geschiedenis van het Rijksmuseum voor Volkenkunde 1837–1937, Leiden, pp. 63–9.

36. Siebold, "Kort begrip," p. 64.
37. Effert, *Royal Cabinets*, pp. 38–9. See Siebold, "Kort begrip," pp. 63–9.
38. Philipp Franz Balthasar von Siebold, 1843, *Lettre sur l'utilité des musées ethnographiques et sur l'importance de leur creation dans les états Européens qui possèdent des colonies ou qui entretiennent des relations commerciales avec les autres parties du monde*, Benjamin Duprat. Reprinted in Hamy, *Les Origines du Musée d'Ethnographie*. Available online in Googlebooks.
39. Hamy, *Les Origines du Musée d'Ethnographie*, pp. 232–3.
40. Hamy, *Les Origines du Musée d'Ethnographie*, pp. 234–5.
41. For a detailed comparison of the classificatory schemes of Jomard and Siebold, see Nélia Dias, *Le Musée d'ethnographie du Trocadéro: Anthropologie et Muséologie en France*, CNRS, pp. 135–8.
42. Hamy, *Les Origines du Musée d'Ethnographie*, pp. 239–41.
43. Hamy, *Les Origines du Musée d'Ethnographie*, p. 241.
44. Hamy, *Les Origines du Musée d'Ethnographie*, pp. 241–3.
45. Effert, *Royal Cabinets*, pp. 152–64.
46. Alphonse Daudet, 1873, *L'Empereur aveugle* in *Contes de Lundi*, Alphonse Lemerre.
47. Effert, *Royal Cabinets*, p. 135.
48. Kasper Risbjerg Eskildsen, 2012, "The Language of Objects: Christian Jürgensen Thomsen's Science of the Past," *Isis* 103(1), 24–53. Citation, p. 45.
49. Eskildsen, "The Language of Objects," 41.
50. Tove Benedikte Jakobsen, in collaboration with Jans Holme Andersen and Christian Adamsen, 2007, *Birth of a World Museum*, Acta Archaeologica Suplementa, vol. VIII, Wiley-Blackwell, pp. 21–2.
51. Eskildsen, "The Language of Objects," 44–5.
52. Kasper Risbjerg Eskildsen, 2008, "Leopold Ranke's Archival Turn: Location and Evidence in Modern Historiography," *Journal of Modern Intellectual History* 5, 425–53. See pp. 431–2.
53. Eskildsen, "The Language of Objects," 30–31.
54. Matthew Goodrum, 2008, "Questioning Thunderstones and Arrowheads: The problem of recognizing and interpreting stone artefacts in the Seventeenth Century," *Early Science and Medicine*, 13(5), 482–508.

55. Eskildsen, "The Language of Objects," 32.
56. Eskildsen, "The Language of Objects," 34.
57. Jakobsen, *Birth of a World Museum*, pp. 153–7.
58. Christian Jurgensen Thomsen, 1836, "Kortfattet Udsigt over Mindesmærker og Oldsager fra Nordens Fortid" [A Brief View of Prehistoric Nordic Memorials and Antiquities], in *Oldkyndighed*, Copenhagen, pp. 27–90. German translation, 1837. Translated into English, 1848, as *Guide to Northern Archaeology*, John Bain.
59. Eskildsen, "The Language of Objects," 39.
60. B. Gräslund, 1981, "The background to C. J. Thomsen's Three-Age system," in G. Daniel (ed.), *Towards a History of Archaeology*, Thames and Hudson, pp. 45–50. See also Bo Gräslund, 1987, *The Birth of Prehistoric Chronology: Dating Methods and Dating Systems in Nineteenth-century Scandinavian Archaeology*, Cambridge University Press.
61. Peter Rowley-Conwy, 2007, *From Genesis to Prehistory: The Archaeological Three Age System and Its Contested Reception in Denmark, Britain, and Ireland*, Oxford University Press, p. 298.
62. Rowley-Conwy, *From Genesis to Prehistory*, pp. 65–81.
63. Rowley-Conwy, *From Genesis to Prehistory*, p. 75.
64. Rowley-Conwy, *From Genesis to Prehistory*, pp. 108–9.
65. Jakobsen, *Birth of a World Museum*, p. 154.
66. Bruce Trigger, 1989, *A History of Archaeological Thought*, Cambridge University Press, p. 86.

Chapter 3

1. Philippe Taquet, 2007, "Establishing the paradigmatic museum: Georges Cuvier's Cabinet d'anatomie comparée in Paris," in Simon Knell et al. (eds.), *Museum Revolutions: How Museums Change and Are Changed*, Routledge, pp. 3–14, p. 11.
2. James Delbourgo, 2017, *Collecting the World: Hans Sloane and the Origins of the British Museum*, Harvard University Press, p. 173.
3. Delbourgo, *Collecting the World*, pp. 315–16.
4. Delbourgo, *Collecting the World*, p. 162.
5. Delbourgo, *Collecting the World*, p. 307.
6. Delbourgo, *Collecting the World*, p. xxiii.
7. Delbourgo, *Collecting the World*, p. 202.
8. Delbourgo, *Collecting the World*, p. 200.
9. Delbourgo, *Collecting the World*, p. 266.

10. H. J. Braunholtz, 1953, "The Sloane Collection: Ethnography," *The British Museum Quarterly*, 18(1), 23–6. See pp. 24–5.

11. H. J. Braunholtz, "History of ethnography in the Museum after 1753," *The British Museum Quarterly*, 18(3,) 1953, pp. 90–93.

12. Neil Chambers, 2007, *Joseph Banks and the British Museum: The World of Collecting, 1770–1830*, Pickering & Chatto, p. 12.

13. Chambers, *Joseph Banks and the British Museum*, p. 13.

14. Delbourgo, *Collecting the World*, pp. 177–80, 211–12, 282–5.

15. Delbourgo, *Collecting the World*, p. 324.

16. John Mack, 1977, "Antiquities and the Public: the Expanding Museum, 1851–96," in Marjorie Caygill and John Cherry (eds.), 1997, *A. W. Franks: Nineteenth-Century Collecting and the British Museum*, British Museum Press, pp. 34–50, 37.

17. Stephen Briggs, 2007, "Prehistory in the nineteenth century," in Susan M. Pearce (ed.) *Visions of Antiquity: the Society of Antiquaries of London 1707–2007*, Society of Antiquaries of London, pp. 227–66.

18. David Hughson, 1805–9, *London; being an accurate history and description of the British metropolis and its neighbourhood, to thirty miles extent, from an actual perambulation*, W. Stratford, four volumes. Citation vol. 4, p. 390.

19. H. J. Braunholtz, 1953, "History of Ethnography in the Museum 1753–1938" (part II), *British Museum Quarterly*, 18(4), 109–20. See pp. 110–11.

20. Jill Cook, 1997, "A Curator's Curator: Franks and the Stone Age Collections," in Marjorie Caygill and John Cherry (eds.), *A. W. Franks: Nineteenth-Century Collecting and the British Museum*, British Museum Press, pp. 115–29, p. 115.

21. David M. Wilson, 1984, "The Forgotten Collector: Augustus Wollaston Franks of the British Museum," Thames and Hudson, p. 12.

22. Marjorie Caygill, 1997, "Franks and the British Museum—the Cuckoo in the Nest," in Marjorie Caygill and John Cherry (eds.), *A. W. Franks: Nineteenth-Century Collecting and the British Museum*, British Museum Press, pp. 51–114. Citation, p. 136.

23. Max Bryant, 2016, "'The Progress of Civilization': the pedimental sculpture of the British Museum by Richard Westmacott," *Sculpture Journal*, 25(3), 315–27.

24. Bryant, "The Progress of Civilization," 323.

25. Mack, "Antiquities and the Public," pp. 40–41.

26. *Handbook to the Ethnographical Collections*, 1910, British Museum, p. 1.

27. R. R. Marett, 1936, *Tylor*, Chapman and Hall, p. 31.

28. J. C. H. King, 1997, "Franks and Ethnography" in Marjorie Caygill and John Cherry (eds.), *A. W. Franks: Nineteenth-Century Collecting and the British Museum*, British Museum Press, pp. 136–59. See p. 140.

29. Caygill, "Franks and the British Museum," p. 72.

30. Caygill, "Franks and the British Museum," p. 72.

31. Braunholtz, "History of Ethnography in the Museum," part I, 91.

32. Caygill, "Franks and the British Museum," p. 71.

33. Braunholtz, "History of Ethnography in the Museum," part II, 115–16.

34. *The Geologist*, 1859, vol. 2, p. 397.

35. Donald R. Kelley, 2003, "The rise of prehistory," *Journal of World History* 14, 17–36.

36. Bruce Trigger, 1989, *A History of Archaeological Thought*, Cambridge University Press.

37. Mack, "Antiquities and the Public," p. 42.

38. Charles Caverno, 1898, *Chalk Lines Over Morals*, C. H. Kerr, p. 50.

39. William Ryan Chapman, 1985, "Arranging ethnology: A. H. L. F. Pitt Rivers and the typological tradition," in George W. Stocking Jr. (ed.), *Objects and Others: Essays on Museums and Material Culture*, University of Wisconsin Press, pp. 15–48. Citation, p. 23.

40. Asa Briggs, 1965, *Victorian People*, Penguin Books, p. 43.

41. Briggs, *Victorian People*, p. 23.

42. Briggs, *Victorian People*, pp. 46–7.

43. Mark Bowden, 1991, *Pitt Rivers*, Cambridge University Press, p. 7.

44. Bertrand Russell and Patricia Russell (eds.), 1937, *The Amberley Papers: Bertrand Russell's Family Background*, Allen & Unwin, vol. 1, p. 22.

45. A. H. Lane Fox, 1875, "On the principles of classification adopted in the arrangement of his anthropological collection, now exhibited in the Bethnal Green Museum," *Journal of the Anthropological Institute* 4(1), 293–308; A. H. Lane Fox, 1891, "Typological Museums, as exemplified by the Pitt-Rivers Museum at Oxford, and his provincial museum at Farnham, Dorset," *Journal of the Society of Arts*, 18 December 1891, 115–22.

46. Lane Fox, 1874, "An address to the Anthropological Society of

London," *Journal of the Anthropological Institute.* http://web.prm.ox
.ac.uk/Kent/musantob/display4.html

47. William Ryan Chapman, 1982. *Ethnology in the Museum: A. H. L. F. Pitt Rivers (1827–1900) and the Institutional Foundations of British Anthropology*, DPhil thesis, Oxford University. Chapter 4, http://web.prm.ox.ac.uk/rpr/index.php/ethnology-in-the-museum.html

48. Lane Fox, "On the principles of classification."

49. Mack, "Antiquities and the Public," p. 46.

50. W. R. Chapman, 1983, "Pitt Rivers and his collection, 1874–1883: the chronicle of a gift horse," *Journal of the Anthropological Society of Oxford*, 14(2), 181–202.

51. Chris Gosden, Frances Larson and Alison Petch, 2007, *Knowing Things: Exploring the Collections at the Pitt Rivers Museum 1884–1945*, Oxford University Press, p. 68.

52. Letter from Pitt Rivers to Mr. Rudler, 23 May 1898, Virtual archive of the Pitt Rivers Museum, Primary Documents, S&SWM PR PAPERS L2096A.

53. Michael O'Hanlon, 2014, *The Pitt Rivers Museum: A World Within*, Scala Arts and Heritage Publishers, pp. 73–86.

54. O'Hanlon, *The Pitt Rivers Museum*, pp. 76–7.

Chapter 4

1. Andrea Wulf, 2016, *The Invention of Nature: The Adventures of Alexander von Humboldt, The Lost Hero of Science*, John Murray, p. 189.

2. Dolores L. Augustine, 1998, "Arriving in the upper class: the wealthy business elite of Wilhelmine Germany," in David Blackbourn and Richard J. Evans (eds.), *The German Bourgeoisie: Essays on the Social History of the German Middle Class from the Late Eighteenth to the Early Twentieth Century*, Routledge, pp. 46–86.

3. Chris Manias, 2012, "The growth of race and culture in nineteenth-century Germany: Gustav Klemm and the Universal History of Humanity," *Modern Intellectual History*, 9(1), 1–31. Citation, p. 8.

4. Otis T. Mason, 1874, "The Leipsic 'Museum of Ethnology,'" *Annual Report of the Board of Regents of the Smithsonian Institution for 1873*, Government Printing Office, pp. 390–410, p. 396.

5. Manias, "The growth of race and culture," p. 20.

6. Manias, "The growth of race and culture," p. 26.

7. Manias, "The growth of race and culture," 5.

8. Arnoldo Momigliano, 1990, "The rise of antiquarian research," in *Classical Foundations of Modern Historiography*, University of California Press, p. 54.

9. Peter N. Miller, 2013, "The missing link: 'Antiquarianism,' 'Material Culture,' and 'Cultural Science' in the work of G. F. Klemm," in Peter N. Miller (ed.), *Cultural Histories of the Material World*, University of Michigan Press, pp. 263–81, 267.

10. Gustav Friedrich Klemm, 1843, "Fantasie über ein Museum für die Cultur-Geschichte der Menshheit," *Allgemeine Culturgeschichte der Menschheit*, volume 1, B. G. Teubner, pp. 352–62.

11. Miller, "The missing link," pp. 267–8.

12. Manias, "The growth of race and culture," 10–11.

13. Manias, "The growth of race and culture," 9.

14. Manias, "The growth of race and culture," 9–10.

15. Matti Bunzl, 1996, "Franz Boas and the Humboldtian tradition: From Volksgeist and Nationalcharakter to an Anthropological Concept of Culture," in George W. Stocking, Jr. (ed.), *Volksgeist as Method and Ethic: Essays on Boasian Ethnography and the German Anthropological Tradition*, History of Anthropology, vol. 8, University of Wisconsin Press, pp. 17–78. Citation, p. 50.

16. Edward B. Tylor, 1905, "Professor Adolf Bastian," *Man* 5, pp. 138–43.

17. Robert H. Lowie, 1937, *The History of Ethnological Theory*, Farrar & Rinehart, pp. 32–3, 35.

18. Lowie, *The History of Ethnological Theory*, pp. 32–3, 35.

19. Klaus-Peter Koepping, 1983, *Adolf Bastian and the Psychic Unity of Mankind*, University of Queensland Press, pp. 37, 49.

20. Bunzl, "Franz Boas and the Humboldtian tradition," p. 49.

21. Koepping, *Adolf Bastian*, p. 61.

22. Koepping, *Adolf Bastian*, Chapter 5, pp. 60–68; Bunzl, "Franz Boas and the Humboldtian tradition," p. 49.

23. Koepping, *Adolf Bastian*, p. 62; cf. W. Smith, 1980, "Friedrich Ratzel and the Origins of Lebensraum," *German Studies Review*, 3(1), 51–68.

24. H. Glenn Penny, 2002, *Objects of Culture: Ethnology and Ethnographic Museums in Imperial Germany*, University of North Carolina Press, pp. 187–90.

25. Penny, *Objects of Culture*, p. 51.

26. H. Glenn Penny, 2019, *In Humboldt's Shadow: A Tragic History of German Ethnology*, Princeton University Press, p. 47.

27. Lowie, *The History of Ethnological Theory*, p. 30.
28. O. M. Dalton, 1898, *Report on Ethnographic Museums in Germany*, Her Majesty's Stationery Office.
29. Koepping *Adolf Bastian*, p. 215.
30. Penny, *Objects of Culture*, p. 186.
31. Penny, *Objects of Culture*, p. 196.
32. Penny, *Objects of Culture*, p. 103.
33. Penny, *Objects of Culture*, p. 186.
34. Penny, *Objects of Culture*, p. 153.

Chapter 5

1. Walter Benjamin, 1999 [1982], *The Archive Project*, translated by Howard Eiland and Kevin McLaughlin, Belknap Press of Harvard University Press, p. 7.
2. E.-T. Hamy, 1890, *Les Origines du Musée d'Ethnographie: Histoire et Documents*, Ernest Leroux, p. 52.
3. Hamy, *Les Origines du Musée d'Ethnographie*, p. 57.
4. Hamy, *Les Origines du Musée d'Ethnographie*, p. 2.
5. Hamy, *Les Origines du Musée d'Ethnographie*, p. 51.
6. Nélia Dias, 1991, *Le Musée d'ethnographie du Trocadéro (1878–1908)*, Editions du CNRS, pp. 164–5.
7. Dias, *Le Musée d'ethnographie du Trocadéro*, pp. 163–6.
8. For an intellectual biography of Hamy see Dias, *Le Musée d'ethnographie du Trocadéro*, pp. 207–35.
9. Dias, *Le Musée d'ethnographie du Trocadéro*, pp. 176–7.
10. Dias, *Le Musée d'ethnographie du Trocadéro*, pp. 176–7.
11. Dias, *Le Musée d'ethnographie du Trocadéro*, pp. 177–80.
12. Hamy, *Les Origines du Musée d'Ethnographie*, p. 363. See also E.-T. Hamy, 1897, *La galerie américaine du Musée du Trocadéro*, two volumes, Paris.
13. Dias, *Le Musée d'ethnographie du Trocadéro*, pp. 187–91.
14. Dias, *Le Musée d'ethnographie du Trocadéro*, pp. 158–62.
15. Dias, *Le Musée d'ethnographie du Trocadéro*, pp. 194–5.
16. Annie Dupuis, 1999, "À propos de souvenirs inédits de Denise Paulme et Michel Leiris sur la création du musée de l'Homme en 1936," *Cahiers d'etudes africaines*, 39, 511–38. Citation, p. 522.
17. Marcel Mauss, [1907] 2011, "L'ethnographie en France. Une science négligée, un musée à former," *Revue européenne des sciences sociales*, 49(1), 209–34. Citation, p. 229.

18. Mauss, "L'ethnographie en France," 223–4.

19. Marcel Fournier, [1994] 2005, *Marcel Mauss: A Biography*, Princeton University Press, chapter 13, "The Institut d'Ethnologie," pp. 233–45.

20. Lucien Lévy-Bruhl, *La mentalité primitive* (1922), translated as *Primitive Mentality* (1923); *L'âme primitive* (1927), translated as *The "Soul" of the Primitive* (1928).

21. Thomas Hirsch, 2017, "'I'm the whole show': Marcel Mauss professeur à l'Institut d'ethnologie," in André Delpuech, Christine Laurière and Carine Peltier-Caroff (eds.), *Les années folles de l'ethnographie: Trocadéro 1928–1937*, Muséum national d'Histoire naturelle, pp. 341–403. Citation, p. 343.

22. Christine Laurière, 2008, *Paul Rivet, le savant et le politique*, Muséum national d'histoire naturelle.

23. Henri Lévy-Bruhl, 1951, "In Memoriam, Marcel Mauss," *L'Année Sociologique*, 3e serie, 1948–9, 2.

24. Hirsch, "I'm the whole show," p. 390.

25. Hirsch, "I'm the whole show," pp. 374–5.

26. James Clifford, 1981, "On Ethnographic Surrealism," *Comparative Studies in Society and History*, 23(4), 539–64; Vincent Debaene, 2002, "Les surréalistes et le musée d'ethnographie," *Labyrinthe*, 12(2), 71–94.

27. Debaene, "Les surréalistes et le musée d'ethnographie," 73.

28. Hirsch, "I'm the whole show," p. 367.

29. Benoît de L'Estoile, "Can French anthropology outlive its museums?," Unpublished lecture.

30. Sally Price and Jean Jamin, 1988, "A Conversation with Michel Leiris," *Current Anthropology*, 29(1), 157–74. Citation, p. 158.

31. Bernard Dupaigne, 2016, *Histoire du musée de l'Homme. De la naissance à la maturité (1880–1972)*, Sépia, chapter 7, "Esthétisme ou science?"

32. Alice L. Conklin, 2013, *In the Museum of Man: Race, Anthropology and Empire in France, 1850–1950*, Cornell University Press, p. 105.

33. G. H. Rivière (1968), "My Experience at the Musée d'Ethnologie," *Proceedings of the Royal Anthropological Institute of Great Britain and Ireland*, 1968, 17.

34. Rivière, "My Experience at the Musée d'Ethnologie," 17, 19.

35. Rivière, "My Experience at the Musée d'Ethnologie," 18.

36. Bernard Dupaigne, 2006, *Le scandale des arts premiers: La veritable histoire du musée du quai Branly*, Mille et Une Nuits, p. 17.

37. Marja Warehime, 1986, "'Vision sauvage' and Images of Culture: Georges Bataille, Editor of Documents," *The French Review*, 60(1), 39–445. Citation, p. 41.

38. Christine Laurière, 2015, "Une Musée sous tensions (1938–1949)," in Claude Blanckaert (ed.), *Le Musée de l'Homme : histoire d'un musée laboratoire*, Muséum national d'histoire naturelle/Éditions Artlys, pp. 47–76. See p. 50.

39. Hélène Ivanoff, 2018, "Le Trocadéro au miroir allemande: Entre art, préhistoire et ethnologie," in André Delpuech, Laurière and Peltier-Caroff (eds.), *Les années folles de l'ethnographie*, pp. 203–33.

40. Christine Laurière and Carine Peltier-Caroff, 2017, "La sale du Trésor: Un petit royaume de l'art primitive," in Delpuech, Laurière, and Peltier-Caroff (eds.), *Les années folles de l'ethnographie*, pp. 186–91.

41. Alice L. Conklin, 2013, *In the Museum of Man: Race, Anthropology and Empire in France, 1850–1950*, Cornell University Press, p. 130.

42. Price and Jamin, "A Conversation with Michel Leiris," 158.

43. Clifford, "On Ethnographic Surrealism," 546.

44. Clifford, "On Ethnographic Surrealism," 549.

45. Jacques Soustelle, 1936, "Musées vivants, pour une culture populaire," *Vendredi*, 26 August 1936.

46. Rivière, "My Experience at the Musée d'Ethnologie," p. 18.

47. Christine Laurière, 2017, "L'épreuve du feu des futurs maîtres de l'ethnologie," in Delpuech, Laurière and Peltier-Caroff (eds.), *Les années folles de l'ethnographie*, pp. 405–47. See also, in the same volume, André Delpuech, "Collectes, collecteurs, collections dans les années trente," pp. 449–79.

48. Dupuis, "À propos de souvenirs inédits de Denise Paulme et Michel Leiris." Citation, p. 518.

49. Patrick Wilcken, 2010, *Claude Lévi-Strauss: The Poet in the Laboratory*, Bloomsbury, pp. 56–74, 79–105.

50. Benoît de L'Estoile, 2007, *Le Goût des Autres: De l'exposition coloniale aux arts premiers*, Flammarion, pp. 160–71.

51. Michel Leiris, [1934] 2017, *Phantom Africa*, Seagull Books, 267.

52. Price and Jamin, "A Conversation with Michel Leiris," 159–62.

53. Dupuis, "À propos de souvenirs inédits de Denise Paulme et Michel Leiris," 521.

54. Hirsch, "I'm the whole show," p. 376.

55. Mauss, "L'ethnographie en France," 22.

56. Charles-Robert Ageron, 1984, "L'exposition colonial," in Pierre Nora, *Les lieux de mémoires 1. La république*, Gallimard.
57. Christine Laurière, 2017, "Le banquier et mécène du musée," in Delpuech, Laurière, and Peltier-Caroff (eds.), *Les années folles de l'ethnographie*. Citation, p. 194.
58. Debaene, "Les surréalistes et le musée d'ethnographie."
59. Conklin, *In the Museum of Man*, p. 212.
60. De l'Estoile, *Le Goût des Autres*, p. 71.
61. Brent Hayes Edwards, 2017, Introduction to the English translation, Michel Leiris, *Phantom Africa*, Seagull Books, p. 3.
62. Michel Leiris, 1938, "Du musée d'Ethnographie au musée de l'Homme," *La Nouvelle Revue Française*, pp. 344–5.
63. Isac Chiva, 1992, "Entretien avec Claude Lévi-Strauss: Qu'est-ce qu'un musée des arts et traditions populaires?," *Le Débat* 70, 156–63. Citation, p. 156.
64. De l'Estoile, "Can French anthropology outlive its museums?"
65. Laurière, "Une Musée sous tensions," pp. 61–76; Dupaigne, *Histoire du musée de l'Homme*, chapter X, "Les sombre années de la France."
66. Laurière, "Une Musée sous tensions," pp. 68–9.
67. F. Weber, 2000, "Le folklore, l'histoire et l'état en France" (1937–1945), *Revue de synthèse* 121, 453–67.
68. Weber, "Le folklore, l'histoire et l'état en France," 457.
69. Christine Laurière, 2019, "Jacques Soustelle, de Mexique terre indienne à l'Algérie, terre française," in Christine Laurière and André Mary (eds.), *Ethnologues en situations coloniales*, Les Carnets de Bérose no. 11, Bérose Encyclopédie internationale des histoires de l'anthropologie, pp. 109–64, https://www.berose.fr/article1675.html
70. Emmanuelle Loyer, 2015, *Lévi-Strauss*, Flammarion, p. 682.
71. Nathan Schlanger, 2016, "Back in business: history and evolution at the new Musée de l'Homme," *Antiquity* 90, 1090–99.

Interlude

1. Sally G. Kohlstedt, 2008, "Otis T. Mason's Tour of Europe: Observation, Exchange and Standardization in Public Museums, 1889," *Museum History Journal*, 1(2), 181–208; Catherine A. Nichols and Nancy J. Parezo, 2017, "Social and Material Connections: Otis T. Mason's European Grand Tour and Collections Exchange," *History and Anthropology*, 28(1), pp. 58–83.

2. Nichols and Parezo, "Social and Material Connections," 72.
3. Curtis M. Hinsley, Jr., 1981, *Savages and Scientists: The Smithsonian Institution and the Development of American Anthropology*, Smithsonian Institution Press, pp. 109–10.
4. Benoît de L'Estoile, 2007, *Le Goût des Autres: De l'exposition coloniale aux arts premiers*, Editions Flammarion, p. 34.
5. Paul Greenhalgh, 1988, *Ephemeral Vistas: The Expositions Universelles, Great Exhibitions and World's Fairs, 1851–1839*, Manchester University Press, p. 20.
6. Otis T. Mason, 1890, "Anthropology in Paris during the Exposition of 1889," *American Anthropologist*, 3(1), 27–36. Citations, p. 31 and p. 35.
7. Nichols and Parezo, "Social and Material Connections," 64.
8. Nichols and Parezo, "Social and Material Connections," 64.
9. Nichols and Parezo, "Social and Material Connections," 69.
10. Nichols and Parezo, "Social and Material Connections," 73.
11. Nichols and Parezo, "Social and Material Connections," 74.
12. Hinsley, *Savages and Scientists*, pp. 109–10.

Chapter 6

1. William J. Rhees, 1880, *James Smithson and His Bequest*, Smithsonian Institution. (See the "Advertisement" by Spencer Baird.)
2. Heather Ewing, 2007, *The Lost World of James Smithson: Science, Revolution, and the Birth of the Smithsonian*, Bloomsbury.
3. Rhees, *James Smithson*, p. 12.
4. Ewing, *The Lost World of James Smithson*, p. 271.
5. Rhees, *James Smithson*, p. 12.
6. Ewing, *The Lost World of James Smithson*, p. 20 and p. 358 n. 4.
7. Ewing, *The Lost World of James Smithson*, p. 14.
8. Rhees, *James Smithson*, p. 24; Ewing, *The Lost World of James Smithson*, pp. 294, 316.
9. Ewing, *The Lost World of James Smithson*, p. 22.
10. The will is available at: https://siarchives.si.edu/history/featured-topics/stories/last-will-and-testament-october-23-1826
11. Ewing, *The Lost World of James Smithson*, pp. 324, 330; G. Brown Goode, 1892, "The Genesis of the National Museum," in *Report of the United States National Museum for the year ending June 30, 1891*, p. 281.
12. Rhees, *James Smithson*, pp. 21–2.

13. Ewing, *The Lost World of James Smithson*, p. 327.
14. Rhees, *James Smithson*, pp. 31–50, summarises the Congressional debates.
15. Rhees, *James Smithson*, p. 34.
16. Ewing, *The Lost World of James Smithson*, p. 329.
17. Ewing, *The Lost World of James Smithson*, p. 330.
18. Goode, "The Genesis of the National Museum," pp. 273–4.
19. Regna Darnell, 2000, *And Along Came Boas: Continuity and Revolution in Americanist Anthropology*, John Benjamin, p. 21.
20. Goode, "The Genesis of the National Museum," p. 333.
21. Curtis M. Hinsley, 1981, *Scientists and Savages: The Smithsonian Institution and the Development of American Anthropology, 1846–1910*, Smithsonian Institution, p. 64.
22. Goode, "The Genesis of the National Museum," p. 329.
23. Henry Adams, 1907, *The Education of Henry Adams*, privately printed. First trade edition, 1918. Quotations from chapter III: "Washington (1850–1854)."
24. *Historical Census Statistics on Population Totals by Race*, 1790 to 1990 (PDF), United States Census Bureau.
25. *Memoirs of John Quincy Adams, comprising portions of his diary from 1795 to 1848*, J. B. Lippincott, p. 29.
26. Hugh Brogan, 2006, *Alexis de Tocqueville: Prophet of Democracy in the Age of Revolution*, Profile Books, p. 204.
27. Frederick J. Turner, 1893, "The Significance of the Frontier in American History," *Annual Report of the American Historical Association*, 1893, pp. 197–227.
28. Frederick William True, 1897, "The United States National Museum," in George Brown Goode (ed.), *The Smithsonian Institution, 1846–1896*, Smithsonian Institution Press, p. 333.
29. Donald Worster, 2001, *A River Running West: The Life of John Wesley Powell*, Oxford University Press, p. 196.
30. Worster, *A River Running West*, p. 209.
31. Worster, *A River Running West*, p. 287.
32. Worster, *A River Running West*, p. 113.
33. Worster, *A River Running West*, p. 436.
34. Adams, *The Education of Henry Adams*, chapter XIX, "Chaos."
35. Adams, *The Education of Henry Adams*, chapter XV, "Darwinism."
36. Adams, *The Education of Henry Adams*, chapter XV, "Darwinism," and chapter XXXI, "The Grammar of Science."

37. Worster, *A River Running West*, p. 604, n. 30.

38. Worster, *A River Running West*, p. 463.

39. John Wesley Powell, 1888, "Competition as a Factor in Human Evolution," *American Anthropologist* 1, 297–321. Citation, pp. 301–2.

40. Joan Mark, 1980, *Four Anthropologists: An American Science in Its Early Years*, Science History Publications, p. 144.

41. Worster, *A River Running West*, pp. 397–8.

42. Darnell, *And Along Came Boas*, p. 90.

43. Worster, *A River Running West*, p. 398.

44. E. B. Tylor, 1884, "How the Problems of American Anthropology Present Themselves to the English Mind," *Science*, 4(98), 545–51. Citation, p. 550.

45. Worster, *A River Running West*, p. 398.

46. Darnell, *And Along Came Boas*, pp. 37–8. See 14th Annual Report, Bureau of Ethnology, for 1892–3, 1896, pp. xxviii–xxix.

47. Darnell, *And Along Came Boas*, p. 23.

48. Worster, *A River Running West*, pp. 403–5.

49. William De Buys (ed.) 2001, *Seeing Things Whole: The Essential John Wesley Powell*, Island Press, p. 4.

50. Hinsley, *Savages and Scientists*, p. 233.

51. Orin Starn, 2004, *Ishi's Brain: In Search of America's Last "Wild" Indian*, W. W. Norton, p. 185.

52. Leslie A. White, 1957, "How Morgan Came to Write Systems of Consanguinity and Affinity," *Papers of the Michigan Academy of Sciences, Arts, and Letters* (xlii), 257–68. Citations, pp. 257 and 262.

53. Lewis Henry Morgan, 1877, *Ancient Society: Researches in the Lines of Human Progress from Savagery through Barbarism to Civilization*, Holt, p. xxix.

54. Morgan, *Ancient Society*, p. 6.

55. Carl Resek, 1960, *Lewis Henry Morgan: American Scholar*, University of Chicago Press, p. 141.

56. Mark, *Four Anthropologists*, p. 165, n. 33.

57. Darnell, *And Along Came Boas*, p. 89.

58. Thomas C. Patterson, 2001, *A Social History of Anthropology in the United States*, Berg, p. 38.

59. Worster, *A River Running West*, pp. 270–71.

60. Hinsley, *Savages and Scientists*, p. 149.

61. Worster, *A River Running West*, p. 277.

62. Worster, *A River Running West*, p. 285.

63. J. W. Powell, 1885, "From Savagery to Barbarism," *Transactions of the Anthropological Society of Washington*, vol. 3, pp. 173–96. Citation, p. 193.

64. Hinsley, *Savages and Scientists*, p. 149.

65. Worster, *A River Running West*, p. 392.

66. Hinsley, *Savages and Scientists*, pp. 64–5.

67. Marc Rothenberg, et al. (eds.), 2007, *The Papers of Joseph Henry, Volume 11: The Smithsonian Years: January 1866–May 1878*, Smithsonian Institution, pp. 458–9.

68. Hinsley, *Savages and Scientists*, 67.

69. Debra Lindsay, 1993, *Science in the Subarctic: Trappers, Traders, and the Smithsonian Institution*, Washington, DC: Smithsonian Institution Press, pp. 5–6.

70. Lindsay, *Science in the Subarctic*, p. 75, and see chapter 5: "Northern collectors and Arctic anthropology," pp. 77–88.

71. Robert Rydell, 1984, *All the World's a Fair: Visions of Empire at American International Expositions, 1876–1916*, University of Chicago Press, p. 20.

72. Rydell, *All the World's a Fair*, pp. 21–2.

73. Rydell, *All the World's a Fair*, p. 23.

74. Rydell, *All the World's a Fair*, pp. 33–4.

75. Mark, *Four Anthropologists*, p. 21.

76. Otis T. Mason, 1882, "What Is Anthropology?" A Lecture Delivered in the National Museum, Judd and Detweiler, p. 14.

77. Nancy J. Parezo, 1985, "Cushing as Part of the Team: The Collecting Activities of the Smithsonian Institution," *American Ethnologist*, 12(4), 763–74. Citation, p. 769.

78. Darnell, *And Along Came Boas*, p. 76.

79. Darnell, *And Along Came Boas*, p. 75.

80. Parezo, "Cushing as Part of the Team," 767.

81. Parezo, "Cushing as Part of the Team," 766.

82. Letter dated May 1881, cited by Parezo, "Cushing as Part of the Team," 766.

83. Mark, *Four Anthropologists*, p. 104.

84. Hinsley, *Savages and Scientists*, p. 180.

85. Darnell, *And Along Came Boas*, p. 77.

86. Hinsley, *Savages and Scientists*, pp. 196–7.

87. R. Lowie, 1956, "Reminiscences of Anthropological Currents in

America Half a Century Ago," *American Anthropologist*, 58(6), new series, 995–1016.

88. C. Hinsley, 1999, "Life on the Margins: The Ethnographic Poetics of Frank Hamilton Cushing," *Journal of the Southwest*, 41(3), pp. 371–82. Citation, p. 377.

89. Parezo, "Cushing as Part of the Team," 771.

90. Parezo, "Cushing as Part of the Team," 765.

91. Parezo, "Cushing as Part of the Team," 766.

92. Frank Hamilton Cushing, 1886, "A Study of Pueblo Pottery as Illustrative of Zuni Cultural Growth," in *Fourth Annual Report of the Bureau of Ethnology for 1882–1883*, Government Printing Office, pp. 467–521.

93. Hinsley, *Savages and Scientists*, p. 94.

94. Hinsley, *Savages and Scientists*, p. 119, n. 27.

95. Mason, "What Is Anthropology?," p. 13.

96. G. Brown Goode, 1901, "The Museums of the Future," *Report of the U.S. National Museum*, Pt. 2, Government Printing Office, pp. 437–45. Citations, pp. 427, 428, 432.

97. Hinsley, *Savages and Scientists*, p. 94.

98. Goode, "The Museums of the Future," p. 443.

99. Ira Jacknis, 1985, "Franz Boas and Exhibits: On the Limitations of the Museum Method in Anthropology," in George W. Stocking, Jr. (ed.), *Objects and Others: Essays on Museums and Material Culture*, University of Wisconsin Press, pp. 75–111. Citation, p. 81.

100. Walter Hough, 1908, "Otis Tufton Mason," *American Anthropologist*, 10(4), 661–7. See pp. 662–3.

101. Hinsley, *Savages and Scientists*, pp. 97–8.

102. G. Carroll Lindsay, 1965, "George Brown Goode," in Clifford L. Lord (ed.), *Keepers of the Past*, University of North Carolina Press.

103. 1st Annual Report, Bureau of Ethnology, for 1879–80, 1881. Citation, p. 80.

104. 14th Annual Report, Bureau of Ethnology, for 1892–3, 1896. Citation, p. xxix.

105. Darnell, *And Along Came Boas*. See chapter 4: "The Mapping of North America," pp. 45–67.

106. Ewing, *The Lost World of James Smithson*, pp. 336–42; Nina Burleigh, 2012, "Digging up James Smithson," *American Heritage*, 62(2). See also the website of the Smithsonian Institution ("Mr. Smithson Goes to Washington").

107. Burleigh, "Digging up James Smithson."
108. Burleigh, "Digging up James Smithson."
109. Ewing, *The Lost World of James Smithson*, pp. 10–11.
110. Mitch Toda, 2012. "James Smithson, *c.* 1765–1829," *Smithson Institution Archives*, siarchives.si.edu/blog/james-smithson -c–1765–1829.

Chapter 7

1. Regna Darnell, 1998, *And Along Came Boas: Continuity and Revolution in Americanist Anthropology*, John Benjamins.
2. Darnell, *And Along Came Boas*, pp. xi–xii.
3. Ira Jacknis, 1985, "Franz Boas and Exhibits: On the Limitation of the Museum Method in Anthropology," in George W. Stocking, Jr. (ed.), *Objects and Others: Essays on Museums and Material Culture*, History of Anthropology, vol. 3, University of Wisconsin Press, p. 80.
4. Annual Report, United States National Museum, Smithsonian Institution, 1914, p. 15.
5. E. B. Tylor, 1884, "How the Problems of American Anthropology Present Themselves to the English Mind," *Science*, 4(98), 545–51.
6. Tylor, "How the Problems of American Anthropology Present Themselves," 546.
7. Tylor, "How the Problems of American Anthropology Present Themselves," 547.
8. Tylor, "How the Problems of American Anthropology Present Themselves," 549.
9. O. T. Mason, 1887, "The Occurrence of Similar Inventions in Areas Widely Apart," *Science*, 9(226), 534–5.
10. Rosemary Lévy Zumwalt, 2019, *Franz Boas: The Emergence of the Anthropologist*, University of Nebraska Press, pp. 133–4.
11. Brooke Penaloza Patzak, 2018, "An Emissary from Berlin: Franz Boas and the Smithsonian Institution," 1887–1888, *Museum Anthropology* 41, 30–45, 32.
12. Patzak, "An Emissary from Berlin," 32.
13. Patzak, "An Emissary from Berlin," 33.
14. Franz Boas, 1887, "The Occurrence of Similar Inventions in Areas Widely Apart," *Science*, 9(224), 485–6.
15. Douglas Cole, 1999, *Franz Boas: The Early Years, 1858–1906*, University of Washington Press, p. 127.

16. Boas, "The Occurrence of Similar Inventions," 485.
17. Boas, "The Occurrence of Similar Inventions," 485.
18. Boas, "The Occurrence of Similar Inventions," 485–6.
19. Patzak, "An Emissary from Berlin," 34.
20. Mason, "The Occurrence of Similar Inventions in Areas Widely Apart," 534.
21. Wm. H. Dall and Franz Boas, 1887, "Museums of Ethnology and Their Classification," *Science*, 9(228), 587–9, 588.
22. Dall and Boas, "Museums of Ethnology," 612.
23. Dall and Boas, "Museums of Ethnology," 613–4.
24. Dall and Boas, "Museums of Ethnology," 614.
25. Patzak, "An *Emissary* from Berlin," p. 34.
26. Cole, *Franz Boas*, p. 129.
27. Patzak, "An *Emissary* from Berlin," 41.
28. Jacknis, "Franz Boas and Exhibits," p. 107.

Chapter 8

1. Ralph W. Dexter, 1965, "Contributions of Frederic Ward Putnam to Ohio Archaeology," *The Ohio Journal of Science*, 65(3), 315–32, 110.
2. F. W. Putnam, 1898, *Guide to the Peabody Museum of Harvard University with a Statement Relating to Instruction in Anthropology*, Salem Press, p. 4.
3. Curtis M. Hinsley, 1985, "From Shell-heaps to Stelae: Early Anthropology at the Peabody Museum," in George W. Stocking, Jr. (ed.), *Objects and Others: Essays on Museums and Material Culture*, University of Wisconsin Press, pp. 49–74.
4. Henry James, 1914, *Notes on Novelists with Some Other Notes*, Scribner, pp. 413–15.
5. Hinsley, "From Shell-heaps to Stelae," p. 56.
6. Phoebe Sherman Sheftel, 1979, "The Archaeological Institute of America, 1879–1979: A Centennial Review," *American Journal of Archaeology*, 83(1), 3–17, 4.
7. Curtis M. Hinsley, 1993, "In Search of the New World Classical," in Elizabeth Hill Boone (ed.), *Collecting the Pre-Columbian Past*, Dumbarton Oaks Research Library and Collection, Washington, DC, p. 112.
8. William R. Taylor, 1969, "Francis Parkman," in Marcus Cunliffe and Robin W. Winks (eds.), *Pastmasters: Some Essays on American Historians*, Harper & Row, p. 4.

9. Hinsley, "From Shell-heaps to Stelae," pp. 54–5.

10. Letter from Darwin to Charles Lyell, 30 July 1860, Darwin Correspondence Project, University of Cambridge.

11. Letter from Darwin to Asa Gray, 22 May 1860, Darwin Correspondence Project, University of Cambridge.

12. Louis Agassiz, 1851, "Contemplations of God in the Kosmos," *The Christian Examiner and Religious Miscellany*, vol. 50, pp. 1–17.

13. Letter from Gray to Darwin, 10 January 1860, Darwin Correspondence Project, University of Cambridge.

14. Mary P. Winsor, 1979, "Louis Agassiz and the Species Question," in William Coleman and Camille Limoges (eds.), *Studies in the History of Biology*, volume 3, Johns Hopkins University Press, pp. 89–117. See p. 112.

15. Louis Menand, 2001, *The Metaphysical Club*, Farrar, Straus & Giroux. See pp. 124–8.

16. Letter from Gray to Darwin, 10 January 1860, Darwin Correspondence Project, University of Cambridge.

17. Toby A. Appel, 1988, "Jeffries Wyman, Philosophical Anatomy, and the Scientific Reception of Darwin in America," *Journal of the History of Biology*, 21(1), 69–94.

18. Rewriting Origin: The Later Editions, Darwin Correspondence Project, University of Cambridge.

19. Jules Marcou (ed.), 1896, *Life, Letters, and Works of Louis Agassiz*, two volumes, Macmillan. Citation, vol. 1, p. 142.

20. Hinsley, "From Shell-heaps to Stelae," p. 51.

21. Henry Adams, [1918] 1999, *The Education of Henry Adams*, Oxford University Press, chapter XV, p. 196.

22. David L. Browman and Stephen Williams, 2013, *Anthropology at Harvard: A Bibliographical History, 1790–1940*, Harvard University Press, p. 44.

23. *First Annual Report of the Trustees of the Peabody Museum of American Archaeology and Ethnology*, Cambridge MA, 1868, pp. 8–9.

24. David L. Browman, 2002, "The Peabody Museum, Frederic W. Putnam, and the Rise of U.S. Anthropology, 1866–1903," *American Anthropologist*, 104(2), 508–19, 509.

25. Hinsley, "From Shell-heaps to Stelae," p. 52.

26. Henry Adams, *The Education*, chapter IV, "Harvard College (1854–8)."

27. Steven Conn, 1998, *Museums and American Intellectual Life, 1876–1926*, University of Chicago Press, p. 42.

28. Joan Mark, 1980, *Four Anthropologists: An American Science in Its Early Years*, Science History Publications, p. 16.

29. Alfred M. Tozzer, 1933, "Biographical Memoir of Frederic Ward Putnam, 1839–1915," *National Academy of Sciences*, volume XVI, pp. 125–53. Citations, p. 130.

30. See Mark, *Four Anthropologists*, p. 151; William Henry Holmes, 1894, "Stone Implements of the Potomac-Tide-Water Province," in *Annual Report of the Bureau of Ethnology*, 1893–4.

31. For a review of twentieth-century controversies over the first settlement of the Americas see Gary Haynes, 2002, *The Early Settlement of North America: The Clovis Era*, Cambridge University Press, especially chapters 1 and 7.

32. Bruce Trigger, 1989, *A History of Archaeological Thought*, Cambridge University Press, pp. 104–5.

33. Edward Watts, 2020, *Colonizing the Past: Mythmaking and Pre-Columbian Whites in Nineteenth-Century American Writing*, University of Virginia Press.

34. Dexter, "Contributions of Frederic Ward Putnam to Ohio Archaeology," 115.

35. Lewis Henry Morgan, 1876, "Houses of the Mound-Builders," *The North American Review*, 23(252), 60–85, 61.

36. Mark, *Four Anthropologists*, p. 23.

37. J. W. Powell, 1885, "The Indians Are the Mound-Builders," *Science*, 5(113), 267.

38. Cyrus Thomas, 1894, "Report on the Mound Explorations of the Bureau of American Ethnology," *Twelfth Annual Report of the Bureau of American Ethnology, 1890–1891*, Washington, DC, 3–370.

39. Trigger, *A History of Archaeological Thought*, pp. 104–5.

40. Hinsley, "From Shell-heaps to Stelae," pp. 70–71.

41. Rubie Watson, n.d., *Opening the Museum: The Peabody Museum of Archaeology and Ethnology*, Occasional Papers, vol. 1, Peabody Museum of Archaeology and Ethnology, Harvard University, pp. 7–8.

42. Mark, *Four Anthropologists*, p. 30.

43. Mark, *Four Anthropologists*, p. 29.

44. Mark, *Four Anthropologists*, p. 22.

45. Hinsley, "From Shell-heaps to Stelae," p. 61.

46. D. Browman, 2002, "The Peabody Museum, Frederic W. Putnam, and the Rise of U.S. Anthropology, 1866–1903," *American Anthropologist*, 104(2), 508–19. See p. 512.

47. Mark, *Four Anthropologists*, p. 53.

48. Regna Darnell, 1998, *And Along Came Boas: Continuity and Revolution in Americanist Anthropology*, John Benjamins, p. 122.

49. Darnell, *And Along Came Boas*, p. 122.

50. Curtis Hinsley, 2016, "Anthropology as Education and Entertainment," in Curtis M. Hinsley and David R. Wilcox (eds), 2016. *Coming of Age in Chicago: The 1893 World's Fair and the Coalescence of American Anthropology*, University of Nebraska Press, p. 4.

51. Mark, *Four Anthropologists*, p. 32.

Chapter 9

1. Curtis M. Hinsley and David R. Wilcox, 2016, "Introduction: The Chicago Fair and American Anthropology in 1893," in Curtis M. Hinsley and David R. Wilcox (eds.), 2016, *Coming of Age in Chicago: The 1893 World's Fair and the Coalescence of American Anthropology*, University of Nebraska Press, p. xvii.

2. Melissa Rinehart, 2012, "To Hell with the Wigs! Native American Representation and Resistance at the World's Columbian Exposition," *American Indian Quarterly*, 36(4), 403–42, 420.

3. Erik Larson, 2003, *The Devil in the White City. Murder, Magic, and Madness at the Fair that Changed America*, Vintage Books, pp. 247–8.

4. Robert Rydell, 1984, *All the World's a Fair: Visions of Empire at American International Expositions, 1876–1916*, University of Chicago Press, p. 45.

5. Rydell, *All the World's a Fair*, p. 56.

6. Rydell, *All the World's a Fair*, p. 57.

7. Curtis M. Hinsley, 2016, "Anthropology as Education and Entertainment," in Curtis M. Hinsley and David R. Wilcox (eds.), 2016, *Coming of Age in Chicago: The 1893 World's Fair and the Coalescence of American Anthropology*, University of Nebraska Press, p. 16.

8. See David Brown, 2020, *The Last American Aristocrat: The Brilliant Life and Improbable Education of Henry Adams*, Scribner, chapter 37, "Chicago," pp. 283–7.

9. Henry Adams, 1919, *The Education of Henry Adams*, chapter XXII, "Chicago (1893)."

10. Rydell, *All the World's a Fair*, p. 68.

11. Ira Jacknis, "Refracting Images: Anthropological Display at the Chicago World's Fair 1893," in Curtis M. Hinsley and David R. Wilcox (eds.), 2016, *Coming of Age in Chicago: The 1893 World's Fair and the Coalescence of American Anthropology*, University of Nebraska Press, p. 272.

12. Jacknis, "Refracting Images," p. 272.

13. Frederick J. Turner, 1893, "The Significance of the Frontier in American History," *Annual Report of the American Historical Association*, 1893, pp. 197–227.

14. Rydell, *All the World's a Fair*, p. 55.

15. John C. Ewers, 1958, "A Century of American Indian Exhibits in the Smithsonian Institution," *Annual Report of the Board of Regents of the Smithsonian Institution*, pp. 513–26.

16. Otis T. Mason, 1894, "Ethnological Exhibits of the Smithsonian Institution at the World's Columbian Exposition," in C. Staniland Wake (ed.), *Memoirs of the International Congress of Anthropology*, Schute Publishing Company, pp. 208–16; Jacknis, "Refracting Images," 17–18.

17. Jacknis, "Refracting Images," p. 315.

18. Rosemary Lévy Zumwalt, 2019, *Franz Boas: The Emergence of the Anthropologist*, University of Nebraska Press, pp. 211–39; Frederic Ward Putnam, 1893, "Ethnology, Anthropology, Archaeology," in Trimball White and William Igleheart (eds.), *The World Columbian Exposition: Chicago 1893*, John K. Hastings, p. 415.

19. Nancy L. Fagin, 1984, "Closed Collections and Open Appeals: The Two Anthropology Exhibits at the Chicago World's Columbian Exposition of 1893," *Curator*, 27(4), 249–64, 256–7.

20. Douglas Cole, 1999, *Franz Boas: The Early Years, 1858–1906*, University of Washington Press, pp. 127, 154.

21. Franz Boas, 1893, "Ethnology at the Exposition," *A World's Fair: A Special Issue of Cosmopolitan Magazine*, December 1893, 78–83, 81.

22. Boas, "Ethnology at the Exposition," 79.

23. Boas, "Ethnology at the Exposition," 80.

24. Zumwalt, *Franz Boas*, p. 218.

25. Hinsley, "Anthropology as Education and Entertainment," p. 23.

26. Ralph W. Dexter, 1966, "Putnam's problems popularizing anthropology," *American Scientist*, 54(3), 315–32, 317.
27. Jacknis, "Refracting Images," pp. 276–95.
28. Hinsley, "Anthropology as Education and Entertainment," p. 38.
29. Hinsley, "Anthropology as Education and Entertainment," p. 27.
30. Hinsley, "Anthropology as Education and Entertainment," pp. 38–44.
31. Hinsley, "Anthropology as Education and Entertainment," p. 47.
32. Hinsley, "Anthropology as Education and Entertainment," pp. 33–5; Dexter, "Putnam's problems."
33. Cole, *Franz Boas*, p. 156.
34. Hinsley, "Anthropology as Education and Entertainment," p. 59.
35. Erik Larsen, 2003, *The Devil in the White City: Murder, Magic, and Madness at the Fair That Changed America*, Crown Publishers, pp. 311–15.
36. Hinsley, "Anthropology as Education and Entertainment," p. 75.
37. Hinsley, "Anthropology as Education and Entertainment," p. 70.
38. Bluford Adams, 1996, "'A Stupendous Mirror of Departed Empires': The Barnum Hippodromes and Circuses, 1874–91," *American Literary History*, 8(1), 34–56.
39. H. Glenn Penny, 2002, *Objects of Culture: Ethnology and Ethnographic Museums in Imperial Germany*, University of North Carolina Press, p. 61.
40. C. M. Hinsley and B. Holm, 1976, "A cannibal in the National Museum: The early career of Franz Boas in America," *American Anthropologist*, 78, 306–16.
41. Joan Mark, 1980, *Four Anthropologists: An American Science in its Early Years*, Science History Publications, p. 38.
42. Zumwalt, *Franz Boas*, p. 235.
43. Zumwalt, *Franz Boas*, p. 229.
44. Zumwalt, *Franz Boas*, p. 252.
45. Ira Jacknis, 1985, "Franz Boas and Exhibits: On the Limitation of the Museum Method in Anthropology," in George W. Stocking, Jr. (ed.), *Objects and Others: Essays on Museums and Material Culture*, History of Anthropology, vol. 3. University of Wisconsin Press, p. 76.
46. Regna Darnell, 1998, *And Along Came Boas: Continuity and Revolution in Americanist Anthropology*, John Benjamins, p. 94.
47. Hinsley, "Anthropology as Education and Entertainment," p. 47.

48. Jacknis, "Franz Boas and Exhibits," p. 87.
49. Jacknis, "Franz Boas and Exhibits," p. 86.
50. Jacknis, "Franz Boas and Exhibits," p. 93.
51. Mark, *Four Anthropologists*, p. 44.
52. Hinsley, *Savages and Scientists*, p. 251.
53. F. Boas, 1907, "Some principles of museum administration," *Science* 25, 921–23, 928.
54. Powell and Boas, "Museums of Ethnology," 613–14.
55. Mark, *Four Anthropologists*, pp. 48–9.
56. William C. Sturtevant, 1969, "Does Anthropology Need Museums?," *Proceedings of the Biological Society of Washington* 82, 619–49, 622.
57. Franz Boas, 1919, "Scientists as spies," reprinted in George Stocking, 1974, *A Franz Boas Reader: The Shaping of American Anthropology*, University of Chicago Press.
58. Mark, *Four Anthropologists*, pp. 161–2.
59. See, for instance, Leslie. A. White, 1966, *The Social Organization of Ethnological Theory*, Rice University Studies, no. 52.

Chapter 10

1. Frances Larson, 2014, *Severed: A History of Heads Lost and Heads Found*, Granta, p. 151.
2. Wendy Moore, 2005, *The Knife Man: Blood, Body-Snatching and the Birth of Modern Surgery*, Bantam Books, p. 25.
3. Moore, *The Knife Man*, p. 86.
4. Moore, *The Knife Man*, Chapter 12 "The Giant's Bones," pp. 397–428.
5. Moore, *The Knife Man*, p. 422.
6. Moore, *The Knife Man*, pp. 421–6.
7. Moore, *The Knife Man*, p. 450.
8. Moore, *The Knife Man*, p. 474.
9. Moore, *The Knife Man*, pp. 467–9.
10. Richard Steckel, Clark Spencer Larsen, Paul Sciulli and Phillip Walker, 2006, "The Scientific Value of Human Remains in Studying the Global History of Health," in Jack Lohman and Katherine Goodnow (eds.), *Human Remains and Museum Practice*, UNESCO, pp. 60–70. See pp. 63–4.
11. A. Hrdlička, 1914, "Physical Anthropology in America: An Historical Sketch," *American Anthropologist*, 16(4), new series, 508–54, 513.

12. S. Gould, 1978, "Morton's Ranking of Races by Cranial Capacity," *Science*, 200(4341), 503–9, 503; cf. Paul Wolff Mitchell, 2018, "The fault in his seeds: Lost notes to the case of bias in Samuel George Morton's cranial race science," *PLOS Biology*, https://doi.org/10.1371/journal.pbio.2007008

13. Sanford B. Hunt, 1861, "Samuel George Morton," in Samuel D. Gross (ed.), *Lives of Eminent American Physicians and Surgeons of the Nineteenth Century*, Lindsay and Blakiston, 591.

14. R. Jameson, 1850, "Remarks on Dr. Morton's Tables on the Size of the Brain," *Edinburgh New Philosophical Journal* 48, pp. 330–33.

15. Gould, "Morton's Ranking of Races by Cranial Capacity"; see also Stephen Jay Gould, 1981, *The Mismeasure of Man*, W. W. Norton and Company; cf. Michael Weisberg and Diane B. Paul, 2016, "Morton, Gould, and Bias: A Comment on 'The Mismeasure of Science.'" PLOS https://doi.org/10.1371/journal.pbio.1002444

16. Gary Laderman, 1996, *The Sacred Remains: American Attitudes Toward Death, 1799–1883*, Yale University Press, pp. 145–6.

17. Laderman, *The Sacred Remains*, p. 146.

18. Samuel J. Redman, 2016, *Bone Rooms: From Scientific Racism to Human Prehistory in Museums*, Harvard University Press, pp. 28–9.

19. Ann Fabian, 2010, *The Skull Collectors: Race, Science and America's Unburied Dead*, University of Chicago Press, p. 183.

20. Fabian, *The Skull Collectors*, p. 176.

21. Fabian, *The Skull Collectors*, p. 175.

22. Fabian, *The Skull Collectors*, p. 175.

23. United States National Museum, annual report for the year ending 30 June 1898, p. 4.

24. Fabian, *The Skull Collectors*, pp. 210–11.

25. A. Hrdlička, 1900, "Arrangement and Preservation of Large Collections of Human Bones for Purpose of Investigation," *American Naturalist*, 34(397), 10.

26. Stanley A. Freed, 2012, *Anthropology Unmasked: Museums, Science, and Politics in New York City, volume I: The Putnam-Boas Era*, Orange Frazer Press, p. 182.

27. Rosemary Lévy Zumwalt, 2019, *Franz Boas: The Emergence of the Anthropologist*, University of Nebraska Press, p. 181; Douglas Cole, 1985, *Captured Heritage: The Scramble for Northwest Coast Artifacts*, University of Washington Press, p. 119.

28. Zumwalt, *Franz Boas*, pp. 180–81.

29. J. S. Huxley and A. C. Haddon, 1935, *We Europeans: A Survey of "Racial" Problems*, Jonathan Cape, p. 13.
30. Sherwood Washburn, 1962, "The study of race," *American Anthropologist* 65, 521–31.
31. I. De Vore and S. Washburn, 1992, "An Interview with Sherwood Washburn," *Current Anthropology*, 33 (4), 411–23, 422.
32. A. Kuper, 1993, "Racial science," *Nature* 364, 754.
33. Patricia Pierce Erikson, 2008, "Decolonizing the 'Nation's Attic,'" in Amy Lonetree and Amanda J. Cobb (eds.), 2008, *The National Museum of the American Indian: Critical Conversations*, University of Nebraska Press, p. 56.
34. 101st Congress, Second Session, Senate Report, pp. 101–473: "Providing for the Protection of Native American Graves and the Repatriation of Native American Remains and Cultural Patrimony."
35. Chip Colwell, 2017, *Plundered Skulls and Stolen Spirits: Inside the Fight to Reclaim Native America's Culture*, University of Chicago Press, p. 105.
36. Colwell, *Plundered Skulls*, p. 121.
37. S. Powell, C. Garza and A. Hendricks, 1993, "Ethics and Ownership of the Past: The Reburial and Repatriation Controversy," *Archaeological Method and Theory*, 5, 1–42.
38. David Hurst Thomas, 2000, *Skull Wars: Kennewick Man, Archaeology, and the Battle for Native American Identity*, Basic Books, p. 231.
39. 136th Congress, 1990, Rec S17,173.
40. Erikson, "Decolonizing the 'Nation's Attic,'" p. 60.
41. Colwell, *Plundered Skulls*, p. 83.
42. Colwell, *Plundered Skulls*, p. 113.
43. Margaret M. Bruchac, 2021, "Colonizing the Indigenous Dead," *History of Anthropology Review* 45.
44. Redman, *Bone Rooms*, p. 281.
45. M. F. Brown and M. Bruchac, 2006, "NAGPRA from the Middle Distance: Legal Puzzles and Unintended Consequences," in J. H. Merryman (ed.), *Imperialism, Art and Restitution*, University of Cambridge Press, pp. 193–217, 198.
46. Redman, *Bone Rooms*, p. 5.
47. Redman, *Bone Rooms*, p. 279; Colwell, *Plundered Skulls*, pp. 7–9.
48. Colwell, *Plundered Skulls*, p. 222.
49. Thomas, *Skull Wars*, p. 226.

50. Colwell, *Plundered Skulls*, p. 221.
51. I. K. Jordan, Lavanya Rishishwar and Andrew B. Conley, 2019, "Native American admixture recapitulates population-specific migration and settlement of the continental United States," *PLOS Genetics*. https://journals.plos.org/plosgenetics/article?id=10.1371/journal.pgen.1008225
52. Philip Deloria, 2022, "When Tribal Nations Expel Their Black Members," *New Yorker*, 25 July 2022.
53. Thomas, *Skull Wars*, p. 228.
54. Bruchac and Brown, "NAGPRA from the Middle Distance," p. 209.
55. Bruchac and Brown, "NAGPRA from the Middle Distance," p. 211.
56. Michael Kammen, 2010, *Digging Up the Dead: A History of Notable American Reburials*, University of Chicago Press, p. 191.
57. *The New York Times*, 20 February 2009, "Geronimo's descendants sue secret society at Yale."
58. Personal communication.
59. Thomas, *Skull Wars*, p. 77.
60. Thomas, *Skull Wars*, pp. 82–3.
61. Thomas, *Skull Wars*, p. 219.
62. Orin Starn, 2004, *Ishi's Brain: In Search of America's Last "Wild" Indian*, W. W. Norton, p. 147.
63. Starn, *Ishi's Brain*, p. 28.
64. Starn, *Ishi's Brain*, p. 171.
65. Starn, *Ishi's Brain*, pp. 215–16.
66. James Chatters, 2001, *Ancient Encounters: Kennewick Man and the First Americans*, Simon and Schuster.
67. Douglas Preston, 1997, "The Lost Man," *New Yorker*, 16 June.
68. Thomas, *Skull Wars*, p. xxii.
69. Thomas, *Skull Wars*, p. 240.
70. U.S. Senate, Committee on Indian Affairs, 109th Congress, First Session, 28 July 2005.
71. S. Bruning, 2006, "Complex Legal Legacies: The Native American Graves Protection and Repatriation Act, Scientific Study, and Kennewick Man," *American Antiquity*, 71(3), 501–21, 508.
72. M. Rasmussen, M. Sikora, A. Albrechtsen, 2015, "The ancestry and affiliations of Kennewick Man," *Nature* 523, 455–8.
73. Colwell, *Plundered Skulls*, pp. 228–9.
74. https://ropercenter.cornell.edu/paradise-polled-americans-and-afterlife

75. Carl Sagan, 1974, *Broca's Brain: Reflections on the Romance of Science*, Random House, p. 4.

76. Sagan, *Broca's Brain*, pp. 5–6.

77. Stephen Jay Gould, 1987, "The Hottentot Venus," in *The Flamingo's Smile: Reflections in Natural History*, Penguin Books, pp. 291–305.

78. P. V. Tobias, 2002, "Sara Baartman: Her life, her remains, and the negotiations for their repatriation from France to South Africa," *South African Journal of Science* 98, 107–10, 109.

79. Clifton Crais and Pamela Scully, 2011, *Sara Baartman and the Hottentot Venus: A Ghost Story and a Biography*, Princeton University Press. For the early years, see chapter 1: "Winds of the Camdeboo."

80. Crais and Scully, *Sara Baartman*, p. 27.

81. Crais and Scully, *Sara Baartman*, p. 57.

82. Crais and Scully, *Sara Baartman*, p. 78; Sadiah Qureshi, 2004, "Displaying Sara Baartman, The Hottentot Venus," *History of Science* 42, 233–57.

83. Crais and Scully, *Sara Baartman*, chapter 4: "Before the law," pp. 82–102.

84. Crais and Scully, *Sara Baartman*, p. 89.

85. Z. S. Strother, 1999, "Display of the Body Hottentot," in Bernth Lindfors (ed.), *Africans on Stage*, Indiana University Press, pp. 1–61, pp. 30–31.

86. Crais and Scully, *Sara Baartman*, p. 135.

87. Tobias, "Sara Baartman," p. 108.

88. Tobias, "Sara Baartman," 108–9.

89. Gould, "The Hottentot Venus," pp. 295–6.

90. Crais and Scully, *Sara Baartman*, pp. 160–61.

91. Crais and Scully, *Sara Baartman*, pp. 166–7.

92. Crais and Scully, *Sara Baartman*, pp. 167–9.

93. Kammen, *Digging up the Dead*, p. 15.

94. https://www.ucl.ac.uk/bentham-project/who-was-jeremy-bentham/auto-icon/extract-benthams-will

Chapter 11

1. J. A. Kelly, 2015, "'Dahomey! Dahomey!': African art in Paris in the late 19th century," *Journal of Art Historiography*.

2. https://www.elysee.fr/emmanuel-macron/2020/12/18/restitution-des-biens-culturels-une-promesse-tenue-pour-une-nouvelle-page-des-relations-entre-lafrique-et-la-france

3. Nicolas Truong, 2018, "Restitutions d'art africain," *Le Monde*, 28 November 2018.

4. Felwine Sarr and Bénédicte Savoy, translated by Drew S. Burk, November 2018, *The Restitution of African Cultural Heritage. Towards a New Relational ethics*, Ministère de la Culture.

5. Sarr and Savoy, *The Restitution of African Cultural Heritage*, p. 2.

6. Sarr and Savoy, *The Restitution of African Cultural Heritage*, p. 61.

7. Sarr and Savoy, *The Restitution of African Cultural Heritage*, p. 58.

8. Sally Price, 2020, "Has the Sarr-Savoy report had any effect since it was first published?," *Apollo*, 6 January 2020.

9. Philippe Baqué, 2020, "Polémique sur la restitution des objets d'art africaines," *Le Monde diplomatique*, August 2020.

10. Baqué, "Polémique sur la restitution des objets d'art africains."

11. Baqué, "Polémique sur la restitution des objets d'art africains."

12. Vincent Noce, 29 November 2018, "Senegal and Ivory Coast will ask for return of objects in French museums," *The Art Newspaper*.

13. S. Memel-Kassi, 2020, "The Illicit Circulation of Ivorian Collections: Challenges and Prospects," *Journal for Art Market Studies*, 4(1). https://doi.org/10.23690/jams.v4i1.97

14. Thomas Phillips, 1694, "Voyage of the Hannibal, 1693–1694," in Elizabeth Donnan (ed.), 1931, *Documents Illustrative of the History of the Slave Trade to America, volume 1: 1441–1700*, pp. 392–410.

15. J. Dupuis, 1824, "Journal of a Residence in Ashantee," pp. 163–4. Cited in Ivor Wilks, *Asante in the Nineteenth Century*, Cambridge University Press, pp. 679–80.

16. Herbert S. Klein, 1999, *The Atlantic Slave Trade*, Cambridge University Press, p. 129.

17. C. Newbury, 1959, "A Note on the Abomey Protectorate," *Africa: Journal of the International African Institute*, 29(2), 146–55, 148.

18. R. Law, 1993, "The 'Amazons' of Dahomey," *Paideuma* 39, 245–60. See also Suzanne Preston Blier, 2004, "Les Amazones à la rencontre de l'Occident," in Nicolas Barcel (ed.), *Zoos humains: Au temps des exhibitions humaines*, La Découverte, pp. 136–41.

19. Eva L. R. Meyerowitz, 1944, "The Museum in the Royal Palaces at Abomey, Dahomey," *The Burlington Magazine for Connoisseurs*, 84(495), 147–51, 148, 149.

20. Francesca Pique and Leslie H. Rainer, 1999, *Palace Sculptures of Abomey: History Told on Walls*, The Getty Conservation Institute and the J. Paul Getty Museum. https://www.getty.edu

/conservation/publications_resources/pdf_publications/pdf/palace1.pdf

21. Kevin Sieff, 2018, "An African country reckons with its history of selling slaves," *Washington Post*, 29 January 2018.

22. Theodore R. Johnson, 2014, "How to apologize for slavery: What the U.S. can learn from West Africa," *Atlantic Monthly*, 6 August 2014.

23. https://www.france24.com/en/20200811-benin-restores-slavery-monuments-to-testify-to-brutal-past

24. Ivor Wilks, 1975, *Asante in the Nineteenth Century: The Structure and Evolution of a Political Order*, Cambridge University Press, p. 201.

25. Wilks, *Asante in the Nineteenth Century*, pp. 200–202.

26. R. Addo-Fening, 2013, "Ghana under colonial rule: An outline of the early period and the interwar years," *Transactions of the Historical Society of Ghana* 15, new series, pp. 39–70.

27. Kathryn Wysocki Gunsch, 2018, *The Benin Plaques: A 16th Century Imperial Monument*, Routledge. Annex 4: List of Plaques by Institution.

28. P. Igbafe, 1970, "The Fall of Benin: A Reassessment," *The Journal of African History*, 11(3), 385–400, 395.

29. Igbafe, "The Fall of Benin," 397.

30. Barnaby Phillips, 2021, *Loot: Britain and the Benin Bronzes*, Oneworld Publications, p. 53.

31. Barnaby, *Loot*, p. 72.

32. Barbara Plankensteiner, 2007, "Benin: Kings and Rituals: Court Arts from Nigeria," *African Arts*, 40(4), 74–87. See p. 77.

33. Girshick Ben-Amos, 2021, *Benin: Kingdom of*, Grove Press, Oxford Arts Online, https://www.oxfordartonline.com/groveart/view/10.1093/gao/9781884446054.001.0001/oao-9781884446054-e-7000007886

34. Phillips, *Loot*, p. 104.

35. A. E. Coombes, 1994, *Reinventing Africa: Museums, Material Culture, and Popular Imagination in Late Victorian and Edwardian England*, Yale University Press, pp. 7–29.

36. Philip A. Igbafe, "Slavery and Emancipation in Benin, 1897–1945," *The Journal of African History*, vol. 16, no. 3, 1975, pp. 409–29.

37. Coombes, *Reinventing Africa*, p. 159.

38. William Fagg, 1957, "The Seligman Ivory Mask from Benin: The

Royal Anthropological Institute Christmas Card for 1957," *Man* 57, 113.

39. H. Glenn Penny, 2002. *Objects of Culture: Ethnology and Ethnographic Museums in Imperial Germany*, University of North Carolina Press, p. 77.

40. F. von Luschan, 1919, *Die Altertümer von Benin*, Museum für Völkerkunde.

41. Penny, *Objects of Culture*, p. 75.

42. H. Ling Roth, 1903, *Great Benin: Its Customs, Art and Horrors*, F. King & Sons. See pp. xviii–xxi.

43. Phillips, *Loot*, pp. 121–7.

44. F. Willett, 1973, "Kenneth Murray," *African Arts*, 6(2), 65–6.

45. Phillips, *Loot*, p. 219.

46. Phillips, *Loot*, pp. 217–18.

47. J. Povey, F. Willett, J. Picton, & E. Eyo, 1988, "Bernard Fagg: 1915–1987," *African Arts*, 21(2), 10–12.

48. John Picton, 1994, "A tribute to William Fagg," *African Arts*, 27(3), 26–9, p. 26.

49. Phillips, *Loot*, p. 226.

50. Wole Soyinka, 2021, *Chronicles From the Land of the Happiest People on Earth*, Bloomsbury Circus. Ben Okri's review appeared in the *Guardian*, 27 September 2021.

51. *The Economist*, 2 April 2022, "Red Line: Kidnappers brazenly derail a train." See also Kazeem Ugbodaga, 24 November 2020, "Kidnappers on the prowl in Edo: Five hotspots to avoid," *PM News Nigeria*.

52. Kwame Anthony Appiah, 2009, "Whose Culture Is It?," in James Cuno (ed.), *Whose Culture? The Promise of Museums and the Debate over Antiquities*, Princeton University Press, p. 73.

53. Phillips, *Loot*, p. 225.

54. Phillips, *Loot*, p. 223.

55. Folarin Shyllon, 2011, "Looting and illicit traffic in antiquities in Africa," in Stefano Manacordo and Duncan Chappell (eds.), *Crime in the Art and Antiquities World: Illegal Trafficking in Cultural Property*, Springer, p. 135.

56. Frank Willett, 2000, "Restitution or Re-circulation: Benin, Ife and Nok," *Journal of Museum Ethnography* 12, 125–31.

57. Suzanne Preston Blier, 1982, "Treasures of Ancient Nigeria," *Art Journal*, 42(3), 234–6.

58. Willett, "Restitution or Re-circulation," 126.

59. Gregory Austin Nwakunor, 11 July 2021, "Rumble in Benin over looted artefacts," *Guardian Nigeria*.

60. Meyerowitz, "The Museum in the Royal Palaces at Abomey," 151.

61. Phillips, *Loot*, p. 3.

62. Mark R. Lipschutz and R. Kent Rasmussen, 1989, "Johnson, James (Holy Johnson)," *Dictionary of African Historical Biography*, Oxford University Press.

63. Charles Gore, 2007, *Art, Performance and Ritual in Benin City*, Edinburgh University Press, p. 199.

64. B. Kundrus, 2005, "From the Herero to the Holocaust? Some Remarks on the Current Debate," *Africa Spectrum*, 40(2), 299–308.

65. J. Torpey, 2001, "'Making Whole What Has Been Smashed': Reflections on Reparations," *The Journal of Modern History*, 73(2), 333–58, 338.

66. https://www.bbc.com/news/world-africa-65531736

67. https://culturalpropertynews.org/nigeria-gives-benin-ruler-exclusive-ownership-of-bronzes/

68. Brigitta Hauser-Schäublin, 2023, "Benin-Bronzen gehen an den Oba: War das der Sinn der Restitution?," *Frankfurter Allgemeine Zeitung*, 5th May, 2023.

69. https://news.artnet.com/art-world/benin-bronze-lawsuit-restitution-study-group-smithsonian-2221312

70. https://www.bbc.com/news/world-africa-63504438

Chapter 12

1. Philippe Dagen, 2019, *Primitivismes: Une Invention Moderne*, Gallimard; 2021, *Primitivismes 2: Une Guerre Moderne*, Gallimard. See "Se declarer pour le primitive," *Primitivismes: Une Invention Moderne*, pp. 133–42.

2. William Rubin, 1984, "Modernist Primitivism: An Introduction," in William Rubin (ed.), *"Primitivism" in 20th-Century Art*, volume 1, Museum of Modern Art, p. 1–84, 7, 17.

3. Dagen, *Primitivismes: Une invention moderne*, p. 136.

4. Dagen, *Primitivismes: Une invention moderne*, p. 16.

5. Elizabeth A. Williams, 1985, "Art and Artefact at the Trocadero: Ars Americana and the Primitivist Revolution," in George W. Stocking (ed.), 1985, *Objects and Others: Essays on Museums and Material Culture*, University of Wisconsin Press, pp. 146–66, 156.

6. Fondation Dapper, 1989, *Objets interdits*, Fondation Dapper, p. 10.

7. Jack Flam and Miriam Deutch (eds.) 2003, *Primitivism and Twentieth-century Art: A Documentary History*, University of California Press, p. 27.

8. Flam and Deutch, *Primitivism and Twentieth-century Art*, p. 27.

9. Robert Goldwater, 1968 [enlarged edition. First published 1938], *Primitivism in Modern Art*, Belknap Press of Harvard University Press, p. 89.

10. Flam and Deutch, *Primitivism and Twentieth-century Art*, p. 32.

11. Flam and Deutch, *Primitivism and Twentieth-century Art*, p. 31.

12. Hilary Spurling, 2009, *Matisse: The Life*, Penguin Books, p. 149.

13. Spurling, *Matisse*, p. 150.

14. Flam and Deutch, *Primitivism and Twentieth-century Art*, pp. 33–4.

15. Suzanne Preston Blier, 2019, *Picasso's* Demoiselles: *The Untold Origins of a Modern Masterpiece*, Duke University Press, pp. 111–13.

16. John Richardson, 1991, *A Life of Picasso: The Early Years, 1881–1906*, Random House, p. 519, n. 44.

17. Richardson, *Life of Picasso*, p. 459.

18. Goldwater, *Primitivism in Modern Art*, p. 126.

19. Dagen, *Primitivismes: Une invention moderne*, p. 12.

20. Frances Spalding, 1980, *Roger Fry: Art and Life*, University of California Press, p. 233.

21. Jill Lloyd, 1991, *German Expressionism: Primitivism and Modernity*, Yale University Press, p. 161.

22. Lloyd, *German Expressionism*. See chapter 3 "The Brücke Studios: A Testing Ground for Primitivism," pp. 21–49; chapter 9 "Emil Nolde and the Paradox of Primitivism," pp. 161–88; chapter 10 "A South Seas Odyssey: Max Pechstein's Visionary Ideals," pp. 191–212.

23. Barry Schwabsky, 2019, "The Perfect Victim: How should we remember the art of Emil Nolde?," *The Nation*, 19 September 2019.

24. Alain Buisine, 2012, *Passion de Gauguin*, Presses Universitaires de Septentrion, p. 46.

25. R. Swedberg, 2016, "The literary author as a sociologist? Among French Peasants by August Strindberg," *Journal of Classical Sociology*, 16(1), 124–30.

26. Goldwater, *Primitivism in Modern Art*, pp. 66–7.

27. Dagen, *Primitivismes: Une Invention Moderne*, chapter 6, "Gauguin pour preuve," pp. 306, 310.

28. Philippe Dagen, 2021, *Primitivismes 2: Une Guerre Moderne*, Gallimard, pp. 91–2.

29. Flam and Deutch, *Primitivism and Twentieth-century Art*, pp. 33–5.

30. Anon. 1920, "Opinions sur l'art nègre," *Action*, iii, April 1920.

31. Flam and Deutch, *Primitivism and Twentieth-century Art*, p. 33.

32. Lloyd, *German Expressionism*, p. 85.

33. Guillaume Apollinaire, 1912, "Exotisme et ethnographie," *Paris-Journal*, 10 September 1912.

34. Maureen Murphy, 2020 (revised edition), *De l'imaginaire au musée: Les arts d'Afrique à Paris et à New York (1931 à nos jours)*, Les presses du reel, p. 34.

35. Flam and Deutch, *Primitivism and Twentieth-Century Art*, pp. 148–66.

36. J. Clifford, 1981, "On Ethnographic Surrealism," *Comparative Studies in Society and History*, 23(4), 539–64; Vincent Debaene, 2002, "Les surréalistes et le musée d'ethnographie," *Labyrinthe*, 12(2), pp. 71–94.

37. See Debaene, "Les surréalistes et le musée d'ethnographie."

38. Guillaume Apollinaire, 1917, "A propos de l'Art des Noirs, Melanophilie ou Melanomanie," *Mercure de France*, 1 April 1917.

39. Christopher B. Steiner, 1994, *African Art in Transit*, Cambridge University Press, p. 104.

40. Peter Read (ed.), 2016, *Guillaume Apollinaire/Paul Guillaume: Correspondence*, Gallimard.

41. Steiner, *African Art in Transit*, p. 6.

42. Y. Biro, 2013, "African Art, New York, and the Avant-Garde," *African Arts*, 46(2), 88–97, p. 92.

43. Murphy, *De l'imaginaire au musée*, pp. 104–5.

44. Paul Guillaume and Thomas Munro, 1926, *Primitive Negro Sculpture*, Harcourt Brace, p. 7.

45. Murphy, *De l'imaginaire au musée*, p. 180.

46. Paul Guillaume, 1919, "Une esthétique nouvelle. L'art nègre," *Les Arts á Paris* 4 (May 15). Cited in Biro, "African Art, New York, and the Avant-Garde," p. 95.

47. Murphy, *De l'imaginaire au musée*, pp. 129–30.

48. Goldwater, *Primitivism in Modern Art*. Citations, pp. xvi, xvii, xxi, xxiv.

49. N. C. Lutkehaus, 2015, "The Bowerbird of Collectors: On Nelson A. Rockefeller and 'Collecting the Stuff That Wasn't in the

Metropolitan,'" *Bulletin of the Buffalo Society of Natural Sciences*, vol. 42, pp. 125–36, 125.

50. Patrick Wilcken, 2010, *Claude Lévi-Strauss: The Poet in the Laboratory*, Bloomsbury, p. 40.

51. Emmanuelle Loyer, 2015, *Lévi-Strauss*, Flammarion, pp. 227–9.

52. Loyer, *Lévi-Strauss*, pp. 278–83.

53. Claude Lévi-Strauss, 1982 [original French edition in two volumes, 1975, 1979], *The Way of the Masks*, Douglas & McIntyre Ltd, p. 9.

54. Lévi-Strauss, *The Way of the Masks*, p. 4.

55. Lévi-Strauss, *The Way of the Masks*, p. 3.

56. Lévi-Strauss, *The Way of the Masks*, p. 10.

57. Jennifer Lena, 2020, "The omnivore paradox," *Times Literary Supplement*, 27 March 2020.

58. Geoffrey Hellman, 1960, "Imperturbable Noble," *New Yorker*, 7 May 1960.

59. Hellman, "Imperturbable Noble."

60. Richard Norton Smith, 2014, *On His Own Terms: A Life of Nelson Rockefeller*, Random House, p. 97.

61. Norton Smith, *On His Own Terms*, pp. 90–93, 95–9.

62. Hellman, "Imperturbable Noble."

63. Murphy, *De l'imaginaire au musée*, pp. 156, 299, n. 51.

64. Murphy, *De l'imaginaire au musée*, p. 300, n. 54.

65. Norton Smith, *On His Own Terms*, p. 248.

66. Norton Smith, *On His Own Terms*, p. 361.

67. Norton Smith, *On His Own Terms*, p. 368.

68. Norton Smith, *On His Own Terms*, p. 642.

69. S. Vogel, 1982, "Bringing African Art to the Metropolitan Museum," *African Arts*, 15 (2), 38–45, 41.

70. Rubin, "Modernist Primitivism," p. 7.

71. Rubin, "Modernist Primitivism," p. 1.

72. Rubin, "Modernist Primitivism," p. 17.

73. Rubin, "Modernist Primitivism," p. 73.

74. Rubin, "Modernist Primitivism," p. 18.

75. Arthur C. Danto, 1984, "Defective affinities: 'Primitivism' in 20th Century Art," *New Republic*, 239(18), pp. 590–2.

76. Alfred Gell, 1996, "Vogel's Net: Traps as Artworks and Artworks as Traps," *Journal of Material Culture*, 1(1), pp. 15–38.

77. Danto, "Artifact and Art," p. 31.

78. http://news.bbc.co.uk/1/hi/entertainment/4059997.stm

79. A. Jones, 1993, "Exploding Canons: The Anthropology of Museums," *Annual Review of Anthropology*, 22, 201–20. See p. 208.

80. Nélia Dias, 2001, "Esquisse Ethnographique d'un Projet: Le Musée Du Quai Branly," *French Politics, Culture & Society*, 19(2), 81–101.

81. Cited in Bernard Dupaigne, 2006, *Le Scandale des arts premiers la véritable histoire du musée du quai Branly*. Paris, Mille et une nuits, p. 35.

82. Jacques Kerchache, 1990, *Les chefs-d'œuvre du monde entier naissent libres et égaux*, Adam Biro.

83. Sally Price, 2007, *Paris Primitive: Jacques Chirac's Museum on the Quai Branly*, University of Chicago Press, p. 35.

84. See Dias, "Esquisse Ethnographique d'un Projet."

85. Claude Lévi-Strauss, 1996, "Une synthèse judicieuse," *Le Monde*, 9 October 1996.

86. Dupaigne, *Le Scandale des arts premiers*.

87. Malraux, *La Metamorphose des dieux*, vol. III, *L'Intemporel*, Gallimard, p. 262.

88. Krzysztof Pomian, 2000, "Un musée pour les arts exotiques: Entretien avec Germain Viatte," *Le Débat*, 70(1), 75–84; Dias, "Esquisse Ethnographique d'un Projet"; Benoît de L'Estoile, 2007, *Le Goût des Autres: De l'exposition coloniale aux arts premiers*, Flammarion, p. 11.

89. Dubuc, "Le future antérieur du Musée de l'Homme," 89.

90. Dupaigne, *Le Scandale des arts premiers*, p. 150.

91. De l'Estoile, *Le Goût des Autres*, p. 416.

92. De l'Estoile, *Le Goût des Autres*, pp. 24–5.

93. "Le musée du quai Branly rejette Darwin," interview with Emmanuel Desveaux, first director of the museum, *Le Monde*, 19 March 2002.

94. De l'Estoile, "Can French anthropology outlive its museums?" Unpublished lecture.

95. De l'Estoile, *Le Goût des Autres*, p. 416.

96. "Le musée du quai Branly rejette Darwin."

97. Dias, "Esquisse Ethnographique d'un Projet," 95.

98. Fabrice Grognet, 2007, "Musées Manqués, Objets Perdus? L'Autre Dans Les Musées Ethnographiques Français," *L'Homme* 181, 173–87, p. 174.

99. Edwin Heathcote, 2001, "Berlin's Humboldt Forum: a palace in search of a purpose," *Financial Times*, 4 January 2021.

100. Karl-Heinz Kohl, Fritz Kramer, Johann Michael Möller, Geroen Sievernich and Gisela Völger, 2019, *Das Humboldt Forum und die Ethnologie*, Kula Verlag, p. 13.
101. Interview with Bénédicte Savoy, 2017, "Das Humboldt-Forum ist wie Tschernobyl," *Süddeutsche Zeitung*, 20 July 2017.
102. Götz Aly, 2023, *The Magnificent Boat: The Colonial Theft of a South Seas Cultural Treasure*, Harvard University Press.
103. Katja Geisenhainer, 2021, Ein Kind des Kolonialismus? *Paideuma*, Vol. 67, pp. 193–210
104. https://www.metmuseum.org/press/news/2018/rockefellerwing -announcement
105. Peggy Levitt, 2015, *Artifacts and Allegiances: How Museums Put the Nation and the World on Display*, University of California Press, p. 27.
106. Wole Soyinka, 2019, *Beyond Aesthetics: Use, Abuse and Dissonance in African Art Traditions*, Yale University Press, p. 109.

Chapter 13

1. Enrique Florescana, 1993, "The Creation of the Museo Nacional de Antropología of Mexico and its Scientific, Educational, and Political Purposes," in Elizabeth Hill Boone, *Collecting the Pre-Columbian Past*, Dumbarton Oaks Research Library and Collection, Washington, DC, pp. 81–101.
2. David A. Brading, 1988, "Manuel Gamo and Official Indigenismo in Mexica," *Bulletin of Latin American Research*, 7(1), 75–89, 82.
3. Alan Knight, 1990, "Racism, Revolution and Indigenismo: Mexico, 1910–40," in Richard Graham (ed.), *The Idea of Race in Latin America, 1870–1940*, University of Texas Press, pp. 71–113, 85.
4. Brading, "Manuel Gamo," 86.
5. Barbara Braun, 1993, "Diego Rivera's Collection: Pre-Columbian Art as a Political and Artistic Legacy," in Elizabeth Hill Boone, 1993, *Collecting the Pre-Columbian Past*, Dumbarton Oaks Research Library and Collection, Washington, DC, pp. 251–70.
6. George M. Foster, 1965, "The New National Museum of Anthropology in Mexico City," *American Anthropologist* 67, 734–6.
7. Octavio Paz, [1950] 1985, *The Labyrinth of Solitude and the Other Mexico*, Grove Press, p. 298.
8. Paz, *The Labyrinth of Solitude*, pp. 322–4.

9. Carlos Fausto, 2020, "Under Heavy Fire: Brazil and the Politics of Anti-Memory," *Latin American Antiquity*, 31(2), 247–55, 248.

10. See Thiago Lopes da Costa Oliveira, 2020, "Lost Objects, Hidden Stories: On the Ethnographic Collections Burned in the National Museum of Rio de Janeiro," *Latin American Antiquity*, 31(2), 256–72.

11. Samuel P. Huntington, 1996, *The Clash of Civilizations and the Remaking of World Order*, Simon and Schuster.

12. Amy Lonetree and Amanda J. Cobb (eds.), 2008, *The National Museum of the American Indian: Critical Conversations*, University of Nebraska Press, p. 53.

13. Lonetree and Cobb, "The National Museum of the American Indian," p. 54.

14. John Bloom, 2005, "Exhibition Review: The National Museum of the American Indian," *American Studies*, 46(3), 327–38.

15. Bloom, "Exhibition Review," p. 327.

16. Edward Rothstein, 2004, "Museum With an American Indian Voice," *The New York Times*, 21 September 2004.

17. James Lujan, 2005, "A Museum of the Indian. Not for the Indian," *American Indian Quarterly*, 29, 3–4, 510–16, 511.

18. Chavez Lamar, 2008, "Collaborative Exhibit Development at the Smithsonian's National Museum of the American Indian," in Amy Lonetree and Amanda J. Cobb (eds.), *The National Museum of the American Indian: Critical Conversations*, University of Nebraska Press, p. 147.

19. Lamar, "Collaborative Exhibit Development," p. 148.

20. Lujan, "A Museum of the Indian. Not for the Indian."

21. Marc Fisher, 2004, "Indian Museum's Appeal, Sadly, Only Skin-Deep," *Washington Post*, 21 September 2004.

22. Amanda J. Cobb, 2005, "The National Museum of the American Indian: Sharing the Gift," *American Indian Quarterly*, 29(3–4), 361–83. Citation, p. 377.

23. Lonetree and Cobb, *The National Museum of the American Indian*, p. 181.

24. Aldona Jonaitis and Janet Catherine Berlo, 2008, "'Indian Country' on the National Mall: The Mainstream Press versus the National Museum of the American Indian," in Amy Lonetree and Amanda J. Cobb (eds.), *The National Museum of the American Indian: Critical Conversations*, University of Nebraska Press, p. 211.

25. Lujan, "A Museum of the Indian," 511.

26. P. P. Erikson, "Decolonizing the 'Nation's Attic,'" in Amy Lonetree and Amanda J. Cobb (eds.), *The National Museum of the American Indian: Critical Conversations*, University of Nebraska Press, pp. 43–83. Citation, p. 68.

27. Jolene Rickard, 2007, "Absorbing or Obscuring the Absence of a Critical Space in the Americas for Indigeneity: The Smithsonian's National Museum of the American Indian," *RES: Anthropology and Aesthetics* 52, 85–92, 85.

28. Rickard, "Absorbing or Obscuring," 86, 87.

29. Erikson, "Decolonizing the '"Nation's Attic,'" p. 68.

30. Lujan, "A Museum of the Indian," 513.

31. Paul Richard, 2004, "Shards of Many Untold Stories," *Washington Post*, 21 September 2004.

32. Lujan, "A Museum of the Indian," 513.

33. Richard, "Shards of Many Untold Stories."

34. Lujan, "A Museum of the Indian," 515.

35. Cited in Lonetree and Cobb, *The National Museum of the American Indian: Critical Conversations*, p. 103.

36. Jonaitis and Berlo, "Indian Country," p. 211.

37. Richard, "Shards of Many Untold Stories."

38. Enid Schildkraut, 2006, "The beauty of science and the truth of art: Museum anthropology at the crossroads," in Cordula Grewe (ed.), *Die Schau des Fremden*, Franz Steiner Verlag Stuttgart, pp. 119–42. See pp. 121–2.

39. See William L. Merrill, Edmund J. Ladd and T. J. Ferguson, 1993, "The Return of the Ahayu:da: Lessons for Repatriation from Zuni Pueblo and the Smithsonian Institution," *Current Anthropology*, 34(5), 523–67. See pp. 532–3.

40. Merrill, Ladd and Ferguson, "The Return of the Ahayu:da," 532.

41. William L. Merrill and Richard E. Ahlborn, 1977, "Zuni Archangels and Ahayu:da," in Amy Henderson and Adrienne L. Kaeppler (eds.), *Exhibiting Dilemmas: Issues of Representation at the Smithsonian*, Smithsonian Books. The negotiations are described in detail in Merrill, Ladd and Ferguson, "The Return of the Ahayu:da."

42. Merrill, Ladd and Ferguson, "The Return of the Ahayu:da," 534.

43. Chip Colwell, 2017, *Plundered Skulls and Stolen Spirits: Inside the Fight to Reclaim Native America's Culture*, University of Chicago Press, pp. 52–3.

44. Merrill, Ladd and Ferguson, "The Return of the Ahayu:da," 547.

45. See Philippe Descola, 1996, *The Spears of Twilight: Life and Death in the Amazon Jungle*, HarperCollins, pp. 273–8; and Carlos Fausto, 2020, *Art Effects: Image, Agency, and Ritual in Amazonia*, University of Nebraska Press, pp. 50–63. Both authors provide detailed analysis of the symbolism of the tsantsa rituals.

46. Fausto, *Art Effects*, p. 55.

47. Steven Lee Rubenstein, 2007, "Circulation, Accumulation, and the Power of Shuar Shrunken Heads," *Cultural Anthropology*, 22(3), 357–99, 376.

48. Daniel Steel, 1999, "Trade Goods and Jivaro Warfare," *Ethnohistory*, 46(4), 745–76.

49. Anne Christine Taylor, 1993, "Remembering to Forget: Identity, Mourning and Memory among the Jivaro," *Man*, 28(4), 653–78, p. 670.

50. Rubenstein, "Circulation, Accumulation, and the Power of Shuar Shrunken Heads," 358, 375.

51. Rubenstein, "Circulation, Accumulation, and the Power of Shuar Shrunken Heads," 382.

52. Rubenstein, "Circulation, Accumulation, and the Power of Shuar Shrunken Heads," 357.

53. Laura Peers, 2011, "Shrunken Heads," Pitt Rivers Museum, p. 9.

54. Larson, Frances, 2014, *Severed: A History of Heads Lost and Heads Found*, Granta, p. 40.

55. https://www.prm.ox.ac.uk/shrunken-heads

56. Peers, "Shrunken Heads," p. 15.

Chapter 14

1. Ben Burt, 2019, *The Museum of Mankind: Man and Boy in the British Museum Ethnography Department*, Berghahn. Appendix: Ethnography Department Exhibitions, 1970 to 2003.

2. Burt, *The Museum of Mankind*, p. 138.

3. Jan Dalley, "Lunch with the FT: John Studzinski," *Financial Times*, 21 January 2011.

4. Claus-Joachim Kind, Nicole Ebinger-Rist, Sibylle Wolf, Thomas Beutelspacher and Kurt Wehrberger, 2014, "The Smile of the Lion Man. Recent Excavations in Stadel Cave (Baden-Württemberg, south-western Germany) and the Restoration of the Famous Upper Palaeolithic Figurine," *Quartär*, 61, 129–45.

5. Jill Cook, 2018, *Living with Gods: Peoples, Places and Worlds Beyond*, British Museum, pp. 4 and 7.

6. Kind et al., 142–4.

7. Kind et al., 139.

8. Matthias Schulz, 2011, "Solving the Mystery of a 35,000 year old Statue," *Spiegel International*, 9 December 2011.

9. Jarrett A. Lobell, 2002, "New Life for the Lion Man," *Archaeology*, 65(2).

10. Kind et al., 142.

11. Christopher Spring, Nigel Barley, and Julie Hudson, 2001, "The Sainsbury African Galleries at the British Museum," *African Arts*, 34(3), 18–93, 18.

12. Spring et al., "The Sainsbury African Galleries," 21.

13. Spring et al., "The Sainsbury African Galleries."

14. Philippe Dagen, 2021, *Ex Africa*, Gallimard: Musée du quai Branly–Jacques Chirac.

15. Enid Schildkraut, 1991, "Ambiguous Messages and Ironic Twists: Into the Heart of Africa and the Other Museum," *Museum Anthropology*, 15(2), 16–22, 16.

16. Simon Ottenberg, 1991, (Review) "Into the Heart of Africa," *African Arts* 24(3), 79–82, 80.

17. Schildkraut, "Ambiguous Messages and Ironic Twists," 20–21.

18. *Toronto Globe and Mail*, 1990, Arts Weekend, 29 December 1990.

19. "The Truth About Africa," pamphlet produced by the Coalition for the Truth about Africa, cited by Ottenburg, "Into the Heart of Africa."

20. Mary Jo Arnoldi, 1999, "From the Diorama to the Dialogic: A Century of Exhibiting Africa at the Smithsonian's Museum of Natural History," *Cahiers d'études africaines*, 39(155), 701–26, 711–16.

21. Arnoldi, "From the Diorama to the Dialogic." See pp. 704, 710.

22. U.S. House of Representatives 129 (15 September 1992, p. 46). Cited by Arnoldi, "From the Diorama to the Dialogic."

23. Mary Jo Arnoldi, Christine Mullen Kreamer and Michael Atwood Mason, 2001, "Reflections on 'African Voices' at the Smithsonian's National Museum of Natural History," *African Arts*, 34(2), 16–35, 16–18.

24. Arnoldi et al., "Reflections on 'African Voices,'" 19.

25. Arnoldi et al., "Reflections on 'African Voices,'" 20–21.

26. Arnoldi, "From the Diorama to the Dialogic," 718.

27. Arnoldi et al., "Reflections on 'African Voices,'" 19–20.

28. Arnoldi et al., "Reflections on 'African Voices,'" 28–30.

29. Arnoldi et al., "Reflections on 'African Voices,'" 22.

30. Arnoldi et al., "Reflections on 'African Voices,'" 22.

31. Arnoldi et al., "Reflections on 'African Voices,'" 25.

32. Jean-Luc Vellut, 2006, "In response to 'In the Heart of Darkness' by Adam Hochschild," *New York Review of Books*, 12 January 2006.

33. Bogomil Jewsiewicki, 2010, *The Beautiful Time: Photography by Sammy Baloji*, Museum for African Art, New York, p. 12.

Chapter 15

1. *The Economist*, 14 August 2018, Special Report: "Museums: Temples of Delight."

2. 2021, Visitor Figures 2020, *The Art Newspaper*, 30 March 2021.

3. Statista Research Department, 4 January 2022. https://www
.statista.com/statistics/1174784/museum-industry-market-size-us/

4. Nicholas Thomas, 2016, *The Return of Curiosity: What Museums Are Good for in the 21st Century*, Reaktion Books, pp. 85–6, 92.

5. Roberta Colombo Dougoud, 2013, "Les bambous gravés, objets ambassadeurs de la culture kanak," *Journal de la Société des Océanistes*, 119–32. Citation, p. 131.

6. Dmitry Kostyukov, 2020, "A New Museum Director's First Challenge: Which Exhibits to Give Back," *The New York Times*, 30 September 2020.

7. Margarita Valdovinos. Forthcoming. "Beyond the history of ethnographic collections: A complex approach to the Cora objects gathered by Konrad Theodor Preuss in view of a restitution process."

8. Valdovinos, "Beyond the history of ethnographic collections."

9. https://insightshare.org/maasai/

10. Spears and Spires, *The Economist*, 14 February 2020.

11. Edward Said, 1979, *Orientalism*, Pantheon, p. 95.

12. Edward Said, 1993, *Culture and Imperialism*, Chatto and Windus, p. 35.

13. Paola Ivanov and Jonas Bens, 2020, "Colonial Alexithymia: Affect and Colonialism in the German Humboldt Forum Debates." Paper presented at the EASA 2020 conference in Lisbon, in the panel "Making and Remaking Anthropology Museums: Provenance and Restitution."

14. C. Kusimba, 2004, "Archaeology of Slavery in East Africa," *The African Archaeological Review*, 21 (2), 59–88. See p. 65.

15. Peggy McGlone, 2022, "Smithsonian to give back its collection of Benin Bronzes," *Washington Post*, 8 March 2022.

16. A. Adogame, 2010, "How God became a Nigerian: Religious impulse and the unfolding of a nation," *Journal of Contemporary African Studies*, 28(4), 479–98.

17. Kwame Anthony Appiah, 2009, "Whose Culture Is It?," in James Cuno (ed.), *Whose Culture? The Promise of Museums and the Debate over Antiquities*, Princeton University Press, pp. 71–86, p. 74.

18. Barbara Plankensteiner (ed.), 2018, *The Art of Being a World Culture Museum: Futures and Lifeways of Ethnographic Museums in Contemporary Europe*, Kerber: Welt Museum Wien.

19. Tobias Harding, 2020, "World culture, world history and the roles of a museum," *International Journal of Cultural Policy*, 330–43. Citation, p. 334.

20. Writing in *Svenska Dagbladet*, 4 November 2016. Cited by Harding, "World culture," 339.

21. Peggy Levitt, 2015, *Artifacts and Allegiances: How Museums Put the Nation and the World on Display*, University of California Press, p. 18.

22. Nigel Barley, 1987, "Pop Art in Africa? The Kalabari Ijo Ancestral Screens," *Art History*, 10(3), 369–80. Citation, p. 373.

23. Herman Melville, 1850, "Hawthorn and his mosses," *The Literary World*, 17 and 24 August 1850.

INDEX

A

Adams, Henry 114–15, 118–19, 164, 166, 174–5

Adams, John 112, 114,

Adams, John Quincy 112, 113, 114, 115, 164

Adams, Robert McCormick 202–4, 298–9

Africa Museum, Tervuren
"Memory of Congo: The Colonial Era" exhibition 337–9

Agassiz, Louis 162–3, 164, 166–7, 187, 195

American Indians 116–18, 120–28, 134–5, 140, 161, 165, 167, 175, 183
Burials and reburials 213–14
Classification of languages 139–40, 177–8, 186, 206–8
See also (National) Museum of the American Indian; NAGPRA
American Museum of Natural History 267–8, 276, 306, 311, 328
Boas at 157, 172, 186–9, 209, 210, 268

Apollinaire, Guillaume 16, 257, 260–64

Appiah, Kwame Anthony 24, 349

Archaeological Institute of America 159–61

Army Medical Museum (U.S.A.) 197–8

Arnoldi, Mary Jo 331–6

Art and ethnography 93–4, 275–7, 288–9
See also primitive art, primitivisme

L'art nègre 90, 253, 259, 260, 261, 263–4
Picasso and 255, 260

Asante 226, 227, 228–9, 233–5

Aztec 43, 93, 179, 291–5

B

Baartman, Sara 215–20

Baird, Spencer 109, 114, 122, 127–9, 131–5, 150

Balfour, Henry 70, 105, 251

Banks, Joseph 19, 55–6, 57, 111

Barley, Nigel 355

Barthélemy, André de Courcay 33–4, 35

Barthes, Roland 9

Bastian, Adolf 77, 78–83, 105, 150, 152, 178, 189
Elementary ideas 80
Lowie on 79
On race 80

Bataille, Georges 92, 97
Bateson, Gregory 22
Beard, Mary 26
Beckmann, Max 260
Bell, Alexander Graham 136,
  140–41, 150
Benin, Nigeria (also known as
  Edo) 226, 227, 234–41
  Benin City 247–8
  British punitive expedition
    236–8, 245
  See also Oba of Benin
Benin Bronzes 26, 234–41, 245,
  260, 286–7, 343, 348–9, 353
  In Nigerian museums 241–5
Bénin, Republic of 16, 223, 225,
  227, 232–3
  And slavery 230–32, 233
Benjamin, Walter 84
Bentham, Jeremy 221–2
Berlo, Janet Catherine 302, 304
#BlackLivesMatter 15–16, 17
Boas, Franz 8, 134, 292
  At the American Museum of
    Natural History, 186–8, 268
  And the development of
    American anthropology 143–4
  Classification of museum
    artefacts 143–4, 149–57, 172
  And evolutionism 143–4, 187–8
  And human remains 199, 209–10
  And Frederic Putnam 171–2, 186
  And museum anthropology
    188–9
  And World's Columbian
    Exposition 177–80, 182–3,
    185–6
Braque, Georges 97, 251, 260
Braunholtz, H. J. 55

Breton, André 261, 267
Briggs, Asa 67
British Museum 1, 2, 5, 10, 11, 12,
  17, 26, 51, 53–63, 105, 137, 342
  And Benin Bronzes 26, 238, 241,
    245, 248, 326
  Ethnography at 55, 57–63, 317–26
  Museum of Mankind 317–18
  Sainsbury gallery 325–6
  Wellcome gallery 324–5
Brixham Cave 51, 64, 168
Broca, Paul 3–4, 89, 198, 214
Broekhoven, Laura van 312, 315,
  345–7
Brooklyn Museum 264
Bruchac, Margaret 204–5, 208
Bureau of Ethnology,
  Smithsonian Institution 2,
  120–26, 133, 139–40, 169, 177–8,
  184, 186

C
Cabinet des médailles 31–6
Cannizzo, Jeanne 327–30
Chapman, William Ryan 69
Chirac, Jacques 101, 278–82
Christian VIII, King of Denmark
  49–50
Christy, Henry 61–2, 65, 70, 148
Civilisation 3, 5, 6–8, 59–61, 297
Classification of museum
  artefacts
  At the British Museum 55–8, 63
  At the Great Exhibition 66–7
  Boas and 143–4, 149–57
  Evolutionary and geographical
    models 36–8, 41–3, 68–9, 82–3,
    95–6, 98–9, 143–9
  Klemm and 76–7

Pitt Rivers and 69, 138
Three Age System 47–9, 65
At the Museum of Natural
    History, Smithsonian
    Institution 135–8, 143–9
At the Peabody Museum of
    American Archaeology and
    Ethnology 169–70
At the World's Columbian
    Exposition, 1893 177–80
Cobb, Amanda 301
Colonialism 2, 6, 10
    Acquisitions made by
        metropolitan museums in
        the colonial period 17–22
    Anti-colonialism in French
        ethnology 96–7
    Ministry of Colonies and
        ethnology in France 96
    Colonial Exhibition, Palais de
        la Port Dorée, Paris, 1931 97–8
    Colonial Museum, Paris 98
    Colonisation of the trans-
        Mississippi 117–18, 120
    Also see Imperialism
Colwell, Chip 214, 308
Congo Free State 331, 336–8
Conklin, Alice 91, 93
Cook, Captain James 11, 19, 55, 57
Cook, Jill 58, 320, 323
Coon, Carleton 200–201
Cosmopolitan Museum 355–6
Cosmos Club 118–19
Cuno, James 15
Cushing, Frank 129, 131–5, 189
Cuvier, Georges 36, 37–8, 42, 53
    And the Hottentot Venus
        217–18, 219
Cyrus Cylinder 25

D
Dagen, Philippe 251–3, 326–7
Dahomey 16, 223, 226, 227,
    229–33
    Abomey Palace Museum 230
Danto, Arthur 276–7
Darnell, Regna 122, 143–4
Darwin, Charles 63, 73, 119, 159,
    162–4
    Theory of human evolution 4,
        5–6, 64, 162–4, 175
    Race and civilisation 5–6
Darwinism at Harvard
    University 161–4
Darwinism, opposition to 65–6,
    198, 284
Daudet, Alphonse 44–5
Delbourgo, James 53–5
Deloria, Philip 207
Derain, André 25, 251, 254, 258,
    260
Désveaux, Emmanuel 283
Dodds, Alfred-Amédée 223, 225,
    229, 230
Dorlech, Harmut 17
Duchamp, Marcel 267, 276,
    277

E
Edison, Thomas 136, 173
Edo *see* Benin
Edo Museum of West African
    Art 246
Elgin (Thomas Bruce, 7th Earl
    of Elgin) 11
Elgin (James Bruce, 8th Earl of
    Elgin) 12
Elgin Marbles 11, 26, 59
Evans, Richard 12–14

Evolution and evolutionism 5, 51, 52, 64–9, 74, 86, 90, 95, 99, 119, 136–8, 143
  Boas and 143–4, 148, 171, 172
  Darwin and Spencer 5
  Evolutionary models of cultural progress 52, 68, 69, 74, 95, 99, 137, 148
Ewing, Heather 110, 112, 113
Exposition Universelle, Paris (1855) 84–5
Exposition Universelle, Paris (1878) 85–6
Exposition Universelle, Paris (1889) 103–4, 253
Eyo, Ekpo 244–5, 246

F
Fagg, Bernard 71–3, 241, 242, 247
Fagg, William 240, 241, 243, 245
Fagin, Nancy 179
Family of Man Exhibition 9–10
Farmer-Paellman, Deadria 250
Fausto, Carlos 296, 309–10
Ferry, Jules 86–7
Fischer, Hartwig 17
Fisher, Marc 301
Foucault, Michel 2
Franks, Augustus Wollaston 58–9, 61, 62–3, 65–6, 69, 77, 104, 169
Frobenius, Leo 20, 21, 23, 255

G
Gamio, Manuel 292–3
Garfield, James A. 120
Gauguin, Vincent 218, 253, 255, 258–9, 265
Gaulle, Charles de 99, 101, 278

Geronimo 209
Gilbert, Davies 110
Goethe, Johann Wolfgang 73
Goldwater, Robert 256, 265, 266, 271–5
Goode, George Brown 104, 106, 148–9, 174, 189
  Policy on museums 136–8
Gould, Stephen Jay 196–7, 214–15
Grant, Ulysses S. 117, 120
Gräslund, Bo 48
Gray, Asa 162–3, 164, 165
Great Exhibition of the Works of Industry of All Nations (1851) 61, 66–7, 84
Griaule, Marcel 89, 92, 93–4, 100–101
Grotius, Hugo 12
Guillaume, Paul 262–4

H
Hacking, Ian 2
Hague Conventions, 1899 and 1907 13
Hague Convention for the Protection of Cultural Property in the Event of Armed Conflict 14, 15
Hamy, Enest-Théodore 85–8, 171, 189
Harnoncourt, René d' 269–73
Hastrup, Kirsten 209, 210
Hauser-Schäublin, Brigitta 250
Hazoumé, Romuald 226
Henry, Joseph 113, 126–7, 129
Herder, Johann Gottfried von 6
Herskovits, Melville 22
Hicks, Dan 11
Hinsley, Curtis 127, 134, 138, 160

Hitler, Adolf 13, 200, 241
Hochschild, Adam 337–9
Holmes, William Henry 104, 147, 167, 178, 185, 186, 189
Horniman Museum 26
Hottentot Venus *see* Sara Baartman
Hrdlička, Aleš 167, 198, 210, 211
Hugo, Victor 12
Human remains, collection, repatriation and burial 202–8
Boas and 199, 209–10
At U.S. Museum of Natural History 195, 198, 204, 310–11
Humboldt, Alexander von 38, 39, 43, 52, 73, 78–80, 162, 291
Humboldt Forum 17, 83, 284–7, 288
Hunt, James 4
Hunter, John 193–4
Huntington, Samuel 297
Huxley, Julian 200
Huxley, Thomas Henry 4, 64, 66, 70

I
Identity Museums 2, 10, 290, 297–8, 305, 350, 356
Imperialism 2, 6, 8, 11, 16–18, 27, 248, 297, 328, 337, 342
also see Colonialism
Indigenous peoples 9, 218, 219, 259, 281, 290, 295–6, 303, 305, 314, 344
Problems of definition 212–13, 259, 271–2
also see Primitive peoples
Ishi 210–12

J
Jacknis, Ira 186, 303
Jefferson, Thomas 73, 112, 168
Jesup, Morris K. 157, 187–8
Jomard, Edme-François 34–6, 52, 85
Plan for a museum of ethnography 36–8, 41–3, 68–9, 87
Jonaitis, Aldona 302, 304

K
Kahlo, Frida 270, 293
Kalabari 354–5
Kandinsky, Wassily 256
Kant, Immanuel 80
Kasarhérou, Emmanuel 343–4
Kasteele, Rainier Pieter van de 40
Kennewick Man 212–13
Kerchache, Jacques 279–80
Kérékou, Mathieu 232–3
Kirchner, Emil Ernst Ludwig 256
Klemm, Gustav 74–8, 105
Theory of cultural history 74–7
Collection of 76, 77
On race 74–5
Knight, Alan 292–3
Koepping, Klaus–Peter 80
Kramer, Fritz 286
Kroeber, Alfred 209
And Ishi 210–12

L
Lamar, Chavez 300
Lane-Fox, Augustus *see* Pitt Rivers
Laurière, Christine 92

Leiris, Michel 17–18, 91, 92, 93, 94, 96–7, 98, 100, 200

Leopold II, King of Belgium 331, 336, 337–8

L'Estoile, Benoît de 1, 99, 282, 282

Lévi-Strauss, Claude 94, 99, 101, 200, 265–8, 279, 280, 283

Levitt, Peggy 351–2

Lévy-Bruhl, Lucien 89, 91, 97

Lewitzy, Anatole 100

Lifschitz, Deborah 100

Lincoln, Abraham 117, 126, 198

Lindsay, G. Carroll 139

Linnaeus, Carl 37

Lion Man 320–24

Lipschitz, Jacques 93, 97

London Ethnological Society 4, 66

Louvre 1, 5, 13, 16, 31, 33, 34, 84, 85, 342
  Ethnography in 35, 86–7, 279– 80

Lowie, Robert 79, 81

Lubbock, John 4–5, 64–5, 66, 70
  Pre–Historic Times 51, 64, 164

Luf Boat 287

Lujan, James 300–304

Luschan, Felix von 240–41

Lyell, Charles 63, 64, 159, 162, 164

M

MacGregor, Neil, 25, 285, 318–19, 320–23

Macie, Elizabeth 109–11

Macron, President Emmanuel 16, 17, 223–4, 233

Malraux, André 260, 278, 281

Manhyia Palace Museum, Ghana 234

Manias, Chris 77

Marsh, Othniel Charles 159, 168

Martin, Stéphane 16, 224

Mason, Otis T. 129, 148–9, 150, 171
  And Boas 149, 151–4, 186
  Curator of ethnology, U.S. National Museum 135–8
  Visits European museums 103–6
  At World's Columbian Exposition 177

Matisse, Henri 97, 254, 258, 260

Mauss, Marcel 88–90, 94, 96, 97, 100, 101
  And the Institute for Ethnology 89–91

Mayenne, Villar de la 32–3

McCain, John 203, 213

McGee, William 123, 186

McLeod, Malcolm 317–18

Memel-Kassi, Silvie 226

Merrill, William 298, 307

Merryman, John Henry 14–15

Metropolitan Museum of Art 5, 269, 273–4
  Michael C. Rockefeller Wing 273–4, 288

Meyerowitz, Eva 230, 246–7

Miller, Peter N. 76

Momigliano, Arnoldo 76

Moore, Wendy 193–4

Morgan, Lewis Henry 123–6, 160, 169, 170, 189

Morton, Samuel George 195–7

Murphy, Maureen 24, 260–61

Murray, Kenneth 241–2

Museum of African and Oceanian Art, Paris 98

Museum of African American
History and Culture,
Washington, DC 298, 305
Museum of the American Indian,
Washington, DC 298–305
Museum of Anthropology,
Mexico City 290–95
Musée des Arts et Traditions
Populaires, Paris 99
Museum of Cultures: European
and non-European Ethnology,
Basel 339–40
Museum of Ethnology
(Völkerkunde), Berlin 79, 81–3,
85, 150, 152, 286, 344–5
Museum of Ethnography,
Copenhagen 49, 105–6, 288
Museum of Ethnography
(Trocadéro) Paris 86–8, 90, 97,
223
    Collecting expeditions
    94–5
Musée de l'Homme, Paris 88,
98–9, 102, 266, 280, 282
    During the Second World War
    99–101
Musée de la Marine (Naval
Museum), Paris 35
Musée du quai Branly-Jacques
Chirac, Paris 16, 282–4, 285–6,
343–4
    Ex Africa exhibition 327
Museum of Modern Art, New
York 93, 264, 265, 268–9, 270–71,
272
    "Primitivism in 20th century
    art" 274
Museum of Natural History,
Paris 31, 33, 34, 37, 84, 90, 99

Museum of Natural History, Rio
de Janeiro 295–6
Museum of Natural History, U.S.
National Museum,
Smithsonian Institution 113,
135–8
    Africa Hall 330–36
    Boas and 143–57
    Human remains at 195, 198,
    204, 310–11
Museum of Natural History,
Vienna 201
Museum of Nordic Antiquities,
Copenhagen 47–9
Museum of Primitive Art, New
York 271
Museum of Other People
    Characterised 1–2, 5
    Exhibitions in 317, 352
    History of 1–2, 9–10
    Crisis of 2, 27, 305–6,342, 349–51
Museums: *see* Abomey Palace
Museum; Army Medical
Museum (U.S.A.); (National)
Museum of African American
History and Culture,
Washington, DC; (Royal) Africa
Museum, Tervuren; (National)
Museum of the American
Indian, Washington, DC;
American Museum of Natural
History; British Museum;
Brooklyn Museum; Manhyia
Palace Museum; Museum of
Cultures: European and non-
European Ethnology, Basel;
Edo Museum of West African
Art; Museum of Ethnography,
Paris; Horniman Museum;

Musée de la Marine (Naval Museum); Musée du quai Branly-Jacques Chirac; Museum of Anthropology, Mexico City; Museum of Modern Art, New York; Museum of Natural History, Paris; Museum of Natural History, Rio de Janeiro; Museum of Natural History, Vienna; (Royal) Ontario Museum; Museum of Nordic Antiquities, Copenhagen; Museum of Primitive Art, New York; Museum of Völkerkunde, Berlin; Peabody Museum of American Archaeology and Ethnology, Harvard University; Pitt Rivers Museum, Oxford; Pompidou Centre, Paris; Teheran Museum of Contemporary Art *See also* Classification of museum artefacts; Cosmopolitan Museum; Identity Museums; The Museum of Other People; World Culture Museums

N
NAGPRA (Native American Graves Protection and Repatriation Act) 15, 202–3, 206, 208, 212–13
Napoleon Bonaparte 11–13, 34, 40
Napoleon III 44–5, 84–5
Newell, Jenny 18–20
Nigeria 348–9

Nigerian museums 71, 241–4
Nolde, Emile 257–8
Norton, Charles Eliot 159–60
Nyerup, Rasmus 47

O
Oba of Benin 235, 236, 238, 249, 250
  Claims Benin Bronzes 349
Oehlenschläger, Adam Gottlob 46
O'Hanlon, Michael 71
Omai 19
Ontario Museum, "In the Heart of Africa" 327–30
Owen, Richard 61, 65

P
Parezo, Nancy 134–5
Parkman, Francis 161
Paz, Octavio 294–5
Peabody, George 158, 164
Peabody Museum of American Archaeology and Ethnology, Harvard University 158–9, 164–6, 272
  Arrangement of exhibits 169–70
Pechstein, Max 257–8
Peers, Laura 312, 314
Penny, Glenn 81, 83
Phillips, Barnaby 243, 244
Phillips, James 235–6
Picasso, Pablo 16, 24, 97, 251–3, 254–5, 256, 257
  And *L'art négre* 255, 260
  At the Museum of Ethnography 255
  Les Demoiselles d'Avignon 255–6, 277

Picton, John 24, 245
Pitt Rivers, Augustus Lane-Fox 4,
  65, 66–71, 109, 240
  Evolutionary typology 68–9
Pitt Rivers Museum, Oxford
  70–71, 105, 138, 240
  Conditions of donation 72
  Maasai visit 345–7
  On the treatment of dead
    enemies 70, 308–9, 312–15
  Plans for development 71–2
  See also Broekhoven, Laura
    van; Peers, Laura
Playfair, Lyon 66–7
Pompidou Centre, Paris
  277–8
Powell, John Wesley 117–20, 129,
  131, 133, 136, 144–7, 160–61, 169,
  171, 188, 189, 204, 211
  And Bureau of Ethnology,
    Smithsonian Institution
    120–26, 131, 139–40
  Classifying American Indian
    groups 121–2, 124–5, 139–40
  And Lewis Henry Morgan
    124–5
  On museum displays 154–5
Prehistory 46–7, 51, 62–5, 167, 168,
  283, 290
Preuss, Konrad Theodor 344–5
Price, Sally 225
Primitive mentality 8, 91, 91
Primitive peoples 3, 5–9, 38, 49,
  61, 82, 89, 91, 96, 99, 138, 168,
  175, 187, 201, 251, 319, 330, 334,
  350
  And civilised peoples 5, 9, 38,
    61, 96, 99, 168, 187, 350
  Defined 3, 5, 9, 138, 319

Primitive art, *Primitivisme* 93–4,
  251–3, 260–61, 262–5, 268, 269,
  271–2, 274–5, 276–8, 279–80, 289,
  327
Pritchard, James Cowles 3
Putnam, Frederic 160, 166–9,
  171–2, 186
  And Franz Boas 171–2, 186
  And World's Columbian
    Exposition 174, 177, 178–85

R
Race 3, 4, 6, 74–6, 79–80, 124, 128,
  143, 149, 152, 155, 164, 178, 180,
  195–6, 199–201, 204, 208
Ratzel, Friedrich 80–81, 189
Rau, Charles 129, 135
Rawson, Harry 236–7
Read, Charles Hercules 63,
  104
Redman, Samuel J. 205–6
Restitution of cultural treasures
  11, 15, 25–26, 27, 219, 224, 225,
  248–9, 286–7, 343–4, 358–9
  Attitudes in Germany 248–9
  Sarr-Savoy report 224–5
Restitution Study Group 250
Reynolds, Joshua 19, 194
Richard, Paul 304, 305
Rickard, Jolene 303
Rivera, Diego 270, 293
Rivet, Paul 89, 90, 91, 92, 96, 98,
  99–100, 101
Rivière, Georges Henri 90, 91–3,
  94, 99, 100, 101
Robertson, Geoffrey 10–11
Rockefeller, Abby Aldrich 268–9,
  272
Rockefeller, Michael 272–3

Rockefeller, Nelson 240, 264, 269–74
Rosetta Stone, 11, 12
Rothstein, Edward 300, 301
Rousseau, Henri 257
Rowley-Conwy, Peter 51
Rubenstein, Steven 311
Rubin, William 274–5

S
Sandahl, Jette 351–2
Sarr, Felwine 224
Savoy, Bénédicte 224, 286–7
Schaefner, André 91, 92, 94, 97, 100
Schildkraut, Enid 20, 276, 306, 328–9
Schiller, Francis 3
Schlözer, August Ludwig 46
Schmid, Anna 339–40
Schmid, Elizabeth 321, 323–4
Seeley, J. R. 7–8
Sickles, Emma 183–4
Siebold, Philipp Franz Balthasar von 38–45, 52
  Plan for a museum of ethnography in Leiden 41–3
Sieff, Kevin 230–31
Silko, Leslie Marmon 302
Slavery, in West African kingdoms 228–9, 230–32
Slave trade 228, 305, 336
Sloane, Hans 17, 53–5, 57, 109
Smith, Richard Norton 272
Smithson, James 109–12, 113
  Bequest 111–12
  Body exhumed and moved to Washington, DC 140–42

Smithsonian Institution 2, 9, 26
  In the nineteenth century 109–42
  Anthropology and ethnology at 113–14, 127, 129
  At the Centennial Exhibition in Philadelphia 128–9
  Collection of Native American artefacts 126–8, 131–5
  Also see U.S. National Museum of Natural History
Soustelle, Jacques 94, 100
Soyinka, Wole 243, 288
Spencer, Herbert 5, 119–20, 157
Starr, Frederick 20–21
Stein, Gertrude 254–5, 260
Stieglitz, Alfred 263–4
Stravinsky, Igor 91, 97
Sturtevant, William C. 9, 189
Surrealism and surrealists 97–8, 261

T
Talon, Patrice 16, 223, 225, 233
Taylor, Anne Christine 310
Tehran Museum of Contemporary Art 24–5
Thomas, David Hurst 206, 207
Thomas, Nicholas 342–3
Thomsen, Christian Jürgensen 45–52, 57
  Three Age System 47–9, 65
Tijani, Abba Isa 348
Tillion, Germaine 100
Tjibaou, Marie Claude 343
Tocqueville, Alexis de 116
Torday, Emil 20

Trigger, Bruce 52, 64, 168
Tsantsa 309–15
Turner, Frederick J. 116, 175–6
Tylor, Edward Burnett 6, 7, 61–2, 70, 78, 105, 121, 188
  On invention and diffusion 144–51

U
UNESCO 13, 26, 200, 282, 285
  1970 Convention on the Means of Prohibiting and Preventing the Illicit Import, Export and Transfer of Ownership of Cultural Property 14, 15

V
Valdonivos, Margarita 344–5
Van Gogh, Vincent 24, 253
Viatte, Germain 281
Victoria and Albert Museum 27, 57, 69, 316
Vildé, Boris 100
Virchow, Rudolf 78, 79, 189
Vlaminck, Maurice de 253–4
Vogel, Susan Mullin 275–6

W
Waitz, Theodor 80
Ward, Herbert 331

Warhol, Andy 24, 277
Watson, Ruby 169–70
Watteville, Oscar-Amédée de 85
Wellington, Arthur Wellesley, 1st Duke of Wellington 13, 40
West, Richard 203, 303, 304–5
Westmacott, Richard 59–60
Wetzel, Robert 321
Willett, Frank 242, 246
Williams, Jonathan 26
World Culture Museums 351–2
World's Columbian Exposition, Chicago, 1893 173–88
World's Fairs 84
  See also The Great Exhibition of the Works of Industry of All Nations, 1851; Exposition universelle, Paris, 1855, 1878, 1889; World Columbian Exposition, Chicago, 1893
Worsaae, Jens 49–50, 51, 52
Worster, Donald 118, 120–21
Wundt, Wilhelm 80
Wyman, Jeffries 162–4, 165

Z
Zand, Roxane 25
Zayas, Marius de 263, 264
Zuni 131, 135, 145, 208, 306–8
  Ahayu:da 306–8